by a friend. She lists beauty shops, and saunas, Parisian plastic surgeons, jazz clubs, theaters, and opera houses. And she includes shops from haute couture to boutiques, perfumes, jewelry, leather goods, and shops for toys, porcelains, or men's wear.

Gerie has concentrated on the most popular areas in France—Paris, the château country, and the Riviera. And she includes an area newly popular after its former glory, Deauville, with its beaches and casinos. For each, she lists a calendar of events around the year, useful local addresses, sightseeing tours, and special places you'll want to see by yourself.

A special introductory section includes Gerie's expert advice on packing, health and beauty hints, French currency and clothes sizes, telephone service and tipping practices—all the information to make your trip easier and more enjoyable.

France Especially for Women gives more than 400 stores and shops, over 80 beauty salons, and hundreds of hotels and restaurants, divided into three age groups and three price ranges, with up-to-date detailed information.

If you're a woman planning to travel to France, or if you know one, **France Especially for Women** is for you.

France Especially for Women is the first in a new series of travel guides for women, by Gerie Tully. Coming soon: **England Especially for Women** and **Italy Especially for Women.**

Acknowledgments

I could not have gathered all the research for this book without the help of the following people:

In New York: Peter Karman, Daniel Dorian, Maria Fritz.

In Paris: M. B. Juster, M. Renart, Mme. Boursin.

On the Riviera: M. Sabatier, M. Robert Blanc, Mme. Soubeyran (the "lady with the smile").

And last but not least my very special thanks to Ed Finkel for his unfailing support and multifaceted assistance.

DC
16
.T84

Designed by Jack Meserole

Manufactured in the United States of America

LIBRARY OF CONGRESS CATALOGING IN PUBLICATION DATA

Tully, Gerie.
   France especially for women.

   1. France—Description and travel—1945–   —Guide-
books. I. Title.
DC16.T84   914.4'04'83   73–18544
ISBN 0-200-04020-0

1 2 3 4 5 6 7 8 9 10

FRANCE

Especially for Women

Gene Tully

Abelard-Schuman   NEW YORK

Dedication
To my precious Heatherkins
and the day I can take her
to this beautiful country
for her very first visit

Contents

Introduction   1

Part I
Before You Go

1   Making the Most of Your Trip   5

2   Tips for Travelers   9

Packing Hints   9   /   What to Take   12   /   Health Hints   12   /   Relax   14   /   Beauty Hints   15   Extra Tips   16

3   From Here to There   18

4   Useful Information   21

Trains   21   /   Eurailpass   22

FRENCH GOVERNMENT REGULATIONS   22

Visa   22   /   Health   22   /   Customs   23

CLIMATE   24

SIZE CHARTS   24

WEIGHTS AND MEASURES   26

Time Conversion   26   /   Telephone Service   27   Telegrams and Cables   27   /   Postal Service   27   Currency   27   /   Accommodations   28   /   Hotel Taxes   28   /   Tipping   29   /   Electric Current   29   Emergency Medical Services   30   /   Pharmacies   30   Lost Property   30

IF YOU ARE IN DIFFICULTY . . .   30

5   Useful French Phrases   31

Part
II
Paris

6   Welcome to Paris   37

THE BEST TIME FOR PARIS   37

HOW TO GET AROUND   38

Subways   40   /   Buses   41   /   Taxicabs   42
Rental Cars   43

USEFUL ADDRESSES   43

Police   43   /   Emergency Medical Services   43
Pharmacies   43   /   Ambulances   43   /   Post Offices
43   /   Consulates   43

CALENDAR OF EVENTS   44

7   Where to Stay   46

RIGHT BANK HOTELS   47

Deluxe   47   /   Four Star NN   50   /   Three Star
NN   56   /   Two Star NN   58

LEFT BANK HOTELS   60

Deluxe   60   /   Three Star   60   /   Two Star   62

8   Wining and Dining   65

FRENCH DISHES   65

FOOD AND COOKING VOCABULARY   68

RESTAURANTS: EXPENSIVE   70

RESTAURANTS: MODERATE   74

RESTAURANTS: INEXPENSIVE   83

1st Arrondissement   83   /   2nd Arrondissement   86
3rd Arrondissement   86   /   4th Arrondissement   87
5th Arrondissement   87   /   6th Arrondissement   88
7th Arrondissement   90   /   8th Arrondissement   91
9th Arrondissement   92   /   10th Arrondissement   93
16th Arrondissement   93   /   18th Arrondissement   94

RESTAURANTS NEAR FAMOUS MONUMENTS   95

Arc de Triomphe (L'Etoile)   95   /   Les Invalides   95
Musée du Louvre (Carrousel)   96   /   Notre Dame and
Île-St.-Louis   96 / Opéra—Madeleine—Concorde   96

Panthéon—Latin Quarter   96   /   Sacré-Coeur   96
St.-Germain-des-Prés   97   /   Tour Eiffel—École
Militaire   **97**

RESTAURANTS OPEN IN AUGUST   97

9   Nighttime Entertainment   **100**

DANCE   101

MUSIC HALLS   101

OPERA   102

CONCERTS   102

ORGAN RECITALS   103

THEATER   103

CINEMAS   103

NIGHT CLUBS   103
"In" Clubs   106   /   For Jazz Fans   107

10   Sightseeing   **109**

COACH TOURS   109
Day Tours   109   /   Night Tours   110   /   Tours by
Boat   111

ON YOUR OWN   112

MUSEUMS   122

PARKS AND GARDENS   127

Botanical Gardens   129

11   Excursions Out of Paris   **130**

VERSAILLES   130

FONTAINEBLEAU AND BARBIZON   133

CHARTRES   135

COMPIÈGNE   136

CHANTILLY   136

ROUEN   137

12   Beauty Comes First   **139**

BEAUTY SALONS   139

SPECIAL PROBLEMS   143

Obesity and Cellulite   144   /   Plastic Surgery   145
Chemosurgery   147   /   Body Surgery   147

13   Shopping   **149**

Shopping Tips   150

MAIN SHOPPING STREETS AND AREAS   151

Main Department Stores   151   /   Couturiers   151
Boutiques   151 / Shoe Boutiques   151 / Jewelers
151 / Art Galleries and Art   151 / Antique Dealers
151   /   Copies of Antiques and Furniture   152
Crystal and China   152

DEPARTMENT STORES   152

BOUTIQUES   153

HAUTE COUTURE   159

SALE SHOPS   162

KNITWEAR   163

FOR LARGE SIZES   164

LEATHER GOODS   164

FOR HIM   167

FOR CHILDREN   168

JEWELRY   169

PERFUMES AND GIFTS   170

ANTIQUES   171

CRYSTAL / PORCELAIN / CERAMICS   172

KNICKKNACKS / GADGETS / GIFTS   172

MISCELLANEOUS MARKETS   173

CLEANERS   174

REPAIR SERVICES   174

Part
III
The
Château
Country

14   Welcome to the Château Country   **177**

HOW TO GET THERE   178

CALENDAR OF EVENTS   178

15 Where to Stay   180

HOTELS IN ANGERS   180
Four Star   180 / Three Star   180 / Two Star   180
CHÂTEAUX IN THE VAL DE LOIRE   181

16 Wining and Dining   183

RESTAURANTS   183
Expensive   183   /   Moderate and Inexpensive   184

17 Nighttime Entertainment   185
NIGHT CLUBS   185

18 Sightseeing   186

THE CHÂTEAUX   186

Blois   187 / Chambord   187 / Cheverny   187
Valençay   188 / Chaumont   188 / Amboise   188
Chenonceaux   188 / Azay-le-Rideau   189 / Chinon
189 / Langeais   189 / Loches   189 / Saumur   189
Montgeoffroy   190 / Brissac   190 / Plessis Bourré
191 / Le Plessis-Mace   191 / Serrant   191
WINE-TASTING   191

Part IV
Deauville

19 Welcome to Deauville   195

HOW TO GET THERE   196
USEFUL ADDRESSES   196
Physicians   196 / Dentists   196 / Hospital   197
Drugstores   197
CALENDAR OF EVENTS   197

20 Where to Stay   198

HOTELS IN DEAUVILLE   198
Deluxe   198 / Four Star   199 / Three Star   199
Two Star   200
HOTELS IN TROUVILLE   201
Deluxe   201

21 Wining and Dining   202

RESTAURANTS IN DEAUVILLE   202

Expensive   202 / Moderate   203 / Inexpensive   204

RESTAURANTS IN TROUVILLE   204

22 Nighttime Entertainment   205

BARS AND NIGHT CLUBS   205

23 Excursions Out of Deauville   206

CAEN   206

TOUQUES   206

CHÂTEAUX AND MANOR HOUSES   207

ECCLESIASTICAL ARCHITECTURE   207

WORLD WAR II SITES   208

24 Sports   209

Golf   209 / Mini-Golf   209 / Horseback Riding   209
Swimming   209   /   Tennis   209   /   Yachting   209

25 Beauty Comes First   210

BEAUTY SALONS   210

MASSAGE   210

PEDICURES   210

SPA   211

26 Shopping   212

DEPARTMENT STORES   212

BOUTIQUES AND SMALL SHOPS   212

LEATHER GOODS   213

SHOES   213

JEWELRY   213

GIFTS / GAMES / SOUVENIRS   213

SPORTS EQUIPMENT   213

LAUNDRY AND DRY CLEANING   214

Part
V
The
Riviera

27 Welcome to the French Riviera   **217**

CLIMATE   **220**

HOW TO GET THERE   **220**

HOW TO GET AROUND   **221**

Trains **221**   /   Buses **221**   /   Taxis **222** Boat Trips **222**

GAMBLING   **222**

TOURIST OFFICES (SYNDICATS D'INITIATIVE)   **222**

TOUR AGENTS   **222**

CALENDAR OF EVENTS   **223**

28 Wining and Dining   **225**

29 Sightseeing   **227**

30 Beauty Comes First   **230**

31 Shopping   **231**

Shopping Hours **231** / Shopping Tips **231** / Nice —Côte d'Azur Airport **232**

32 Welcome to Nice   **233**

33 Where to Stay in Nice   **234**

HOTELS   **234**

Deluxe **234** / Four Star NN **235** / Three Star NN **236** / Two Star NN **238**

34 Wining and Dining in Nice   **241**

RESTAURANTS   **241**

Expensive **241** / Moderate **242** / Inexpensive **243**

35 Nighttime Entertainment in Nice   **244**

OPERA   **244**

THEATERS   244

CINEMAS   244

CABARETS   245

NIGHT CLUBS   245

GAMBLING   245

36   Sightseeing in Nice   246
IN CIMIEZ   247

37   Sports in Nice   248
Beaches   248 / Skin Diving   248 / Tennis   248
Water Skiing   248

38   Beauty Comes First in Nice   249

39   Shopping in Nice   250
DEPARTMENT STORES   250

BOUTIQUES AND SMALL SHOPS   250

LEATHER GOODS   252

FOR HIM   252

JEWELRY   253

PERFUMES / GIFTS   253

ANTIQUES   254

40   Welcome to Cannes   255

41   Where to Stay in Cannes   256
HOTELS   256
Deluxe   256 / Four Star   257 / Three Star   258
Two Star   260

42   Wining and Dining in Cannes   262

43   Nighttime Entertainment in Cannes   265
CONCERTS AND SHOWS   265

CINEMA   265

CABARETS AND NIGHT CLUBS   266

GAMBLING   266

44   Sightseeing in Cannes   267

45   Sports in Cannes   268

Public Beaches   269   /   Private Beaches   269
Golf   269   /   Horseback Riding   270   /   Horse-
racing   270   /   Ice Skating   270   /   Polo   270
Skin Diving   271 / Swimming Pools   271 / Tennis
271   /   Water Skiing   271

46   Beauty Comes First in Cannes   272

HAIRDRESSERS   272

SAUNAS   272

THALASSO THÉRAPIE   273

47   Shopping in Cannes   274

DEPARTMENT STORES   274

BOUTIQUES AND SMALL SHOPS   274

LEATHER GOODS   275

FOR HIM   276

JEWELRY   276

PERFUMES / GIFTS   276

ANTIQUES   277

48   Welcome to Monte-Carlo   278

CALENDAR OF EVENTS   278

49   Where to Stay in Monte-Carlo   280

HOTELS   280

Deluxe   280   /   Three Star   281

50   Sports in Monte-Carlo   282

Beaches   282 / Tennis   282 / Water Skiing   282

xvi Contents

51 Sightseeing in Monte-Carlo 283

52 Shopping in Monte-Carlo 284

BOUTIQUES AND SMALL SHOPS 284

LEATHER GOODS 285

JEWELRY 285

PERFUMES / GIFTS 285

ANTIQUES 285

53 Other Riviera Towns 286

ST.-TROPEZ 286

Shopping 286

FRÉJUS 287

ST.-RAPHAËL 288

GRASSE 288

VALLAURIS 288

VENCE 288

BIOT 289

JUAN-LES-PINS 289

ANTIBES 289

CAGNES 290

Index 293

France
Especially
for
Women

Note to the Reader

It is very important for you to understand that during the writing of this book the dollar value has been jumping all over the place. When I began it, there were four francs to the dollar, and that is the figure I am using as a rough guide. It is also a handy figure to use because of its easy division. However, please remember that it is only a guide. The best thing that can happen is that the dollar will be worth more by the time you visit France, and at the moment it looks as if it will be. If so, you will get *better* value for your money than what is reflected in this book.

As for hotels and restaurants, their prices are difficult to predict. Some hotels say they will be raising their prices and others say not; it is safest to assume that they will. Restaurant prices fluctuate with the price of food. Please keep these possibilities in mind, and remember that I am giving you the most accurate information I can. Use it as a guide. I watch my budget as carefully as you watch yours; I am always on the lookout for bargains, and want to share as many with you as is possible in these days of the fluctuating dollar.

Introduction

The main purpose of this book is to act as a very personal, hand-holding guide for every woman who travels. Not only single women, but married women who *think* single. It is the only book on the market today that caters to the special interests of women and to the very particular problems a woman encounters while traveling. Without help, some of these problems can be rather disconcerting if you are a novice at this wonderful game of "gallivanting."

Often a woman traveling alone hopes to run into a fascinating man. And why shouldn't she? One of the secondary purposes of this book is to act as a catalyst between those who are seeking and the sought-after, bringing them together, hopefully, for their mutual enjoyment.

You will find that the book is addressed to three different age groups: 18 to 25 indicated in the listing by letter A; 26 to 40 indicated by letter B; 40 and up indicated by letter C. If a woman of 40 desires company (especially male) she will obviously be more likely to find it at the hotels, etc., suggested under that age bracket, rather than that of the 18 to 25ers. This does not mean, however, that in reading the book you must concentrate on any one particular age group. The groupings merely act as a guide to help you find the kind of people you are interested in. Nor does it mean that this is written only for man-hunters. But it's nice to know the information is there if you want it.

A woman has special needs when traveling that are seldom taken into account by travel agencies, tourist bureaus, or guidebooks. She may want to know, for instance, where she can safely have her hair bleached, get a good facial, have a handbag repaired, or have a dress made inexpensively or altered; how to get a ticket to see the *haute couture* collections, or even where to find a spa for a week's reducing or a plastic surgeon for reshaping.

This book will give in detail all the information necessary to make a woman's trip as easy, comfortable, and as much fun as possible. It will cover three price ranges, from budget to luxury class, so that there is something for everyone.

All information is given on a personal, woman-to-woman

1

basis. It is keyed to the particular needs of all traveling fe-
males, with or without a man, alone, with a friend, or with
several other women.

Since we all have different taste and ideas, you can help
me as well as other travelers. If you find some lovely little
hotel, restaurant, or shop that you were particularly thrilled
with, won't you write me and tell me about it? My research
is kept very up to date, and I will check out your suggestion
for the next edition.

On the other hand, if you have had problems you couldn't
find answers to, or complaints about any of the establishments
listed here, I would like to hear from you on that too. Perhaps I can help you with the problems, and I will definitely
check into your complaints. Management often changes, and
when that happens the service may change as well, so we like
to hear about it in order to reevaluate the situation before
making a recommendation again.

We recognize how important your vacation time and money
are to you and therefore make every effort to suggest only
those places we feel you can surely enjoy. But naturally there
are places we miss, since it would be impossible to cover
every hotel or restaurant in a city, and that's why we welcome any suggestions or tips from our readers. Complaints
are every bit as constructive, and all are taken very seriously.
With your help, the next edition can be even bigger and better.

Part
I
Before
You
Go

Making the Most of Your Trip

Any vacation should be considered an investment in the future. If you'd like to find a man either as a *copain* (friend) or as more permanent company, make the most of your time. Go where the opportunities are best and then spend every minute of your time as if it were money.

Forget about digging up a friend to go with you. You'll do much better on your own and meet people more quickly and easily. Also, you'll be able to be flexible enough to change your plans and follow his itinerary (if you meet him) without having any guilt about leaving your friend. Furthermore, traveling alone away from home, you can be anyone you wish, and that's kind of fun at times. Break your usual bonds and try a new role for a change. Who will know?

Traveling alone requires a lot of initiative. Don't wait for people to speak to you first; men are sometimes leery of approaching a lone woman. But if you extend a touch of friendliness, say to the businessman sitting next to you on the plane, you will more than likely find a willing escort when you land. And if you are staying on after he leaves he may even introduce you to his friends or business colleagues to squire you around after his departure. This, my dears, is precisely how it's done. In Paris, the American Express office is a second home to most travelers, a place where they pick up their mail, book their tours, and cash checks. It's a crowded and informal place where somebody interesting could well turn up. Also, around breakfast time, in any city, your hotel lobby is a good place to be when people stand around awaiting their tours and making plans. Some nice, lonely guest may ask you to join him. It happens all the time.

The dinner hour tends to be later in France than it is at home, so check your hotel about this as soon as you register,

5

as it will determine all your plans. You don't want to dine too early, miss the all-important apéritif hour, and find you have the whole dining room to yourself because you jumped the gun. If you are going to snare a drink- or mealtime companion, you have to be in the right place at the right time—in this case, the pre-dinner apéritif hour. Hotel cocktail lounges allow female guests unescorted, so don't hesitate to take a table and have a drink or two. You will no doubt meet a lot of American men this way, though rarely Europeans, as they do their imbibing at dinner.

During the spring and summer seasons do your relaxing and drinking at the sidewalk cafés, either near your hotel or at one that attracts guests from other first-class establishments. It is quite common to share tables, so keep yours free until the right chap comes along and then flash him a sweet, inviting smile. Very often a man will walk alongside you and start a conversation, asking how long you are staying and offering to show you the sights. Be pleasant to him and enjoy it. You can always cut him off if you want to.

You must decide early on in your travels if you want to find just pleasant company or a serious romance. If it is just company, which is the wisest attitude, accept all offers initially and take the opportunity to see the city with a resident. After all, he can't get past the hotel lobby if you don't want him to. But chances are he will prove interesting and you will see things firsthand that will enhance your store of knowledge about France as well as your memory book. Just remember that the foreign standard of living is not always up to ours. And whether your date is a Frenchman or an American, rich or poor, gold-digging is *verboten*.

Let your escort suggest the restaurant or entertainment. European men are particularly eager to meet American women. There are a couple of reasons for this, and in each case it is best to be forewarned. To begin with, many of them still seem to believe that old story about the streets of America being paved with gold. Either they want to find a woman with some of it stuck to her fingers so they can do the spots with her in style, or they want a chance to come to America legally and make some money of their own; so beware. Many have married American women for position or passport, only to replace them with something better once they are here. If you can't avoid falling head over heels, at least have the presence of mind to think it over carefully. Second, since European women are relatively restricted socially, European men are attracted by the comparative strength and independence of the American woman who is free to do and go as she pleases. With her he can give full vent to his emotions, fall in love if he likes, with no obligation to marry. And when a European shows affection, my dears, that is something you will *never* forget.

However, don't spend all your time man-hunting or your vacation may be completely lost. Being so intense about the man thing can cause you to lose sight of what you have come for—a knowledge and enjoyment of France. Try to forget about being an American and learn to accept what you find, no matter where you go. Don't cling to your expectations or fantasies; if you give up your preconceived ideas, you can enjoy the individual personality and charm that each place offers.

Being a good traveler also involves what you might call "tourist manners," the heart of which is really a consideration for others and their ways. A good rule to start with is to learn the French for "Good morning" and "Good evening," "Please," "Thank you," and "You're welcome." Use them with everyone you deal with, from the bank clerk at the airport where you cash your traveler's checks, to the anonymous chambermaid you may pass in the hotel corridor.

When you are being introduced to anyone at all, including children, be sure to shake hands, and be prepared for another round-robin of hand-shaking, starting with your hosts and continuing with the eldest of the guests, when you leave. The romantic custom of hand-kissing still persists in Europe, thank heaven. So don't put off some gallant chap by thrusting forward your hand for a manly shake. Extend it graciously and gently and let him decide whether to kiss or shake.

People abroad seldom drink mixed drinks before dinner as we do here at home. If, in a private home, you are asked what you will have, it is best to ask for a sherry or vermouth. Smoking is also a touchy subject in many foreign homes, and it is safest to wait until your hostess or host offers cigarettes and you see that other women have accepted them. If there is a man around, never light your own; this is considered very bad form. Thank-you notes are definitely *de rigueur* for any hospitality extended you, whether a dinner in someone's home or a weekend visit. A phone call is simply not sufficient in any situation, as it is here at home. And it goes without saying that you send a gift if you stay overnight. Need I remind you that the subject of politics is strictly forbidden? Whatever you may think, keep it to yourself. You cannot hope to change anyone's mind about his own country's policies, and frankly I don't think you have any right to. Furthermore, you are unlikely to be well-informed enough to discuss the subject intelligently.

Be prepared for all sort of delays, changes, and frustrations on your travels and take them good-naturedly. It doesn't help to complain and will only waste your breath or raise your blood pressure. Another good rule is to keep smiling. This will get you through any difficulty whether you speak the language or not. People always welcome an attitude of warmth and friendliness and will go out of their way to make you feel comfortable. And when this happens you will find that traveling is one of the best and most exciting means of broadening not only your knowledge and experience, but also your circle of friends.

2
Tips for Travelers

Traveling can be interesting, invigorating, and fun. It can also be hectic and debilitating if it's your first trip and you still lack the information and knowledge that we veteran travelers have picked up along the way. Having traveled the world under all conditions—from luxury cruise to African safari—I shall now pass on to you my gems of wisdom.

Packing Hints

This may be the most important part of your preparations, because whatever you pack will have to take care of your needs throughout your entire trip, and in some cases serve triple duty.

When selecting your wardrobe, go over the temperature chart provided on page 38 to see what your requirements will be, and then coordinate accordingly. Remember too that few people are likely to see you in the same thing twice, so you can virtually repeat the same two or three outfits in every city. Unless you can wear at least part of an outfit for every occasion and it can be intermatched, forget it. That lovely dress for which you need a special pair of shoes is best left at home. This means that much more room for goodies you may wish to buy along the way, which, I warn you, will be a strong temptation!

Keeping in mind that you will be living out of a suitcase, packing and repacking it, fishing through it for something when you are in a hurry, or having to find just one little item when you arrive at your destination late and want to flop right into bed, you will understand why I consider your choice of suitcases a major decision.

First, you will need two bags: one large and one small. Today's tote bags are not only good and roomy but very convenient. If you play your cards right, you can get a tote bag

9

through the check-in desk without weighing it. Of course, you will have to carry it with you on board the plane, but that's better than having to check it through and pay overweight charges, isn't it?

I put my heaviest things in a tote bag and leave it on a chair somewhere when I check in, then collect it before boarding. It's also convenient to keep some toiletries, cosmetics (you never know when you may meet some gorgeous male and want to freshen up in a hurry to make points before landing), reading material, and stationery for use in-flight.

Another reason a tote bag is convenient is that you may wish to spend a day at the beach or take an overnight trip somewhere, and it is much easier to carry a tote bag than a weekender-size suitcase.

I will get back to the large suitcase in a minute, but first, another suggestion. A lightweight, plastic garment bag is invaluable, either to carry a few dresses in for a weekend trip without all your luggage, or packed full, several dresses on each hanger, to carry on board over your arm if your luggage is too overweight. Just pack it flat in the bottom of your case until you need it. For a trip of several days, you can pack it with all your hanging things, use the tote bag for all the other essentials, and check the rest of your luggage with the hotel bell captain.

Now for the large case. The very best type of bag to use is one made of light but very strong fiber, that has some "give" to it. The locks, too, are important. These must be sturdy and reliable, or you will have your things spilling out all over the off-loading ramps.

After a lot of experimenting with many different types, my favorite (this is not a plug!) is Samsonite's Fashionaire which opens up flat, like a man's suitcase, allowing you to pack all your dresses and hanging things on one side, and lingerie, accessories, cosmetics, etc., on the other.

On the hanging side, I generally put several garments on one hanger to save space and to keep them from jostling around. The cheap wire hangers are best because they are lightweight and convenient. You can lift them right out and hang them up in your hotel-room closet, and pack them just as quickly. Since you will very seldom find enough hangers in your closet, carrying your own is a good precaution.

Pack the dresses flat into the case, lengthwise, folding at the waistline, and alternating the position of each hanger to evenly distribute the weight and bulk. Leave your nightie and dressing gown for last so you can get at them easily.

Lingerie is best either sorted into coordinate sets and then placed in a plastic bag, or separated according to bras, slips, panties, and stockings, each again slipped by group into a plastic bag. This keeps them all together and all you have to do when packing or unpacking is to slip the bag into your case or a drawer, without having to gather up each piece and fold it. The plastic bags also keep them clean and free of snags.

Two cosmetic bags can separate your toiletries into the things that you use daily, and those that you keep for spares or use only occasionally—suntan lotions, medications, band-aids, shampoo, and the like.

A hanging mirror with a magnifying side to use around your neck is a "must." That way, you can see the back of your hair while using both hands, or take it over to a window for a better light to make up by.

A sewing kit, extra bobby pins, a nail kit, Scotch tape, extra plastic bags, and a laundry kit (portable line, inflatable hangers for drying "drip-drys," and packets of soap powder), plus a travel iron with adapters, complete the necessity list. A tube of Duco Cement also comes in handy for mending fingernails as well as dozens of other things.

Under the heading of medical supplies, remember to take your prescriptions and extra medication if possible. Also: band-aids, bandages, antacid tablets, aspirin, something for constipation and diarrhea, eyedrops, and suntan lotion. A knife, spoon, and fork are also handy for "in-room" snacks and a dozen other uses.

Remember that you are entitled to 66 pounds free baggage allowance in first class and 44 pounds in economy class. Weigh your empty bags first and deduct their total weight from your total allowance. Then eliminate all the things you do not absolutely need, pack the essentials, and leave plenty of room for the irresistibles that you'll find en route.

The moment you arrive in your hotel room you will want to hang all your clothes in the bathroom and turn on the hot water in the tub to steam out the wrinkles. Close the door and leave them in there for at least 15 minutes. Then you won't have to worry about having each dress pressed as you need it. For deep creases, or if there isn't enough steam, wet a face cloth and dampen the creases thoroughly. As the dress dries, the creases will disappear. Be sure, though, that the fabric can stand water.

What to Take

Take the same type of clothes you would wear in a similar season at home, but be sure to add a packable raincoat or all-weather coat, since you are likely to have some rain, especially in Paris. A folding umbrella is also useful.

A neutral or coordinated color scheme in your choice of clothes will help to extend your wardrobe. Separates with matching skirts or slacks are ideal, plus a jacket or sweater, and a couple of basic evening things that pack well. Comfortable, basic shoes and a good roomy handbag that goes with everything are absolutely essential.

Though any manner of dress is acceptable on the streets of France, please don't insult the natives by sashaying into their churches with bare arms, backs, fronts, or whatever. Remember to pack a conservative dress or two.

Being comfortable is most important if you want to relax and sleep on the plane. Avoid wearing tight slacks, dresses, belts, or girdles; a loose-fitting skirt with a jacket or sweater is just the ticket. Take along a pair of slipper socks and put them on as soon as you get on the plane.

Health Hints

Many travelers spoil their trip by failing to observe a few basic dos and don'ts, so take a few moments to go through these tips before you leave home and you should have no problem.

Diarrhea is the usual souvenir of less-than-cautious travelers. Water used to be the number one problem, but, thank heaven, it is now safe to drink the tap water in just about any major city. This is good news for the budget too, since the bottled water we have always been cautioned to drink at all times, even for brushing the teeth, starts adding up after a while. Mind you, I said *tap water*; that doesn't mean you can safely drink at a quaint little spring you may find in some village. In villages or outlying towns it is still wise to stick with bottled water or wine.

The possibility of food contamination is generally a matter of where you eat. Most of the smaller bistros are perfectly safe because they are usually family affairs, with Mama doing the cooking and cleaning, and they are generally pretty fussy about their food and kitchen. You can tell how clean the kitchen or chefs are by the general appearance of the public areas. If these are less than satisfactory, chances are the kitchen isn't any better. In that case, either leave or stick to basic foods that are thoroughly cooked. Cheese and bread with a glass of wine should hold you until you can scout for something a bit more acceptable.

Stay away from any foods of an indeterminate nature, even in the better restaurants. You wouldn't eat hamburger or meatloaf in some places in the United States; follow that rule in foreign countries and you should be able to avoid food poisoning.

Since pasteurization is still not done everywhere, be cautious. Dairy products such as milk or cream, or even custard or cream-filled pastries, require a good sniff and a careful scrutiny before you eat them. The latter may not have been properly refrigerated; or, left out in the open to entice the customer, may have gone bad.

Shellfish should only be eaten when you know for a fact that it has been freshly caught and refrigerated, and that means either at a seaside resort or a good hotel or restaurant.

No raw vegetables or fruit should be eaten without thorough washing. It's wiser to have them cooked first, and also to peel all fruit (which is the European way, anyway). The best bet is not to eat any fresh, raw vegetables at all. Normally this doesn't present a problem in France but it's always better to be on the safe side.

Even with all these precautions one can still get a tummy upset just from the change in eating habits and all the hectic and unaccustomed running around, not to mention a possible change of climate. All those irresistible and delicious French sauces and the fabulous wines can also wreak havoc with the intestinal tract. So carry along a bottle of Kaopectate or similar medication, because nothing can make you feel worse than a case of the "tourista trots" when you are on holiday. I want to stress the fact that you should take along your own anti-diarrhea medication—*don't* buy it in Europe. It has recently been discovered that some of the most popular medications are dangerous, and since they are sold there under several brand names, you won't know what you are buying.

Relax

Nothing is as tiring as sightseeing and shopping. The only way to survive is to stay as fit as possible. Don't rush around like an idiot, trying to see a dozen places in one day—and very likely not remembering a thing about them. Wear comfortable clothes, especially shoes! Sore feet have ruined many a holiday. Try to arrange your sightseeing so that you go first, in the morning, while you are feeling fresh, to a place that requires a lot of walking and stair-climbing; then, in the afternoon, to a place where you can sit or be fairly inactive. Also alternate what you see between the indoors and the outdoors. This will give you enough change of pace and surroundings to conserve your energy and your interest. For lunch, have a light snack: a heavy meal makes you too sluggish afterward to pull your poor body around, especially if you drink wine.

When you return to your room take off all your clothes and stand in the tub. Take the hand shower (most hotels have them) and play a spray of cool-to-tepid water on your legs from the thighs down to the ankles. Use it full force to take full advantage of its therapeutic powers. The heavy spray will relax those knotted muscles, stimulate the circulation, and refresh you to the point where you're ready to go off to your next destination. If there is no hand shower, stand in the tub under the faucet, positioning your legs so that the flow of the water is directed at the calf, gradually working down to the feet. The bidet too (that extra fixture in the bathroom that looks like a seatless john) can also be a big help. Fill it with warm water and massage your feet and toes. (I was taught that trick by Madama Oeri, the directress of the Juvena Beauty Clinic in Zurich, and have blessed her ever since. You will too, once you try it.)

For summertime sightseeing you may want to dispense with stockings, which is fine, but keep a small tin or box of talc to dust your feet and prevent blisters that can make it too painful to carry on. If you get stuck without it, don't stand on formality—whip out your compact and press it into double duty. Use a tissue to dust the powder on your feet, though— save the puff for your face.

Beauty Hints

I believe in using every moment to advantage while traveling, and that's why I prefer to do my own hair and nails, using the time normally spent in beauty salons for shopping or sightseeing instead.

If you can manage your own hair, you're in luck. Roll it around your fingers, stick in a few bobby pins instead of curlers, and wrap it up in a lovely scarf (luckily they're "in" so you will be right in style). You won't have the obvious lumps of rollers and it won't be uncomfortable to sleep on. Just brush out your hair when you get ready and you'll look fresh and neat instead of a mess.

For those who prefer going to a hairdresser, why not do it the day you arrive in the city instead of before you leave home, so you won't have to squash your hairdo sleeping on the plane. Most large hotels have a beauty salon and you can ask for an appointment when you make your reservation. It would be good timing to have it done shortly after you arrive so the shampoo and massage will relax you after your flight.

Broken nails can be such a bother while traveling when you don't want to waste your time with a manicurist. I always carry Duco Cement with me for quick patch-ups. Cover the nail with the glue, then peel off a tiny piece of tissue and pat it over the break. Now put on the nail patch, bringing it right up to the edge on top and on the side to give it more strength. Spread more glue over it. When thoroughly dry, file it down smooth on the top and sides and you're all set. A coat of polish hides all traces of the patch and it will last quite some time.

Rather than carry extra bottles with you that you really don't use every day, take advantage of your hotel room service for your beauty treatments. Here's how:

FACIAL MASK   Tighten and refine the pores by covering the face and neck with simple honey. Order it with your breakfast and put the remainder in your medicine chest so the maid won't take it away.

CLEANSER   Naturally you will want to carry your own with you, but should you run out, regular cooking oil can be used for the same purpose. When you order a salad, ask for vinegar and oil dressing and hang onto the cruets of both.

ASTRINGENT   Cucumber will remove the traces of oil and

act as the perfect tonic, closing the pores and tightening the skin.

TIRED OR BURNING EYES   Here again cucumber comes to the rescue. A slice on each eye will give you soothing relief and take down the swelling. Good for under the eyes, too, when they puff up.

BATH OIL   The same salad oil can be used in the bath to moisturize your skin. Have the water quite hot so you open all the pores and allow it to penetrate, so that when you wipe off the excess as you get out of the tub there is a sufficient amount left in the pores to work.

BUBBLE BATH   Plain shampoo gives you a rich bubble bath and, depending on the type used, can also moisturize and clean.

SHINY HAIR   To give your hair new life, sheen, and body, beat up a raw egg with a fork and work it through your hair, letting it sit for a while before washing it out.

HAIR RINSE   To remove all traces of oil and soap (very difficult in hard-water areas), use the vinegar left over from your salad for guaranteed "squeaky clean" hair.

DRY, SUN-BLEACHED HAIR   Ask room service to heat a half-cup of salad oil for you, or put it in a glass and then into a basin of hot water. Daub it all over the scalp and the rest of your hair. Wrap a towel around your head for a couple of hours (at least one), then shampoo. You will need two or three sudsings to get it all out, but it will be worth it. Your hair will gleam like a new penny and be as soft as silk.

MOISTURIZING MASK   Plain yogurt can do wonders for your skin. Just leave it on as long as you like and rinse off. Your skin will feel soft and silky, and firm.

Extra Tips

Your Duco Cement will also come in handy for dozens of other things: a stone popped out of its setting, a shoe sole or strap that has pulled open, the broken cap of a cosmetic bottle, cracked mirror in a compact—any number of things.

Scotch tape is another indispensable, great for a hem that has come undone until you can fix it. And speaking of hems, like most women you may buy something on your trip that you wish to wear while traveling. If you want to hem it yourself and don't have any straight pins, just use bobby pins to hold it in place while you hem it. They also make good paper clips or bookmarks. When using a guidebook it's a good idea to clip a bobby pin on the top of important pages you want to refer to that day—a map of the city, local transport, certain shops or monuments you may want to see, etc. You can also clip your sales receipts together this way to keep them all in place for the time when you have to make out your customs declaration. Try scotch-taping a hotel envelope to the inside cover of your guidebook to keep them in. Another on the other cover could hold business cards of people you meet along the way and want to write to later.

To make sure you have handy all the names and addresses of people you want to see, write them in the back of this book so you won't have to look all over for separate slips of paper or address books.

3
From Here to There

Vacation time being as precious as it is, the most logical way to get where you are going is to fly. I highly endorse flying via the national carrier of the country of your destination; that's why I recommend Air France when going to France or French-speaking countries. Pricewise, it's the same as all other international airlines. The service is excellent, as are the meals. But just as important is the fact that you have about seven hours to accustom yourself to the sound of French, and even to practice whatever phrases you know. These will come in handy when you arrive in France, so look at the chapter of French phrases in this book, and learn a few more. There's no time like the present.

To get down to the question of how much the flight will cost you, even the experts are having difficulty in figuring out air fares these days. The airlines have been plagued with one problem after another, from a fare hike to the dollar devaluation, and now the fuel crisis. All these have of course been reflected in the fares given below, which I hope will still apply when you book your reservation.

All fares are round trip and will be listed on the basis of New York as the embarkation point. Fares change from Peak to Shoulder to Winter Season:

Peak Season is from June 1 to August 31.
Shoulder Season is from April 1 to May 31, and from September 1 to October 31.
Winter Season is from November 1 to March 31.

Standard Fares

	TO PARIS	TO NICE
First Class	$1,206	$1,328
Economy Class:		
Peak	824	916
Shoulder	652	762
Winter	612	724

If you plan to stay at least 14 days but no more than 21 days, you may go on the 14-to-21-day excursion fare. This fare also allows you one free stop between New York and your final turnaround city, and another stop between your turnaround city and New York. For example, if you were flying from New York to Paris, you would be allowed a free stopover in London on the way over.

14-to-21-Day Excursion Fare

	TO PARIS	TO NICE
Peak Season: June 1 to August 31	$642	$714
Basic Season: September 1 to May 31	554	627

If you plan to stay between 22 and 45 days, you are eligible for yet another lower fare rate, the 22-to-45-day excursion fare. No stopovers are allowed on this.

22-to-45-Day Excursion Fare

	TO PARIS	TO NICE
Peak	$526	$560
Shoulder	428	458
Winter	388	426

There are also additional plans such as GIT fares and Affinity Groups. GIT fares require that you guarantee a certain expenditure in your land arrangements in addition to the air fare. Also, on the 14-to-21-day GIT, there must be 15 passengers; on the 7-to-8-day winter GIT, there must be ten passengers. You can make arrangements for such tours through the airline office or your travel agent. Affinity Groups (all members of the same club, company, or organization) can travel in groups of a minimum of 40 passengers.

There is an additional saving if you live in any of the gateway cities in America that Air France or other international airlines fly to, such as Anchorage, Boston, Chicago, Houston, Los Angeles, Philadelphia, and Washington, D.C. In this case, you would book your ticket directly from your home city to Paris, rather than booking a domestic flight between your city and New York, and then your international ticket from New York to Paris. You pay only the add-on fares listed below, *added to* the New York–Paris fare. As you can see, these savings are sometimes quite substantial.

Gateway Cities Add-on Fares

FROM	First Class	Economy	14-to-21-Day Excursion	22-to-45-Day Excursion
Anchorage	$430	$250	$147	$133
Boston	deduct $18	deduct $10	deduct $7	deduct $5
Chicago	130	104	100	76
Houston	246	200	208	199
Los Angeles	450	306	207	P 225
				S 180
				W 170
Philadelphia	30	20	17	17
Washington, D.C.	58	38	31	31

To complicate matters even further, there is a weekend surcharge which applies to all these fares. You must pay an additional $15 if you leave New York for Paris on a Friday or Saturday, and an additional $15 if you arrive in New York from Paris on a Saturday or Sunday.

4
Useful Information

Though Paris is the focal point for most tourists coming to France, if you have the time it would be a shame not to explore other regions. I don't recommend driving to female tourists for many reasons which I won't go into here, but with the French National Railways as good as it is, there is no reason why you cannot visit other areas in the greatest of comfort and in the least amount of time. The trains are speedy, clean, and very comfortable, and food service is available on most. There are many districts I could recommend, but it's unlikely that you will have time to see everything—so I will suggest just a few of the most important places that I think every woman will be delighted with: the château country south of Paris; Deauville, to the north, on the English Channel; and the famous Riviera on the coast of southern France.

Trains

The French National Railways are excellent; they are fast and very comfortable. You can take the coach, a *couchette,* or a sleeping compartment. There is an additional fee of about $5 for the couchette, which has six bunks. Here you can lie down but can't undress, so if you want more comfort and security you will need a sleeping compartment, which runs quite a bit more.

Round trips up to 1,500 kilometers (about 1,000 miles) are just double the price of the one-way ticket, but if you are traveling between 1,500 kilometers and 1,800 kilometers (about 1,000 to 1,200 miles), there is a saving of 20%. One-day Sunday and three-day weekend tickets up to 50 miles offer a 30% to 50% saving.

French express trains are super lickety-split and *très, très* comfortable. The Rapide will get you from Paris to London in 6 hours.

Hang onto your ticket because it will not be collected until the end of your trip, and if you lose it you will have to pay again. A ticket is valid for from 10 to 30 days. If you don't use it, don't expect to get an immediate refund; what with the red tape, it can take up to four months before you get your money.

Meals are no problem on French trains as there are several different services. The dining car has three sittings and requires reservations, which you can make on the platform outside the dining car before the train leaves; failing that, ask the steward. There are also cafeterias where the food is quite good and half the price of the dining car. Some trains even have an inexpensive tray service at your seat.

Eurailpass

If you are going to do a lot of traveling by train it is definitely to your advantage to buy a Eurailpass. This allows you unlimited first-class travel in 13 countries without tickets. You merely show your pass and you're off. Costs are: 21 days: $150; 1 month: $190; 2 months: $260; 3 months: $300.

Validity of the Eurailpass begins the date you have it stamped, so don't have this done until you are ready for your first trip. They are only available in North America. Buy one before you leave at any travel or railway ticket office, or from Eurailpass, P.O. Box 191, Madison Square Station, New York, N.Y. 10018.

FRENCH GOVERNMENT REGULATIONS

Visa

No visas are required for U.S. or Canadian visitors, just a valid passport.

Health

U.S. and Canadian citizens need no inoculations to enter France. However, a smallpox vaccination is required by the United States upon reentry to the country, so get this before you leave. For a time, this requirement was dropped, but after a recent outbreak of smallpox in Europe it was reinstated, so get it anyway just to be on the safe side.

Customs

Articles of personal wear can be brought into France duty-free, provided they are for the traveler's own use and conform to normal needs.

TOBACCO Travelers entering France from non-European countries can import duty-free: 400 cigarettes or cigarillos, or 125 cigars, or 1 pound of tobacco. These must be carried in hand luggage to avoid paying duty, and women are not allowed to bring in cigars or tobacco duty-free.

OTHER CONCESSIONS

1 quart of liquor
3 bottles of wine
2 still cameras of different sizes or make
1 movie camera
10 rolls of black-and-white film for each camera or 20 rolls of color film for each
10 rolls of film for movie camera
1 portable musical instrument
1 phonograph with 4 LP records
1 recording machine with 2 rolls of tape or wire or 10 records
1 portable radio
1 pair of binoculars, or field or opera glasses
1 baby carriage
1 set of small camping equipment and 1 tent
1 set of sports equipment (skis, tennis rackets, golf clubs, 2 hunting guns with 50 rounds of ammunition)
1 portable typewriter
1 each of the usual portable electrical appliances (iron, hair curlers, hair dryer), as well as medical apparatus, personal jewelry, toilet articles, souvenirs, etc.

Certain goods are strictly banned and must be reexported or be deposited or abandoned at the Customs Office. These include especially: spurious printed matter; drugs; books, writings, and pictures banned by the French government; powder and ammunition (except a concession of 100 cartridges for sportsmen).

CLIMATE

Temperatures in Europe are quoted in Centigrade, which can be pretty confusing. To convert to Fahrenheit there is a formula that you just have to memorize. It seems difficult at first, but once you've set it in your mind it's really quite easy to remember. Here's the rule:

Double the Centigrade figure, subtract 10%, and add 32.

For instance, if the Centigrade reading is 20°, double it and you get 40; 10% of 40 is 4, which subtracted from 40 gives you 36. Add 32 and the Fahrenheit reading becomes 68°.

It's a good idea to try to remember just a few conversions so you automatically know them without having to calculate. I find it convenient to remember the Centigrade figures for 75° and 85° because if it's the former I know I can wear a dress with sleeves and should perhaps carry a light sweater or shawl; if it's the latter I dress as coolly as possible. The Centigrade figures of 30° (86°F) and 25° (77°F) tell the story automatically for me. But here's a comparison table for quick reference:

Centrigrade	Fahrenheit
—18	0
—15	5
—10	14
—5	23
0	32
5	41
10	50
15	59
20	68
25	77
30	86
35	95
50	122

SIZE CHARTS

Sizes can be a problem in Europe until you memorize the ones that are important to you, so use the following charts until then.

Hosiery

American, Australian, English	European
8½	1
9	2
9½	3
10	4
10½	5
11	6

Shoes

American and Australian	English	European
3½	2	33
4½	3	34
5–5½	3½–4	35
6–6½	4½–5	36
7–7½	5½–6	37
8–8½	6½–7	38
9–9½	7½–8	39–40

Blouses, Sweaters, Slips

American	European
10–30	38
12–32	40
14–34	42
16–36	44
18–38	46
20–40	48

Coats, Dresses, Suits, Skirts

American	European
7–8	38
9–10	40
11–12	42
13–14	44
15–16	46
17–18	48

WEIGHTS AND MEASURES

Liquid Measure

1 liter = 1.057 quarts
1 pint = 0.56 liters
1 quart = 1.136 liters
1 gallon = 4.54 liters

Weight

1 kilogram or kilo (1,000 grams) = 2.2 pounds
1 metric ton (1,000 kilograms) = 2,204.62 pounds

Area

1 square meter = 10.76 square feet
1 square kilometer = 0.3861 square miles
1 hectare = 2.471 acres

Distance

1 kilometer (1,000 meters) = approx. ⅝ mile
1 meter = approx. 39 inches or 3.28 feet
1 centimeter (.01 meter) = .4 inch
1 millimeter (.001 meter) = approx. .04 inch

TO CONVERT KILOMETERS TO MILES: Divide by 3 and multiply by 2. Thus, 60 kilometers becomes: 60 ÷ 3 = 20; 20 × 2 = 40 miles.

Time Conversion

Paris is 6 hours ahead of the eastern United States. Therefore, when it is 6 P.M. in Paris, in the United States it is:

EST	CST	MST	PST
12 noon	11 A.M.	10 A.M.	9 A.M.

Telephone Service

You won't find telephone booths on every corner as at home. You will have to make your calls from a hotel, restaurant, or post office. In many places you go to a desk and give the attendant the number you want and she will get it for you, directing you to an empty booth when you take the call. In other telephones you need a special coin—a *jeton*—which you buy at newsstands, a tobacconist's, or from the cashier at a restaurant or café.

To make a call, put the *jeton* into the slot, lift the receiver, and dial your number. The ringing tone sounds like our busy signal. When your party answers, press the button *A* and begin speaking. Their busy signal is sort of a *bip-bip-bip* sound. The price of the *jeton* has been changing with the recent fluctuation of international currency but at the time of writing is about 40 centimes at a post office, 50 centimes at a café or restaurant, and maybe a bit more when purchased at a hotel. To call the United States it costs $12 for 3 minutes, person-to-person, and $3 for every minute after that.

Telegrams and Cables

These are sent either from your hotel or from the post office. A straight wire to the United States is $2.14 for up to 7 words and 30 cents for every word thereafter. A night letter cost $3.40 for up to 22 words and 20 cents for each additional word.

Postal Service

Letters weighing ¾ of an ounce cost 50 centimes within France and most of Europe. Postcards are 1.10F for airmail abroad. An airmail letter to Canada and the United States is 1.40F for one sheet of airmail paper and envelopes, plus half that for each extra sheet. Stamps can be purchased at your hotel, the post office, or a tobacconist's.

Currency

With the value of the dollar fluctuating like a yo-yo as I write this, I strongly urge you to check on current prices before leaving on your trip so you'll know the worst. Call your local bank or a French Tourist Office or embassy if you have one in your city. The *Wall Street Journal* and many other newspapers carry the latest currency values, too. At the moment $1 = 4F and I hope it doesn't go any lower. For easy calculation think of 1F as approximately $.25, or useful for tipping just about anyone to whom you would give a quarter in the United States. That way you lose the tendency to think of the French currency as "play money," as travelers so often do.

If possible, try to buy some French francs at your bank before you leave so you will have enough when you arrive to avoid having to stand in the long lines at the airport to get them. You will need enough to tip the porters and for your cabfare to the hotel; $15 worth of francs should be more than sufficient. When you get to your destination, go to the bank for the best rate of exchange. You would be surprised at the difference it makes.

Accommodations

In the cheaper hotels or pensions you must specify that you want a room with a bath; they don't come automatically equipped with same. In fact, some don't even have toilets in the room, so that's another point to check on, as no bath is one thing but a room without a john isn't worth the savings to the budget. If you do book a room without a bath and want to use the public facilities, you will have to recognize the signs on the door so you know what room you're going into:

Bain = bath   *Douche* = shower   *W.C.* or *Toilette* = toilet

Continental breakfast is usually included in the price of your room at first-class and deluxe hotels, even in some second-class hotels or pensions. It consists of *croissants* (luscious, flaky, crescent-shaped rolls) or *brioches* (which look like popovers but aren't as light or flaky), butter, jam, and coffee, tea, or hot chocolate. Anything other than that you pay for.

Hotel Taxes

In France you will be taxed 22% of your total bill. Keep this in mind when figuring the cost of your room into your budget. *Caution:* Try to pay for meals ordered from room service in cash. That way you pay the tax only once. If you sign for it, it goes onto your total bill, so you not only pay the tax on the meal check but again on the total hotel bill, making for an unreasonable total of 44%, which is outrageous. If you do sign, always see that the bill is fully filled out *and totaled* before you sign it! Many waiters have been known to have you sign and then add on whatever they wish. This is quite a racket in the hotel business.

Tipping

Most restaurants automatically add a 15% service charge to your check and it's not necessary to tip any more than that unless you feel you have had special service, in which case 5% extra is sufficient. If the service is included you will see *"service compris"* or *"tout compris"* on the menu. If it's not included (*"service non-compris"*), tip 12% to 15% of the total. Be sure to check each item on the bill before you pay it, as mistakes are made too often to always be considered mistakes. You will be charged for bread and butter if you touch it, so if you don't, make sure it isn't on your bill. The wine steward, if he serves you, gets another 12% to 15% of the cost of the wine, or one or two francs.

At your hotel tip the chambermaid .50F per day; leave it on the dresser when you leave. The concierge will virtually be your "French connection" because you can go to him for everything you need. He will tell you how to get where you want to go, get tickets for you, make reservations—just about everything. Tip him when you leave, depending on the services he has performed for you. One or 2F per day will usually do.

Give 1F per day to the waiter who brings your breakfast in the morning. In Europe it's customary to put your shoes outside your door at night for the porter to shine, so give him 1 or 2F depending on how often you have used his services.

A bellboy gets 1F per bag at either the hotel or the airport. Washroom attendants and theater ushers get .50F, and taxi drivers, beauticians, and manicurists each get about 15%.

Electric Current

Most of France uses 110–115 volts AC, although more and more places are switching to 220–230 volts. If you are taking an electrical appliance with you such as an iron or hair dryer, make sure that it has a switch for both currents. If not, buy a converter for about $10 or you will blow out your appliance. If your appliance is designed to work on foreign voltages, you must still be sure to take a set of adaptor plugs as there is no set type of outlet in Europe. Every hotel has a different kind. One may require a three-pronged plug, another a two-pronged type requiring either flat sides or round plugs. If you forget you can always get them in Europe but you're better off getting them before you leave home.

Emergency Medical Services

During the night or on Sunday, the nearest police station will give you the name and address of a doctor who is on call, or of a pharmacy that is open.

If you have to be hospitalized, the doctor who attends you will advise you on the hospital or nursing home you should enter, and will make the necessary arrangements.

Pharmacies

Every pharmacy displays a notice when it is closed, giving the names and addresses of pharmacies in the area which are open.

Lost Property

PASSPORT   Inform your embassy immediately, and you will be advised what steps to take.

TRAVELER'S CHECKS   Immediately notify a branch of the bank that issued the checks, giving them a list of the serial numbers; also declare your loss to the police station in your area.

PERSONAL EFFECTS   If you know exactly where the loss occurred, notify the police station in that quarter. If the item is found, you will have to pay a small charge, about 10% of its value, to reward the person who handed it in. Losses must be reported within three months of the date of loss.

IF YOU ARE IN DIFFICULTY . . .

Contact your embassy or legation, which will refer your case to the attaché who is knowledgeable about the particular problem you may have. But in certain cases, you may wish to make use of the various public services listed on page 43.

5
Useful French Phrases

If you can't pronounce these phrases, just point to the one you need.

Greetings

Bonjour. Je m'appelle————.	Good morning. My name is _____.
Bonsoir.	Good evening.
Je suis heureuse de faire votre connaissance.	I am happy to meet you.
Comment allez-vous?	How are you?
Très bien, merci. Et vous?	Very well, thank you. And you?
Je me suis très bien amusée.	I (have) enjoyed myself very much.
S'il vous plaît.	Please.
Merci.	Thank you.
Pas de quoi.	You're welcome.

Traveling

Combien de temps le voyage à _____ va-t-il durer?	How long will it take to go to _____?
Quand arriverons-nous à _____?	When will we arrive at _____?
Appelez-moi un taxi, s'il vous plaît.	Please get me a taxi.
Quelle est cette rue?	What street is this?
Est-ce la bonne direction?	Am I going in the right direction?
Dois-je changer d'autobus?	Do I have to change buses?
Veuillez me dire où il faut descendre.	Please tell me where to get off.
Voici mes bagages.	Here is my baggage.
Dois-je tout ouvrir?	Must I open everything?
Je n'ai rien à déclarer.	I have nothing to declare.
A quelle heure et à quel quai est le train pour_____?	What time and at what platform is the train for_____?
Veuillez mettre ceci dans le filet.	Please put this on the rack.
Où est le wagon-restaurant?	Where is the diner?

Hotel

Je veux le petit déjeuner dans ma chambre.
I want breakfast in my room.

Veuillez m'appeler à____heures.
Please call me at____o'clock.

Puis-je faire laver des affaires?
Could I have some laundry done?

J'ai des choses à repasser.
I want some things pressed.

Veuillez préparer ma note.
Please make out my bill.

Apportez-moi, s'il vous plaît, encore une couverture [un oreiller, des cintres, du savon, des serviettes, du papier hygiénique].
Please bring me another blanket [pillow, more hangers, soap, towels, toilet paper].

Theater

Avez-vous des places pour ce soir?
Have you any seats for tonight?

Je veux un fauteuil d'orchestre [une place réservée, un fauteuil au balcon, une loge].
I want a seat in the orchestra [a reserved seat, a balcony seat, a box].

Shopping

Voulez-vous me diriger à une pharmacie [une épicerie, une quincaillerie, un cordonnier, un horloger, un tailleur]?
Will you direct me to a pharmacy [a grocery store, a hardware store, a shoemaker, a watchmaker, a tailor]?

Combien est-ce?
How much is it?

Je préfère quelque chose de moins cher.
I prefer something less expensive.

Pharmacy

Je veux du sparadrap [une brosse à dents, de la pâte dentifrice, du produit détachant, un peigne, des toiles anticor, de la lotion antimoustique, un laxatif, du rouge à lèvres, des lames de rasoir, des serviettes hygiéniques, du shampooing, de la savonnette, de l'huile de soleil, un thermomètre].
I want to buy some adhesive tape, [a toothbrush, toothpaste, cleaning fluid, a comb, corn pads, mosquito repellant, a laxative, lipstick, razor blades, sanitary napkins, shampoo, soap, suntan oil, a thermometer].

Time

Quelle heure est-il?
What time is it?

Il est____heures et demie.
It is half past____.

Il est___heures et quart.	It is a quarter past___.
Il est___heures moins le quart.	It is a quarter to___.
à___heures moins dix	at ten minutes to___

Numbers

un	one	*vingt*	twenty
deux	two	*vingt et un*	twenty-one
trois	three	*vingt-deux*	twenty-two
quatre	four	*trente*	thirty
cinq	five	*quarante*	forty
six	six	*cinquante*	fifty
sept	seven	*soixante*	sixty
huit	eight	*soixante-dix*	seventy
neuf	nine	*soixante-et-onze*	seventy-one
dix	ten	*soixante-douze*	seventy-two
onze	eleven	*quatre-vingts*	eighty
douze	twelve	*quatre-vingt-un*	eighty-one
treize	thirteen	*quatre-vingt-dix*	ninety
quatorze	fourteen	*quatre-vingt-onze*	ninety-one
quinze	fifteen	*cent*	one hundred
seize	sixteen	*cent un*	one hundred and one
dix-sept	seventeen	*trois cents*	three hundred
dix-huit	eighteen	*mille*	a thousand
dix-neuf	nineteen		

Months of the Year

janvier	January	*juillet*	July
février	February	*août*	August
mars	March	*septembre*	September
avril	April	*octobre*	October
mai	May	*novembre*	November
juin	June	*décembre*	December

Days of the Week

dimanche	Sunday	*jeudi*	Thursday
lundi	Monday	*vendredi*	Friday
mardi	Tuesday	*samedi*	Saturday
mercredi	Wednesday		

Part
II
Paris

6
Welcome to Paris

So here you are in Paris! You've had a tantalizing glimpse of the city on the way from the airport; your bags are unpacked, your dresses steaming in the bathroom where you've had a fascinated look at the bidet, and now, forgetting all about jet lag, you're ready to go out and see for yourself the most beautiful city in the world.

Paris is a city of fascinating contrasts: modern buildings that speak of tomorrow, 17th-century mansions that whisper of the intrigues of yesterday. Its history is everywhere—at the Louvre, or in the Tuileries Gardens which date back to 1564, with images of Louis XIII, Napoleon and Josephine, and other members of the French royal family who strolled there. Or at the Conciergerie, where Marie-Antoinette was imprisoned before her trip to the guillotine, with Madame du Barry.

Paris is also in the present moment, having coffee at the Café des Deux Magots, watching the students and the *types* stroll by; it's having a late night snack at the café tucked away behind the Renault showroom on the Champs-Elysées, or strolling along the beautiful tree-lined boulevards.

THE BEST TIME FOR PARIS

Lately, it seems that the weather has changed inexplicably all over the world, and what used to be a good time of the year to be in a particular region may not be today. So please don't hold me responsible if it drops into the 50s when I have said it should be warm and sunny.

There are four seasons in Paris and the temperatures are fairly close to those in the Midwest or East of the United States. The average maximum temperatures are (in Fahrenheit):

Jan.–Feb.	Mar.–Apr.	May–June	July–Aug.	Sept.–Oct.	Nov.–Dec.
44°F	55°F	70°F	75°F	65°F	46°F

In my opinion, April to June and September through October are the best times to visit Paris, not only because the weather is better then but because the tourists are scarcer, and you can enjoy the city much more. No waiting in lines for tickets or to see the sights.

In the summer Paris is jammed, and mainly with tourists because the Parisians evacuate the "City of Light" as if there were a plague. In August you will be hard pressed to find many Parisians, except the few who stay behind to keep the city breathing—if not vibrating.

However, if you have always wanted a designer gown and couldn't afford the usual sky-high prices, July and August or January through March are your best bets because then the designers cut their prices almost in half to make way for the new collections. So it could be a very propitious time for your visit.

If meeting interesting men is your cup of tea, early October and June are excellent, provided you have a hotel reservation well in advance. In October Paris is packed with visitors to the Auto Show, and in June to the Air Show.

HOW TO GET AROUND

The first thing to do is pick up a copy of the *Plan de Paris par Arrondissement* for about 7F ($1.75) at any big bookstore or newsstand. It gives you all the maps and information you need to find your way around, including a map of the city and one for each arrondissement.

Arrondissements are separate, numbered districts that divide the city. Every address carries the number at the end: 1er (1st), 2e (2nd), 3e (3rd), etc. This helps you find the part of the city where the address is located, so make a habit of looking for it.

If you are staying at a hotel in the 8th arrondissement and want a beauty salon nearby, just check the addresses in the phone book until you find those with "8e" after them—*voilà*, instant tracking service!

The districts fan out from the center of the city (the first arrondissement). The Seine acts as the dividing line between the Right and Left banks, the Right Bank being the north side of the river. There are 20 arrondissements.

The 1st arrondissement could be the logical starting point of your first tour of Paris, but it's easier and more pleasant to start at the top of the Champs-Elysées (8th arrondissement), and work east along the Right Bank, then cross the Seine and come back up the Left Bank to complete the circle. And, with a few exceptions, you will only be concerned with arrondissements 1 through 9 anyway.

The 8th arrondissement is most famous for the Arc de Triomphe at the Place de l'Étoile, better known as simply "Étoile," and it is aptly named as it acts as the center of a star formation of 12 streets all extending, spoke-like, from this beautiful arch, whose twin is in Greenwich Village in New York.

The 8th arrondissement is also the area where you will find the poshest beauty and couturier salons, and it is worth walking around just to look in the windows.

Ambling east on the beautiful Champs-Elysées we come to the 1st arrondissement on the Right Bank and here is where you will find Place de la Concorde, and Place Vendôme, Jardin des Tuileries, and the Louvre. Then north to the 2nd for the Opéra and Place de la Madeleine. The 3rd is nothing special so we will skip it and carry on to the east and the 4th which brings you back to the Seine again. This district takes in the Ile de la Cité, the little island in the middle of the Seine on which stands the famed Cathedral of Notre Dame; and the second island, Ile St.-Louis, home of many famous celebrities, notably the Aga Khan.

Crossing the river now to the Left Bank, you are in the 5th arrondissement—the Latin Quarter—glorified in so many songs, stories, and films as the mecca of artists. Here you will find the famous art and book stalls side by side, the Seine ambling along behind them as the perfect backdrop. Farther south from the river, the Boulevard St.-Germain and its surrounding area will boggle your mind with their mad "mod" boutiques. The Sorbonne also makes its home here; the pulse of Paris and perhaps the world in general can be taken in the 5th arrondissement and neighboring 6th, because it is the traditional meeting ground for the youth and artists not only of

France but of all countries. Here they congregate at sidewalk cafés, bistros, and cellar clubs to eat, drink, dance, paint, sculpt, write, revolt, and discuss the problems of the universe.

In the 7th arrondissement Napoleon's Tomb, in Les Invalides, and the Eiffel Tower (Tour Eiffel) are the main attractions. Not national landmarks but, I find, just as interesting, are the beautiful old mansions once belonging to the élite of Paris and now housing foreign embassies. To walk the streets taking in each architectural detail is to conjure up an image of what life once was in the days of the aristocracy.

Actually the 7th arrondissement completes our circle tour of the heart of Paris, but there are a few other districts that have a place in your plan of exploration. The 16th arrondissement on the Right Bank, adjacent to the 7th and 8th, is another "must" as it is the site of the magnificent Bois de Boulogne, one of Paris's most famous and beautiful parks, encompassing seven lakes and ponds, camping grounds, racecourses, restaurants, and a Shakespearean theater. In this district, too, you will find the Palais de Chaillot with its anthropological, naval, and French monument museums. And again some elegant mansions—the Duchess of Windsor and Omar Sharif being examples of the caliber of the residents.

The 18th arrondissement takes us to Montmartre with its lingering memories of Toulouse-Lautrec, Utrillo, and others. The little sidewalk cafés and bistros around the Place du Tertre are still there where they once painted, along with the basilica of Sacré-Coeur and Pigalle.

This will give you a brief preview of where things are, and I hope you will thoroughly explore each district.

Subways

Or, *le Métro,* as it is called in France. No need to fear it because you don't speak French. I guarantee you won't get lost and you will enjoy the experience to boot. There is something especially exciting about finding your way around successfully in a strange city.

At the entry of each station and again on each platform there is a map of Paris with all the subway lines indicated. Find the station you want to get to and look for the last stop on that line, which will give you the name of the line you want to look for. (Each line is named after its last stop: e.g., *Direction Nation* is the line that ends at Nation.) Next find the red circle that indicates where you are at present. It's a simple matter now to trace your course. You just keep going in the *"direction"* you selected on the map and get off at the station you want. You may have to transfer to another line; here again, you select the right one and go in that *"direction."* When you change trains follow the signs that say *"Correspondance."* They will lead you to the transfer points at which you get the train going in your new *direction.* Don't be concerned if the signs lead you through tunnels, up and down stairs, etc.; just have faith that you will wind up exactly where you want to go.

The Métro has nowhere near the seating capacity of our own subways, and the infirm and aged get first chance at the seats there are. However, the cars are much roomier than ours and there is plenty of room to stand.

First-class tickets are 1.50F and second-class 1.30F. You must keep them until you disembark at your final station, as periodic checks are made to make sure that only first-class ticket holders are riding those coaches.

The Métro runs from 5:30 A.M. to 1:15 A.M. Books of tickets at discount prices are available for the tourist. You have a choice of a 10-ticket book, 2nd class, for 8F ($2) or a "Tourist Ticket" (1st class) for about 30F ($7.50) which is valid for 7 days and entitles you to travel on the suburban Sceaux Line, as well as the subways and buses in Paris and certain suburbs.

To get one of these books go to any of the offices of the RATP, the public transportation company, at the Office de Tourisme de Paris at 127, avenue des Champs-Elysées (8th); Syndicat d'Initiative de Paris, 7, rue Balzac (8th); and Tourist Offices of the RATP, 53 bis, quai des Grands-Augustins (6th), and on the Place de la Madeleine (8th) next to the church, near the flower market.

Buses

Not the best means of getting around if you want to save time, but you do get to see more of Paris topside than on the subways below. Try taking a double-decker with no destination in mind except to see the sights. Some buses have an open air platform in the back where you can station yourself for a better view in all directions. The route I enjoy runs along the Boulevard St. Germain, then out along the Seine to the

Bois de Bologne (Bus #63). It's a trip that gives you a real feel of this interesting area.

Buses begin running from 6:00 to 6:30 A.M. and the last one leaves the terminal between 9:00 and 9:30 P.M., though some run until 12:50 A.M. This is indicated at the bus stops. Service is not as frequent on Sundays and holidays. You can buy a ticket for 1.30F or a book of 10 for 8F at the bus terminal, on the bus, and at a tobacconist's bearing the red RATP sign.

There will be a line at the bus stop and you must wait your turn. At some stops there is even a ticket machine such as you find in stores at home, where you take a number and wait for it to be called before you board the bus. Now *that* is French practicality!

Taxicabs

Taxi stands are generally located near street corners, outside railroad stations or official buildings, and at air terminals and airports. Take the first cab at the head of the line. You can also flag one on the street if you can find one. Cab drivers usually understand enough English to get by, but if you want to try your French go right ahead.

Always make sure the cab has a meter and that it doesn't start until you get in. The initial drop is 2.50F ($.62) and about .50F ($.13) per kilometer after that.

Normal luggage will usually be carried free if it fits into the cab, but drivers have the right to charge you .50F extra per bag. Tip about 15%.

The fare between the airport and Paris is between 18F and 30F ($4.50 to $7.50) depending on where your hotel is. After 11 P.M. prices are quite a bit higher.

HANSOM CABS   Obviously you won't be taking a horse-drawn cab for purposes of transport, but purely as a romantic venture, so you will be willing to pay for the privilege. Don't pay the first price the driver asks for; you have to negotiate the price. Offer less and, if he refuses, walk away slowly as if disinterested. If he wants you he'll come after you. You will find these carriages at: the Opéra, the Eiffel Tower, the Tuileries Gardens, the Rond-Point des Champs-Elysées, and the Bois de Boulogne.

Rental Cars

I am not going to give you any details on driving in Paris because I don't want to be responsible for anyone who attempts it. All I can say is—*don't!!*

USEFUL ADDRESSES

Police

COMMISSARIAT CENTRAL   9, boulevard du Palais (4th)   Tel: 17
At the principal intersections in the city, there are emergency call boxes; by breaking the glass, you can call the nearest police station. You may also call the police by dialing 17 on any phone.

Emergency Medical Services

Tel: 83.01.01
Call the above number; or, during the night or on Sunday, the nearest police station will give you the name and address of a doctor who is on call, or of a pharmacy that is open.

Pharmacies

Every pharmacy displays a notice when it is closed, giving the names and addresses of pharmacies in the area which are open.

Ambulances

You can call an ambulance by telephoning the Poste Central des Ambulances Municipales Urbaines, 6, quai de Gesvres (4th), Tel: 272.94.00.

Post Offices

Most post offices are open from 8 A.M. to 11 P.M.
MAIN POST OFFICE   52, rue du Louvre (1st)
No. 8   49, rue La Boëtie (8th)
No. 7.   Aérogare des Invalides (7th)
No. 102   40, boulevard de Vaugirard (15th)
No. 118   15, rue d'Amsterdam (8th)

The following post offices accept cables or telegrams day or night:
No. 44   103, rue de Grenelle (7th)
No. 47   Place de la Bourse (2nd)
AÉROPORT D'ORLY
ANNEX I   71, avenue des Champs-Elysées (8th)   (up until 9 P.M.)

Consulates

U.S. CONSULATE   2, rue St.-Florentin (7th)   Tel: RIC. 03.03

U.S. EMBASSY   2, avenue Gabriel (8th)   Tel: ANJ. 74.60
BRITISH CONSULATE   3, rue d'Aguesseau (8th)   Tel: ANJ. 27.10

CALENDAR OF EVENTS

It's important to know just what's going on in Paris so that, for instance, if you only have a couple of days to spend and want to do some shopping, you don't pop in over a national holiday and find all the stores closed. It's happened to me on many occasions, and I have often heard women complain that their travel agent should have told them. Of course, some of these events you may want to be on hand for. Here is an approximate list for the year.

Autumn

FÊTE DES VENDANGES (Grape Harvest Festival)   Place du Tertre, Montmartre (18th)   Métro stop: Abbesses   October
The grapes are gathered from one remaining old vineyard on the Rue des Saules, and it is most interesting to see as there is a lot of festivity.
CONCERTS by visiting foreign orchestras at the Salle Gaveau, Salle Pleyel, and Théâtre des Champs-Elysées   October
MOTOR SHOW   Porte de Versailles (15th)   Métro stop: Porte de Versailles   October
This is one of the several times during the year that Paris is completely sold out. If you must go to Paris at that time you must absolutely have a reservation several months in advance. The city is very crowded and you may find, even though you've booked a reservation, that by the time you get there it's gone, so be sure to reconfirm it before your arrival.
SALON DES ARTISTES-DÉCORATEURS   Grand Palais, Avenue Winston Churchill (8th)   Métro stop: Champs-Elysées   October–November
CHRYSANTHEMUM SHOW   Porte d'Auteuil (16th)   Métro stop: Porte d'Auteuil   October–November
PARIS INTERNATIONAL DANCE FESTIVAL Théâtre des Champs-Elysées   15, avenue Montaigne (8th)   November

Winter

INTERNATIONAL BOAT SHOW   C.N.I.T. Exhibition Hall, Rond-Point de la Défense (18th)   January
Another busy time in Paris.

Spring

PERFORMANCE OF THE ST. JOHN PASSION Church of St.-Germain-des-Prés   March or April

ESSCA-PADE (jazz festival and ball)   Pavillon d'Ermenonville
March or April
HOLIDAY ON ICE   Palais des Sports   April
SPRING FLOWER SHOW   Parc de Bagatelle   April–May
FAIR   Ermenonville Amusement Park   Late May
Featuring a full variety show, lotteries, cinema, and theater stars,
etc.

Summer

FESTIVAL DU MARAIS   Music and dramatic performances in the
courtyards of the Hôtel de Sully, Hôtel de Rohan, and Hôtel
d'Aumont   Nightly at 9:15 P.M.   May, June, and July
Also concerts in local churches.
PROGRAM FROM THE MAISON DU MARAIS   46, rue François
Miron (4th)   Tel: 887.74.31
THÉÂTRE DES NATIONS   International drama festival with visiting foreign companies   Odéon Théâtre de France   Nightly at
9 P.M.   May, June, and July

Bastille Day: July 14

The French national holiday, a particularly gay and noisy
one. You probably won't get any sleep at all. It is also a time
when most stores and businesses are closed, so plan accordingly.

The following events take place on that day:
MILITARY PARADE   From the Étoile to the Place de la Concorde
9:30 A.M.
PUBLIC BALLS   Place de l'Hôtel de Ville, Place de la Bastille,
Place Voltaire, Place Armand-Carrel, and Place Gambetta
Starting at 9 P.M.
FIREWORKS   Eiffel Tower, Pont-Neuf, Auteuil Viaduct, Buttes-
Chaumont, Porte Brancion, Parc Montsouris, and Montmartre
Starting at 10 P.M.

May–October

VERSAILLES MUSIC AND DRAMA FESTIVAL   Nightly at 9 P.M.
PARIS INTERNATIONAL TRADE FAIR   Parc des Expositions

June–October

SON ET LUMIÈRE   Sound-and-light spectacle   Hôtel des Invalides

7
Where to Stay

There is no doubt that hotels in Paris are pricey indeed, as everything else in Paris, but—if this is any consolation at all—they are so well regulated by the government that at least you know you are getting what you pay for, and prices are restricted. In 1970, the government took a very firm stand on the control of the service and rates of all hotels. They use the star system for classification: Deluxe, four star, two star, and one star, and now they have added the NN notation as well, which indicates that the hotel has been recently renovated. A double N before a four-star classification means that it is better than a plain four-star without the NN.

This control by the government is particularly valuable to travelers on a budget. Naturally, deluxe hotels offer the best of everything, but if your budget dictates a less than top-class establishment, you can breathe easier knowing that even the cheapest hotels have to meet rigid standards.

The price of a room usually includes taxes and a continental breakfast, which consists of *croissants,* rolls, jam, coffee, tea, or hot chocolate. At the moment, some of the hotels I have inspected have not yet heard if their new prices will be approved for next year, but half have already been notified that they will be allowed a 5% increase. Accordingly, I have taken the liberty of adding the same rates to the hotels that were not too sure, as I am almost positive they will be granted the same increase. If not, well, you'll have a nice surprise in store when you pay less than you expected. However, don't count on it.

You will find it much easier to select a hotel if you first decide what part of Paris you wish to be in. If shopping is your pleasure you may want to be in an area that offers *haute couture* salons, department stores, or boutiques. Or you may prefer to be near museums or parks. In any case, just choose the area of your interest and then select a hotel listed below for that particular location.

You will find only the hotels in the more touristy parts of Paris listed here—areas that are safe and convenient for women. So, though there may be very inexpensive hotels in the outlying districts, I have not included them. Since hotel space in Paris is always at a premium, it is wise to book at least a month in advance for even the most modest hotel, for somehow even they manage to be full to the brim. Should you arrive in Paris without reservations, call the Comité de Tourisme de Paris at 127, Champs-Elysées (8th), Tel: ELY. 52.78, and they will help find a room for you. They will only guarantee one night, but at least that gives you a chance to find something on your own. There is no charge involved.

All prices have been figured at the rate of 4F per dollar, but this may change by the time you read this. High season runs from March 15 to the end of July and again from September 1 to November 15.

The letter A, B, or C after an address refers to the age group of the clientele at that particular establishment. This means that if a hotel is marked *A* you will find mostly young people from 18 to 25 staying there, which may not be your cup of tea if you are 40.

A = 18 to 25   B = 26 to 40   C = over 40

RIGHT BANK HOTELS

Deluxe

LE BRISTOL   112, rue du faubourg St.-Honoré (8th)   B-C Tel: 359. 23.15   Cable: BRISTOTEL   Métro stop: Champs-Elysées–Clemenceau

In the heart of shopping on the poshest street and near the Place Madeleine. They have lots of diplomats and businessmen since they are also near the embassies. Room rates: double with bath, 320F to 500F ($80 to $125); for a single it's 200F ($50) for a small single bed, and 340F ($85) for a double bed in a larger room. Breakfast, taxes, and services are included. All rooms have phones, wall-to-wall carpeting, twenty-four-hour room service, air conditioning. The doubles are large and done in traditional French décor. All double rooms are huge with mirrored wardrobe doors and entry hall. There is a dressing alcove and every bath has a dressing table with magnifying mirror and a separate little basin for brushing your teeth, no less. All baths are marble. Singles vary in size, but they are nicely done as well. They have a restaurant, the Bristol, open 12 to 3 for lunch and 7 to 10 for dinner. There is also a nice bar and lounge. One-day dry-cleaning service. Beauty salon, open 9 to 6:30 Monday through Friday, and just a block away you will find the Alexandre Salon, which is open on Saturday.

HÔTEL GEORGE V 31, avenue George-V (8th) B-C Tel: 225.35.30 Cable: GEORGEOTEL-PARIS 086 Métro stop: George-V

Very posh clientele with a lot of businessmen. Rates for a single room, low season, are: 230F ($57.50); high season, 250F ($62.50). Doubles, low season: 330F ($82.50); high season, 360F ($90). Taxes are included but no breakfast or service. Continental breakfast is 16F ($4). All rooms have a phone, radio-TV, wall-to-wall carpeting, mini-bar, twenty-four-hour room service, and a very large bath. Rooms are large and mostly done in the traditional French manner—except for the sixth, seventh, and eighth floors, which were all redone in 1972 in a modern style. All are different, and every one is as beautiful as the others. Restaurant Les Princes: lunch and dinner, and snacks all day long. It is really a very pretty restaurant. The main dishes run from 24F to 45F ($6 to $11.25). Twenty-four-hour cleaning service. The beauty salon is open from 9 to 7, closed on Sunday, with English-speaking attendants. The bar is open from 11 A.M. to 3 A.M., and is a good place to meet people. Little sitting areas all around an outdoor patio make it a very relaxing place to sit and write letters or just to sit and enjoy.

HÔTEL INTER-CONTINENTAL 3, rue de Castiglione (1st) B-C Tel: 073.18.00 Cable: INHOTELCOR-PARIS Métro stop: Tuileries and Concorde

They get a lot of businessmen, especially American. The rates for a single room are 142F to 190F ($35.50 to $47.50); for a double 182F to 238F ($45.50 to $59.50). No breakfast, taxes, or service included. All rooms have a phone, radio, wall-to-wall carpeting, mini-bar, and twenty-four-hour room service. The singles are small and the doubles are medium size. All are furnished very nicely in the traditional French style, and most of the rooms are quite different. The coffee shop is ultramodern and features American snacks. The Rôtisserie is open 12 to 3 and 7 to 10, with excellent French cuisine. The Bistro is a very comfortable bar with a harpist at the cocktail hour. Twelve-hour cleaning service and they do have a beauty salon. The Inter-Continental is just across from the Tuileries, which are the gardens in front of the Louvre. It is ideally located just off the Rue du Faubourg St.-Honoré with *haute couture* shops all around it. This hotel has a great deal of history. It was originally the Hôtel Continent, built in 1878 on the ruins of the old Ministry of Finance, constructed under Napoleon I. It became the favorite place of all the greats in succeeding years: King Peter I of Serbia, King Fouad of Egypt, and Empress Eugénie, the last crowned resident of the Tuileries, who used to come here to meditate and to dream. During the war it was closed as a hotel and used for some time by the Germans—not to resume activity again until 1968 when it was taken over by the Inter-Continental chain, and fully refurbished to become once again the epitome of elegance and splendor.

THE LANCASTER 7, rue de Berri (8th)   B-C   Tel: 359.90.43
Métro stop: George-V

This is a smaller hotel, tucked away on a side street rather than on a major thoroughfare, so the hotel is quiet and gets a very reserved clientele. All rooms are done in typical French décor and are really quite lovely. Rates for a single room are: 215F to 276F ($53.75 to $69); double: 277F to 357F ($69.25 to $89.25); including breakfast, taxes, and service. All rooms have telephones, wall-to-wall carpeting. Baths are modern with tub-shower and double basin.

HÔTEL MEURICE 228, rue de Rivoli (1st)   B-C   Tel: 073.32.40
Cable: MEURICEOTEL   Métro stop: Tuileries

Lots of businessmen and just a few small tourist groups. Single: 215F to 240F ($53.75 to $60); double: 330F to 350F ($82.50 to $87.50); taxes are included, but no breakfast or service. Continental breakfast 13F ($3.25). All rooms have phone, radio-TV, wall-to-wall carpeting, twenty-four-hour room service. The single rooms are medium size and surprisingly nice. Doubles are large and are all attractively furnished in the French traditional manner. Very large baths with double basins and separate glass door showers, make-up tables, and lots of good long mirrors all over. The Copper Bar serves drinks and snacks from 11 A.M. to midnight. There will be a restaurant, though it's being refurbished at the moment; it will be open for lunch from 12 to 3 and dinner from 7 to 10. Twelve-hour dry-cleaning service. Beauty salons are open from 9:30 to 6:30; closed on Sunday. The cost of a shampoo and set there: 30F ($7.50); cut 15F and up ($3.75); color and bleach 50F ($12.50); manicure 20F ($5). The lobby and lounges are very elegant, with huge crystal chandeliers and beautiful traditional French furniture, antiques, tapestries, and paintings. Even the elevator doors are lacquered in the Chinese style. A lovely hotel in an excellent location, just across from the Hôtel Inter-Continental and the Tuileries Gardens, near the Louvre and good shopping including Rue du Faubourg St.-Honoré, the street of all the elegant *haute couture* shops.

PLAZA-ATHÉNÉE 25, avenue Montaigne   (8th)   B-C   Tel: 359.85.23   Telex: 65092   Métro stop: Alma-Marceau

This is a very popular hotel with South American millionaires. The rates for a single room are: 245F to 268F ($61.25 to $67); for a double: 375F to 432F ($93.75 to $108); including breakfast, taxes, and service. All rooms have a phone, TV, wall-to-wall carpeting, twenty-four-hour service. They are large and beautifully appointed throughout with a very comfortable, happy tone. The restaurant, grill, and English bar are a favorite meeting place for high society, models, actresses, etc.

HÔTEL PRINCE DES GALLES 33, avenue George-V (8th)   B-C   Tel: 225.39.90   Métro stop: George-V

Next door to the George V with the same sort of clientele—lots of interesting businessmen. Single: 247F to 305F ($61.75 to $76.25); double: 379F to 402F ($94.75 to $100.50); including taxes, but not service or breakfast, which is 15F ($3.75). All rooms have phone, radio, TV, wall-to-wall carpeting, twenty-four-hour room service, and baths. The rooms are done in Regency or Empire style and have that elegant feeling of the best of Paris living. The hotel is constantly being refurbished and has just completed a large portion of the rooms. The colors are beautifully coordinated and bright. The rooms are quite large and roomy, even the singles. Off the back there is a charming garden restaurant with flowers growing profusely in sculptured patterns. The main dining room is the height of elegance, in a quiet manner, with pink linen, crystal chandeliers, and, of course, excellent service. There are little alcoves around for sitting and reading and a paneled bar which is a good place to meet new people. Beauty salon, open from 9 to 7, closed on Sunday.

RITZ   15, place Vendôme (1st)   B-C   Tel: 073.28.30   Telex: 22262   Métro stop: Opéra
Very, very posh clientele. Single: from 175F to 210F ($43.75 to $52.50); double: from 255F to 315F ($63.75 to $78.75). All plus 15% service charges. All rooms include a phone, radio, wall-to-wall carpeting, twenty-four-hour room service. They are large and beautifully done in the French traditional manner—big baths and all the goodies one would expect at the Ritz Hotel. The restaurant is very famous and difficult to get into; I would definitely suggest a reservation. It is open 12 to 3 for lunch, 7 to 10 for dinner, and very expensive. The hotel is beautifully situated on the Place Vendôme. The buildings on the Place Vendôme were originally the sumptuous mansions of rich financiers who had vied for homes in this little circle, then called Place Louis-le-Grand. The hotel blends inconspicuously into the other buildings around it and you really have to look to find it. The epitome of elegance! It is grandly furnished with original period pieces and is famous for the ultimate in service, cuisine, and comfort. This is one of the most distinguished hotels in the world.

Four Star NN

BEDFORD   17, rue de l'Arcade (8th)   B-C   Tel: 265.40.32
Cable: BEDFORTEL-PARIS   Métro stop: Madeleine
Near the Madeleine. They have a lot of businessmen. The rate for a single is 114F ($28.50); for a double: 142F ($35.50). Breakfast, taxes, and service included. Every room has a phone, wall-to-wall carpeting. The singles are medium size, but very nice and bright. Doubles are large. The old-style doubles are very large and well done, but the renovated rooms are furnished in the modern style. The restaurant is the Relais Victoria, open for lunch from 12 to 2:30, dinner 7 to 9:30. It also serves snacks, sandwiches, omelets, pastries, etc., from 11 A.M. to midnight. Steak from 18F to 24F ($4.50 to $6). One-day cleaning

service or express. They also have a bar. The halls need a paint job and look a bit dirty, but the rooms are bright.

THE CALIFORNIA 16, rue de Berri (8th)   B-C   Tel: 359.93.00 Telex: 66634   Métro stop: F.-D.-Roosevelt
The rates for a single room are: 116F to 147F ($29 to $36.75); for a double: 155F ($38.75); all including breakfast, taxes, and service. Wall-to-wall carpeting, telephone, and twenty-four-hour room service. The rooms are large, simply furnished, and very convenient. Some of the furniture is genuinely antique, but the rest are reproductions. The dining room opens onto a lovely courtyard with a fountain and lots of plants, making it a lovely spot in the summertime. The hotel is large and just opposite the *Paris Herald-Tribune,* so there are usually lots of journalists popping in for a drink or a meal. It is just a short distance from the Champs-Elysées.

HÔTEL CASTILLE 37, rue Cambon (1st)   B-C   Tel: 073.48.20 Métro stop: Concorde
The rates for a single room are: 87F to 97F ($21.75 to $24.25); for a double: 128F to 153F ($32 to $38.25); all including breakfast, taxes, and service. Every room has a telephone and wall-to-wall carpeting and is very large. Done in the simple, old-fashioned French manner, they are very comfortable and extremely clean. All baths are well equipped. Here, it is suggested that you look at the room before you agree to take it because they do vary a bit; some have been redone and some not. The great feature of the hotel is its gorgeous flowered patio, which makes it especially nice in the summer. The dining salon is quite nice with a fireplace and chandeliers, but the rest of the rooms are rather simple. This hotel is owned by the same company as the Ritz Hotel and that sort of service prevails.

THE CECILIA 11, avenue Mac-Mahon (17th)   B-C   Tel: 380.32.10   Métro stop: Étoile
The rates for a single room are: 75F to 115F ($18.75 to $28.75); for a double: 85F to 125F ($21.25 to $31.25); breakfast, taxes, and service included. All rooms are large and have high ceilings and splashy wallpaper, fireplaces, chandeliers, wall-to-wall carpeting, and telephone. Sparkling bathrooms. This is very convenient to the Arc de Triomphe and is family owned, so you'll have very personal service. They really treat you very, very well, especially a woman alone.

THE CELTIC HOTEL 6, rue Balzac (8th)   B-C   Tel: 225.09.25 Cable: CELTIC-PARIS   Métro stop: George-V
The rates for a single room are: 110F to 130F ($27.50 to $32.50); for a double: 140F to 160F ($35 to $40); all including breakfast, taxes, and service. Every room has a phone, wall-to-wall carpeting, a twenty-four-hour service and is nicely furnished. Just a few steps off the Champs-Elysées and very convenient. It does have a restaurant and bar.

CLARIDGE HOTEL 74, avenue des Champs-Elysées (8th)   B-C Tel: 359.33.01   Telex: 28412   Métro stop: George-V
The rates for a single: 115F to 145F ($28.75 to $36.25); for

a double: 170F ($42.50); all including breakfast, taxes, and service. All rooms have a phone, wall-to-wall carpeting, and old-fashioned furniture and are medium to large. Location-wise you can't beat this hotel since it is right in the middle of the Champs-Elysées. The decor is turn-of-the-century and a welcome change from all the modern skyscrapers. There is a colorful rotunda lounge for drinks or coffee and a huge marble hallway with lots of crystal and old-fashioned, overstuffed furniture. There is also a marble Turkish bath and a swimming pool. The restaurant is open from 12 to 3 and 7 to 10. Fixed-priced dinner 37F ($9.25).

ÉTOILE PARK   10, avenue Mac-Mahon   (17th)   A-B-C   Tel: 755.69.63   Métro stop: Étoile
Single: 84F to 95F ($21 to $23.75); double: 102F to 108F ($25.50 to $27); breakfast, taxes, and service included. All rooms have a phone and wall-to-wall carpeting, are of medium size and comfortably decorated. The hotel was renovated in 1969 and all baths are now modern. Some of the rooms have balconies, which is very romantic at night, when you can see the Arc de Triomphe all lit up. Convenient location and good value for the money.

CHÂTEAU FRONTENAC   54, rue Pierre-Charron (8th)   B-C   Tel: 359.35.07   Métro stop: F.-D.-Roosevelt
The rates for a single are: 98F to 105F ($24.50 to $26.25); for a double: 71F to 157F ($17.75 to $39.25); all including breakfast, taxes, and service. Clientele here includes a lot of businessmen and some groups. The hotel has recently been renovated and offers every convenience. It's only one block from the Champs-Elysées, so the location is perfect. All rooms have a telephone, TV, and refrigerator. They are medium size and all modern.

LE GRAND HÔTEL   12, boulevard des Capucines (8th)   B-C   Tel: OPE.05.40   Telex: 22-875   Métro stop: Opéra
Just opposite the Opéra and all good shopping. This hotel gets a lot of international businessmen. Rates for a single are: 160F ($40) for the standard room and 180F ($45) for the new modern rooms; for a double: 200F to 250F ($50 to $62.50). All rates include breakfast but not tax and service. Telephone, radio, TV, wall-to-wall carpeting in all rooms. Doubles are medium size and have automatic bellboy for drinks, large baths, and mirrored wardrobe doors. Singles are small but attractive, especially the new modern studio rooms. The demi-suite 264F ($66) is particularly nice—very modern with grass wallpaper, modern bath, and antique writing table. The famous Café de la Paix Restaurant is located in the Grand Hôtel. It is said that this is the meeting place of the world; if you sit there long enough you are bound to see someone you know. There is also the Pacific Grill, several other little cafés grouped together, and an outside terrace. The hotel has been renovating regularly and doing a very good job of it. A very modern lobby and an en-

larged sunken lounge for drinking, meeting, etc. It's convenient
to everything and really a good selection.

HÔTEL LOTTI   7, rue de Castiglione (1st)   B-C   Tel: 742.93.84
Cable: OTELOTTI   Métro stop: Tuileries and Concorde
The rates for a single room are: 142F to 173F ($35.50 to
$63.25); for a double: 242F to 273F ($60.50 to $68.25). All in-
clude breakfast and taxes, but not service. All rooms are very
large, have phones, wall-to-wall carpeting, and twenty-four-hour
room service. The modern baths have magnifying make-up mirrors and are done in the French traditional manner. Very good
value here. The restaurant, Le Cadran, is open from 7 to 10 A.M.
for breakfast, 12 to 3 for lunch, and 7 to 10 P.M. for dinner.
Fixed-price menu: 40F ($10). Twenty-four-hour service for
dry cleaning. No beauty salon but you have Berger right around
the corner and the Inter-Continental just down the street. There
is also a bar. Every winter they remodel twenty to thirty rooms,
so the hotel is always kept up-to-date. It is beautifully located,
just up the street from the Tuileries Gardens.

HÔTEL LOUVRE CONCORDE   Place du Théâtre-Français (1st)
A-B-C   Tel: 508.43.00   Cable: LOUVROTEL, PARIS   Métro
stop: Palais-Royal
Near the Louvre, Palais Royal, and Avenue de l'Opéra. Type
of clients: mostly businessmen and groups, especially Japanese.
The rate for a single with a bath is 129F ($32.25); for a double
with bath: 123F ($30.75); all including breakfast, taxes, and
service. Rooms have phones, wall-to-wall carpeting, and twenty-
four-hour service. They are large, modern, and have mirrored
wardrobe doors. The coffee shop is open from 7 until midnight,
the restaurant from 12 to 3 and 7 to 10; they also have a bar.
Frankly, all these facilities are lacking in atmosphere and are
not pleasant at all. If you have to have a snack, they're sufficient, but that's about all I can say for them. Laundry: 12-hour
service express. Beauty salon: open 9 to 7, closed on Sundays.
The hotel was renovated in 1972 with new baths and modern
furniture. They also have a massage unit, so for 1F ($.25) you
can have fifteen minutes of comfort.

HÔTEL MÉRIDIEN   81, boulevard Gouvion-St.-Cyr (17th)   B-C
Tel: 758.12.30   Métro stop: Porte Maillot
This hotel gets a lot of businessmen and groups. Single room:
164F to 213F ($41 to $53.25); double: 205F to 256F ($51.25
to $64); breakfast, taxes, and service included. All rooms have
phones, radio, television, wall-to-wall carpeting, modern baths,
and mini-bars. They are not too large but have a good view of
the city. This is the largest hotel in the country and brand new,
with all the modern conveniences of a new American hotel—
shops, restaurants, beauty salons, etc.—which make it unneces-
sary even to leave the hotel if you don't wish to.

NORMANDY   7, rue de l'Echelle (1st)   Tel: 073.04.80   Cable: NOR-
MANDY PARIS OO   Métro stop: Pyramides and Palais-Royal
Near the Louvre and the Avenue de l'Opéra. A lot of business-

men. The rate for a single is 100F ($25); for a double, 137F to 200F ($34.25 to $50). Rates do *not* include breakfast, taxes, or service. The doubles are large and done in the traditional French manner. Half of the singles are modern and very large, and half have not yet been redone. Breakfast is 10F ($2.50). The restaurant is open for lunch 12 to 3 and for dinner from 7 to 11. One-day service on dry cleaning. Beauty salon open from 9 to 7, closed Sunday and Monday. There is a bar. The sixth and seventh floors will be renovated by the end of 1974 and all rooms will have mini-bars then.

P.L.M. ST.-JACQUES 17, boulevard St.-Jacques (14th) B-C Tel: 589.89.80 Métro stop: St.-Jacques
Single: 120F ($30); double: 150F to 190F ($37.50 to $47.50); breakfast, taxes, and service included. All rooms have telephone, radio, TV, wall-to-wall carpeting, modern bath, and mini-bar. Again, this is a new hotel and, with its modern shops and even a Jerry Lewis Cinema Theatre in the building, its feeling is far more American than French. It is owned by the Rothschilds and features a kind of service the Rothschilds are perhaps quite used to themselves. The Café Français is right out of the Gay '90s; you can also have a snack at the Petit Café or an exotic meal at Le Tempura. Then too, there is a Polynesian Bar and a garden bar, so one wants for nothing here. The only problem is, I find, that it's a bit out of the way and taxi fares do tend to run up if you are not a Métro rider.

RÉGENCE-ÉTOILE 24, avenue Carnot (17th) A-B-C Tel: 380.75.60 Métro stop: Étoile
Single: 32F to 82F ($8 to $20.50); double: 50F to 128F ($12.50 to $32); no taxes, service, or breakfast included. The rooms are tiny but very gay, clean, and comfortable, all with tubs or showers. No restaurant. This is a very handy place just off the Arc de Triomphe, convenient to everything.

THE REGINA 32, place des Pyramides (1st) B-C Tel: 073.74.00 Métro stop: Tuileries
The rates for a single room are: 108F to 129F ($27 to $32.25); for a double: 138F to 300F ($34.50 to $75); all including breakfast, taxes, and services. All rooms have a phone and wall-to-wall carpeting and are rather large. Old-fashioned French traditional décor with many antiques, very authentic flavor. There is a courtyard with a fountain and lots of flowers, and private little salons if you wish to write letters or visit quietly. There is a restaurant for lunch and dinner—12 to 3 and 7 to 10.

HÔTEL ROBLIN 6, rue Chauveau-Lagarde (8th) B-C Tel: 265.57.00 Cable: HOTEL ROBLIN Métro stop: Madeleine
Near the Madeleine. The clientele here is just single people, no groups. Double with bath: 150F to 160F ($37.50 to $40); single without bath: 120F ($30). Room service 7 A.M. to 10 P.M. The single rooms are very small, the double medium to large. All are simply furnished but nice, very bright and colorful; modern baths. The #2 line rooms are magnificent, absolutely huge! They have make-up tables, mirrored wardrobes, fireplace, velvet spreads,

and all the finer touches. There are five like this so if you can, try to get one. They all face the front. (A #2 line room is 160F or $40.) The manager, Mr. Kauffmann, is very kind and charming and you can go to him for any information or service. The restaurant, Le Mazagran, is open from 12 to 3 for lunch and 7 to 9:30 for dinner. *À la carte* dishes just 40F to 60F ($10 to $12).

HÔTEL SCRIBE   1, rue Scribe (9th)   B-C   Tel: 742.03.40
Cable: SCRIBOTEL PARIS   Métro stop: Opéra
Near the Opéra, just across the street from the Grand Hôtel. Type of clients: primarily businessmen and groups. The rate for a single room is 169F ($42.25); for a double, 198F to 224F ($49.50 to $56). These rates include breakfast, taxes, and service. All rooms have phones, wall-to-wall carpeting, and twenty-four-hour room service. Most rooms are old-fashioned and I don't find them too interesting. But the new deluxe, modern rooms are very nice: medium size with TV, mini-bar, and large baths. Singles are large whether they are the modern or old-fashioned type. Scribe coffee shop is open for breakfast 7 to 10 A.M., lunch 12 to 3, and dinner 7 to 11:30 P.M. Fixed-price meals: 35F ($8.75). Twenty-four-hour service for laundry. The beauty salon, with English-speaking attendants, is open 9:30 to 6:30, closed on Sunday. They also have a large selection of perfumes. A shampoo and set is 29F ($7.25), cut 14.50F ($3.63), color 59.50F ($16.88), manicure 18F ($4.50). There is also a bar. The second floor will be totally remodeled by May, 1974, by which time two-thirds of the hotel will have been redone. But the ill-lit halls and lobby are still dreary and uninteresting! Of the two, I feel the Grand, across the street, is a far better buy.

HÔTEL LA TRÉMOILLE   17, rue de la Trémoille (8th)   Tel: 225.64.95   Métro stop: Alma-Marceau
A favorite of visiting nobility and dignitaries. Single: 100F to 110F ($25 to $27.50); double: 110F to 250F ($27.50 to $62.50). Rates do *not* include breakfast, taxes, or service. A continental breakfast is 9F ($2.25). Rooms are medium to large with telephones and wall-to-wall carpeting. Very near to the Champs-Elysées in a rather nice residential area, the hotel is quiet and dignified. The rooms are done in a comfortable French traditional manner. No restaurant.

VICTORIA PALACE   6, rue Blaise-Desgoffe (6th)   B-C   Tel: 548.80.40   Métro stop: St.-Placide
Single: 115F ($28.75); double: 150F ($37.50); both including breakfast, taxes, and service. All rooms include telephone, TV, wall-to-wall carpeting, Louis XVI–style beds and chairs, and lovely marble-top tables with black hardware. Most of the baths are done in Italian marble and are very modern. There is a beautiful green courtyard opening off the dining room, which is open for lunch 12 to 3, and dinner 7 to 10. Fixed-price meals 40F ($10). There is also an American bar. The management takes particularly good care of its clients, which is why they get repeats year after year after year.

Three Star NN

HÔTEL DE L'ARCADE 7–9, rue de l'Arcade (8th) A-B-C Tel: 265.43.85 Cable: ARCADHOTEL-PARIS Métro stop: Madeleine

They get all types of clients, from all over the world. Single: 82F to 91F ($20.50 to $22.75); double: 105F ($26.25); including breakfast, taxes, and service. All rooms have phones and wall-to-wall carpeting, and modern baths. The singles are small but modern and very nice. The doubles are small to medium. There is no restaurant in the building, but a few doors down at the Bedford Hotel, which is under the same management, you can sign your check and they will put it on your bill at the Hotel de l'Arcade. The Bedford also has a small bar. TV and radio are expected to be in all rooms by the end of 1974. This is a good value and a very nice hotel; excellent service.

HÔTEL BRIGHTON 218, rue de Rivoli (8th) B-C Tel: 073.27.80 Métro stop: Tuileries

Single: 78F to 100F ($19.50 to $25.00); double: 109F to 115F ($27.25 to $28.75); breakfast included. The rooms have a phone, wall-to-wall carpeting, fireplaces, mirrored wardrobe, and make-up tables. The doubles are large and very attractive, with modern baths, with two basins. If you're taking a double, ask for a twin-bedded room rather than one with a double bed; it's much nicer. The singles are plain but have good, modern baths, though not too big. Twenty-four-hour dry-cleaning service. The restaurant is open only from April 1 to November 1. The bar is open all day until midnight. Excellent value for the price; and the location, just opposite the Tuileries, the deluxe hotels, and all the famed *haute couture* shopping, makes it well worth considering.

HÔTEL LIDO 4, passage de la Madeleine (8th) A-B-C Tel: 266.27.37 Métro stop: Madeleine

Single with bath: 91F ($22.75); single with shower: 83F ($20.75); single without bath: 57F ($14.25); double with bath: 110F ($27.50); double with shower: 90F ($22.50); all including breakfast, taxes, and service. All rooms have phones and wall-to-wall carpeting. Singles have double beds but are rather small, especially those without a bath; however, even these have toilet, wash basin, and bidet. The rooms here are simply furnished, very pleasant and colorful, and a good bargain. The hotel was renovated in 1972. Its lobby is very modern, and in the rooms they have even thought of special little touches like a hanging pincushion, shoe cleaners, and a clothes brush. On a little side street, a passage really, off the Place de la Madeleine.

MADELEINE-PLAZA 33, place de la Madeleine (8th) B-C Tel: 265.20.63 Métro stop: Madeleine

Facing the back of the Madeleine and the most centrally located of all the Madeleine area. Single: 79F to 95F ($19.75 to $23.75); double: 93F to 110F ($23.25 to $27.50); including breakfast, taxes, and service. All rooms have phones, wall-to-wall carpeting, new modern baths that are quite spacious. One-day service for dry cleaning. Should you happen to be driving or have friends visiting, there is parking right next door and directly across the street. The manager, Madeleine Berthelin, is extremely kind and charming as are Françoise and Elaine, both of whom speak English.

HÔTEL MONT-THABOR   4, rue du Mont-Thabor (1st)   B-C   Tel: 073.22.73   Cable: HOTEL TABOH   Métro stop: Tuileries and Concorde

Large numbers of South American businessmen stay here. Single: 91F ($22.75); double: 122F ($30.50); triple: 150F ($37.50); breakfast, taxes, and service included. All rooms have a phone, wall-to-wall carpeting, and room service until 1 A.M. The singles all have showers but no baths; they are very small but quite convenient. The doubles are medium to large, all furnished in traditional French style and rather nice. The triple is lovely: there is a paneled alcove for the third bed and the style of the room, done in colorful grass wallpaper, is very interesting. By the time this book is published, the restaurant will be remodeled and open from 12 to 3 and 7 to 10. All the lobby and salons will be renovated as well, though work had not been started at the time I saw the hotel. The manager, Mr. Juan Alvarez, is very kind indeed and will be only too happy to help you. The hotel is conveniently located just behind the Hotel Meurice and near the Tuileries and all good shopping.

HÔTEL OPAL   19, rue Tronchet (8th)   A-B-C   Tel: 265.77.97   Métro stop: Havre-Caumartin

Single: 43F to 73F ($10.75 to $18.25); double: 50F to 80F ($12.50 to $20); breakfast, taxes, and service included. Every room has a telephone, radio, wall-to-wall carpeting. Rooms are medium size, done in the French traditional style, and are extremely charming. It is close to the Madeleine, Opéra, and St.-Lazare station, and a very important shopping center; this is right in the heart of Paris.

POWERS   52, rue François-1er   B-C   Tel: 359.64.95   Métro stop: F.-D.-Roosevelt

All the rooms have a phone, wall-to-wall carpeting, and are furnished in the typical French style. The doubles are very large. Single: 95F ($23.75); double: 130F ($32.50); not including breakfast or taxes. Continental breakfast 8F ($2).

HÔTEL VIGNON   23, rue Vignon (8th)   A-B-C   Tel: 073.27.65   Métro stop: Madeleine

Double with bath: 86F to 93F ($21.50 to $23.25); twin with bath: 93F to 123F ($23.25 to $30.75); twin without bath: 57F ($14.25); twin with a shower: 71F ($17.75); all prices including breakfast, taxes, and service. All rooms have phones, wall-to-wall carpeting, and are very simply furnished. The single rooms have no toilet, though they have a bidet, wash basin, and shower. Why, with all that equipment, they skipped the toilet, I don't know! The rooms are very clean and adequate. Grill and Bar (not the hotel's, actually) is in the lobby. There is a beauty salon right across the street, on a side street near the Madeleine.

Two Star NN

ARC ÉLYSÉE   45, rue Washington (8th)   A-B-C   Tel: 359.59.74
Métro stop: George-V
Single (without toilet): 62F ($15.50); double: 72F ($18). Breakfast 6F ($1.50). All rooms have a telephone and wall-to-wall carpeting. Singles are rather small, with a basin and a bidet but no toilets. It is really worthwhile to take the double room because the price isn't that much different and at least you will have a toilet. All doubles have a shower; only five have bath tubs. No elevators, so if you don't feel like hiking, this is not the hotel for you. However, for the price, it is certainly a bargain. Just off the Champs-Elysées and extremely convenient. It gets a very young crowd as well as older people, and requires two to three weeks notice in advance. I recommend more than that because I have written them several times and not had a response for months.

HÔTEL ARROMANCHES   6, rue Chateaubriand (8th)   A-B-C
Tel: 359.39.19   Métro stop: George-V
Single: 16F to 52F ($4 to $13); double: 52F to 97F ($13 to $24.25). Breakfast 7F ($1.75). All rooms are medium size and have telephones, wall-to-wall carpeting, and TV. Each one is furnished differently, and all are very comfortable and homey. No restaurant. The location is very convenient, just off the Champs-Elysées.

HÔTEL CONTINENT   30, rue du Mont-Thabor (1st)   A-B-C
Tel: 073.46.89   Métro stop: Concorde
The prices here are very confusing because they vary from room to room, but I'll try to give you some idea of what they are. None of the singles have toilets though all have bidets. Those with bidet, shower, and wash basin but no toilet are 50F ($12.50). Those with just a bidet and wash basin are 37F to 45F ($9.25 to $11.25). A double without toilet but with basin and bidet is 80F ($20). One with toilet, bath, and all facilities is 95F ($23.75). Taxes and service included, but not breakfast, which is 5F. All the baths are colorful and modern. The singles are small but more attractive than you would expect in a two-star hotel. All rooms have a phone, wall-to-wall carpeting, twelve-hour room service, and mini-bar. Double rooms, too, are small but very well done and very convenient. If you are traveling with someone, ask for a bath with a door; some of them just have curtains. Particularly nice are rooms 16, 26, 36, 46, 50, and 52. Rooms 54, 62, and 64 have the same colorful décor but shower rather than a bath. Some have dormer windows, an interesting touch. Rooms 66 and 68 on the top floor are singles without toilet but with a shower and bidet, and a double brass bed, for only 55F ($13.75). With so many different kinds of rooms, I'd advise you to see whatever ones are available, and make your decision then. The lobby is all paneled, and there is a little sitting area with velvet chairs and a three-table coffee salon.

The hotel is just across the street from the Inter-Continental and for its location and price, it is really quite a bargain. Don't let the two stars put you off; see it first and then make your decision.

FAMILY HÔTEL   35, rue Cambon (1st)   A-B-C   Tel: 742.76.55
Métro stop: Concorde
Single: 35F to 54F ($8.75 to $13.50); double: 57F to 82F ($14.25 to $20.50); including breakfast, taxes, and service. The rooms are medium size, simply furnished but quite adequate, and neat as a pin. The charm of the proprietress, Madame Battesti, is one of the reasons for the popularity of this little place. But secondly, it is in a fantastic location—right in the area of the Ritz Hotel and some of Paris's most elegant people. It's lovely to be able to walk in this area without having to pay the prices that a hotel in this area would ordinarily call for. It's really getting the best location for the biggest bargain.

HÔTEL MARIGNY   11, rue de l'Arcade (8th)   B-C   Tel: 266.42.71
Métro stop: Madeleine
Clientele includes a lot of international businessmen. Single: 70F ($17.50); double with bath: 82F ($20.50); including breakfast, taxes, and service. All rooms have a phone and wall-to-wall carpeting. They are very small but adequately furnished and conveniently located.

MONTPENSIER   12, rue de Richelieu (1st)   A-B-C   Tel: 742.54.34   Métro stop: Palais-Royal
Single: 33F to 95F ($8.25 to $23.75); double: 55F to 102F ($13.75 to $25.50); all including breakfast, taxes, and service. All rooms are medium size and have a phone, wall-to-wall carpeting. Most have large, modern bathrooms. They are furnished with a combination of modern and antique furniture. Most of the rooms face the courtyard, so happily you can avoid some of the traffic noises of the street. It is conveniently located near the Louvre and the gardens of the Palais-Royal.

HÔTEL PEIFFER   6, rue de l'Arcade (8th)   A-B-C   Tel: 266.03.07
Métro stop: Madeleine
Single with bath: 80F ($20); single with shower: 72F ($18); single without bath: 59F ($14.75); double with bath: 86F ($21.50); double with shower: 78F ($19.50); double without bath: 56F ($14); all including breakfast, taxes, and service. All rooms have phones and wall-to-wall carpeting. Singles are small, but they do have a double bed. Doubles are medium to large and all are furnished in modern décor. This is not at all what one would expect for a two-star hotel. It is surprisingly nice, in fact, as nice as a three-star, and very good value indeed. The lobby is modern, and the hotel itself conveniently located for everything.

HÔTEL ST.-LOUIS   75, rue St.-Louis-en-l'Ile (4th)   Tel: 033.10.13
Métro stop: Pt. Marie
Single: 31F to 56F ($7.75 to $14); double: 47F to 82F ($11.75 to $20.50); including breakfast, taxes, and service. All rooms have wall-to-wall carpeting and a telephone. This is a very quaint and charming little place situated on the Ile St. Louis, one of the two islands sitting in the middle of the river Seine.

It has a very warm and friendly ambiance and guests enjoy coming back time after time. Although not convenient to the shopping area, it does give you a feeling of being apart from all the city noises and activity.

LES TUILERIES 10, rue St.-Hyacinthe (1st) A-B-C Tel: 073.81.65 Métro stop: Tuileries
Clientele here includes many British. Single: 40F to 81F ($10 to $20.25); double: 53F to 86F ($13.25 to $21.50); breakfast and taxes included. All of the rooms have telephones and wall-to-wall carpeting. Most are huge and colorful with modern baths. No restaurant. The hotel is very English in appearance, with paneled walls and English-type furniture, but actually it is very French. Though old-fashioned, the rooms are very comfortable and pleasant.

LEFT BANK HOTELS

The Left Bank is known all over the world for its bohemian life. Here are the Sorbonne and the Latin Quarter, where famous artists and writers have lived and worked. The Left Bank is as bohemian as the Right Bank is posh.

Deluxe

PARIS HILTON 18, avenue de Suffren (15th) B-C Tel: 273.92.00 Telex: 20955 Métro stop: Champ-de-Mars
A lot of American businessmen use the Hilton as their home away from home. All rooms are medium size and furnished in good modern taste, with telephone, radio, TV, and wall-to-wall carpeting. Single: 142F to 214F ($35.50 to $53.50); double: 178F to 253F ($44.50 to 63.25); including breakfast, taxes, and service. There are all the unusual shops, beauty salons, and interesting restaurants that one expects to find at the Hilton. The coffee shop is a good place for snacking, as every day they have a different specialty from another part of the world. The restaurant Le Suffren has a Gay '90s feeling; and Le Toit de Paris is absolutely remarkable at night, when you can see all of Paris lit up like twinkling stars. The food is marvelous, and this is a good place for a woman to have dinner alone without a problem.

Three Star

HÔTEL DE BOURGOGNE ET MONTANA 3, rue de Bourgogne (7th) A-B-C Tel: 551.20.22 Métro stop: Varenne
Single: 75F to 140F ($18.75 to $35); double: 64F to 150F ($16 to $37.50); including breakfast, taxes, and services. All rooms have telephones, wall-to-wall carpeting, and new bathrooms. Simply furnished but very comfortable. The lounge is a homey place for writing and watching TV or meeting friends.

The dining room is open for breakfast, lunch, and dinner, except in August and on Saturdays, with a fixed price menu at 24F, which is $6. The hotel is located just across from the building of the President of the National Assembly and a few minutes walk from the air terminal, as well as directly across the river from the Place de la Concorde. The service is very good and one feels quite comfortable here.

MONTALEMBERT 3, rue Montalembert (7th) Tel: 548.68.11
Métro stop: Rue du Bac
Single: 91F to 111F ($22.75 to $27.75); double: 108F to 134F ($27 to $33.50); including breakfast, taxes, and service. All rooms have telephones and wall-to-wall carpeting and are large with very nice furnishings. A lot of them have little entryways and all have modern baths. The wood-paneled lobby gives you a very warm feeling, as does the entire staff who greet you in a most friendly manner. There is an American-style bar and a restaurant for lunch and dinner. Restaurant closed on Sundays and in August.

PARIS-DINARD 29, rue Cassette (6th) A-B-C Tel: 548.63.86
Métro stop: Luxembourg
Single: 45F to 80F ($11.25 to $20.00); double: 55F to 95F ($13.75 to $23.75); *not* including breakfast, taxes, or service. Continental breakfast 6F ($1.50). Most rooms are medium size and very well done, with telephone, wall-to-wall carpeting, and modern baths. The hotel has recently been remodeled. Many of the rooms have balconies in the front overlooking a church garden. The top floors have beautiful views of the city. Ask the receptionist to allow you to see what they call the *chambres rustiques*. These are beautiful, huge, traditional Breton country-house suites, with large bedsteads, heavy furniture, and typical Breton paintings. If you can afford to stay in one, fine; otherwise do see them—it's well worthwhile. The receptionist is happy to boast that Ernest Hemingway and Albert Schweitzer were once guests of the hotel. The hotel is in a very busy area within walking distance of the St.-Germain-des-Prés and if you feel like a stroll, the Luxembourg Gardens are just a couple of blocks away.

HÔTEL DU PAS-DE-CALAIS 59, rue des Sts.-Pères (6th) Tel: 548.78.74 Métro stop: St.-Germain-des-Prés
Single: 74F ($18.50); double: 90F ($22.50); breakfast, taxes, and service included. All rooms have telephones and wall-to-wall carpeting and are very modern and colorful with large bathrooms. The inside rooms face a little courtyard. Conveniently located just off of the Boulevard St.-Germain and a short distance from St.-Germain-des-Prés. Two of its most notable guests have been Jean-Paul Sartre, who wrote the play *Dirty Hands* here, and Chateaubriand, who lived here from 1811 to 1814.

HÔTEL DU QUAI VOLTAIRE 19, quai Voltaire (7th) Tel: 548.42.91 Métro stop: Rue du Bac
This hotel is situated right on the quai overlooking the Seine,

a stone's throw from the heart of the bohemian quarter of Paris. Single: 26F to 40F ($6.50 to $10); double: 77F to 82F ($19.25 to $20.50); all-inclusive. The rooms have telephones and wall-to-wall carpeting, and are large and simply but comfortably furnished. Most important is the beautiful view across the Seine to the Louvre and the Pont-du-Carrousel and Pont-Royal. The public rooms are not very interesting, in fact they're rather dreary, but then at these rates that is less important. There is a bar for snacks and drinks and an outdoor café for people-watching day and night. Some of the luminaries who have graced this old hotel are Richard Wagner, Oscar Wilde, Charles Baudelaire, and Jean Sibelius.

TRIANON-PALACE 1 bis, rue de Vaugirard (6th) A-B-C Tel: 326.88.10 Métro stop: Luxembourg
Single: 42F to 62F ($10.50 to $15.50); double: 55F to 95F ($13.75 to $23.75); including breakfast, taxes, and service. All rooms have telephones and wall-to-wall carpeting. The rooms are large, simple, and comfortable. There are dining rooms on the eighth floor that are very charming and give you an exciting view of the Latin Quarter. The hotel is just a short distance from the Boulevard St.-Michel, and the Boulevard St.-Germain, so you are within walking distance of all the charming little cafés.

HÔTEL DE L'UNIVERSITÉ 22, rue de l'Université (7th) A-B-C Tel: 548.45.62 Métro stop: Rue du Bac
Single: 57F to 78F ($14.25 to $19.50); double: 113F to 159F ($28.25 to $39.75); *not* including breakfast, taxes, or service. Continental breakfast 6F ($1.50). All rooms have telephones, wall-to-wall carpeting, and good, modern baths. The hotel was originally a three-hundred-year-old townhouse that Madame Bermann, the owner, converted into a most intimate and elegant hotel, doing all the redecorating herself. My particular favorite is Room 35, from which you can step right out into the courtyard. It has a big fireplace and beautiful provincial armoire in a bright shade of orange. The breakfast room, too, opens into the little courtyard with a fountain. This hotel has quickly become a little secret that world travelers like to keep to themselves. It is absolutely necessary to make a reservation a month or two in advance.

Two Star

HÔTEL DE L'AVENIR 65, rue Madame (6th) Tel: 548.84.54 Métro stop: St.-Sulpice
Single: 55F to 79F ($13.75 to $19.75); double: 40F to 85F ($10 to $21.25); including taxes, service, and breakfast. All rooms include telephone, wall-to-wall carpeting. Rooms are small to medium size, rather simply furnished but clean. The fifth and sixth floors have balconies, which are about the only special feature of the hotel. However, it is close to the Luxembourg Gardens and is in a quiet district.

HÔTEL CLAUDE-BERNARD 43, rue des Ecoles (5th) A-B-C
Tel: 326.32.52 Métro: Maubert-Mutualité
Single: 32F to 40F ($8 to $10); double: 52F to 85F ($13
to $21.25); including breakfast, taxes, and service. All rooms
have telephones and wall-to-wall carpeting and are simply furnished but clean and comfortable. Some have balconies. There
are lots of mirrors and greenery all over the place, which gives
it a rather warm feeling. The staff, too, is very helpful.

HÔTEL DANUBE 58, rue Jacob (6th) A-B-C Tel: 548.42.70
Métro stop: St.-Germain-des-Prés
Single: 29F ($7.25); double: 31F to 73F ($7.75 to $18.25);
not including the continental breakfast which is 6F ($1.50). All
rooms include telephone, wall-to-wall carpeting, and new bathrooms. The hotel is furnished in old-fashioned, traditional style
and has a very personal, comfortable ambiance. There is a
courtyard, over which some of the rooms look, and a grand
piano in the public lounge for friendly get-togethers.

HÔTEL D'ISLY 29, rue Jacob (6th) Tel: 326.64.41 Métro stop:
St.-Germain-des-Prés
Single: 54F to 71F ($13.50 to $17.75); double: 65F to 137F
($16.25 to $34.25); *not* including breakfast, taxes, or service.
Breakfast 6F ($1.50). All rooms are medium size and very frilly
and feminine. All have telephones, wall-to-wall carpeting, and
good-sized baths. Clean, comfortable, and centrally located, especially for all the lovely boutiques on the Boulevard St.-Germain
and interesting little bistros that pop up on every side street.

LITTRÉ 9, rue de Littré (6th) A-B-C Tel: 222.71.74 Métro
stop: Montparnasse
Single: 155F ($38.75); double: 150F ($37.50); including breakfast, taxes, and service. All rooms have telephones, TV, wall-to-
wall carpeting, and very modern baths—some in Italian marble.
The room is done in reproductions of traditional French pieces
and with very bright colors. There are two salons with paneling,
white columns, and some antiques. The Scottish Bar is a complete departure with bright yellow sofas and chairs and all the
modern touches. There is also a restaurant. The hotel is in the
middle of the Montparnasse area but on a little side street away
from traffic noises. It is a sister hotel to the Victoria Palace Hotel
on the Right Bank, listed above. It is quite popular with American Express and other good travel agencies. Two stops on the
Métro get you to the Boulevard St.-Germain.

THE MADISON 143, boulevard St.-Germain (6th) A-B-C Tel:
326.57.12 Métro stop: St.-Germain-des-Prés and Mabillon
Single: 45F to 76F ($11.25 to $19); double: 51F to 102F
($12.75 to $25.50); including breakfast, taxes, and service. The
rooms have telephones and wall-to-wall carpeting. They are
large, light, and cheerful, and some have balconies. The lobby is
bright and attractive as is the bar. There is also a TV room.

MONT-BLANC 28, rue de la Huchette (5th) A-B-C Tel: 033.
49.44 Métro stop: St.-Michel

Small but extremely clean rooms with telephones and wall-to-wall carpeting. Single: 22F ($5.50); double: 28F to 65F ($7.00 to $16.25); not including breakfast at 7F ($1.75). This is a tiny little place very close to the Place St.-Michel, the stomping ground of students. The receptionist will tell you that here Elliot Paul wrote the popular book, *The Last Time I Saw Paris*.

REGENT'S HÔTEL   44, rue Madame (6th)   A-B-C Tel: 548.02.81   Métro stop: St.-Sulpice

Single: 42F to 87F ($10.50 to $21.75); double: 63F to 93F ($15.75 to $23.25); including breakfast, taxes, and service. All rooms have telephones, wall-to-wall carpeting, and simple but very nice furniture. It is being remodeled right along, and the baths are modern. A lovely patio in the back, overlooked by half of the rooms, makes it very peaceful. Three rooms have little terraces opening out into the courtyard. Good value for the money.

HÔTEL ST.-SIMON   15, rue de St.-Simon (7th)   A-B-C   Tel: 548.35.66   Métro stop: Rue du Bac

Single: 27F to 32F ($6.75 to $8); double: 48F to 113F ($12 to $28.25); including breakfast, taxes, and service. Telephones and wall-to-wall carpeting. An old-fashioned type of hotel, and very quiet and comfortable. Its main feature is a carriage courtyard with lots of flowers. There is another garden in the rear as well. All of this lends a very peaceful atmosphere.

SÉVIGNÉ   6, rue Belloy (16th) Tel: 720.88.90   Métro stop: Trocadéro

Single: 70F to 100F ($17.50 to $25); double: 80F to 110F ($20 to $27.50); including breakfast, taxes, and service. Every room has a telephone, TV, and wall-to-wall carpeting, make-up tables, and balconies on the fifth floor.

SQUARE MONGE   42, rue des Bernardins (5th)   Tel: 033.49.08   Métro stop: Maubert-Mutualité

Single: 36F to 52F ($9 to $13); double: 71F to 77F ($17.75 to $19.25); including breakfast, taxes, and service. All rooms have telephones and wall-to-wall carpeting. Some have fireplaces, others have showers, but *no* private toilets. Just off the Boulevard St.-Germain and very convenient.

8
Wining and Dining

Forget about your diet when you come to France. It would truly be a greater sin to pass up this opportunity to enjoy the world's finest cuisine. From the most expensive restaurants, such as the Tour d'Argent and Maxim's, to the smallest bistro, the one common denominator is a fierce pride in the culinary expertise of the chef.

Dining and wining in Paris is as much a part of "things to do" as seeing the Arc de Triomphe. So take this opportunity to become a gourmet in the hands of the experts and to gain a sophistication about food that will last the rest of your life.

Special Tips

The word *menu* usually means the fixed-price specialty of the day, rather than the list of available dishes as we know it in America. If you want to see what a restaurant offers, ask for *la carte*. However, since the *menu* usually includes soup or appetizer, main course, and dessert or cheese, it is considerably less expensive than when you order *à la carte*.

Check your bill in detail, making sure that every item on it is what you ordered, and if you have any doubts don't hesitate to question the waiter. If the bill says *service non compris,* tip is not included in the total and you should leave approximately 15% in addition to the bill. If it says *service compris,* 15% has already been added on.

FRENCH DISHES

Following is a list of some of the dishes you will find on a French menu, and the names of some of the wines that go well with them.

Soups

bouillabaisse fish soup
consommé a clear broth
potage a cream soup
purée Saint-Germain pea soup
soupe au pistou a white bean
   soup, made with garlic and
   cheese

tourain périgourdin a vegetable soup, made with onions
   and fresh tomatoes
vichyssoise a cold, cream soup,
   made with leaks and potatoes

Note: No wines are served with soup.

Shellfish

coquilles St.-Jacques scallops
écrevisses crayfish
huîtres oysters
langouste lobster

moules mussels, often cooked
   in butter and wine, as in
   moules marinières

WINE A dry white wine from Alsace (Gewurtzraminer or
Muscat), or from the Loire (Pouilly, Saumur, or Muscadet).

Entrées

COLD

harengs marinés marinated
   herring
oeufs en gelée eggs in aspic
pâtés made from chicken or

pork livers or the famous
   truffled goose liver from Périgord and Alsace
saumon fumé smoked salmon

HOT

artichauts farcis stuffed artichokes
escargots snails stuffed with
   butter and flavored with garlic and parsley
quenelles de brochet mousse-
   like fishcakes made with
   ground pike and served with
   a brown sauce

ris de veau à la lyonnaise
   sweetbreads cooked in a tar-
   ragon sauce
rognons flambés kidneys flamed
   in brandy
saucissons aux marquises de
   Sévigné a hot sausage cream
   tart

WINES A white Bordeaux (Tavel, Anjou Rosé), light, red
Beaujolais (Fleury Chirouble, Brouilly), or Côtes-du-Rhône (Châ-
teauneuf-du-Pape).

Fish

filets de sole sole with mussels, shrimp, and white wine
   sauce
homard à l'Armoricaine lobster
   cooked in a spicy sauce of
   tomatoes, garlic, herbs, white
   wine, and cognac

loup au fenouil sea perch
   cooked with fennel
saumon grillé grilled salmon
truite meunière trout poached
   in butter

WINES A dry white wine from Alsace, the Loire, or Champagne
districts.

Poultry

caneton à l'orange duck with orange sauce

coq au vin chicken in red wine

oie à l'alsacienne goose with sauerkraut

pintade farcie stuffed guinea hen

poulet Marengo chicken in a white wine sauce with garlic, mushrooms, and crayfish

suprêmes de dinde farcies stuffed turkey breasts

WINES A rich claret (Haut-Médoc, Châteaux Margaux, Mouton Rothschild, Mouton Cadet). Or a full-bodied, robust Burgundy (Côte de Beaune, Nuits Saint-George, Vosnes Romanée, Chambelle Musigny).

Meat and Game

caille sous la cendre truffled quail, stuffed with pâté, wrapped in grape leaves, and cooked in glowing embers

civet de lièvre jugged hare

côtes de boeuf ribs of beef

cuissot de chevreuil haunch of venison

entrecôte grillée grilled steak

faisan à la flamande pheasant with endive

gigot braisé à la septaine braised spring lamb with vegetables

jambon à la crème ham with cream sauce

paupiettes de veau veal birds

WINES A full-bodied Burgundy (Pommard, Chambertin—the greatest of all Burgundies), Clos Vougeot, Grand Echesaux, or Richebourg.

Cheese

There are no less than three hundred different, delicious cheeses made in France. Don't forget to taste some of the better known: the inimitable Camembert, Brie, Roquefort, Tome from Savoy, blue cheese (*bleu*) from the Auvergne and Bresse, Gruyère from Jura, light and creamy Fontainebleau, and all the delectable goat's milk cheeses that come in every shape and size, with such amusing names as: Bouton de Culotte, Chabichou, Crottin de Chavignol, and Rigotte de Condrieu.

WINES Apart from the goat's milk cheeses, which can be accompanied by a white wine (Sancerre), a red wine such as a claret or burgundy is the perfect companion of most other cheeses.

Desserts

crème caramel baked custard with a burnt-sugar topping

gâteau Saint-Honoré a mound of tiny, cream-filled cream puffs

glaces ice creams in many flavors

mousses rich, creamy, puddinglike

pâtisserie rich pastries

puits d'amour jam- or cream-filled tarts

soufflé a light, fluffy baked dish with fruit or liqueur

WINES Champagne *Brut* or *Sec* (sweet or dry); Vouvray, or a sweet wine, such as Montbazillac or Banyule.

Liqueurs and Brandies

Grand Marnier, Cointreau, Vieille Curé; Cognac and Armagnac, or the fruit brandies, such as *prune, framboise* (raspberry), and *kirsch* (cherry).

Wine

Wines are always served in the same order: light wines at the beginning of the meal; followed by stronger, more robust, and fuller-bodied wines; and a sweeter wine with dessert. Don't drink a Mâcon after a Pommard, or a claret after a Mâcon.

White and rosé wines are served chilled, a Beaujolais is served cool, and a claret at room temperature. Burgundy is served *chambré* (that is, at a temperature slightly warmer than that of the room where it is drunk); sweet wines are chilled and champagne is put on ice (but not iced). Champagne is a wine that can be drunk throughout the meal, for it goes with any course.

To help you in the serious business of wining and dining, here is a brief vocabulary of French terms for various foods, eating utensils, and services.

VOCABULARY

Cooking Terms

à l'indienne curried
à point medium done
au gratin in a cheese sauce
bien cuit well done
bouilli boiled
farci stuffed
flambé flamed

frit fried
grillé grilled
meunière cooked in butter
purée de mashed
rôti roast
saignant rare

Meats and Game

agneau lamb
boeuf beef
cervelles brains
charcuterie cold meats, esp. pork
cuissot de chevreuil leg of venison
entrecôte steak

foie de veau calves' liver
lapin rabbit
moutin mutton
porc pork
ris de veau sweetbreads
rognons kidneys
saucisson sausages
veau veal

Poultry

caille quail
caneton duck
dinde turkey

faisan pheasant
pintade guinea hen
poulet chicken

Fish and Seafood

brochet pike
coquilles Saint-Jacques scallops
crevettes shrimps
cuisses de grenouille frogs' legs
homard lobster
huîtres oysters

moules mussels
palourdes clams
sole sole
thon tuna
truite trout

Vegetables

artichauts artichokes
asperges asparagus
aubergines eggplant
carottes carrots
chou cabbage
chou-fleur cauliflower
épinards spinach

haricots verts green beans
laitue lettuce
navet turnip
oignons onions
petits pois green peas
pommes de terre potatoes

Fruits

cerises cherries
citron lemon
fraises strawberries
framboises raspberries
melon melon

pamplemousse grapefruit
pastèque watermelon
pêche peach
pomme apple
raisins grapes

Desserts

fromage cheese
fruit fruit
gâteau cake

glace ice cream
parfait ice cream with a
    flavored sauce

Miscellaneous

beurre butter
café coffee
café au lait coffee with milk
café crème coffee with cream
café décaféiné decaffeinated
    coffee
confiture jam
crudités raw vegetables
eau minérale mineral water
eau naturelle tap water

miel honey
moutarde mustard
oeufs eggs
pain bread
pain grillé toast
poivre pepper
sel salt
sucre sugar
thé tea
vin wine

Table Setting

assiette	plate	*nappe*	tablecloth
couteau	knife	*plat*	dish
cuillère	spoon	*serviette*	napkin
fourchette	fork	*verre*	glass

Service

à la carte	individually priced dishes from the large menu	*prix fixe*	fixed-price meal
addition	bill	*sommelier*	wine steward
garçon	waiter	*table d'hôte*	fixed-price meal

We will list restaurants in three price ranges, Expensive: 25F ($6.25) and up; Moderate: 15F to 25F ($3.75 to $6.25); Inexpensive: up to 15F ($3.75).

RESTAURANTS: EXPENSIVE

Paris is Paris and its food is beyond comparison, so try to have at least one meal in one of the very famous but expensive restaurants listed below for a very special treat.

LE GRAND VEFOUR   17, rue de Beaujolais   Tel: 742.58.97
Métro stop: Bourse
Raymond Oliver's cooking is rivaled only by his hospitality. His great specialty is his way with eggs, but there is also a choice of other dishes, notably *poulet au homard,* and an extraordinary *timbale de macaronis,* incorporating truffles, foie gras, and lobster. Le Grand Vefour was formerly a café, very much in fashion during the Directoire period. It has an intimate, warm setting which heightens the enjoyment of the meal and your awareness of true gourmet dining. Closed on Tuesdays and throughout August. Meals are served until 9 P.M., and tables must be reserved.

LAPÉROUSE   51, quai des Grands-Augustins (6th)   Tel: 326.68.04   Métro stop: St.-Michel
Magnificently located on the banks of the Seine, this charming restaurant has its habitués, who go there for such specialties as *gratin de langouste Georgette, caneton de Colette Lapérouse, soufflé Grand Marnier,* all typically French dishes. The cellar is particularly well stocked. Open every day except Sunday. Meals served until 10 P.M., and tables should be reserved.

MAXIM'S   3, rue Royale (8th)   Tel: 265.27.94   Métro stop: Concorde
In a décor reminiscent of the Gay '90's, Maxim's upholds the tradition of unrivaled service in fine foods and wines imposed in his day by King Albert. Some of the outstanding dishes are *chartreuse de perdreau, sole Albert, omelette du curé* and *selle*

de veau Orlov. Suppers are served till late at night, but tables should be reserved in advance. Evening dress is compulsory on Friday evenings and recommended on Tuesday evenings. There is music and dancing. Open all year, closed on Sundays.

LA TOUR D'ARGENT   15, quai de la Tournelle (5th)   Tel: 033. 23.32   Métro stop: Maubert-Mutualité
This restaurant, with its fine view of the Cathedral of Notre Dame, is so famous that it is considered by many foreign tourists as the apotheosis of French gastronomy. The star dish is the celebrated *canard au sang;* other specialties include *filet de sole aux écrevisses, filet Marco Polo,* and *noisette de tournelles.* The décor is sumptuous and the service of the highest standard. Open all year daily except Monday. Meals are served until 10 P.M., and tables should be reserved.

The restaurants which follow are not quite in the same class as those listed above, although for reasons which would be difficult to define since in many cases their cuisine can be considered on a par with the previous listings. They all qualify as gourmet establishments and belong in the category of Expensive.

L'ABSINTHE   24, place du Marché-St.-Honoré (1st)   Tel: 073. 68.14   Métro stop: Pyramides
A new bistro decorated in the amusing décor of early 1900s. Here you may still order cold dishes after 12 P.M. Open until 12:30 A.M. and throughout August. Closed Sundays.

L'ARCHESTRATE   84, rue de Varenne (7th)   Tel: 551.47.33 Métro stop: Varenne
A small place just opposite the Rodin Museum, and owned by Alain Senderens, who also does all the cooking. You are always sure of some of the best food in Paris here. A reservation is necessary here. M. Senderens is a young man, rather shy but very charming, who takes a personal interest in his customers. His specialty is the old, traditional recipes one seldom finds in Paris today. The *moules soufflées* are by far my special favorite. If they're not on the menu, ask him when you make the reservation if he can prepare the dish for you.

LE BISTRO   In the Hôtel Inter-Continental   3, rue de Castiglione (1st)   Tel: 073.18.00   Métro stop: Tuileries
Excellent *à la carte* menu and music. Open until 1 A.M. and throughout August.

DROUANT   Place Gaillon   Tel: 073.53.72   Métro stop: 4-Septembre
This has been a very sound restaurant for many years; it is particularly celebrated for its fish and seafood. Specialties include: *bouillabaisse, homard Drouant,* and *sole au gratin.* There is also an excellent *caneton nantais* and *paupiettes de poulet de Bresse.* The décor is discreet and the service excellent. Customers may

lunch either in the Grillroom or in the restaurant. Open every day except in August. Tables should be reserved for lunch.

L'ESPADON 38, rue Cambon (1st) Tel: 073.28.30 Métro stop: Madeleine

Located in the Hotel Ritz. One of the loveliest restaurants in Paris. Expensive but extremely worthwhile for a big night out on the town. Terrace. Open in August.

FOUQUET'S 99, avenue des Champs-Elysées (8th) Tel: 225.59.54 Métro stop: George-V

An elegant restaurant on the first floor. Very Parisian atmosphere on the main floor and on the terrace off Avenue George-V. Open until 1:30 A.M. and throughout August.

GEORGE V 31, avenue George-V (8th) Tel: 225.35.30 Métro stop: George-V

Elegant dining room featuring excellent international cuisine. Particularly beautiful on the grand patio. Excellent service. Open until 10 P.M. and throughout August.

GUY 6, rue Mabillon (6th) Tel: 033.87.61 Métro stop: Mabillon

South American décor and music with some of the best Brazilian cuisine. Open until 2 A.M., and throughout August. Closed Sundays.

L'HÔTEL 13, rue des Beaux-Arts (6th) Tel: 663.89.20 Métro stop: St.-Germain-des-Prés

Jazzy New York style place for Café Society. Abounds with cover girls and golden boys. Open until 2 A.M. and throughout August.

JARDIN DU RITZ 15, place Vendôme (1st) Tel: 673.53.11 Métro stop: Opéra

Dine in front of a lovely flower garden, with excellent cuisine. Open until 10 P.M.

JOUR ET NUIT 2, rue de Berri (8th) Tel: 359.50.65 Métro stop: George-V

One of the best near the Champs-Elysées. Broad choice of dishes on the menu. Open until 2 A.M. and throughout August.

LAMAZÈRE 23, rue de Ponthieu (8th) Tel: 359.66.66 Métro stop: F.-D.-Roosevelt

Truly good cuisine—rare to find, but you pay for it. Open until 1 A.M. and throughout August. Closed Sundays.

LAURENT 41, avenue Gabriel (8th) Tel: 359.14.49 Métro stop: Champs-Elysées–Clemenceau

Located in the gardens of the Champs-Elysées, this elegant restaurant offers a high-quality cuisine in a luxurious setting. Specialties include *sole soufflé Centrillon, cassolette de homard au whiskey, tournedos Prince Albert,* and *médaillons de veau Brillat-Savarin.* It is a fashionable spot frequented by celebrities. Open until 11 P.M. Closed on Sundays and during August. Tables should be reserved.

LEDOYEN carré du Champs-Elysées (8th) Tel: 265.47.82

The service, tableware, and décor are all of a high standard. So is the cuisine. Particularly recommended are *délices impériales, sole soufflé,* and *canard aux pêches.* Closed on Sundays. Meals served until 10 P.M.

LUCAS-CARTON 9, place de la Madeleine (8th) Tel: 265.22.80 Métro stop: Madeleine

One of the best kitchens in Paris with marvelous wines, a grand old authentic décor of 1900. Open until 11 P.M. and throughout August.

LA MANADE 39, rue Galande (5th) Tel. 033.94.85 Métro stop: Maubert-Mutualité

Folklore décor for atmospheric dining. Fish soup and other favorites here. Open until 2 A.M. and throughout August. Closed Tuesdays.

LE MERCURE GALANT 15, rue des Petits-Champs (1st) Tel: 742.82.98 Métro stop: Bourse

A new restaurant done in style of the "Fin de Siècle," this is really worthwhile for its décor and its excellent cuisine. Open until 1 A.M. and throughout August. Closed Sunday.

PARIS 25 16, rue de la Grande Truanderie (1st) Tel: 508.44.72 Métro stop: Les Halles

A new bistro in the style of the early 1900s. Very warm and charming. Open until 1 A.M. and throughout August. Closed Sundays.

LE PETIT BEDON 38, rue Pergolèse (16th) Tel: 727.23.66 Métro stop: Argentine

This is a fashionable restaurant patronized by numerous Parisian celebrities. The cuisine is excellent, notably its delicious *truffes sous la cendre, canard sauvage au poivre vert, faisan rôti en volière,* and *omelette aux queues d'écrevisses Curnonsky.* The last-named is the leading specialty of the house. Open every day. Meals served until 10 P.M. Tables should be reserved.

PRUNIER DUPHOT 9, rue Duphot (1st) Tel: 073.11.40 Métro stop: Madeleine

Prunier ranks among the leading restaurants in Paris for shellfish and seafood. Its *belons* oysters, *marmite dieppoise, bar farci à l'angevine,* and *filet de turbot Vérilhac* are outstanding. Closed on Mondays and from June 15 to August 31. They also serve until 11 P.M.

PRUNIER TRAKTIR 16, avenue Victor-Hugo (16th) Tel: 727. 01.45 Métro stop: Victor-Hugo

This is a branch of Prunier Duphot mentioned above. Here, too, seafood is a specialty. Particularly recommended is *le mouclade,* a sensational mussel soup. At the bar you can savor all kinds of shellfish. Open daily until 10:30 P.M., except Mondays, closed in July.

RÉGENCE-PLAZA 27, avenue Montaigne (8th) Tel: 225.14.90 Métro stop: F.-D.-Roosevelt

Great cosmopolitan atmosphere and cuisine. In summer, have lunch or dinner on the plant-filled patio. Open in August.

RELAIS PARIS-EST 4, boulevard de Strasbourg (10th) Tel: 667.87.63 First floor of the Gare de l'Est (railroad station), Métro stop: Strasbourg-St. Denis

Elegant restaurant with marvelous cuisine. Open until 10 P.M. and throughout August. Closed on Sunday.

SABOT DE BERNARD 2, rue du Sabot (6th) Tel: 222.84.90
Métro stop: St.-Sulpice
A lovely place for dining and dancing to soft sweet music. A very romantic place indeed, the interior is done in stone work, hand worked woods, and soft velvets. Open until 1:30 A.M. and throughout August. Closed Sundays.

TAILLEVENT 15, rue Lamennais (8th) Tel: 235.05.08 Métro stop: George-V
This restaurant is located in a former private residence near the Etoile. The service is courteous and attentive, the clientele fashionable, and the décor draws its inspiration from the Palace of Versailles. Outstanding dishes include *soufflé au fromage, truffes en pâté, turbot Taillevent,* and *soufflé glacé Lamennais.* Closed on Sundays and August. Tables should be reserved.

TOUR EIFFEL Champ de Mars (7th) Tel: 551.19.59
First floor of the Tour Eiffel. Paris at your feet. Specializes in provincial dishes. The cuisine is superb. Open until 10 P.M. and throughout August.

RESTAURANTS: MODERATE

ALEXANDRE 53, George-V (8th) Tel: 359.17.82 Métro stop: George-V
Just off the Champs-Elysées and near the TWA office. This is a typical Parisian restaurant featuring many typical dishes. Not only is it convenient from the point of view of location, but it also stays open until 1:30 A.M. Very elegant atmosphere, excellent food and service, and not too expensive. Weather permitting, take advantage of the outdoor café and watch Paris stroll by.

CHEZ ANDRÉ 53, boulevard St.-Marcel (13th) Tel: 331.71.18
Métro stop: St.-Michel
This is a particularly interesting place because all the journalists, designers, and models from the nearby *haute couture* district have their meals here. It looks very much like the kind of restaurant one sees in the old movies about newspapermen; shirt-sleeved waiters, partitions between the tables, noise, smoke, and all the hustle and bustle that add to the atmosphere.

CHEZ LES ANGES 54, boulevard Latour-Maubourg (7th) Tel: 705.89.86 Métro stop: Latour-Maubourg
Specializing in dishes from Burgundy. Closed from August 15 to September 15. Closed on Mondays.

ANGKOR 3, rue des Petites-Ecuries (10th) Tel: 770.34.79
Métro stop: Château-d'Eau
A choice of 120 dishes. Open in August.

L'ASSIETTE AU BEURRE 11, rue St.-Benoit (6th) Tel: 222.88.47
Métro stop: St.-Germain-des-Prés
Early nineteenth-century décor. This is a very "in" place during

the season, and reservations are suggested. Open until 12 midnight, and throughout August.

L'AUBERGE BASQUE   51, rue de Verneuil (7th)   Tel: 548.51.98
Métro stop: Solférino and Rue du Bac
A small place with only 12 tables, situated on a little street between the Boulevard St.-Germain and the Gare d'Orsay. The fireplace adds to the *intime* atmosphere, as does the Spanish guitar music. A good place to relax and let your hair down. Open for lunch and dinner. Closed in August.

AUBERGE DU VERT-GALANT   42, quai des Orfèvres (1st)   Tel: 326.83.68   Métro stop: St.-Michel
In summer there are not many as lovely and quiet as this terrace. Closed Saturdays. Open in August.

THE BERKELEY   7, avenue Matignon (8th)   Tel: 225.47.79
Métro stop: F.-D.-Roosevelt
Just off the Champs-Elysées, this is a charming place, with terraces furnished in white wrought iron and lots of shrubbery for outdoor dining, coffee, or drinks. The restaurant inside is on different levels, with balconies that overlook the central area. There are tufted-leather booths with brown and gold marble floors and ceilings, low-hanging fringed light fixtures, and music. A great atmosphere any time of the day or night. It's quite inexpensive too, serving anything from snacks, such as sandwiches or salads, to hot dishes; from hamburgers 14F ($3.50) to *châteaubriand* 26F ($6.50) or lobster 30F ($7.50). For dessert you can take your choice of French pastries or American-style ice-cream sundaes. Open from 9 A.M. to 2 A.M.

LE BISTROT DE PARIS   33, rue de Lille (7th)   Tel: 548.32.44
Métro stop: Rue du Bac
Owned and personally watched over by Michel Oliver, son of Raymond Oliver, who owns the famous Le Grand Vefour. In the kitchens of his father's famous restaurant, Michel developed his love of good cuisine and finally decided to branch out on his own. Not at all like Le Grand Vefour, Le Bistrot de Paris takes one back to the early 1900s. A charming place, with its brass light fixtures and dark paneling, the restaurant emanates a very warm, personal ambiance. M. Oliver himself is a young, extremely handsome gentleman who personally greets his patrons and makes them feel at home.

While in Paris you should try to get his cookbook, *La Cuisine est un jeu d'enfants,* a very fine and interesting cookbook intended for children, but I find it to be a great gift for anyone who speaks even a little French. The illustrations are adorable. Ask M. Oliver if he can show you a copy while you are there and then run out to the nearest bookstore and buy one. Closed Sundays and in August.

CHEZ BOSC   7, rue Richepanse (8th)   Tel: 073.65.91   Métro stop: Concorde
A family-owned restaurant where Meurice cooks and his brother, Lucien, is the waiter. The service is absolutely exceptional. Meurice even took the time to come and sit with us and explain

how he does his shopping. He also adds a note for my readers which I think is rather important. From October to April is the best time to order *coquilles* (scallops), otherwise they are not fresh. After April is the best time for fresh fish; earlier than that, what you will get is frozen seafood. It is necessary to call for reservations here as it is a very popular restaurant, by virtue of word of mouth. A specialty of theirs is *châteaubriand*, served for only one, which is unusual; most places serve it for two. Closed Sundays, holidays, and August. Open 12 to 3 for lunch, 7 to 3 A.M. for dinner.

BOUGNAT'S CLUB   15, rue Séguier (6th)   Tel: 033.21.55   Métro stop: St.-Michel

Charming sophisticated atmosphere of an old salon. Very smart clientele and excellent cuisine. Open until 2 A.M.

BRASSERIE BOFINGER   5, rue de la Bastille (4th)   Tel: 272.87.82   Métro stop: Bastille

Good brasserie cuisine, magnificent décor. Open until 2 A.M. and throughout August. Closed Sundays.

BRASSERIE LIPP   151, boulevard St.-Germain (6th)   Tel: 548.53.91   Métro stop: St.-Germain-des-Prés

Good brasserie cuisine with a unique décor and atmosphere. Open until 1 A.M. and throughout August. Closed Mondays.

BRASSERIE MUNICHOISE   5, rue Danielle Casanova (1st)   Tel: 073.66.25   Métro stop: Pyramides

Very good German beer. Open until 2 A.M. and throughout August. Closed Sundays.

CAFÉ DE LA PAIX   Place de l'Opéra (9th)   Tel: 073.35.44   Métro stop: Opéra

In the same building that houses the Grand Hôtel, though not a part of the hotel itself. It has often been said that if you sit in the Café de la Paix long enough you're bound to see someone you know. Also an excellent place to meet someone you don't. Frequented in their day by famous celebrities, such as Oscar Wilde, F. Scott Fitzgerald, and Ernest Hemingway, it has a grand old history. There are several different areas to the restaurant: the outside café, a snack area inside, and the main restaurant. Waitresses come around with trays of gorgeous pastries. Don't be fooled by the name; this place is much more expensive than the average café. Open 9:30 A.M. until 1:30 A.M. and throughout August.

LE CASSEROLE   10, rue des Sts.-Pères (7th)   Tel: 222.16.33   Métro stop: St.-Germaine-des-Prés

Under the management of the well-known Don Camillo. Excellent terrines. Open until 3 A.M. for dinner only.

CHAMPOLLION   3, rue Champollion (5th)   Métro stop: Maubert-Mutualité

Just a block from the Place de la Sorbonne, this place naturally gets scads of students from the university. Nonetheless, it's well worth a try if you're in the area. They feature several Russian dishes that are quite good. The service is not too personal, as they are generally in a rush, but the food is good, and I guess that's all that counts. Closed Wednesdays.

À LA CIGOGNE   17, rue Duphot (1st)   Métro stop: Madeleine

An old inn going back to the early 1920s, this has long been a favorite of Parisians who know and enjoy good food. Very Portuguese in décor, but with excellent traditional French dishes. You can't go wrong with just about anything on the menu. The quantity of food will leave you gasping for breath. Open for lunch from 12 to 3 and dinner 7 to 10. Closed on Sundays.

CLOSERIE DES LILAS   171, boulevard du Montparnasse (6th)
Tel: 033.21.68   Métro stop: Vavin

Dine in the shadows on the terrace or at the very agreeable bar. Open until 1:15 A.M. and throughout August.

COCONNAS   2 bis, place des Vosges (4th)   Tel: 272.58.16
Métro stop: Chemin-Vert

If you happen to be visiting the Victor Hugo Museum, this is an excellent place to stop for lunch. As you walk through this beautiful area with its brick townhouses and beautiful arcades, you can almost picture Victor Hugo stepping out of his home and strolling to the restaurant for lunch or dinner. Situated in this charming and ancient square, the restaurant, with its terrace, is very much in keeping with the atmosphere of the area. It has been known for its excellent French cuisine for decades, and I'm sure the chef won't disappoint you. Closed Tuesdays. Open in August.

COPENHAGUE   142, avenue des Champs-Elysées (8th)   Tel: 359.20.42   Métro stop: George-V

Sponsored by the Danish Government, this restaurant specializes in all the delicious foods from their country. Conveniently located, it is particularly nice in the summertime when you can sit out on the rear terrace beyond the noise of the traffic out front. This is one of the best places to have good hearty beer, Carlsberg or Tuborg. The Danish Fish Platter is a particular favorite of mine; it contains all the goodies one likes as an hors d'oeuvre: caviar, herring, smoked salmon, etc. Generally, after such an appetizer, I have no desire for anything else—except perhaps a good rich dessert.

CORSAIRE BASQUE   15, rue de l'Arc-de-Triomphe (17th)   Tel: 380.43.82   Métro stop: Étoile

A very homey, country type of place reminiscent of a small village restaurant. Mouthwatering dishes are displayed on a center table for your selection.

LE COUPE-CHOU   9–11, rue de Lanneau (5th)   Tel: 633.68.69
Métro stop: Maubert-Mutualité

Women in particular like this little place because of its lovely 17th-century, candlelit décor, the warm hearth of the fireplace, and the romantic music. There are two dining rooms, one on the main floor and one on the second floor. Open until 2 A.M. and throughout August.

AUX DEUX DRAGONS 24, rue Monsieur-le-Prince (6th) Métro stop: Odéon
This place, just off the Boulevard St.-Germain, was recommended to me by a friend who adores good Chinese food and claims that this is one of the best in Paris. I must agree. Comparatively reasonable as well. Closed Wednesdays.

AUX DEUX MAGOTS 170, boulevard St.-Germain (6th) Métro stop: St.-Germain-des-Prés And **CAFÉ DE FLORE** at 172 right next door
Two very special and popular cafés in Paris. They go way back in history and have often been the scenes of political plotting, the haunt of starlets, and now for many decades, the hub of the intellectual world. They both serve food, but people generally go there just to sit, and sip a coffee or an apéritif, and watch others go by or to make new friends. You can sit as long as you like without the waiters bothering you. Aux Deux Magots closes in August and de Flore in July.

LE DRUGSTORE
There are several of these offbeat and amusing places, each one different from the other: These are a real must—if only to see what they are like.

LE DRUGSTORE ST.-GERMAIN 140, boulevard St.-Germain (6th) Métro stop: St.-Germain-des-Prés

LE DRUGSTORE OPÉRA Place de l'Opéra (9th) Métro stop: Opéra

LE DRUGSTORE DE L'AVENUE MATIGNON (8th) Métro stop: F.-D.-Roosevelt

LE DRUGSTORE OUEST 79, avenue des Champs-Elysées (8th) Métro stop: F.-D.-Roosevelt

LE DRUGSTORE BERRY 13, rue de Berri (8th) Métro stop: George-V

LE DRUGSTORE ST.-LAZARE (8th) Métro stop: St.-Lazare
This one is particularly interesting for several reasons, not the least of which is the restaurant itself. Very Victorian in its décor, the walls are hung with plaques of the lips of famous women and panels with the eyes of famous men. The food isn't really bad, but I think they are rather overpriced. At the St.-Germain-des-Prés branch, there is a movie house on the lower level, and all sorts of shops winding snake-like throughout the establishment, for gifts, cigarettes, liquor, magazines, even watches, and jewelry. Open daily from 9 A.M. to 2 A.M., all year round.

CHEZ EDGARD 4, rue Marbeuf (8th) Tel: 359.85.92 Métro stop: F.-D.-Roosevelt
Excellent cuisine. *À la carte* menu. Open till 2 A.M. and throughout August.

ÉLYSÉES-BRETAGNE 4, avenue F.-D.-Roosevelt (8th) Tel: 359.20.63 Métro stop: F.-D.-Roosevelt
Crêperie—snacks—*charcuterie* (cold meats). Open until 2 A.M. and throughout August.

ÉLYSÉES MATIGNON 2, avenue Matignon (8th) Tel: 225.73.13 Métro stop: F.-D.-Roosevelt
Very conveniently located near the Rond-Point of the Champs-

Elysées, here they specialize in the typical French cuisine that one expects in Paris, right through the *crêpes Suzette*. A most romantic place in the summertime, when one can dine on the terrace. Inside, you sink into the velvet chairs and relax between one delicious course after another. Closed in August.

À FEIJOADA 76, quai de l'Hôtel de Ville (4th) Tel: 508.09.02
Métro stop: Pont-Marie

Just on the Right Bank, this little place specializes in Brazilian food and music. It's tiny but it's great fun. The owner, Annie Faure, is charming and very kind to her customers. There is a rather limited menu of Brazilian dishes: *feijoada,* which is the national dish of beans and rice, *picandinha* (my favorite), a combination of finely chopped steak, corn, tomatoes, and spices, served with a fried egg on top and rice. If you want to try the *picandinha,* you must order it when you reserve your table because the meat is all finely chopped by hand in advance. Generally they have live Brazilian music as well as records. Unfortunately, last time I was there the guitarist wasn't, but my memories of my first visit were sufficient. The food is still of the same high quality and the service is beautiful. They serve until after midnight and are closed on Sundays.

CHEZ ISIDORE 13, rue d'Artois (8th) Tel: 225.01.10 Métro stop: St.-Philippe-du-Roule

Also known as Artois, this richly decorated restaurant is very popular. Done in red velvet with a large fireplace, it offers the charming elegance one often associates with Paris. The food is excellent, as is the service. Being a chocoholic, I particularly like the chocolate éclairs, which in size are much like our foot-long hot dogs. If you are a late diner, say after 8:30 or so, be sure to make a reservation. Closed Sunday and from July 14 to September 1.

LE JACQUES-COEUR 6, place St.-Michel (5th) Métro stop: St.-Michel

Don't be put off by the jam of bohemian types out front at the bar, or at the snack bar for that matter. Persevere and keep going until you come to the dining room in the rear. You'll be glad you did, for the atmosphere here is very different. Assorted greenery and soft music will soon relax you as you settle down to a delicious dinner. Open from 12 to 3 for lunch and 7 to 10 for dinner. Closed on Mondays.

LA MAISON DU VALAIS 20, rue Royale (8th) Tel: 260.23.75
Métro stop: Concorde

A perfectly charming little restaurant in the style of a Swiss chalet, with shutters on the tiny windows, plants on the sills, calfskin booths, and rough-timbered walls. All the waitresses wear the traditional costumes of Evolène in Valais. Everyone is so gay and kind and eager to explain the dishes to you. Mr. Gaillard, the host and manager, is particularly kind and will be happy to help you select your wines or explain the history of different regional dishes. One of their specialties is *râclette* (a dish made from a large round cheese from the Valais that is partially melted over a fire and then shaved onto your plate with boiled potatoes)—simply delicious! For an appetizer try the *viande séchée,* thin slices of dried beef. With your *à la carte* meat dishes, you have a chance to try the *rosti,* another traditional Swiss dish similar to our hash-browned potatoes. There are two fixed-price menus, one at 38F ($9.50) and one at 42F ($10.50). Both are three-course dinners and include a choice of Swiss or French wine. There is a bar on the first floor and the restaurant itself is up a flight of stairs. Behind the restaurant there is a shop where you can buy Swiss carvings, wines, cheese, smoked ham and beef, and other Valaisan products. The shop is open from 10 A.M. to 6 P.M.; the restaurant is open only for lunch from 12 to 3 and dinner from 7 to 10.

LA MÉDITERRANÉE   2, place de l'Odéon (6th)   Tel: 326.46.75
Métro stop: Odéon
Just opposite the Théâtre de France on the 18th-century Place de l'Odéon, La Méditerranée is well-known for its excellent fish dishes, especially the *bouillabaisse provençale.* Monsieur Subernat, the proprietor, is very proud of the fact that Jean Cocteau and his friends were frequent visitors to his establishment. The place is charming. It has an excellent Mediterranean menu, and a small terrace for *tête-à-têtes.*

LE MENESTREL   51, rue St.-Louis-en-l'Ile (4th)   Métro stop: Pont-Marie
On the Ile St.-Louis, this tiny and very typical little French restaurant is the favorite of Parisians who appreciate good food at reasonable prices. A friend who lives on the Ile St.-Louis advises that it's best to get there just at the beginning of the dinner hour or much, much later, in order to get a table. Closed Tuesdays.

AU MOUTON DE PANURGE   17, rue de Choiseul (2nd)   Métro stop: 4-Septembre
A bit shocking for most women, this restaurant is nevertheless quite a talking point when you return home, because of its setting, which is very erotic! The murals are sexy enough to begin with, but even the food takes on a pornographic turn. Snails are served in chamber pots and the rolls are miniature penises. And that's just for starters! The staff wears medieval costumes, and the general atmosphere is one of fun.

MUNICHE   27, rue de Buci (6th)   Tel: 633.62.09   Métro stop: St.-Germain-des-Prés
Excellent brasserie with quick service and generous portions. Open until 3 A.M. and throughout August.

LE PACTOLE   44, boulevard St.-Germain (5th)   Tel: 326.92.28
Métro stop: Cluny
The homey atmosphere here revolves around the fact that you pretty much have to take pot luck. The menu features whatever Jacques Manière, the proprietor and chef, was able to find at the markets that day. Nonetheless, it's a very popular restaurant known for its good homey food. The interior is rather masculine with its oak paneling and antlers on the wall. The front half of the restaurant opens onto the Boulevard St.-Germain where you

can sit and watch all the interesting types that the area is famous for. It is necessary to book a table well in advance.

LA PÊCHERIE   24, rue Pierre-Lescot (1st)   Tel: 235.92.41
Métro stop: Etienne-Marcel
Very pleasant modern décor, centered around an aquarium with exotic fish. Good food. Open until 2 A.M.

PETIT BOSSO   20, rue Quincampoix (4th)   Tel: 887.82.48
Métro stop: Rambuteau
Sophisticated bistro-like décor. Open until 1 A.M. and throughout August.

LA PETITE DUCHESSE   15, rue Marbeuf (8th)   Tel: 359.78.69
Métro stop: F.-D.-Roosevelt
At the corner of Rue Clément-Marot, this is really two restaurants in one. On the main floor is a very elegant establishment with soft colors and velvety chairs. There is also an American bar on this floor. Downstairs, equally elegant, is an excellent Italian restaurant which, strangely enough, is very inexpensive considering its lovely fittings. No checked tablecloths here! I had veal scallopini with ham and cheese for $2. A real bargain. Both restaurants stay open until 2 A.M. and throughout August.

LE PROCOPE   13, rue de l'Ancienne-Comédie (6th)   Tel: 326.99.20   Métro stop: Odéon
Built at the end of the 17th century by Francesco Procopio, this is probably the oldest café-restaurant in Paris. Voltaire is said to have come here to eat ice cream. Very moderate prices. Try the fixed-price menu: Hors d'oeuvres Procope, tripe in white wine, chicken livers à la Basquaise, pork chops, Provençal stew. Bottled red wine. Closed Mondays.

PUB RENAULT   53, avenue des Champs-Elysées (8th)   Métro stop: F.-D.-Roosevelt
Be sure not to miss this extremely popular restaurant-cum-snackery where you can find just about anything you want all day and night. A little hard to find unless you are looking for it, of all places, behind the Renault car showroom. You enter the showroom itself, walking to the rear, and all of a sudden, there it is. The décor is to the last detail that of old-fashioned cars, the booths representing the car interior, the ceiling the under-carriage, and the lights are all old lanterns. Strictly an *à la carte* menu, but with a wide selection of choices, including American-style ice cream sodas and sundaes. This is the popular stopping-off place after a movie on the Champs-Elysées and it is generally always packed, but it's worth waiting for a booth. Upstairs is a showroom of old Renault models. Next to the Pub is a boutique where you can buy odds and ends.

LE RELAIS DE LA BUTTE   12, rue Ravignan (18th)   Tel: 606.16.18   Métro stop: Abbesses
A charming little Montmartre bistro, furnished in rustic style and with a pleasant atmosphere. The dishes are prepared with skill and care and you can sample a wonderful garlic soup followed by frogs' legs, lobster, or young guinea fowl. The wines are also very good. Closed Thursdays and in August.

LA RESSERRE   94, rue St.-Martin (4th)   Tel: 272.01.73,   Métro stop: Châtelet

Francis Nini, who created "Le Coupe-Chou" listed below, is now taking good care of this lovely little Louis XVIII-style restaurant. Open until 3 A.M. and throughout August. Closed Sundays.

RÔTISSERIE DE LA REINE PÉDAUQUE   6, rue de la Pépinière (8th)   Tel: 522.86.90   Métro stop: Saint-Lazare

There are six separate dining rooms here, all very warmly and charmingly decorated with beamed ceilings and stone fireplaces. Burgundy-style cooking is the specialty and they offer three fixed-price dinners. The Bourguignon menu features white, red, and rosé wines, all included in the fixed price, which is a good way to experiment with various wines.

ST.-ANTOINE   1, place du Louvre (1st)   Tel: 231.50.12   Métro stop: Louvre

I found this place, just next to the Louvre, one day after spending hours inside the museum working up a tremendous appetite. A small but charming little place, squeaky clean, with delicious food. If you have trouble with your French, the proprietress speaks English and is only too happy to help you. Closed Mondays and from the middle of October to December 1.

LE SOUFFLÉ   36, rue du Mont-Thabor (1st)   Tel: 073.44.38   Métro stop: Tuileries

This is the spot for one of the best soufflés in all of Paris, especially the huge *soufflé Grand-Marnier,* the specialty of proprietor André Faure. A favorite spot of businessmen, certain politicians, and a steady clientele who know the food is consistently good and the service very personable.

TASSÉE DU CHAPITRE   36, rue St.-Louis-en-l'Ile (4th)   Tel: 633.56.09   Métro stop: Pont-Marie

Charming cave-like atmosphere with candlelight. Open until 1 A.M. for dinner only. Closed on Sundays and from August 5 to August 30.

TOURTOUR   20, rue Quincampoix (4th)   Tel: 887.86.48   Métro stop: Rambuteau

Elegant décor and clientele in this old house in the district of Les Halles. Open until 2 A.M. and throughout August. Closed Sundays.

LE TROU DANS LE MUR   23, rue des Capucines (1st)   Tel: 073.66.63   Métro stop: Opéra

This picturesque little restaurant acquired its name in 1848 during the revolution, when a cannonball knocked a hole in the wall of the building. So many people came to see it that the concierge began to make coffee and sandwiches for them. From then on it was just a natural progression to its present status. Edith Piaf and Ernest Hemingway are two of the notables who often dined here. The manager, "Max," is charming. He is particularly kind to women alone and keeps you in a gay mood throughout your meal. The small, undistinguished entrance is a bit deceptive; downstairs the cave-like, candle-lit restaurant, with its vaulted ceilings and stone walls, is most attractive. There are only fifteen tables so it's very comfortable and cosy. There are two fixed-price dinners, one at 19.50F ($4.87) that offers you a three-course dinner and one at 33F ($8.25) that offers you five courses. My favorite dish is the *coquilles Saint-Jacques,* but my companion had the *entrecôte à la bordelaise* (steak simmered in white wine sauce and shallots) and raved about it. *Cuisses de grenouilles provençale* (frogs' legs) are also excellent for 16F ($4). Max will even give you coffee beans and lemon to chew on to dismiss the garlic smell after your dinner. Open for lunch 12 to 3 and dinner 7 to 11.

CHEZ VANIA   25, rue Royale (8th)   Tel: 265.13.52   Métro stop: Madeleine

In a little alleyway just off the Rue Royale, near the Madeleine, is a very tiny place with only six tables downstairs and six more upstairs. The food far surpasses its size. The proprietor, Yuri Nardellof, has been here for sixteen years and is a very personable chap. Ask him to tell you the story of Prince Yousoupoff, one of the assassins of Rasputin. He dined here regularly two or three times a week until he died in 1973. This was also a hangout for Anatol Litvak and other famous Russian names. The cuisine is authentic Russian as well as some French, and all is excellent. There are three fixed-price meals; for 18F ($4.50) you could have *hors d'oeuvres russe,* borscht, Hungarian goulash, cheese or dessert, and coffee. I have several favorites here, one of which is *kaulibac,* a dish made of smoked salmon, mushrooms, hard-boiled eggs, rice, and onions in a pastry crust; a very filling appetizer for 10F ($2.50) a slice. After this I very rarely have room for anything else but if you do, try the Cutlet Pejoisky (mixed chicken and veal croquette with white paprika sauce and rice) for 16F ($4). For dessert the specialty is what Yuri calls *"crème caramel,"* but this is a misnomer because it is nothing at all like *crème caramel,* but is a sweet yogurt, vanilla-flavored, with real fruit—strawberries, apricots, raisins, etc.—sliced into it. This unusual and absolutely delicious dish is a must! Even the drinks here are unique. Try the Ural Skay, an apéritif of Vodka and Russian cherry liqueur at 6F ($1.50). On Fridays and Saturdays they have Balalaika music, from 9 or 10 P.M. to midnight. Yuri and his wife are very attentive to single women dining here, so you need not worry about coming in alone. Chez Vania is open from 12 noon to midnight and serves hot dishes at all times, which is very unusual in Paris. I like to drop by in the middle of the afternoon and have the *crème caramel.*

RESTAURANTS: INEXPENSIVE

1st Arrondissement

AUX ARCADES   18, rue du Louvre   Tel: 236.10.78   Métro stop: Louvre

No fixed-price, but varied, moderate menu. Hors d'oeuvres, main course (broiled red snapper, *sole meunière,* leg of lamb, steak with Bercy sauce), delicatessen specialties such as sauerkraut dishes, cheese tray, desserts. Closed Mondays.

LE BALTARD 11, rue St.-Denis Tel: 231.74.03 Métro stop: Châtelet
Small, gay little bistro where you can have a pleasant meal. Open until 2 A.M. and throughout August. Closed Sundays.

BISTRO DES HALLES 7, rue de Roule Tel: 231.33.20 Métro stop: Louvre
A very sympathetic native of Pas-de-Calais maintains this lovely modern bistro for his clientele of students and employees of the quarter. The cuisine is based on various sauces, dishes, and grills from Pas-de-Calais. His *foie de veau provençale* for 11F ($2.75) is made of veal liver with garlic sauce. There is even a small *menu* for 10F ($2.50) and a carafe (½ pint) of red wine goes for only 1F ($.25). Closed Sundays. Open in August.

BRASSERIE DE L'OPÉRA 10, rue Gomboust Tel: 073.10.85 Métro stop: Pyramides
Nice little bistro. Lyonnaise specialties. *Menu:* hors d'oeuvres (raw carrots, sausage, country pâté), main course (steak, calf's head vinaigrette) or *plat du jour,* cheese or dessert, carafe of red wine. Varied *à la carte:* hot sausages in pastry, *coq au vin,* leg of lamb with French fries. Closed Sundays.

L'ÉCUELLE 28, rue de l'Arbre-Sec Tel: 231.97.82 Métro stop: Pont-Neuf
A charmingly decorated salon on the first floor. Friendly, simple, and fast service. Everyday features a tempting "day's special" for 11F ($2.75) including salad, terrine, steak with herbs, French fries and the house pastry specialty, "Tarte Maison." Closed Sundays. Open in August.

ETCHEGORRY 41, rue Croulebarbe (13th) Tel: 331.63.05 Métro stop: Place d'Italie
Near the Avenue de Gobelins, this is a very rustic provincial type of place with brass pots and huge hams hanging from the ceiling. There is a restaurant on the first and second floors and the food is excellent, as is the service. Closed Tuesdays and August 15 to September 15.

FERME ST.-HUBERT 6, rue Cochin (5th) Tel: 326.21.03 Métro stop: Maubert-Mutualité
Rich and various cheeses. Excellent cuisine and wines. Open all year and until 2 A.M. for dinner only. Closed Sundays and holidays.

LE LOUIS XIV 1 bis, place des Victoires Tel: 508.07.35 Métro stop: Bourse
The restaurant takes its name from the statue of King Louis XIV in the famous square outside. From the moment you step through the door, you are transported back to the 1800s, especially as you climb the wrought iron staircase to the second floor. The proprietor, M. Fédy, specializes in Lyonnaise cuisine from the gastronomic capital of France. Take his suggestion to me and order the beef Bourguignon in wine, and, for a different salad, the dandelion leaves with a hot bacon dressing that

was delicious. All pastries are baked fresh each day. The fixed-price menu includes a good Beaujolais and service. Closed Sundays and Saturday nights and throughout August.

RESTAURANT DE MADAME FAURÉ   40, rue du Mont-Thabor Tel: 073:39.15   Métro shop: Tuileries
Very picturesque, country style, big portions. *Menu:* hors d'oeuvres or "giant" omelettes, *plat du jour* (*coq au vin,* sautéed rabbit, steak with shallots, and, "for delicate stomachs," roast chicken or steak), cheese, dessert, all the barrel wine you can drink. Closed Sundays.

CAFÉ-RESTAURANT DE LA MAIRIE   1, rue Perrault (Place du Louvre)   Tel: 231.88.59   Métro stop: Pont-Neuf
Fixed-price menu: hors d'oeuvres (platters of sausages); *plat du jour* or ¼ chicken, broiled tenderloin with French fries; cheese or dessert; red Corbières wine, beer, or mineral water. Closed Sundays and evenings.

LE PANORAMA   14, quai du Louvre   Tel: 231.32.37   Métro stop: Louvre
Perfect name. Beautiful views of Seine, quays, palaces. *Menu:* appetizer (soup, jellied eggs, herring fillets, potato salad), main course (steak with French fries, chicken and rice), cheese or dessert.

PAUL   15, place Dauphine (another entrance on Quai des Orfèvres)   Tel: 033.21.48   Métro stop: Pont-Neuf
Typical Parisian restaurant. *Menu:* hors d'oeuvres (country pâté, tomato salad), *plat du jour* (grilled steak, quenelles, roast chicken with watercress), cheese or dessert, small carafe of red or white wine. Closed Mondays and August.

LE PROVENÇAL   34, rue de l'Arbre-Sec   Tel: 508.51.05   Métro stop: Pont-Neuf
Menu: hors d'oeuvres (head cheese), main course (calf's head, *Gribiche,* pickled pork and lentils, steak with French fries), vegetables, cheese or dessert. Carafe of wine. *À la carte:* steak with French fries, boiled beef.

LE RICHEPANSE   9, rue Richepanse   Tel: 073.97.77   Métro stop: Concorde
Menu: entrée, cheese, or dessert, carafe of wine, beer, or mineral water. *À la carte: plat du jour,* mackerel fillets with Provençal sauce; steak, cold meat mayonnaise. Closed Sundays and evenings.

RESTAURANT ST.-ANTOINE   21, rue des Prêtres-St.-Germain-l'Auxerrois and 1, place du Louvre   Tel: 231.50.12   Métro stop: Pont-Neuf
Excellent little restaurant with three fixed-price menus. The least expensive includes hors d'oeuvres, pork chop *charcutière,* French fries and rice, cheese and dessert. The most expensive *menu:* hors d'oeuvres *filet maître d'hôtel,* French fries and rice, cheese and dessert, wine.

SALON DE THÉ-PÂTISSERIE HAMMES   2, rue du Louvre   Tel: 508.19.18   Métro stop: Louvre
Beautiful view of the Louvre Palace. *À la carte:* omelette, ham omelette, creamed chicken in puff pastry, quiche Lorraine, *plats*

du jour, cheese, desserts. Bordeaux, carafe of white Sancerre wine. Closed Sundays and evenings.

LE VIEIL ÉCU   166, rue St.-Honoré   Tel: 231.03.24   Métro stop: Palais-Royal

Burlap covered walls, posters of Sali-Bruant, even the tables and chairs make this a true bistro. In the evening, candlelight changes the atmosphere to one of a more romantic nature. Very wide choice of dishes and charming, speedy young waitresses make this a good choice for lunch or dinner. Fixed-price menu 11F ($2.75) including wine and service. Closed Sundays. Open in August.

2nd Arrondissement

BROUILLET   5, rue Paul Lelong   Tel: 236.26.08   Métro stop: Bourse

A vast and deep cave, usually frequented by the journalistic world. The atmosphere is one of friendliness and relaxation with smiling waitresses as well as clientele. The *menu* at an unbelievable 10F ($2.50) including service, consists of *crudités* (raw vegetables), veal kidneys sauté, potatoes *boulangère, tarte aux pommes* (apple tart), and a half-pint of red wine, plus espresso. All is delicious and fresh. The *à la carte* menu, too, offers a wide selection and is really not too expensive. Open from 11 A.M. to 2:30 P.M. Closed evenings.

AUX LYONNAIS   32, rue St.-Marc   Tel: 742.65.59   Métro stop: Montmartre

Just off the Boulevard des Italiens near the Opéra Comique. A very busy and sometimes noisy place, this is an excellent choice for typical Lyonnaise cuisine. I particularly like the chicken, in a cream sauce with mushrooms from the *à la carte* menu. However the fixed-price menu also offers a delicious selection. Closed from mid-July to September.

PARIS-ATHENS   35, avenue de l'Opéra   Tel: 073.66.66   Métro stop: Opéra

Menu: hors d'oeuvres (eggs mayonnaise, country pâté), main course (steak with French fries, ¼ chicken, pork chop), cheese or dessert, carafe of red wine. *À la carte,* garnished omelette, veal sauté Marengo. Closed Sundays.

3rd Arrondissement

AUX ROUTIERS   29, rue Beaubourg   Tel: 887.95.18   Métro stop: Arts-et-Métiers

You will not get bored at this lively place with all the chatting going on at all the tables. Soft lights and old paintings create a lovely atmosphere. Usually crowded with local shop girls and clerks. Fixed-price menu 8F ($2), but even if you have *mousse au chocolat* and a coffee, you will not go beyond 12F ($3). Closed Sundays.

TOUR DE JADE   20, rue de la Michodière   Tel: 742.07.56   Métro stop: Opéra
Pretty décor, but you might have a rather indifferent welcome as is the tradition here. Open in August.

4th Arrondissement

BRASSERIE DE L'ÎLE-ST.-LOUIS   55, quai de Bourbon   Tel: 033.02.59   Métro stop: Pont-Marie
Interesting clientele. Delightful setting with polite, quick service. *Menu:* hors d'oeuvres, *plat du jour* or specialties (tripe in Riesling wine), cheese or dessert. Carafe of red wine. *À la carte:* bacon omelette, herrings with potato salad, *ray au beurre noir.* Highly recommended cassoulet, pork knuckles with lentils. Closed Thursdays.

À L'ENCLOS DE NINON   21, boulevard Beaumarchais   Tel: 272.22.51   Métro stop: St.-Sébastien
Very pleasant menu. Closed Tuesdays. Open in August.

LE MONDE DES CHIMBÈRES   69, rue St.-Louis-en-l'Ile   Tel: 033.45.27   Métro stop: Pont-Marie
Popular for its charm and kind, speedy service, the great wooden desk and bistro style tables make this a typical spot. Fixed-price menu: 13.50F ($3.37) including beer or wine. Closed Sundays.

LE TRUMILOU   84, quai de l'Hôtel de Ville   Tel: 277.63.98   Métro stop: Pont-Marie
A characteristic bistro with great charm and friendliness. The service may sometimes be a trifle slow, but it certainly is worthwhile considering the quality and quantity of the food. Fixed-price menu with four courses, from 12F to 14F ($3 to $3.50) including service. A half-pint of wine is only 1F ($.25). Closed Mondays. Open in August.

5th Arrondissement

LA COQUILLE ST.-JACQUES   1, rue St.-Jacques   Tel: 033.97.39   Métro stop: Maubert-Mutualité
Stays open until dawn. Restaurant on second floor above café. Try the "kir" apéritif, white wine with black currant liqueur, coquilles St.-Jacques (scallops) or crayfish mayonnaise, guinea hen Normandie, or steak with shoestring potatoes and green beans, salad, cheese, and dessert. Bottle of Bordeaux. Closed Tuesdays.

LA GRILLERIE   3, rue du Petit-Pont   Tel: 633.08.32   Métro stop: St.-Michel
Medieval setting. Four *menus,* including walnut salad, charcoal broiled steak with shoestring potatoes. Cheese, dessert extra. Red wine. Open to 11:30 P.M.

CHEZ PAULETTE   28, rue des Bernardins   Tel: 033.63.84   Métro stop: Maubert-Mutualité
A warm atmosphere with lots of greenery, lovely paintings, and a very kind welcome, make this a favorite in the St.-Germain area. Fixed-price menu at 10F ($2.50) including service and a half-pint of wine. Closed Sundays. Open in August.

PUB ST.-MICHEL 19, quai St.-Michel Tel: 633.30.41 Métro stop: St.-Michel
Comfortable pub. Intimate dining-room, unusual décor. Lunch served 12 to 3 P.M. *Menu:* appetizers (relishes, country pâté, eggs mayonnaise, beef muzzle vinaigrette), *plat du jour* or prime steak, cheese or dessert. Wine, beer, mineral water. Open daily to 2:00 A.M.

LE ROUSSIN D'ARCADE (THE JACKASS) 6, place de la Sorbonne Tel: 033.48.18 Métro stop: Sorbonne
Italian specialties. In keeping with name, the doorman is literally a small donkey. *Menu:* hors d'oeuvres (peasant soup, tomato salad, spaghetti, pizza), *plat du jour* (lasagne, veal scallopini with spaghetti, steak with French fries, liver *Vénitienne*), cheese or dessert. Valpolicella or Mâcon red wine. Closed Thursdays.

SAMOURA 8, rue Xavier-Privas Tel: 325.46.08 Métro stop: St.-Michel
Little Japanese spot with good food. During the week, dinner only. Lunch and dinner on Sundays and holidays. Open in August.

LA TABLE D'HÔTE 28, rue de la Montagne-Ste.-Geneviève Tel: 033.14.87 Métro stop: Maubert-Mutualité
A small, picturesque, inn-like place, with a series of amusing rooms. No fixed price, but amazingly low prices. *À la carte:* eggs jellied in whiskey, snails, rabbit sauté hunter style, rib steak *maître d'hôtel,* camembert, Pont L'Evêque. Pitcher of red wine. Bar, discothèque, library, and bridge tables in basement. Open 11:30 A.M. to 2:00 A.M., and throughout August.

6th Arrondissement

ALLARD 41, rue St.-André-des-Arts Tel: 326.48.23 Métro stop: St.-Michel
One of the most famous bistros in Paris, presided over by Monsieur André Allard and his lovely wife Fernande. Fernande herself is the chef in residence and does a noble job. The building in which the restaurant is located goes back to the days of Marie de Medici and Cardinal Richelieu, and is still a stopping-off place for many French celebrities, including Madame Pompidou herself as well as many silver screen luminaries. The front room features sawdust and marble tables with a paneled bar up front. But if you prefer a less noisy meal, try the back room instead. Fernande specializes in Burgundian dishes and one of her favorites is *Canard aux Olives* (duck with olives). Accompany your meal with one of the excellent Burgundy wines which the Allard family itself bottles. Closed Sundays and from July 20 to September 1.

RESTAURANT DES ARTS 73, rue de Seine Tel: 326.11.79 Métro stop: Odéon
A small country cottage type of place with voile curtains in the window and excellent food. It generally gets a lot of nearby stu-

dents. Fixed-price menu: 11F ($2.75). Closed Saturdays and Sundays and August 1 to August 15.

LA BOUCHERIE   6, rue des Ciseaux   Tel: 326.11.67   Métro stop: St.-Germain-des-Prés

In heart of St.-Germain-des-Prés. Very picturesque. *Menu:* appetizer (relishes, cold cuts), main course (steaks, hamburger, steak tartar, veal cutlet), cheese or dessert. Extras: pepper steak; special desserts. Closed Sundays.

RESTAURANT DU DRAGON   14, rue du Dragon   Tel: 548.75.58   Métro stop: St.-Germain-des-Prés

Located in narrow, amusing Rue du Dragon. *Menu:* hors d'oeuvres (eggs mayonnaise, pâté maison), main course (paella Valenciana, veal sauté with mushrooms, steak and parslied potatoes), cheese or dessert, carafe of Corbières red wine. Closed Sundays.

LE MEDICIS   4, place Edmond-Rostand   Tel: 326.46.06   Métro stop: Luxembourg

Nice spot opposite Luxembourg Gardens. *Menu:* hors d'oeuvres (rissoles, eggs mayonnaise, celery remoulade), *plat du jour* (grilled pork chops, chicken with rice and sauce supreme, tripe à la mode de Caen), cheese or dessert. Pitcher of Muscadet, Côtes-du-Rhône, beer.

LE PETIT ST.-BENOÎT   4, rue St.-Benoît   Tel: 548.99.60   Métro stop: St.-Germain-des-Prés

Family cooking, *à la carte* only. Moderate prices. *Menu: plat du jour* (haddock, veal stew, beef with endives, hash with mashed potatoes), cheese or dessert. Bottled red wine. Closed Saturdays, Sundays, and August 15 to August 30.

PETIT ZINC   25, rue de Buci   Tel: 033.79.34   Metro stop: St.-Germain-des-Prés

Bistro décor with simple cuisine and excellent wine. Open until 3 A.M. and throughout August.

SÉLECT LATIN   25, boulevard St.-Michel   Tel: 033.98.90   Métro stop: St.-Michel

Menu: hors d'oeuvres, *plat du jour* (scallops Saint-Jacques, veal), salad or cheese or dessert. Carafe of red, white, or rosé wine. *Menu:* hors d'oeuvres, main course (roast chicken, Alsatian sauerkraut, steak, pork chop), salad or cheese, dessert.

VAGENENDE   142, boulevard St.-Germain   Tel: 326.68.18   Métro stop: St.-Germain-des-Prés

One of the few restaurants retaining the "Belle Epoque" (1900) setting. A real museum of the "modern style." *Menu:* hors d'oeuvres, *plat du jour* (roast goose, roast chicken, calves' liver), cheese and dessert. Bottle of white wine, Beaujolais.

ZÉRO DE CONDUITE   64, rue Monsieur-le-Prince   Tel: 033.50.79   Métro stop: Odéon

Famous Latin Quarter gathering place. *Menu:* hors d'oeuvres (Russian eggs, salad, chorizo sausage), *plat du jour* (charcoal-broiled steak, curried chicken, beef stew, hot North African sausage), dessert (old-fashioned pie). Pitcher of red or rosé wine, beer.

7th Arrondissement

BLANC   24, avenue de Tourville, place de l'Ecole Militaire   Tel: 705.50.15   Métro stop: St.-Francis-Xavier

Pleasant little place, wide menu choice. Fixed-price menu: hors d'oeuvres or relishes, broiled meats or *plat du jour* (e.g., roast guinea hen), cheese or dessert (chef's pies), red wine, beer, mineral water included.

BRASSERIE DE LA TOUR EIFFEL   Métro stop: Champ de Mars

Fixed-price menu: hors d'oeuvres or soup, choice of roast chicken, hamburger or beefsteak, and dessert. Carafe of red wine included.

BRASSERIE-TABAC DES INVALIDES   52, rue Fabert   Tel: 705. 51.93   Métro stop: Invalides

At corner of Rue de Grenelle on the same esplanade as Invalides. This friendly brasserie is run by Mme. Boucheron. Her husband, Firmin, a great restaurateur, won his name at the famous "Hôtel de France" in Champagne. Eggs, omelettes, entrées. *Plat du jour* (sauerkraut, veal kidneys, home-made tripe, *blanquette de veau, coq au vin*). Nice wines. Closed Saturdays.

LA CIGALE   11 bis, rue Chomel   Tel: 548.87.87   Métro stop: Sèvres-Babylone

There is a good *à la carte* menu which is not too expensive and very worthwhile. Closed Sundays, open in August.

LES COPAINS   44, rue de Verneuil   Tel: 548.49.91   Métro stop: Rue du Bac

Lovely spot with a small but good menu. Closed Sundays, open in August.

LE DÔME   47, avenue de la Bourdonnais   Tel: 551.45.41   Métro stop: Ecole-Militaire

Close to Place de l'Ecole. Pleasant; a few steps from Eiffel Tower. *Plat du jour,* cheese or dessert. Varied *à la carte;* steak.

L'ESCALE BLEU   136, rue de Grenelle   Tel: 551.40.32   Métro stop: Varenne

Nothing special in terms of décor but people come here because they enjoy eating like one of the family. Everything is fresh and served with a smile. This is probably why even well-knowns such as Mylène Demongeot and the like come here for a pleasant meal. The proprietress likes to see her clients happy, and you will make her so in return if you compliment her on the quality of the meat or the sweetness of her pie—and you certainly won't have to lie about it. Fixed-price menu: 11F ($2.75) including service. Closed Sundays.

LA FONTAINE DE MARS   129, rue St.-Dominique   Tel: 705. 46.44   Métro stop: Ecole-Militaire

Short way from Champ de Mars and Eiffel Tower. Perfect example of Parisian bistro. Its Cahors wine, regional and country specialties, are famous. Outstanding *à la carte* dishes; broiled fresh sardines, country ham, lamb's tongue Milanaise. Closed Sundays.

RESTAURANT DE L'HÔTEL DE LA BOURDONNAIS   113, avenue de la Bourdonnais   Tel: 705.45.42   Métro stop: Ecole-Militaire

Just off the Place de l'Ecole Militaire. Fixed-price menu: hors d'oeuvres (hard-boiled eggs, cold cuts), *plat du jour* (calves' liver, rabbit, with prunes), cheese or dessert. Carafe of red wine. Bottle Sylvaner included. Closed Saturdays.

MARIUS   25, rue Duvivier, leads into Avenue de la Motte-Picquet, between Ecole Militaire and Les Invalides Tel: 551.72.58 Métro stop: Ecole-Militaire

Menu: hors d'oeuvres (mackerel in white wine), main course (veal scallops in cream, *coq au vin*), cheese or dessert.

LE PETIT TONNEAU 20, rue Surcouf Tel: 486.09.01 Métro stop: La Tour-Maubert

(On a little street parallel to Avenue de la Bourdonnais and Esplannade des Invalides.) Fixed-price menu: hors d'oeuvres, *plat du jour,* cheese or dessert. The chef was formerly at Lucas Carton, a very famous restaurant on the Place de la Madeleine. (See Expensive listing.) Closed Sundays.

LA POULE AU POT 121, rue de l'Université Tel: 551.16.36 Métro stop: Invalides

Corner of Rue Surcouf. Fixed-price menu: first course (soup, mountain sausages), main course (lamb curry, hash with mashed potatoes, broiled meats), cheese or dessert. "Poule au pot" (chicken with herbs and vegetables), a popular French dish, *à la carte*. Also *à la carte,* Beaujolais or Côtes-du-Rhône red wines. Closed Sundays.

LE RÉCAMIER 4, rue Récamier Tel: 548.86.58 Métro stop: Sèvres-Babylone

"Cuisine Bourguignonne." Closed Sundays.

LA RIVE D'OTT 38, avenue de Suffren Tel: 734.80.59 Métro stop: Champ de Mars

Lovely location on west side of Champ de Mars, near Eiffel Tower. *Menu:* hors d'oeuvres, *plat du jour,* cheese or dessert. Closed Saturday evenings and Sundays.

LE VAUBAN 7, place Vauban Tel: 705.52.67 Métro stop: Ecole-Militaire

Facing the entrance to Les Invalides. Beautiful setting, simple cooking. *Menu:* hors d'oeuvres, *plat du jour* (rice-stuffed tomatoes, honeycomb tripe in white wine and onion sauce), cheese or dessert. *À la carte,* usual dishes, roast beef, cold chicken.

8th Arrondissement

BOUTIQUE À SANDWICH 12, rue du Colisée Tel: 359.34.32 Métro stop: F.-D.-Roosevelt

As in all good restaurants, you might find it difficult to get a table on the first floor of this unusual boutique. They feature an exotic selection of sandwiches on the main floor. They also have a fixed-price menu for 15F ($3.75). Closed Sundays.

LE CHAMBIGES 4, rue de Chambiges Tel: 359.34.32 Métro stop: Alma-Marceau

This is a small two-room restaurant at the end of a court. Ask for the 10F *menu* which features egg mayonnaise, steak or chicken, dessert or cheese. Not bad for $2.50. Closed Sundays.

LES CLOYÈRES 9, rue Laborde Tel: 387.93.26 Métro stop: St.-Augustin

This is a new and very charming restaurant with a fixed-price menu at 39F ($9.75) including a Bordeaux wine. That may be a little expensive; however, an area is reserved for self-service where the menu, décor, and presentation of the dishes happily surprised us. For 12F including beer or wine, you can have mushrooms for an appetizer, grilled minute steak with tomatoes and French fries, and a real honest pie or a large choice of cheeses. Again, a bargain at $3. Open for lunch only.

LA MAISON DU CAVIAR 24, rue Quentin-Bauchart Tel: 225.78.62 Métro stop: F.-D.-Roosevelt

A tiny place for very good smoked salmon, caviar from Iran, or Bortsch. Open until 2 A.M. and throughout August. Closed Sundays.

LA PERGOLA 144, avenue des Champs-Elysées Tel: 359.70.52 Métro stop: George-V

Enormous and lively. Three huge *menus*. Prices increase Sundays. *Menu:* tomato salad, lamb curry, pears. *Menu:* stuffed peppers, roast veal with white beets au gratin, cheese and ice cream with fruit. *Menu:* "special" oysters, sautéed chicken, cheese and fruit cup Melba. Carafe of red wine, rosé.

LES PRINCES 29, avenue George-V Tel: 225.35.30 Métro stop: George-V

Very posh and attractive restaurant. Dinner on the flowered covered patio. One of the best *bouillabaisses* in town. Open from midday to midnight and throughout August.

VALENTIN 19, rue Marbeuf Tel: 359.80.11 Métro stop: F.-D.-Roosevelt

A lovely place with an excellent kitchen and very modest prices. The natural and good food makes a very enjoyable lunch but is not suggested for dinner. Closed Sundays.

LE WESTPHALIE 8, avenue F.-D.-Roosevelt Tel: 359.91.20 Métro stop: F.-D.-Roosevelt

Good dishes from Rouergue and Perigord; fish dishes and sea-food are excellent. Open until 2 A.M. and throughout August.

9th Arrondissement

L'ANCIEN CHARTIER 7, rue du faubourg Montmartre Tel: 770.86.29 Métro stop: Montmartre

The décor alone is worth a visit to this lovely restaurant, and the food is surely not secondary. Steak Bourgeois 3F (under a dollar), half-pint of red wine 0.70F (under 25 cents), and other interesting selections. Open in August.

LA BOULE ROUGE 1, rue de la Boule Rouge Tel: 770.43.90 Métro stop: Montmartre

I sometimes wonder how Monsieur Bergeron can still offer such a good honest cuisine with a *menu* at only 12.50F ($3.12) including *assiette de crudités* in the three-course meal. His *à la carte* menu is also very worthwhile and shouldn't be overlooked. Closed Sundays.

L'HORIZON   12, rue Vignon   Métro stop: Madeleine
Menu: hors d'oeuvres (mussels marinière, eggs in aspic), *plat du jour* (poached ray, steak), cheese or dessert. Bottle of wine, pitcher, half-pitcher. Special *couscous*. Closed Sundays.

10th Arrondissement

BAR DU COMBAT ROGGERO   37, avenue Claude-Vellefaux
Tel: 205.30.01   Métro stop: Colonel-Fabien
Marius Roggero doesn't really stick to his fixed-price menu. You may spend a little less than the 12F ($3) he charges or perhaps just a little bit more. But this small bistro has such charisma that it's worth a visit. Try their *bouillabaisse!* Closed Sundays. Open in August.

16th Arrondissement

À L'ANCIEN TROCADÉRO   2, place du Trocadéro   Tel: 727.
42.49   Métro stop: Trocadéro
A reasonable and charming restaurant, located on the Trocadéro, facing the Théâtre National Populaire. *Menu:* hors d'oeuvres, main course (*blanquette de veau*), cheese, dessert, and red wine. Closed Mondays.

LA BIÈRE   9, avenue des Ternes   Tel: 380.09.11   Métro stop: Ternes
Five minutes from Arc de Triomphe going down Avenue de Wagram. Typical local restaurant with self-service on ground floor. *Menu:* hors d'oeuvres (tomato salad, hard boiled eggs, Alsatian sausages), *plat du jour* ("special" sauerkraut, roast chicken and watercress, steak), cheese or dessert. Small carafe red or white wine, beer or mineral water. *À la carte* menu: hors d'oeuvres (snails, Bayonne ham), entrée (pepper steak, half guinea hen), cheese and dessert. Open to 11:30 P.M., Saturday 2 A.M.

RESTAURANT DES CHAUFFEURS   8, chaussée de la Muette
Tel: 288.50.05   Métro stop: Muette
Family cooking. *Menu:* first course (soup, country pâté), *plat du jour* (roast chicken, *pot-au-feu,* or beef and vegetables in rich broth), cheese or dessert. Carafe of red wine. *À la carte* at moderate prices: *pot-au-feu,* broiled sirloin, beef Bourguignon Closed Wednesdays.

MONTE CARLO   9, avenue de Wagram   Tel: 380.02.20   Métro stop: Étoile
Large *menu:* hors d'oeuvres (pâté maison, relishes, meat, birds with olives), main course (hamburger with French fries, breast of veal, fish, steak), cheese or dessert. *Menu:* hors d'oeuvres (chef's pâté), main course (beef ribs, roast chicken, lamb chops), salad, cheese or dessert. Carafe of red, rosé, or white wine with both menus. Bottle Beaujolais or Bordeaux.

LA MUSARDIÈRE   4, avenue Carnot   Tel: 754.80.51   Métro stop: Étoile
Pleasant little restaurant. One or two specialties and some simple dishes. Reasonably priced *à la carte:* omelette, salad niçoise, salad, steak with French fries, fried sausage. *Plat du jour:* veal knuckles, curry with rice.

LE PASSY   2, rue de Passy   Tel: 288.31.02   Métro stop: Muette
Menu: hors d'oeuvres (country pâté, *rissoles*), *plat du jour* (calves' brains, steak with French fries), cheese or dessert. Carafe of red wine. *À la carte:* pickled pork and lentils, etc. Closed August.

LE RELAIS DU BOIS   1, rue Guy-de-Maupassant   Tel: 870.27.60
Métro stop: Pompe
Menu: hors d'oeuvres (tomato salad, country pâté), *plat du jour* (filet mignon), cheese or dessert. Carafe of Côtes-du-Rhône red wine. *Plat du jour à la carte,* boiled beef. Closed Mondays.

LE RUDE   11, avenue de la Grande-Armée   Tel: 727.13.21
Métro stop: Étoile
Little neighborhood restaurant, near Arc de Triomphe. Hors d'oeuvres, main course, cheese and dessert, carafe wine. Typical French specialties: pigs' feet à la Sainte-Menehould, small tripe sausages. Large *à la carte* selection including half-duckling with turnips.

LE TROCADÉRO   8, place du Trocadéro   Tel: 553.75.00   Métro stop: Trocadéro
Menu: hors d'oeuvres (country pâté, salami, sausages), *plat du jour* (steak, tripe, *cassoulet*), cheese or dessert. Carafe of red wine, Touraine rosé.

AU VRAI SAUMUR   1, chaussée de la Muette   Tel: 527.42.84
Métro stop: Muette
Moderate-priced brasserie. *À la carte.* Plat du jour (*choucroute,* beef Bourguignon, duckling with turnips). Bottle of red wine.

18th Arrondissement

CHEZ BABETTE   41, rue Championnet   Tel: 076.71.80   Métro stop: Simplon
Two picturesque rooms. Room 1: *menu:* 20 hors d'oeuvres (self-service), *plat du jour* or steak with French fries, cold meats, cheese or dessert, including all the draft red wine you can drink. Room 2: huge *menu,* including cheese and dessert, wine. *À la carte,* chicken Basquaise, veal cutlets in cream.

LE BON BOCK   2, rue Dancourt   Tel: 606.43.45   Métro stop: Anvers
Famous old-time Montmartre restaurant near Atelier Theater. *Menu:* choice hors d'oeuvres, *plat du jour,* or main course (beef fillet, boiled beef), cheese or dessert (chocolate mousse). Red wine.

LA BONNE TABLE   5, rue Seveste   Tel: 606.96.40   Métro stop: Anvers
Typically Montmartre. *Menu:* lots of hors d'oeuvres, appetizers

(shell-fish, ham), main course (large steak), cheese, fruit or pie. Carafe of red wine. Closed Thursdays and August 15–September 15.

LES BOSQUETS   39, rue d'Orsel   Tel: 606.11.12   Métro stop: Anvers

A bit of a bistro in the heart of Montmartre with a garden for summer dining. Quantity and quality. *Menu:* eight or nine hors d'oeuvres, fish delicacies (*quenelle de brochet, lotte à l'américaine*), meats (*boeuf au poivre, entrecôte Bercy*), desserts (*meringue glacée, mousee au chocolat*). Closed Thursdays and February.

LE CANON DE MONTMARTRE   1, rue Paul-Albert   Tel: 606. 98.30   Métro stop: Château Rouge

On Willette Square at foot of Montmartre Hill. *Menu: plat du jour,* cheese or dessert, carafe red wine. *À la carte: hake* mayonnaise, pork chops. Closed Thursdays.

LE SABOT ROUGE   13, place du Tertre   Tel: 606.96.33   Métro stop: Abbesses

Menu: hors d'oeuvres (soup, herring fillets, relishes), *plat du jour* (*coq au vin,* roast chicken, steak with French fries), cheese or dessert. Carafe of red wine. Closed Wednesdays.

RESTAURANTS NEAR FAMOUS MONUMENTS

While sightseeing, it's handy to know where to drop in for a snack or for lunch, so we offer the following suggestions. Some offer full French meals for as little as two dollars. All fall within the Inexpensive price category. And though none are in the Cordon Bleu class, they speak well, we think, of the art of French cooking. But see for yourself.

Arc de Triomphe (L'Étoile)

LA BIÈRE   9, avenue des Ternes (17th)   Tel: 380.09.11
MONTE CARLO   9, avenue de Wagram (17th)   Tel: 380.02.20
LA MUSARDIÈRE   4, avenue Carnot (17th)   Tel: 754.80.51
LA PERGOLA   144, avenue des Champs-Elysées (17th)   Tel: 359.70.52
LE RUDE   11, avenue de la Grande-Armée (16th)   Tel: 727.13.21

Les Invalides

BRASSERIE-TABAC DES INVALIDES   52, rue Fabert (7th)   Tel: 705.51.93
MARIUS   25, rue Duvivier (7th)   Tel: 551.72.58
LE PETIT TONNEAU   20, rue Surcouf (7th)   Tel: 486.09.01
LA POULE AU POT   121, rue de l'Université (7th)   Tel: 551.16.36
LE VAUBAN   7, place Vauban (7th)   Tel: 705.52.67

Musée du Louvre (Carrousel)

AUX ARCADES　18, rue du Louvre (1st)　Tel: 236.10.78
CAFÉ-RESTAURANT DE LA MAIRIE　1, rue Perrault (1st)　Tel:
231.88.59
LA PANORAMA　14, quai du Louvre (1st)　Tel: 231.32.37
LE PROVENÇAL　34, rue de l'Arbre-Sec (1st)　Tel: 508.51.05
RESTAURANT ST.-ANTOINE　21, rue des Prêtres-St.-Germain-
l'Auxerrois (1st)　Tel: 231.50.12
SALON DE THÉ-PÂTISSERIE HAMMES　2, rue du Louvre (1st)
Tel: 508.19.18

Notre Dame and Île-St.-Louis

BRASSERIE DE L'ÎLE-ST.-LOUIS　55, quai de Bourbon (4th)
Tel: 033.02.59
LA COQUILLE ST.-JACQUES　1, rue St.-Jacques (5th)　Tel: 033.
97.39
LA GRILLERIE　3, rue du Petit-Pont (5th)　Tel: 633.08.32
PAUL　15, place Dauphine (another entrance on the Quai des
Orfèvres) (1st)　Tel: 033.21.48
PUB ST.-MICHEL　19, quai St.-Michel (5th)　Tel: 633.30.41

Opéra / Madeleine / Concorde

BRASSERIE DE L'OPÉRA　10, rue Gomboust (1st)　Tel: 073.
10.85
L'HORIZON　12, rue Vignon (9th)
PARIS-ATHENS　35, avenue de l'Opéra (2nd)　Tel: 073.66.66
RESTAURANT DE MADAME FAURÉ　40, rue du Mont-Thabor
(1st)　Tel: 073.39.15

Panthéon / Latin Quarter

LE MEDICIS　4, place Edmond-Rostand (6th)　Tel: 326.46.06
LE ROUSSIN D'ARCADE (THE JACKASS)　6, place de la Sor-
bonne (5th)　Tel: 033.48.18
SÉLECT LATIN　25, boulevard St.-Michel (6th)　Tel: 033.98.90
LA TABLE D'HÔTE　28, rue de la Montagne-Ste.-Geneviève (5th)
Tel: 033.14.87
ZÉRO DE CONDUITE　64, rue Monsieur-le-Prince (6th)　Tel: 033.
50.79

Sacré-Coeur

CHEZ BABETTE　41, rue Championnet (18th)　Tel: 076.71.80
LE BON BOCK　2, rue Dancourt (18th)　Tel: 606.43.45
LA BONNE TABLE　5, rue Seveste (18th)　Tel: 606.96.40
LES BOSQUETS　39, rue d'Orsel (18th)　Tel: 606.11.12
LE CANON DE MONTMARTRE　1, rue Paul-Albert (18th)　Tel:
606.98.30
LE SABOT ROUGE　13, place du Tertre (18th)　Tel: 606.96.33

St.-Germain-des-Prés

LA BOUCHERIE 6, rue des Ciseaux (6th) Tel: 326.11.67
RESTAURANT DU DRAGON 14, rue du Dragon (6th) Tel: 548.75.58
LE PETIT SAINT-BENOÎT 4, rue St.-Benoît (6th) Tel: 548.99.60
LE PROCOPE 13, rue de l'Ancienne-Comédie (6th) Tel: 326.99.20
VAGENENDE 142, boulevard St.-Germain (6th) Tel: 326.68.18

Tour Eiffel / Ecole Militaire

BLANC 26, avenue de Tourville, Place de l'Ecole Militaire (7th) Tel: 705.45.42
LA BRASSERIE DE LA TOUR EIFFEL First level of Eiffel Tower, Champ de Mars (7th)
LE DÔME 47, avenue de la Bourdonnais (7th) Tel: 551.45.41
LA FONTAINE DE MARS 129, rue St.-Dominique (7th) Tel: 705.46.44
RESTAURANT DE l'HÔTEL DE LA BOURDONNAIS 113, avenue de la Bourdonnais (7th) Tel: 705.45.42
LA RIVE D'OTT 38, avenue de Suffren (7th) Tel: 734.80.59

RESTAURANTS OPEN IN AUGUST

During the month of August you can starve trying to find a place to eat. Most of the city either closes up or changes its hours of closing, and this can be quite a problem for a visitor. Following is a list of restaurants that are open at this time, which is intended to save you the shoe leather and aggravation of tracking them down yourself.

L'ABSINTHE 24, place du Marché-St.-Honoré (1st) Tel: 073.68.14 Expensive
L'ANCIEN CHARTIER 7, rue du faubourg Montmartre (9th) Tel: 770.86.29 Inexpensive
CHEZ LES ANGES 54, boulevard Latour-Maubourg (7th) Tel: 705.89.86 Inexpensive
ANGKOR 3, rue des Petites-Écuries (10th) Tel: 770.34.79 Moderate
RESTAURANT DES ARTS 73, rue de Seine (6th) Tel: 326.11.79 Moderate
L'ASSIETTE AU BEURRE 11, rue St.-Benoît (6th) Tel:222.88.47 Moderate
AUBERGE VERT GALANT 42, quai des Orfèvres (1st) Tel. 326.83.68 Moderate
LE BALTARD 11, rue St.-Denis (1st) Tel: 231.74.03 Inexpensive
LE BISTRO Hôtel Inter-Continental 3. rue de Castiglione (1st) Tel: 073.18.00 Moderate

BOUGNAT'S CLUB 15, rue Séguier (1st) Tel: 033.21.55 Moderate

BRASSERIE BOFINGER 5, rue de la Bastille (4th) Tel: 272.87.82 Moderate

BRASSERIE LIPP 151, boulevard St.-Germain (6th) Tel: 548.53.91 Moderate

BRASSERIE MUNICHOISE 5, rue Danielle-Casanova (1st) Tel: 073.66.25 Moderate

BROUILLET 5, rue Paul-Lelong (2nd) Tel: 236.25.08 Inexpensive

LE CASSEROLE 10, rue des Sts.-Pères (7th) Tel: 222.16.33 Moderate

LA CIGALE 11 bis, rue Chomel (7th) Tel: 548.87.87 Inexpensive

CLOSERIE DES LILAS 171, boulevard du Montparnasse (6th) Tel: 033.21.68 Moderate

COCONNAS 2 bis, place des Vosges (4th) Tel: 342.58.16 Moderate

BAR DU COMBAT ROGGERO 37, avenue Claude-Vellefaux (10th) Tel: 205.30.01 Inexpensive

LES COPAINS 44, rue de Verneuil (7th) Tel: 548.49.91 Inexpensive

LE COUPE-CHOU 9, rue Lanneau (5th) Tel: 633.68.69 Moderate

L'ÉCUELLE 28, rue de l'Arbre-Sec (1st) Tel: 231.97.82 Inexpensive

CHEZ EDGARD 4, rue Marbeuf (8th) Tel: 359.85.92 Moderate

ÉLYSÉES BRETAGNE 4, avenue F.-D.-Roosevelt (8th) Tel: 359.20.63 Moderate

ENCLOS DE NINON 21, boulevard Beaumarchais (4th) Tel: 272.22.51 Inexpensive

ESPADON, HOTEL RITZ 38, rue Cambon (1st) Tel: 073.28.30 Expensive

ETCHEGORRY 41, rue Croulebarbe (13th) Tel: 331.63.05 Moderate

FERME ST.-HUBERT 6, rue Cochin (5th) Tel: 326.21.03 Moderate

FOUQUET'S 99, avenue des Champs-Elysées (8th) Tel: 225.59.54 Expensive

GEORGE V 31, avenue George-V (8th) Tel: 225.35.30 Expensive

GUY 6, rue Mabillon (6th) Tel: 033.87.61 Expensive

L'HÔTEL 13, rue des Beaux-Arts (6th) Tel: 663.89.20 Expensive

JOUR ET NUIT 2, rue de Berri (8th) Tel: 359.50.65 Expensive

LAMAZÉRE 23, rue de Ponthieu (8th) Tel: 359.66.66 Expensive

LAURENT 41, avenue Gabriel (8th) Tel: 359.14.49 Expensive

LUCAS-CARTON 1, place de la Madeleine (8th) Tel: 265.22.80 Expensive

LA MAISON DU CAVIAR 24, rue Quentin-Bauchart (8th) Tel: 225.78.62 Inexpensive

LA MANADE   39, rue Galande (5th)   Tel: 033.94.85   Moderate

MAXIM'S   3, rue Royale (8th)   Tel: 265.27.94   Expensive

LE MERCURE GALANT   15, rue des Petits-Champs (13th)   Tel: 742.82.98   Expensive

MUNICHE   27, rue de Buci (6th)   Tel: 633.62.09   Inexpensive

PARIS 25   16, rue de la Grande Truanderie (1st)   Tel: 508.44.72   Expensive

CHEZ PAULETTE   28, rue des Bernardins (5th)   Tel: 033.63.84   Moderate

LA PÊCHERIE   24, rue Pierre-Lescot (1st)   Tel: 235.92.41   Moderate

LA PERGOLA   144, avenue des Champs-Elysées (8th)   Tel: 359.68.69   Moderate

PETIT BOSSO   20, rue Quincampoix (4th)   Tel: 877.82.48   Moderate

LE PETIT ST.-BENOÎT   4, rue St.-Benoît (6th)   Tel: 548.19.60   Inexpensive

LA PETITE DUCHESSE   15, rue Marbeuf (8th)   Tel: 359.78.69   Moderate

LES PRINCES   29, avenue George-V (8th)   Tel: 225.35.30   Expensive

PRUNIER-TRAKTIR   16, avenue Victor-Hugo (16th)   Tel: 727.01.45   Expensive

LE RÉCAMIER   4, rue Récamier (7th)   Tel: 548.86.58   Inexpensive

RÉGENCE-PLAZA   27, avenue Montaigne (9th)   Tel: 225.14.90   Expensive

RELAIS PARIS-EST   First floor, Gare de l'Est (railroad station)   4, boulevard de Strasbourg (10th)   Tel: 667.87.63   Expensive

LA RESSERRE   94, rue St.-Martin (4th)   Tel: 272.01.73   Moderate

SABOT DE BERNARD   2, rue du Sabot (6th)   Tel: 222.84.90   Expensive

SAMOURA   8, rue Xavier-Privas (5th)   Tel: 325.46.08   Moderate

LA TABLE D'HÔTE   28, rue de la Montagne-Ste.-Geneviève (5th)   Tel: 033.14.87   Inexpensive

TASSÉE DU CHAPITRE   36, rue St.-Louis-en-l'Ile (4th)   Tel: 633.56.09   Moderate

TOUR D'ARGENT   15, quai de la Tournelle (5th)   Tel: 633.23.31   Expensive

TOUR EIFFEL   First floor of the Tour Eiffel (7th)   Tel: 468.19.59   Expensive

TOURTOUR   20, rue Quincampoix (4th)   Tel: 887.86.48   Moderate

LE TRUMILOU   86, quai de l'Hôtel de Ville (4th)   Tel: 277.63.98   Inexpensive

LE VIEIL ÉCU   166, rue St.-Honoré (1st)   Tel: 231.03.24   Inexpensive

LE WESTPHALIE   8, avenue F.-D.-Roosevelt (8th)   Tel: 359.91.20   Inexpensive

9
Nighttime Entertainment

There is certainly no lack of cultural entertainment in Paris and there is something guaranteed for every interest. Some of it may depend upon your knowledge of French, but even at that there are different kinds of entertainment available to you—whether your French is good, moderate, or nonexistent. I have found that many women enjoy the Comédie Française just for the sake of being in this historical theater, even though they may understand not one word. Even if you feel you won't, there are many other choices for you. There are five national theaters as well as dozens of others all over the city catering to different tastes. Generally, you will find announcements plastered on every kiosk or available wall. But the best way to find out what is playing where is to ask the concierge at your hotel, or to buy *Paris Weekly Information* at a nearby newsstand for about $.60.

Of course it's always more convenient to ask the concierge to get the tickets for you, but you will generally get the more expensive seats this way, and it will also cost you a tip. If you go directly to the theater you will still get a good selection of seats at a less expensive price. If the performance is an important one, naturally you will want to do this a few days in advance and reserve your seat. Be sure to check the curtain time of the performance as it varies from theater to theater, ranging anywhere from 8 to 9:30 P.M.

The nice thing about this kind of entertainment is that a woman can be fully occupied every night she is in Paris without having to worry about an escort or what to do with an evening—which is often the case with a woman traveling alone. The entertainment in Paris is so varied and exciting, you never need to feel alone or out of things.

DANCE

Ballet, both classical and modern, has a big following in Paris. Leading dancers perform at the opera, and ballets are also put on at the Opéra Comique and the Théâtre des Champs-Elysées. Some companies even stage performances at unconventional places like the Palais des Sports, where the Maurice Béjart troupe danced Beethoven's *Ninth Symphony* some years ago. Regional folk dancing can be seen at the Palais de Chaillot.

MUSIC HALLS

An exciting and interesting show for you might be one at one of the famous music halls in Paris, similar to those at Radio City Music Hall in New York, only without the movie and with a much more lavish and extensive floor show.

FOLIES-BERGÈRE   32, rue Richer (9th)   Métro stop: Montmartre
This is probably the best known of all the music halls in Paris, and therefore first choice on the list of things to see. It features beautiful nude girls and exciting extravaganzas for them to traipse through. The costumes alone are worth seeing—what there is of them. The girls are beautiful, the sketches, music, and scenery all breathtaking. The box office is open daily from 11 A.M. to 6 P.M. to purchase tickets. The show begins at 8:30 P.M. nightly except Mondays. Cost of seats: balcony or orchestra 55F ($13.75); gallery 30F ($7.50); first and second balcony from 20F to 37F ($5 to $9.25); standing room 15F ($3.75).

LE CASINO DE PARIS   16, rue de Clichy (9th)   Tel: 874.26.22
Métro stop: Trinité
The well-known Zi-Zi Jeanmaire has been holding sway here for several years now, and judging by her popularity, I see no end in sight at the moment. She is a fantastic performer and truly gives you your money's worth. The productions are very exciting and beautiful to behold. This theater was the favorite stomping ground of Maurice Chevalier and Mistinguett, who trod its well-worn boards most of their professional lifetime. Open nightly except Monday. Price of seats: orchestra from 50F to 70F ($12.50 to $17.50); dress circle 35F to 55F ($8.75 to $13.75); balcony 25F to 45F ($6.25 to $11.25); standing room 15F ($3.75).

THE OLYMPIA   28, boulevard des Capucines (1st)   Métro stop: Opéra
The Olympia features more of a variety-type format, with singers, dancers, jugglers, comedians, etc., rather than the beautiful girly extravaganzas of the last two establishments mentioned.

Here is where you will find the greats, such as my favorite, Charles Aznavour. Open nightly except Monday. The price of seats: from 17F to 45F ($4.25 to $11.25).

THE BOBINO   20, rue de la Gaîté (14th)   Métro stop: Gaîté
Similar to the Olympia, and the showcase for most of France's stars. Open nightly except Mondays. Seats from 12F to 35F ($3 to $8.75); standing room 7F $(1.75).

OPERA

OPÉRA   Métro stop: Opéra
Opera buff or not, you should try to take in a performance at the beautiful Opéra. The Chagall ceiling is beautiful to behold as are the paintings, the sweeping staircases, and even the opera-goers themselves, some of whom still dress to the nines as in the grand old days when opera reigned supreme. Aside from posters on the various kiosks around town, there is always the program poster just outside the opera to help you choose the performance you want to see and make your reservations accordingly. Closed between July 25 and September 27. Price of seats 5F to 50F ($1.25 to $12.50).

OPÉRA-COMIQUE   5, rue Favart (2nd)   Métro stop: Richelieu-Drouot
Not quite as elegant as the Opéra, nor as heavy in the drama department, nor as expensive in the ticket department. Closed in July. Price of seats 3F ($.75) to 18F ($4.50). Matinees at 2:30 on Thursday and Sunday.

CONCERTS

Whether you prefer Bach or Beethoven, Stravinsky and the moderns, hot or cold jazz, flamenco, Tzigane, or other forms of folklore music, male choirs, string quartets, religious music, secular music—in short, any kind of music you care to name —you'll find it at one or another of numerous concert halls, churches, and other places where music is performed in Paris.

THÉÂTRE DES CHAMPS-ÉLYSÉES   15, avenue Montaigne (8th)
Métro stop: Alma-Marceau
International music and/or dance programs can be seen here. Price of tickets: 4F to 50F ($1 to $12.50).

O.R.T.F. AUDITORIUM   116, avenue Président-Kennedy   Métro stop: Passy.
This is the auditorium of the French Radio Station and features excellent concerts with guest conductors. Seats from 7F ($1.75) and up.

SALLE PLEYEL   252, rue du faubourg Saint-Honoré (8th)
Métro stop: Ternes

THE SALLE GAVEAU   45, rue La Boëtie (8th) Metro stop: Miromesnil
CONSERVATOIRE   2 bis, rue du Conservatoire (9th)   Métro stop: Montmartre

ORGAN RECITALS

THE PALAIS DE CHAILLOT   Place du Trocadéro (16th)   Métro stop: Trocadéro
ST.-SULPICE CHURCH   St.-Germain-des-Prés (6th)

The last two, and several others, can be checked with your concierge or newspaper listings for available programs. If you are interested in music you will be sure to search out whatever suits your fancy.

THEATER

COMÉDIE-FRANÇAISE   Place du Théâtre Français (1st)   Métro stop: Palais-Royal
As I said before, even if you don't speak or understand French, you may find it well worth the time and money to spend an evening at this lovely theater. This is a national theater dedicated to the French classics, and there you will see all the greats performed. Price of tickets from 4F to 24F ($1 to $6).

CINEMAS

All the major international films are shown on the Champs-Elysées. Generally they are shown with their original sound track in which case they will be marked "V.O." (*version originale*). This means that in English-speaking films, the sound track will remain in English, just the subtitles will be in French. However, if there is a French film you want to see you must check with the concierge of your hotel or look in the *Paris Weekly Information* or the newspapers for the times at which the film will be shown with English subtitles. There is usually a long line, so it is advisable to get there early. Tickets on the Champs-Elysées average about 12F ($3), with neighborhood theaters a bit less.

NIGHT CLUBS

I discuss the Lido, Moulin Rouge, etc., under "Night Tours" in Chapter 10, so we won't go into that now. I really think the best way to see these places is on a tour unless you happen to be with another person or two.

Here are some other clubs not listed later. Again, do go with at least one other person, whether male or female; it's really not proper to go alone.

L'ABBAYE   6 bis, rue de l'Abbaye (6th)   A-B
The big draw here is a duo of American performers, well-known in Paris, who sing both French and English songs and play the guitar. The place is a hangout for English and American tourists, as well as those who live in Paris permanently. The ambience is one of friendliness and togetherness; so it's a good place to meet people. Since the language is no problem, people at the next table will speak to you and it wouldn't be unusual to find a new friend. The place itself is quite interesting, small enough for intimacy, and yet large enough to include a variety of patrons. There are large church-type windows, a rather gaudy fireplace, and everyone sits on church-style benches. The entertainment runs from 10 P.M. to 1 A.M. Drinks are 18F ($4.50), with soft drinks going for 12F ($3). Closed all of February and on Sundays.

LA BUMBARDE   14, rue Xavier Privas (5th)   A
Another youngish spot where the clientele is mostly students from the Sorbonne. Here too is another place where younger women will most definitely meet a man. Good jazz music and rather inexpensive drinks make it a popular spot. Drinks start about 4F ($1).

LA CALVADOS   40, avenue Pierre-1er-de-Serbie (16th)   A-B-C
Open until 6 A.M., this spot gets a lot of the "in" crowd. You can take a choice of the snack bars or the dining rooms on either floor and be entertained by piano music or the guitar accompanied by the singing of "Los Latinos." Drinks are medium price, not too high, but certainly not budget.

CARROUSEL   29, rue Vavin (6th)   Montparnasse   A-B
This club is right next door to the Elle et Lui described below. However, here, instead of women romancing each other, you will find female impersonators, and they are supposed to be the most beautiful ones in the world. If you want to learn a few lessons about make-up and clothes, this is certainly the place to go because these impersonators outdo most of the women I know. Again, the audience is almost as much of a show as the stage show itself, as most of them are transvestites, too, decked out in the latest finery. Here again you would feel more comfortable with a date. Minimum 30F ($7.50).

CAVEAU DE LA HUCHETTE   5, rue de la Huchette (5th)   A-B
A hangout for bohemian types, which may be of interest to the younger visitor. If you fit into that category you'll have no difficulty meeting someone because usually there are a great number of single men around. The *cave* on the lower level, with a dance floor, features a Dixieland combo and is generally so

crowded you're lucky if you can get a place to stand, much less sit. The ground floor is much quieter and makes for more intimate conversation. Entry 8F ($2), 10F ($2.50) on Saturday, plus the price of your drinks. It's open from 9:30 P.M. to 1 A.M. except Saturdays, when they stay open until 2.

CAVEAU DES OUBLIETTES 1, rue St.-Julien-le-Pauvre (5th) A-B-C

An unusual evening is in store for you here if you don't spook easily. This club was originally a 12th-century prison and still retains the dungeons, narrow passages, and even human skulls scattered all over the place. During its prime, prisoners were often pushed out of the little portholes into the Seine to drown. These portholes are called *oubliettes*. Hence the name. The whole atmosphere is medieval, as are the costumes, songs, and the comedy with which you are entertained.

Be sure to take a look at the museum next door, where you will see all forms of medieval torture instruments, including a guillotine. This is certainly worth a stop on your sightseeing program and is an interesting way to spend an evening. Drinks start at 16F ($4).

LE CHAT QUI PÊCHE 4, rue de la Huchette (5th)   A-B

The "Fishing Cat" is a very popular young French jazz spot and draws a lot of American jazz buffs, especially since some American musicians living in Paris will often drop by to sit in on a few sets. The musicians perform in the *cave* on the lower level where the minimum is about 16F ($4). However, if you prefer, you can sit in any of the three rooms on the main floor without paying a minimum or a cover charge, and still listen to the music which is piped up to these rooms as well. First show from 9:30 to midnight, the second from 1 to 2 A.M., with records in between. Closed Wednesday.

CLUB DE L'ETOILE   Avenue Victor-Hugo and Place de l'Etoile (16th)   A-B

If you can find someone else to go with you, there is a good chance you can get into this private club, which gets a lot of the young with-it crowd and is another good meeting ground. A charming woman should be able to talk her way into the place easily enough, as it's done all the time. Aside from being a good place to meet people, there is a good orchestra to seal the relationship. Drinks from 16F ($4).

CRAZY HORSE SALOON   12, avenue George-V (8th)   A-B-C

In complete contrast to the more spectacular shows you will see at the Lido et al., this club features a strictly high-class striptease show. The girls generally work in the nude or at least wind up that way, and the skits are usually played against a plain backdrop. None of the costumes or sets here that you will find in other clubs. When I say striptease I don't mean the kind we have in America, but a more sensual, less gaudy performance. There are also various other acts such as comediennes, musicians, etc., to space out the nude skits. There are two shows nightly, one at 10 and one at 12:30. You are asked to be there at least an hour before the performance to get you seated. And you will see why. The place is so crowded, God help you if you want to cross your legs! Four strangers crowded around one tiny table just big enough to hold four glasses is the general pattern. You're guaranteed to have stiff joints before you leave (but maybe a new friend). Your first drink costs 35F ($8.75), and with the crush of people around you, it's a cinch your waiter won't be bothering you about another.

ELLE ET LUI   31, rue Vavin (6th)   Montparnasse   A-B-C
Here you will definitely want a male escort if you can dig one up because this is a hangout for transvestites, primarily female. It may seem like a strange place to recommend, but I find it very unusual and have spoken to many women who have also found it interesting. Perhaps because it's the kind of thing one doesn't generally see at home, and it gives you something to talk about when you go back. The stage show itself does not begin until about midnight. But the show truly begins the moment you step in the door. The stage show itself is really quite something. It's as sexy and romantic as anything one would expect in a heterosexual relationship of great passion. As I say—it's quite something! The minimum is 30F ($7.50).

LE LAPIN AGILE   4, rue des Saules (18th)   A-B-C
Located near the Place du Tertre, in the heart of Montmartre, this old landmark was once the stomping ground of Toulouse-Lautrec and Picasso as well as many other famous writers, painters, and their hangers-on. The place is very picturesque with wooden tables and benches which you share with the other guests, which makes for a very friendly camaraderie. Entertainments consist of poetry readings and musicians who sing every kind of French song. The fact that it is all done in French doesn't seem to prevent the visitor from having a good time and it is not unusual for the entire audience to join in with the vocalists after a while. Be sure to get there before 10:00 if you want a spot on one of the benches. Since this place is very popular it doesn't take long to fill up. Entry and one drink 18F ($4.50). Matinees Sunday at 3:30 P.M. Closed Monday.

LA MUSETTE   23, rue de Lappe (11th)   A-B-C
A bohemian atmosphere makes this place popular with all age groups and a good place to meet people. Entertainment is rather "iffy," meaning that sometimes they do, and sometimes they don't have musical entertainment.

TROIS NAILLETZ   56, rue Galande (5th)   A-B-C
You have to look hard for this one because it's a little *cave*-type place in an alley near St.-Julien-le-Pauvre. A constantly changing lineup of singers makes this, too, a very popular place and it is often filled to the brim, so try to get there early. Closed on Monday. Entry 4F ($1) and drinks about 9F ($2.25) and up.

"In" Clubs

FRANÇOIS PATRICE   76, rue de Rouen (6th)   B-C

Hosted by François, this elegant club features two bars and a very *soigné* restaurant, isolated from the music by glass walls. There is also a small *club du club* for movie showing and other improvised shows. A rather special touch is the whiskey and champagne fountains disguised by water plants. Expensive.

NEW JIMMY'S   124, boulevard du Montparnasse (14th)   A-B   Tel: 326.74.14

Hosted by Paris's gay Régine. A favorite of the younger crowd, the place vibrates with the echo of rock 'n' roll and pop music. Expensive.

REGINSKAIA   128, rue La Boëtie (8th)   B-C   Tel: 256.20.00

Also owned, managed, and hosted by world-renowned Régine, so popular with the "Beautiful People." She has, in fact, set aside Tuesday as a special "Great Evening" for this set. It's the perfect place for dining and dancing to old songs from 1945 to 1960, and for just plain "people watching." Expensive.

For Jazz Fans

THE PARIS CLUB   14, rue Chaptal (9th)   A-B-C

An information center for all the jazz spots in France if this is your cup of tea. Check with them if you're in the mood for jazz.

THE BLUE NOTE   27, rue d'Artois (8th)   A-B-C

One of the best jazz clubs in town, but a bit expensive. Minimum 20F ($5) for one drink. It gets a mixed bag of the international set and stays open till 4 A.M.

LA CAGE   3, rue Mouffetard (5th)   A-B

Also open till the wee hours, this discothèque, with its continuous pop music, is very popular.

CHERRY LANE   8, rue des Ciseaux (6th)   A-B-C

Unisex bar where lesbians and gay guys mix well together and have a ball.

CHEVAL D'OR   5, rue Descartes (5th)   A-B-C

Two shows, at 11 P.M. and 1 A.M., which will not strain your budget. The breaking-in place of a lot of fledgling French performers.

CIGALE   124, boulevard Rochechouart (18th)   B-C

A discothèque with jazz and pop music. The clientele here is a few notches higher than the blue-jeans type.

CLUB ÉCOSSAIS   4 bis, rue J. Mermoz (8th)   A-B

A discothèque with a very young crowd, a good meeting place. Cover charge of 10F ($2.50). Drinks after that from 5F ($1.25), but you can certainly sit on one for a long time and they won't bother you.

HARRY'S NEW YORK BAR   5, rue Daunou (2nd)   A-B-C

I think just about everybody has heard of this American bar which has always catered to the international set. It wouldn't be too difficult to meet someone from home here, but the main attraction is other English-speaking people of all sexes and the possibility of meeting someone interesting.

CAFÉ DE LA HUCHETTE   5, rue de la Huchette (5th)   A-B
Another popular unisex bar.

LA MÉTHODE   2, rue Descartes (5th)   A-B-C
A casual type of place where performers from all over Paris drop in to break in new acts or just to sit in when they feel like performing.

ORPHÉON   34, boulevard St.-Germain (6th)   A-B
A higher-class discothèque and another good meeting place, with a lot of single people milling about developing new friendships.

LE PETIT BAR   4, rue du Petit-Pont (5th)   A-B
A café-bar that's very campy, and open till the wee hours. A blue-jeans type of place for the young crowd.

PUB ST.-JACQUES   11, rue St.-Jacques (5th)
Open 24 hours a day. Another very popular place for meeting primarily the A and B groups.

10
Sightseeing

Whenever I visit a strange city, the first thing I do is take a daytime city tour, and then the first night tour I can manage. This way you really do get your bearings, and if you make notes as you go along you know exactly what you want to come back and visit more thoroughly.

As for the night tour, well, there is no better way to meet people in a strange city. The chances are that almost everyone else on it will be alone as well. Even if there are couples, it's not at all uncommon for married people visiting Paris to make friends with a lone woman and graciously invite her to join them another time. They might not be your first choice but at least it's a way of getting about without having to be alone.

COACH TOURS

The following tours can be purchased easily from Cityrama at either your hotel or at various places on the street. You will probably see big sandwich boards listing the tours, or you can just drop in to Cityrama at 2, rue du 29 Juillet, Paris (1st), Tel: 742.25.09. The tour is taken in a double-decker bus with multilingual guides. No inside visits but the most complete sightseeing itinerary in Paris.

Day Tours

TOUR K

Departs 9, 10, and 11 A.M. and 1, 2, 3, and 4 P.M.; in the winter (November 12 to March 31) only 10 and 11 A.M. and 2 and 3 P.M. departures. The tour begins on the Rue de Rivoli, then goes to the Place de la Concorde (stop), Tuileries, Louvre (stop), Carrousel, Pont-Neuf, Ile de la Cité, Notre Dame Cathedral (stop), Hôtel de Ville, Place des Vosges, Bastille (stop), Ile St.-Louis; Left Bank: St.-Julien-le-Pauvre, Sorbonne, Latin Quarter, Pantheon (stop), Luxembourg Palace and Gardens (stop), St.-Germain-des-Prés (stop), Chambre des Députés, Invalides (stop), Eiffel Tower (stop); Palais de Chaillot (stop), Arc de

Triomphe (stop), Champs-Elysées, Grand Palais, Palais de l'Elysée, Madeleine church, Montmartre, Sacré-Coeur (stop), Opéra, Rue de la Paix, Place Vendôme (stop), Rue de Rivoli. Tour lasts three hours, cost 25F ($6.25).

Night Tours

I have several suggestions here. One of the "Paris-by-Night" tours is a must, and so is the "Paris Illumination Tour." In the night-club category you have several choices. My suggestion would be either of the following:

TOUR F   Paris by Night, "Lido" (3 cabarets)
This trip includes three different night clubs in three different districts: the Bastille and its "Wild Apache" dances; Montmartre with its "Pigalle" show; and the world-famous Lido on the Champs-Elysées, with its wonderful revue. This year-round tour departs every evening at 9:15 P.M. and lasts for three hours. It is 130F ($32.50).

TOUR T   Grand Tour (dinner included, 3 cabarets)
Every evening, March 11 to December 30 (except Sundays in November and December), this tour takes in the grand dinner show at the Nouvelle Eve in Pigalle (drinks included), the revue of the Moulin Rouge in Montmartre, and the wonderful show at the Lido on the Champs-Elysées. On completion of these tours, the tour members will be taken to their hotel in the center of the city. Unescorted ladies are welcomed. Men are asked to wear a tie and coat. This tour departs at 8:15 P.M., lasts three hours, and costs 230F ($57.50). This one is a bit more costly but it does include your dinner and two of the best shows in Paris. It would cost you more than that to go on your own, and at least in a group you don't have to feel out of place.

At the Lido (and/or Moulin Rouge), reserved ring tables, plus a half-bottle of champagne, are extra. An additional 25F for Tour F ($6.25), and 50F for Tour T ($12.50).

TOUR Y   Paris Illuminations (*Son et lumière* show at the Invalides)
This tour includes: Rue de Rivoli, Place Vendôme, the Louvre, Pont-Neuf, Académie Française, St.-Germain-des-Prés, Latin Quarter, Notre Dame Cathedral, Hôtel de Ville, Conciergerie, Place de la Concorde, Champs-Elysées, Arc de Triomphe, Eiffel Tower, Invalides. At the Invalides you will attend the *son et lumière* show, in a full original version in English. It provides a fascinating and worthwhile evening in the form of an historical pageant projected through the magic of sound and light. In Paris, especially, knowing the history helps one to enjoy so much more the beautiful things to be seen here. After the show the motor coach ends the tour at the Place de l'Opéra. Departure: 9:15 P.M., return: 11:15 P.M.; cost: 26F ($6.50). Daily, May 1 to October 29.

There are several other tour possibilities too lengthy to list here, and you can find them in the Cityrama brochure at the desk of most hotels. The tours described above are my personal suggestions, and those I recommend most highly.

Tours by Boat

BATEAU MOUCHE TOUR   Points of embarkation: Pont-de-l'Alma on the Right Bank   Tel: 225.96.10   Métro stop: Alma-Marceau These are tours up the Seine in a glass-sided boat for easy viewing of the beautiful sights along the way, between the Pont Mirabeau and the Ile de la Cité and the Ile St.-Louis. Multilingual guides explain everything to you.

REGULAR SIGHTSEEING TOURS   Those from 10 A.M. to 12 noon are 5F ($1.25). In the afternoon between 2 and 7 the price is 10F ($2.50).

LUNCHEON CRUISES   These depart at 1 P.M. and cost 50F ($12.50).

TEA PARTY CRUISE   It departs at 4, returns at 6. Cost 20F ($5). Tea and pastry are served during the cruise. From May to the beginning of October.

DINNER CRUISE   This is my favorite, and I don't think any woman should miss it. Your Bateau Mouche becomes a candlelit restaurant with red tablecloths and music. The combination of this atmosphere and the view of Paris at night is unforgettable. During the summer, they have a huge spotlight used to pick up lovers along the banks of the Seine. The menu is excellent for the money. When you arrive there is a platter of hors d'oeuvres at the table, with chips, olives, almonds, cheese, anchovies, and various canapés to have with your apéritif. For dinner, there is a choice of lobster, frogs' legs, or filet of sole, then a choice of Châteaubriand, venison, or lamb. Dessert is a baked Alaska, a special gâteau, or ice cream. In addition to the apéritif, you are served a bottle of red wine, one of white, and champagne with dessert. As you can see, this is well worth the money, and an experience you won't forget, particularly if you saw the film *Charade* where Cary Grant and Audrey Hepburn took the same cruise. Begins at 8:30 P.M., and costs 100F ($25). Runs all week from Easter to November 11; only on Saturday and Sunday November 11 to December 31.

VEDETTES PARIS TOUR EIFFEL   Tel: 468.33.08

This company also runs sightseeing cruises up the Seine, and uses glass-enclosed boats and multilingual guides. The tour lasts one hour and costs 8F ($2). For an additional fee of 4F ($1), they have one that includes a visit to the "Caves de la Tour Eiffel," a very famous wine cellar.

"ILLUMINATION CRUISE"   Run by the same company, it takes you up the Seine at night when the city is all lit up and looking most beautiful. Departure is 9:30 P.M. and 10 P.M. from Pont d'Iéna, a bridge directly in front of the Eiffel Tower. Cost 10F ($2.50).

ON YOUR OWN

After your coach tour of Paris you will want to start wandering around on your own, so this section will deal with the most important sights to see.

ARC DE TRIOMPHE (8th)   Métro stop: Étoile

Standing like a giant at the very top of the Champs-Elysées, in the center of the Place de l'Etoile, is this great monument to the victory of Napoleon's armies. Beneath the arch is the Tomb of the Unknown Soldier of World War I, on which burns a perpetual flame of remembrance. Twelve avenues radiate from the Place de l'Etoile in the shape of a star, which is how the Place got its name (*étoile* means "star" in French). Originally, townhouses, intended for Napoleon's marshals, were built at the intersection of the twelve avenues; but, like the Arc de Triomphe, they were not completed until after Napoleon's reign. The Etoile, like its mate, the Place de la Concorde on the other end of the avenue, is always filled with tremendous traffic jams. It too must be seen once during the day and again at night when it is beautifully flood-lit.

THE CHAMPS-ELYSÉES (8th)

This has got to be one of the most famous and beautiful streets in the world, and one of the first sights people wish to see when they come to Paris. It is a wide, tree-lined boulevard crowned at the top with the magnificent Arc de Triomphe, and at the bottom with the Place de la Concorde. The portion of this grand boulevard nearest the Place de la Concorde reminds one of a beautiful suburban area, with its tree-shaded streets, and parks. Further on, at the Rond-Point, it becomes commercialized by the huge building which houses *Le Figaro,* one of France's leading newspapers. From then on, you will find a great array of cinemas, beautiful shops, and the sidewalk cafés that Paris has become so famous for. Here one can sit for hours and watch the greatest fashion show in the world, meet new people, or just watch Parisian life go by. In the reign of Louis XIV, the Champs-Elysées was the royal route to the palace of Versailles, and at that time it was surrounded only by woods and beautiful fields. Louis XIV assigned his gardener Le Nôtre the task of landscaping this area, and soon it was dotted with charming little lodges standing in well-ordered gardens. Around 1830 the Champs-Elysées was a place of ill repute, where respectable citizens scarcely dared to venture. Later, cafés were built there, and open-air concerts were given. The famous Guignol Lyonnais Marionette Theater made its Parisian début there. A number of aristocrats, including the Duc de Morny and the Duc de la Palva, had sumptuous private residences built that gave tone to the quarter. In 1900 at the time of the Universal Exhibition, the Petit Palais and the Grand Palais were erected.

PLACE DE LA CONCORDE (8th)   Métro stop: Concorde

Once you see the breathtaking beauty of this square, you will realize why it is considered one of the most beautiful in the world. It's the largest square in Paris, but its huge size in no way detracts from its well-balanced proportions. The pity is that it is almost impossible to find a time of day or night when you can really appreciate the Place de la Concorde in its naked beauty because of the huge traffic jams that somehow detract from its beauty. Try to see it once during the daytime, walking completely around the square (really an oval) taking in each historical detail, and then again at night when the flood-lit statues and fountains make it an absolutely stunning spectacle. The first object to catch one's eye is the tall, slender Obelisk from Luxor, Egypt, which has stood here since 1836. It is 33 centuries old. It was sent to King Louis-Philippe from the Sultan Mehemet Ali. Standing symmetrically around the square are eight statues symbolizing the cities of France. Very close to where the Statue of Brest now stands is where the guillotine stood during the French Revolution and where King Louis XVI, Marie-Antoinette, Robespierre, and more than two thousand others were beheaded during that particular reign of terror in French history. From the center of the square you can see the Church of the Madeleine to the north, and in a direct line at the very opposite end stands the Palais-Bourbon (seat of the Assemblée Nationale). To the east are the Tuileries Gardens and to the west, the Arc de Triomphe. Originally, this square was called the Place Louis-XV, then the Place de la Révolution. Subsequently it was named for Louis XVI, and finally called the Place de la Concorde under the reign of King Louis-Philippe. The two outstanding identical buildings on either side of the Rue Royale were built between 1757 and 1776. It's very interesting to see that the buildings still maintain their original, beautiful architecture, and have not become commercialized even though they are, respectively, the Hôtel Crillion and Ministère de la Marine (the French Admiralty).

FAUBOURG ST.-HONORÉ (8th)

The Faubourg St.-Honoré grew out of a very old thoroughfare called the Chaussée du Roule. An interesting feature of this street is that there is no number 13: the Empress Eugénie, who was very superstitious and used to have her hair done in the Faubourg St.-Honoré, ordered the number to be removed. Several of the buildings date from the 18th century. Some of them are now occupied by embassies, including the British Embassy. Number 51 is the Palais de l'Elysée. At the time of the revolution, it was a pleasure spot where country feasts were held. After his divorce, Napoleon made a gift of the building to Josephine. Since 1873, the Palais de l'Elysée has been the residence of the president of the Republic. Today the Faubourg St.-Honoré is a luxury shopping street: antique dealers, art galleries, and boutiques abound, along with fashion houses, perfumers, and distinguished stores like Hermès, Yves St.-Laurent, Cardin, and other great names in fashion.

LA MADELEINE (8th)   Métro stop: Madeleine

This majestic beauty, standing between the Opéra and the Place
de la Concorde, was never intended to be a church at all. Napoleon had originally planned it as a temple of glory to the
soldiers of the Grand Army, and it was not until 1842 that it
became a Catholic church under the Restoration. The huge
bronze doors are 15 feet wide and 33 feet high, and the inside is
crowned by a pediment of great beauty in which there is a relief
of the Last Judgment. Encircling the church is a majestic Cor-
inthian colonnade that gives it more the feeling of a great temple
than a place of Catholic worship.

PLACE VENDÔME (1st)   Métro stop: Opéra

This is a continuous circle of magnificent buildings, once the
elegant mansions of French nobility. The circle is broken only by
one street running through it, which is the Rue de Castiglione on
the south and the Rue de la Paix on the north. In what was once
a private mansion, you will now find the famous Ritz Hotel,
one of the most elegant hostelries in the world today. Here on
the circle you will find Chanel and other luxurious shops cheek
by jowl with the Ministry of Justice, all blending inconspicuously
and uncommercially into this magnificent monument to French
architecture. In the center of the circle stands the slender, tower-
ing Colonne Vendôme, erected as a memorial to Napoleon's
victory at Austerlitz in 1805. The core of the column is stone
but it is covered with bronze melted down from twelve hundred
cannons captured at Austerlitz by the emperor. The statue on top
is naturally of Napoleon himself. He has twice been toppled from
his lofty perch, by two completely different political movements.
However, each time he has been restored to his place of honor
to keep a watchful eye on the beautiful Place Vendôme.

THE OPÉRA AND THE GRANDS BOULEVARDS (9th)

Métro stop: Opéra

This quarter was a maze of small streets until Baron Haussmann
laid out Paris as it exists today. The Opéra was built by the
architect Garnier, and is ornamented with a number of groups of
sculptures, including *The Dance* by Carpeaux. The Grands Boulevards cut through the Place de l'Opéra, extending from the Place
de la Madeleine to the Place de la Bastille, and are successively
known as the Boulevard de la Madeleine, Boulevard des Capucines, Boulevard des Italiens, Boulevard Montmartre, Boulevard
Poissonnière, Boulevard Bonne-Nouvelle, Boulevard St.-Denis,
Boulevard St.-Martin, and—on the other side of the Place de la
République—Boulevard du Temple, Boulevard des Filles du
Calvaire, and Boulevard Beaumarchais. For many years, they
were the favorite Sunday strolling grounds of middle-class
French families. Today they still offer a wide variety of attractions and entertainment, including cafés, concerts, and theaters,
and are crowded with people strolling on Saturdays and Sundays.
Two of the thoroughfares, the Avenue de l'Opéra and the Rue
de la Paix, both famous, begin at the Place de l'Opéra. The latter
is known for its luxury stores, notably jewelers; as is the neigh-

boring Place Vendôme. On the other side of the Place Vendôme is the Rue de Castiglione, named after Napoleon III's mistress who lived there.

THE PALAIS-ROYAL AND PLACE DU THÉÂTRE FRANÇAIS (1st)
Métro stop: Palais-Royal

The Palais-Royal was originally known as the Palais Cardinal and belonged to Cardinal Richelieu. It became known as the Palais-Royal during Anne of Austria's reign as Queen of France. Today, the building surrounds a delightful, tranquil garden. It was here that the famous French writer Colette lived. Adjacent to the Palais-Royal is the Place du Théâtre Français, where the Comédie Française performs classic French plays by Molière, Beaumarchais, Racine, and others; the acting is first-rate.

THE MARAIS (4th)

This is one quarter that must really be walked through thoroughly in order to appreciate all of its ancient history and intrigue, as well as the beautiful architecture that still remains to this day. The Marais is not one particular monument, but a whole quarter that becomes a monument in itself. It owes its name ("the marsh") to the fact that this quarter was originally flooded by the Seine at high water and even as late as the 16th century was still entirely marshland. It is one of the oldest quarters of Paris and the only one which can boast such a great number of treasures of art and architecture in such a small area. Until recently, many of its fine old buildings had fallen into decay, but a great many of them have now been restored. The Marais Festival has also helped to bring new life to this quarter. Since the Middle Ages, it has alternately been the home of aristocrats and artists. Craftsmen flourished in the vicinity of the Temple in the 13th century, when the Marais was the domain of the Knights Templar. It became crown property under Charles V, whose palace was surrounded by noblemen's residences, like the Hôtel de Clisson and the Hôtel de Sens. This is a good place, perhaps, to mention that the word *hôtel* as applied to these buildings is used in its French sense of a private residence or town house; not in the modern English sense of the word. The Marais reached the height of its vogue in the 16th century with the construction of the Hôtel de Lamoignon, the Hôtel Carnavalet, the Hôtel Efficat (which no longer stands) and then the Place Royale in 1605. Financiers and noblemen vied with each other in building sumptuous residences in the Marais. It remained a center of social and intellectual life until the 18th century, when high society gravitated to the Faubourg St.-Germain and the Faubourg St.-Honoré. The Marais was then invaded by artists once again, and the mansions deteriorated into warehouses and workshops. Today many of these fine buildings have been renovated and can once again be admired in their full splendor. They are particularly impressive when flood-lit after dark during the summer months. Another outstanding attraction of the Marais is the Eglise St.-Gervais, where concerts and recitals are frequently given.

PLACE DE LA BASTILLE (In the Marais)   Métro stop: Bastille
Though the building is no longer in existence, this is the spot
where the Bastille Fortress stood. The Bastille was stormed by
the mob on July 14, 1789, during the French Revolution. That
date, July 14th, remains as a French holiday, Bastille Day. It
was in this prison that the Marquis de Sade and the "man in
the iron mask" were imprisoned.

HÔTEL DE SULLY   62, rue St.-Antoine (4th) (In the Marais)
Métro stop: Bastille or St.-Paul-le Marais
Built in 1624 by Androuet Du Cerceau for Madame Gallet, who
lost it at the gaming tables. It was acquired in 1634 by Sully,
who is said to have really lived it up there. Voltaire was arrested coming out of this house one evening after supper and
was imprisoned in the Bastille. Plays are performed in the gardens of the splendid residence during the Marais Festival.

HÔTEL DE SENS   Corner of Rue de l'Hôtel de Ville and Rue du
Figuier (In the Marais)   Métro stop: Pont-Marie
This magnificent medieval residence was built between 1474 and
1519 by Tristan de Salazar to house the Archbishops of Sens.
Henry IV made a gift of it to Queen Margot, who kept her
lovers there. Cardinal Duperron was the next occupant, and
later the building was used by the Burgundian Stage Coach Company. It now houses a public library.

HÔTEL D'AUMONT   7, rue du Jouy (4th) (In the Marais)   Métro
stop: St.-Paul-le Marais
An old house rebuilt by Le Vau for the uncle of the poet Scar-
ron. In 1656 Mansart transformed it for Marshal d'Aumont.
Recently restored, it is undoubtedly the finest private house in
all of Paris. Here, too, performances are put on during the
Marais Festival.

PLACE DES VOSGES (3rd)   Métro stop: Chemin-Vert
Originally named the Place Royale, it was built on the site of the
Hôtel Royal de Tournelles, razed by Catherine de Medici after
the joust in which her husband, Henry II, was killed. The ruins
were later frequented by beggars and vagabonds. In 1605, Henry
IV decided to build the Place Royale, completed in 1625. The
Pavillon du Roi (the King's Lodge) forms a porch facing the
Rue Birague, and the queen's apartments straddle the Rue de
Béarn. Alphonse Daudet. Théophile Gautier, and Victor Hugo
were among the famous people who once lived in the Place des
Vosges. The stone and brick houses around the square still retain
their old-time character and form a remarkable, classical ensem-
ble. This beautiful square is an oasis of calm amid the bustle of
the surrounding streets.

HÔTEL DE BEAUVAIS   68, rue François-Miron (4th)   Métro stop:
St.-Paul-le Marais
This mansion was originally built by Louis XIV for Catherine
Bellier, his very first mistress. In 1763 Mozart also resided here.

ÎLE DE LA CITÉ   (1st and 4th)   Métro stop: Cité
The larger of the two islands sitting in the middle of the Seine,
this one owes its importance partly to the fact that in the Middle
Ages it was the residence of the French court, and partly to
Notre Dame Cathedral (which I've reserved for a separate sec-

tion). The square in front of Notre Dame was once the site of almshouses, the most famous of them being the Hôtel Dieu. The Place Dauphine still remains just as it was built in the 17th century, and is one of the most delightful squares in Paris. From the Square du Vert-Galant, on the top of the Ile de la Cité can be seen the Louvre, on the Right Bank of the Seine. The Palais Mazarin, which stands on the Left Bank, is now the Institut de France. It is a marvel of 17th-century architecture, built on the site of an edifice of sinister reputation called the Tour de Nesle. Also on the Ile de la Cité is the Palais de Justice (the law courts), which surrounds Sainte-Chapelle, another model of Gothic architecture, and the Préfecture de Police.

NOTRE DAME CATHEDRAL   Métro stop: Cité

In 1160 Maurice de Sully, the Bishop of Paris, decided to build a cathedral on a spot formerly occupied by a building dedicated to Jupiter. Work on the cathedral began three years later and continued for some 250 years. No one knows who the architects were, for in those days they always remained anonymous; a building was the work not of one man, but of a corporation, whose members guarded the secrets of their craft and signed their work with esoteric symbols decipherable only by the initiated. Regardless of who was responsible for it, Notre Dame is one of the most beautiful examples of Gothic architecture. It served as a model for St. Patrick's Cathedral in New York. There is no question about it, the beautifully carved doors, the stained-glass windows (including the famous "Rose" window), and the statues are truly magnificent. Yet the interior of Notre Dame always strikes me as cold, somber, and somewhat fearsome, suggesting the fear of God rather than the love of God. I always have the feeling the Hunchback of Notre Dame is peering down at me from some lofty perch high up in a dark, dank corner of the Cathedral. The Cathedral is open daily from 7 A.M. to 6 P.M. Treasury open daily from 10 A.M. to 5:30 P.M. Fee 3F ($.75), Sunday and holidays 1.50F ($.38). Tower open daily 10 A.M. to 5 P.M., in winter to 4 P.M. Fee 3F ($.75), Sunday and holidays 1.50F. Royal buses 47 and 67.

CONCIERGERIE   Métro stop: Cité

Another of the famous sights on the Ile de la Cité is this eerie, bone-chilling medieval building now part of the Palais de Justice. During the French Revolution, after the fall of the Bastille, this royal palace became the infamous prison that all but obliterated any remnants of its origins. You can still visit the small cold, stone cells that imprisoned during their day Marie-Antoinette, the Baron du Barry, the Duke of Orléans, Robespierre, the radical leader Danton, and even an American, Thomas Paine, who was perhaps one of the very few ever to leave the Conciergerie without the usual ride to the Guillotine. Open daily except Tuesdays from 9:30 A.M. to 11:30 A.M., and from 1 to 5.30 P.M. Tours every 20 minutes, admission 3F ($.75), on Sunday 1.50F.

SAINTE-CHAPELLE   Métro stop: Cité

Still in the same area, we finally come to this haven of beauty, warmth, and charm, so different from its neighbors, the Conciergerie and the Palais de Justice. It was commissioned by St. Louis to be built in 1247 as a shrine for the copy of Christ's Crown of Thorns, the original being housed in Notre Dame. But even without its expected treasure, this church is truly a jewel among jewels. It reminds me of a giant jewel box full of emeralds, rubies, and the brightest of rare stones. For everywhere you look there are magnificent stained-glass windows, with the tiniest details so bright and clearly etched that it's impossible to believe that they have been here for so many centuries. When the sun shines through them the church becomes a kaleidoscope of brilliant color. There are 15 of these windows representing the subjects drawn from the Apocalypse. If one had the time, one could actually go over the entire Bible just from the scenes so brilliantly depicted here. Sainte-Chapelle consists of two chapels, one on top of the other. The upper chapel was for the nobility, and the lower chapel for their servants. Be sure not to miss the second floor. American tourists have been known to say "If you've seen one church, you've seen them all." Well, I have seen almost all of the famous churches of Europe, but none as impressive and beautiful as the Sainte-Chapelle. I recommend it most highly as one of *the* sights to see. Open daily except Tuesday from 10 to noon and from 1:30 to 6. Admission 2F ($.50), 1F on Sunday and on holidays.

ÎLE ST.-LOUIS   Métro stop: Cité or Pont-Marie

This little island, the smaller of the two sitting in the middle of the Seine, was formed by the merging of Ile Notre-Dame and the Ile aux Vaches. All its houses date from the 17th century. The main street is the Rue St.-Louis-en-l'Ile. At the corner of the Quai d'Anjou, in the former Hôtel Lambert, Voltaire was the guest of the Marquise du Châtelet, and Rousseau was the guest of Madame Dupin. At number 51, in the Hôtel Chenizot, lived the future Madame Tallien. At the tip of the island, Quai Bourbon, there are a number of splendid old houses. The Hôtel de Lauzun and the Quai d'Anjou were acquired by the city of Paris in 1928, and are still used to entertain distinguished visitors. There are now a number of restaurants and cabarets on the island, but it is still a very tranquil spot with a great deal of charm, and a stroll through its streets takes one back to another, more gracious age.

THE LATIN QUARTER (5th, 6th, 7th)

The Latin Quarter (Quartier Latin) is so called because until 1789 Latin was the language of the university. And ever since the university was founded here in the 12th century, this quarter has been the domain of students. In 1353 a canon of Paris named Robert de Sorbon founded a college for poor students; hence the name Sorbonne. The Latin Quarter as it exists today covers a considerable area and includes substantial parts of the 5th and 6th arrondissements. It is no longer so strongly associated with bohemianism and poverty as it was for centuries. The cafés, bookshops, and stores along the Boulevard St.-Michel are full of well-dressed, prosperous-looking young people. The Boulevard St.-Michel (affectionately known as the Boul' Mich') is the main thoroughfare and focal point of the Latin Quarter. Its pavements are crowded with a noisy and loquacious crowd; all nationalities and races rub shoulders and all languages can be heard. The Place St.-Michel was the focal point of some of the most important fighting of the French Resistance in 1944. And everywhere you can still see tributes to the great heroes of those battles in the inscriptions on various buildings marking the spot where certain heroes had fallen, and the date. The Latin Quarter is a wonderful place to go at night to savor the foods of many lands. On its narrow, winding streets, you will find every possible kind of restaurant: Vietnamese, Chinese, Arabian, Italian, African, Oriental—just name it and you'll find it. At night, these little streets are thronged with students and tourists and there is always a great deal of activity. The Rue de la Bucherie is the favorite meeting place for the long-hairs and guitar types of today. They meet not far from Le Mistral, a bookshop known to impecunious intellectual globetrotters the world over. Its owner, George Whitman, is a descendant of the American poet, and serves tea to his penniless companions. In the Rue St.-Julien is a little museum known as Les Trois Maillets, housing an impressive collection of instruments of torture. The Place Maubert (known as "Black Maube"), once the haunt of thugs, is now a charming and quite harmless little square. In contrast to the atmosphere described above is the Boulevard St.-Germain, lined with stylish modern boutiques and other interesting shops. This is where the "with-it" crowd comes to shop, and it is most interesting to see, no matter what your taste in clothes might be.

PANTHÉON (5th)   Tel: 033.34.51   Métro stop: Luxembourg
Built in the 18th century, this Romanesque building has been at various times in its history a temple, a church, and now a monument in which the heroes of France are entombed. Men such as Voltaire, Victor Hugo, Emile Zola, Rousseau, and Louis Braille, the man who invented the Braille system of reading for the blind, are buried here. Open daily, 10 A.M. to 5 P.M., except Tuesday, and all holidays except January 1, May 1, July 14, December 25. December 1 to January 31: 10 A.M. to 4 P.M. Visits every quarter of an hour. Fee on weekdays 2F ($.50), Sunday 1F ($.25).

ST.-GERMAIN-DES-PRÉS   Métro stop: St.-Germain-des-Prés
The Boulevard St.-Germain, mentioned above, is part of this very interesting quarter, but one should not venture to this part of town merely to look in the shops. It does have a history of its own. In the shadow of the magnificent Abbey of St.-Germain-des-Prés (whose tower dates from the 9th century, and which once contained the sepulcher of the first Merovingian kings), literary and philosophical ideas took shape in the years before and after World War II. These ideas fired the imagination of young intellectuals in search of the meaning and pur-

pose of existence. Triggered by Simone de Beauvoir and Jean-Paul Sartre, Existentialism came into being and the St.-Germain-des-Prés district was its spiritual home. Its temples were the Café de Flore and Les Deux Magots; its muses were Juliette Greco and Anabel, its shrines La Rose Rouge, Le Tabau, and Le Club St.-Germain. Jazz clubs and caves flourished, and at café terraces and other meeting places, faded blue jeans and flapping shirttails were the standard uniform for both sexes. This was the heyday of St.-Germain-des-Prés in the years following World War II. Today, terraces of Le Flore and Les Deux Magots are still crowded; so is the Brasserie Lipp. But in the recently opened St.-Germain Drugstore, the youth is not the same. There is a different awareness of the world, a feeling of wanting to change its ideals and goals. Today, a more serious attitude prevails in St.-Germain-des-Prés that does not detract in any way from the spirit and history of this quarter.

HÔTEL DES INVALIDES   Esplanade des Invalides (7th)   Métro stop: Invalides

Here again, the word *hôtel* is used in its original French sense, as a place of residence, not a hotel as we know it. Originally conceived as a home for retired soldiers, this sober and well-proportioned building faces a vast esplanade and is fronted by the old parade ground with ancient cannons pointing across it, along with two tanks used in the liberation of Paris in 1944. Louis XIV conceived the idea of the building and commissioned Libéral Bruant and Hardouin-Mansart to design it. Under the dome lies the tomb of Napoleon in a crypt, 20 feet deep. It is an impressive monolith of red porphyry, resting on a grand marble base. Next to it is the tomb containing the ashes of Napoleon's son, known as l'Aiglon, a romantic figure immortalized in a famous play by Edmond Rostand. Standing guard around the tomb are twelve figures representing Napoleon's victories and six stands of captured enemy flags. This is actually the second burial place for Napoleon, who was originally buried near his home on St. Helena when he died in 1840. It wasn't until 19 years later that his body was moved to his final resting place here at the Hôtel des Invalides. His brothers, Joseph and Jerome, and Marshal Foch, the Commander of the Allied Armies in World War I, are buried here as well. Le Musée de l'Armée is also here, along with various government offices. Open daily except certain holidays and Tuesdays, 9:30 A.M. to 6 P.M.

THE EIFFEL TOWER (7th)   Métro stop: Champ de Mars or Trocadéro

Built for the Universal Exhibition in 1889, the Eiffel Tower was meant to be a temporary exhibit and not the lasting landmark it has become. It was spared demolition during WWI when it was discovered that its tower made a very good wireless signal station. For your first view of the Eiffel Tower, try standing on the terrace of the Palais de Chaillot. This is far enough away to get a good sense of its enormity, and yet close enough to take in the details of the structure itself. Then go visit the

Tower directly. It rises 985 feet into the air and is most impressive. If you are lucky enough to be there on a clear day, ride up to the third floor for a view of Paris you will never forget. On a cloudy day, you will be lucky if you can see across the river to the Palais de Chaillot. The tower is open daily from 10:30 A.M. to 6:00 P.M. all year round, and from 10:00 A.M. to 6:00 P.M. in July and August. From November 11 to March 15, you can go only as far as the second floor. But during the rest of the year the third floor is open to tourists. Elevator to the first floor: 3F ($.75); to the second floor: 7F ($1.75); to the third floor: 10F ($2.50). Or, if you're made of sturdier stuff, you can climb the stairs, in which case the fee is 1F for the first floor, 2F for the second and the third. Though you may feel fit, this may not be such a good idea; perhaps you should save your energy for further sightseeing! There are several choices for dining right here, so you need not go hungry while exploring this maze of steel lacework. There is a deluxe dining room on the second floor, open daily for lunch; a snack bar on the first floor open daily 10:30 A.M. to 10 P.M.; and a bar open daily from 10 A.M. to 5:30 P.M.

TROCADÉRO (16th)   Métro stop: Trocadéro

This is not a monument in itself, but much like the Marais, a melange of many different points of interest, including the Palais de Chaillot, the Trocadéro gardens stretching out below it with their beautiful fountains, and the view of the Seine in front. As you stand on the vast terrace of the palace, you can look across the Seine to the Eiffel Tower and the Champ de Mars, another beautiful garden with lakes, arches, and grottoes.

The handsome modern-winged Palais de l'Elysée faces the Place Chaillot. On one side of the building are the entrances to the theater, concert hall, Musée de l'Homme (Anthropological Museum), the Musée de la Marine (Naval Museum), Musée des Monuments Français.

MONTMARTRE (18th)

Montmartre is actually a small self-contained village on the top and slopes of a rather high hill, overlooking the rest of Paris. Who has not heard of this famous place, the home of some of the greatest French painters and sculptors, perhaps one of the most famous artist colonies in the world? Utrillo used its streets as a backdrop for so many of his famous paintings that they may look familiar to you when you see them. The great masters have gone, but many would-be geniuses still live here, working and hoping to be discovered one day. You will see them on a weekend all over the Place du Tertre, painting and trying to sell their art to the tourists. The Place du Tertre is quite charming, especially in the summertime when the village band plays for the benefit of the tourists. The square is surrounded by sidewalk cafés and restaurants, and some even have dance floors. The restaurants here are a favorite place for after-theater and late-night dining. In Montmartre, too, is where you will find the Basilica of Sacré-Coeur. Though it is a church it looks far more like an oriental mosque, with its huge white dome. Inside, there is really nothing much worth seeing, but from the terrace outside one gets a marvelous view of Paris stretching out at the foot of the hill. Get off the Métro at Anvers, then walk to Rue de Steinkerque where you will find a funicular to the top of the mountain (unless you feel like walking, which *is* good for the legs). Even if you do take the funicular to the top, try to walk down, as the little winding streets along the way are very quaint and charming and will give you some pleasant moments to remember. By the way, do not get confused by the Boulevard Montmartre, which is not anywhere near the area of the village of Montmartre.

MUSEUMS

On good days when I am in Paris, I like to be out doing things, enjoying the shops, sights, etc. However, on a rainy day a museum is the perfect solution. This is where I spend my time comfortably absorbing the history and culture of this beautiful city. If museums are simply not your cup of tea, so be it; but there is one that everyone must see and that is the Louvre.

In the list that follows here, some museums are marked NM (National Museum) or VP (Ville de Paris, or city museum). These are closed on Tuesdays and on public holidays: January 1, Easter Monday, Whit Monday, May 1, Ascension Day, July 14, August 15, November 1, November 11, and November 25. When one of these holidays falls on a Tuesday, the museums are closed on Monday as well; however, when November 1 falls on a Tuesday, they are closed on Wednesday. On the other hand, if August 15 falls on a Sunday, they remain open. If there is a temporary exhibition in one of the Ville de Paris Museums, it remains open on public holidays. I know that's a lot to remember but since it usually happens that the day that you want to see a museum is the day it's closed, it is better to check first.

THE LOUVRE (1st)   Métro stop: Louvre and Palais-Royal
The Louvre is set on 40 acres (that's three times the area of the Vatican) and has been the home of French kings since the 13th century. From the Place du Louvre, you enter the Cour Carrée, the courtyard of the beautiful Renaissance building which forms the old Louvre. This was an ancient fortress which was transformed into a royal residence by Charles V in the 14th century. Later, François I undertook its reconstruc-

tion, which went on until 1660 under the architects Pierre Lescot, Lemercier, and Le Vau. Much of the sculpture was done by Jean Goujon and Paul Ronce. Passing under the Pavillon Sully you come to the new Louvre, built by Visconti and Lefuel. Its buildings are in the style of the 17th century and are flanked by the Place du Carrousel. The entrance to the museum is to the left through the Pavillon Denon. Much of what you see of the present Louvre was built by Napoleon I and his nephew Napoleon III. It was after the French Revolution that it was converted into a museum displaying the Royal art collection of that time. *Don't* try to see the Louvre in one visit. There are six very important sections (or *départements*) that you will enjoy seeing, and there are antiquities from the Egyptian, Oriental, Greek, and Roman empires, as well as furniture, paintings, sculpture, and other objects of art. One cannot fully appreciate it all in one visit or just drifting by. On the main floor there is a large department for the sale of books, reproductions, and postcards of works included in the Louvre collection. They make particularly nice gifts. Postcards can be mounted in small frames for grouping if you like. The English guidebook is 10F ($2.50); there is also an Audio Guide in English available for 3F ($.75) per person, or 5F ($1.25) per couple, covering each department. This is the recorded voice of an expert who tells you exactly what you are seeing at a particular moment. The Louvre is open from 9:45 A.M. to 5:15 P.M. Admission 3F ($.75); free on Sunday.

GALERIE DU JEU DE PAUME (1st)   Métro stop: Concorde
The Jeu de Paume is bordered by the Rue de Rivoli and the Place de la Concorde at the very opposite end of the Tuileries Gardens. After drifting through the huge and magnificent Louvre with its many wings and courtyards, it seems almost minuscule by comparison. There is a further difference in that it is devoted solely to the works of the great Impressionists: Cézanne, Monet, Pissarro, Van Gogh, Gauguin, Manet, Degas, Renoir, and Sisley. In the 1870s these painters were considered very avant garde. They preferred to break from the traditional way of painting to paint in terms of light and color, in the new way they saw them. Thus, their paintings burst with colors, lines, and curves that appear to have nothing to do with reality. Instead, they express what the painter saw as he painted the subject. The museum is open daily except Tuesday from 10 A.M. to 5 P.M. Admission 5F ($1.25), half-price on Sunday. Audio Guides are available at 3F per person ($.75) or 5F per couple ($1.25).

MUSÉE DE L'ORANGERIE (NM) (1st)   Métro stop: Concorde
Just a short walk from the Jeu de Paume, this museum is for special exhibitions which are changed continually. They do have on permanent display Claude Monet's *Nymphéas,* a series of panels which adorn the walls of the main floor rooms, and which are well worth seeing. Admission 2F ($.50), 1F Sunday ($.25).

The prices change sometimes according to the exhibit being shown.

MUSÉE DE L'ARMÉE   Hôtel des Invalides (7th)   Tel: 468.27.81
Métro stop: Invalides
As the largest collection of military exhibits in the world, this is not exactly a woman's cup of tea, as it were. However, it is an important historical museum in Paris, and one should see it since Napoleon's tomb is also to be found here. The museum itself is open daily, except Tuesday, and Sunday morning, from 10 to 12:15 and 1:30 to 6 P.M. (5 P.M. in winter). Napoleon's tomb may be visited daily from 9:30 A.M. to 5:30 P.M. (5 P.M. in winter); except on January 1, May 1, November 1, and December 25. Admission 3F ($.75).

MUSÉE D'ART MODERNE   13, avenue du Président-Wilson (8th)
Métro stop: Iéna
A large, imposing building with 15 galleries on the first floor and a marvelous collection of sculpture on the main floor. Particularly interesting is the Paris studio of Brancusi, added to the museum after the sculptor's death. In this room, you will see the burlap box which he used as a couch, all his tools, his violin and guitar nearby almost as if ready for him to pick up. Scattered about are various pieces that Brancusi has become famous for. There is a cafeteria-restaurant on the mezzanine for quick refreshments. Open from 10 to 5 daily except Tuesday. Admission 3F ($.75), free on Sunday.

MUSÉE MUNICIPAL D'ART MODERNE (VP)   11, avenue du Président-Wilson (8th)   Tel: 727.93.18   Métro stop: Iéna
Fifteen rooms containing paintings and sculptures of the 19th and 20th centuries. Open daily except Tuesday and public holidays from 10 to 5. Admission weekdays 5F ($1.25); Sundays free.

MUSÉE DES ARTS DÉCORATIFS   107, rue de Rivoli (1st)
Métro stop: Palais-Royal
Furniture and applied arts from the Middle Ages to the present day. Muslim Rooms (Oriental carpets), paintings and drawings by Dubuffet. Open daily except Tuesdays and public holidays from 10 A.M. to noon and 2 to 5 P.M.; Sundays from 11 to 6. Admission 3F ($.75).

MUSÉE CARNAVALET   23, rue de Sévigné (3rd)   Tel: 272.21.13
Métro stop: St.-Paul
The entire history of Paris through the centuries is shown here in exhibits, documents, models, and other reminders of Paris and the Parisians in former days. I find it an extremely interesting museum and I think most women will agree. Open daily except Tuesday and public holidays from 10 to noon and 2 to 6 P.M. (5 P.M. in winter). Admission weekdays 3F ($.75); Sunday free.

MUSÉE CERNUSHI (VP)   7, avenue Vélasquez (8th)   Métro stop: Villiers
Collections of Chinese *objets d'art,* notably old bronzes, specimens of T'ang paintings on silk, a remarkable seated Bodhisattva

as well as contemporary paintings. Open daily except Tuesdays and public holidays from 10 A.M. to noon and 1:30 to 5 P.M. Admission weekdays 1F ($.25); Sundays free.

MUSÉE CLUNY (NM) 25, rue Paul Painlevé (5th) Métro stop: Odéon

A 15th-century Gothic building that lies between Boulevard St.-Michel and Boulevard St.-Germain. Here you will find the craft of the Middle Ages, primarily tapestries, including the tapestry series of the *Lady and the Unicorn,* which is displayed on the second floor. There are two other tapestries of importance, one depicting the life of St. Stephen and the other life at court. As an incurable romantic, it has always intrigued me that the sister of Henry VIII (at 16, the widow of Louis XII) was confined here by the new king to make sure she did not produce an heir to the throne and thus usurp his place. Unfortunately, she chose to have an affair with the Duke of Suffolk, who was forced to marry her and take her back to England. I like to imagine her in these very same rooms, and find this particular story rather haunting. Open daily except Tuesday from 9:45 A.M. to 12:45 P.M. and from 2 to 5:15 P.M. Admission 3F ($.75); half-price on Sunday.

MUSÉE COGNACQ-JAY (VP) 25, boulevard des Capucines (2nd) Tel: 073.55.66 Métro stop: Opéra

Collections of 18th-century French and foreign paintings, sculptures, furniture, and valuable *objets d'art.* Open daily except Tuesday and on public holidays from 10 to noon and 2 to 6 P.M. (5 P.M. in winter). Admission weekdays 1F ($.25), Sunday free.

MUSÉE DE COSTUME (VP) 11, avenue du Président-Wilson (16th) Tel: 727.92.98 Métro stop: léna

This is actually an annex of the Musée Carnavalet, and contains an exhibition of French urban costumes of the 18th, 19th, and 20th centuries. It is interesting to see how much of our current fashions are taken from history, and most women should enjoy this. Exhibits are changed every three months. The museum is open daily except Tuesdays and public holidays, from the beginning of May to the end of September, and from the beginning of December to Easter. Hours: 10 to noon and 2 to 6 P.M. (5 P.M. in winter). Admission: summer weekdays 1F ($.25), Sundays free; winter 2F ($.50).

THE DELACROIX MUSEUM (NM) 6, place de Furstenberg (6th) Métro stop: St.-Germain-des-Prés

Not exactly a museum in the usual sense, but actually the original apartment studio used by Delacroix from 1857 to 1863. It is a lovely little place with a garden and all his things still there. His better works are hanging at the Louvre, but this is worth going to just to see how he lived. Open daily except Tuesday from 9:45 to 5:15. Admission 2F ($.50)

MUSÉE D'ENNERY (NM) 59, avenue Foch (16th) Métro stop: Porte-Dauphine

Chinese and Japanese *objets d'art*. Open Sunday 1 to 5 P.M. (4 P.M. in winter); closed in August. No fee.

LES GOBELINS 32, avenue des Gobelins (13th) Métro stop: Gobelins

Though this is not a museum, be sure to come here following your visit to the Cluny in order to see exactly how the famous tapestries that line the walls of that museum were actually made. Even today, the weavers at Les Gobelins still use the same looms and warp that were used when the castle was built in 1440! I stood in awe as I watched the workers carrying out what looks like a lifetime project. I am told that it sometimes takes three years to complete a single tapestry. In medieval times, apparently it did take a lifetime for a family of weavers to create a single tapestry for one of the palaces. There is also a tapestry museum here, but unfortunately it is primarily only from the 18th century. Tours on Wednesday, Thursday, and Friday, between 2 and 4, though I'm afraid, my dears, that they are in French. However, I don't feel that this is too much of a problem: a woman interested in this sort of thing can easily see for herself what goes on in the weaving process and put it all together without a full explanation in English.

MUSÉE GUIMET (NM) 6, place d'Iéna (16th) Métro stop: Iéna

Just off the Avenue du Président-Wilson, this museum also has an annex at 19, avenue d'Iéna. Its collection features Asiatic art and religious history from China, Japan, Indochina, Afghanistan, Tibet, and India. Illustrated maps indicate the areas in which these objects were found. Pottery and porcelain pieces of the various Chinese dynasties are to be found on the top floor. Open daily except Tuesday from 9:45 to noon and 1:30 to 5:15. Fee 1.50F ($.37), half-price on Sunday. This includes both museums.

MUSÉE INSTRUMENTAL DU CONSERVATOIRE NATIONAL SUPÉRIEUR DE MUSIQUE 14, rue de Madrid (8th) Tel: 522. 30.60 Métro stop: Europe

For music lovers, a fine collection of musical instruments that once belonged to famous performers. Open Thursdays and Saturdays from 2 to 4 P.M. Closed in August. Admission free.

MUSÉE JACQUEMARD-ANDRÉ 158, boulevard Haussmann (8th) Tel: 227.39.94 Métro stop: Miromesnil

French and Italian 18th-century furniture and works of art. Open daily except Tuesday and public holidays from 1 to 6 P.M. Admission 3F ($.75).

MARMOTTAN MUSEUM 2, rue Louis-Boilly (16th) Métro stop: La Muette

Pleasantly situated right next to the Bois de Boulogne. This museum has become very popular with devotees of Monet, ever since Monet's son, Michel, donated over 130 of his father's paintings to the museum in 1966. Prior to this donation the Marmottan was a small mansion owned by the Académie des Beaux-Arts and had no particular distinction. However, it now houses a collection that is considered one of the great art

treasures of the world. Open daily except Tuesday from 10 A.M.
to 6 P.M. Admission 5F ($1.25).

MUSÉE NISSIM DE CAMONDO   63, rue de Monceau (8th)   Tel:
522.12.32   Métro stop: Villiers
In an early 20th-century private residence a faithful reconstruction of an 18th-century home (Louis XV and Louis XVI furniture) which gives one a very good idea of how families lived in
those days. Open daily except Tuesday from 10 to 1 and 2 to 5.
Closed from July 14 to September 15. Admission 3F ($.75).

MUSÉE DE L'OPÉRA   Place Charles-Garnier (9th)   Tel: 073.
90.93   Métro stop: Opéra
Busts, models, costumes, and souvenirs of famous performers.
The library contains all the scores performed at the Paris opera
since its beginning, together with about 80,000 volumes relating
to music, dancing, and drama, plus the archives of the opera
since 1900. This museum has been enriched by the addition of
the former Musée de la Danse. Open daily except Sundays and
public holidays from 10 to 5. Admission 1F ($.25).

MUSÉE RODIN   77, rue de Varenne (7th)   Métro stop: Varenne
Located just across the boulevard from Napoleon's tomb at
Les Invalides. This is the very same mansion in which Auguste
Rodin lived and created many of his beautiful works of art,
and it is virtually jammed with them. Busts and statues pop
out from every wall and corner. Even in the large garden at
the rear of the house various pieces of sculpture are strategically
placed under the trees. Open every day except Tuesday from
10 A.M. to 12:15 P.M. and 2 to 5 P.M. Admission 5F ($1.25).

MUSÉE VICTOR HUGO   6, place des Vosges (4th)   Tel: 272.
16.65   Métro stop: Bastille
The actual residence of Victor Hugo from 1834 to 1848. Here
you will find a lovely collection of his personal souvenirs, books,
drawings, furniture, and other memorabilia. A charming place
to spend an hour or two. Open daily except Tuesdays and public
holidays from 10 to 12:30 and 2 to 6 P.M. (5 P.M. in winter).
Admission weekdays 1F ($.25); Sundays free.

PARKS AND GARDENS

BOIS DE BOULOGNE (16th)   Métro stops: Porte Dauphine,
Porte Maillot, or Porte d'Auteuil   Buses: 63, 43, 47, 52
On the west edge of Paris, *"le Bois"* stretches for 2,180 acres
and is a paradise of racecourses, playgrounds, woods, sporting
areas, gardens, 7 lakes and ponds, restaurants, and even *le camping*. A beautiful place to spend a few hours or a whole afternoon
in the spring, summer, or fall. If you should go there for the
races at Longchamps, you will see all the beautifully dressed
people and realize why Paris is known as the world capital of
chic. No fee.

BOIS DE VINCENNES (18th)   Métro stop: Porte Dorée   Buses:
86 and 125

On the southeast side of Paris, spreading over 2,322 acres, which provide a background for racecourses, the zoo, three lakes and a fine wooded area to relax in, Punch and Judy show, and restaurants. The park is adjacent to the 14th-century Château de Vincennes, which you can also visit. The park is always open and there is no fee.

JARDIN DES TUILERIES Rue de Rivoli (1st) Métro stops: Tuileries and Concorde Buses: 72, 73, 24, 84, 68, 69

This is one of the most important parks in all of Paris. On the Right Bank of the Seine, it begins at the Place de la Concorde and extends all the way to the Louvre. The garden was created in 1564 as part of the royal gardens belonging to the palace of the Louvre. Many kings of France have strolled here, held court, and generally enjoyed themselves. So, sit on a bench and imagine all that has gone before you in this beautiful setting. The gardens consist of 60 acres and contain the Musée du Jeu de Paume, the Orangerie, a carrousel, and a Punch and Judy show. Open daily in May from 6:30 A.M. to 10 P.M.; June, July, and August, 6:30 A.M. to 10:45 P.M. September 1 to October 10, 6:30 A.M. to 10 P.M. October 1 to May 1, 6:30 A.M. to 8 P.M.

PALAIS DE LUXEMBOURG Boulevard St.-Michel (6th) Métro stops: Odéon, Notre-Dame-des-Champs, or Luxembourg

The senate building of the French Republic, it has a really beautifully laid-out park with the Terrace of the Queens, a pool, Punch and Judy shows, tennis, croquet, and a café. This park is very popular with students. It is open 7:30 A.M. to nightfall.

PARC BUTTES-CHAUMONT Rue Manin (19th) Métro stops: Buttes-Chaumont or Botzaris Buses: 75 and 26

Sixty-seven acres in the north section of Paris for fun-lovers to enjoy. Originally created by Napoleon III who built a mountain, a suspension bridge, and even an artificial lake with its own little island in the middle. There is a waterfall, two Punch and Judy shows, Merry-go-Round ("Carrousel"), swings, two restaurants, and a café. It also has 60 acres of rose gardens and 100 varieties of water lilies. Open daily May 1 to October 1, 5 A.M. to 12 P.M. October 1 to May 1, 6 A.M. to 11 P.M. No fee.

PARC MONCEAU Boulevard de Courcelles (17th) Métro stop: Monceau Buses: 30, 84, and 94

Just north of the Arc de Triomphe, this is one of the most fashionable parks in Paris, something you will soon realize when you see all the well-dressed mothers and governesses playing with children dressed by Cardin. It boasts some artificial Roman ruins, a river, and even a Chinese bridge. Open daily in May from 8 A.M. to 10 P.M. June 1 to September 1, 8 A.M. to 11 P.M. September 1–15, 8 A.M. to 10 P.M. September 15 to October 15, 8 A.M. to 9 P.M. October 15 to November 1, 8 A.M. to 8 P.M. November 1 to February 15, 8 A.M. to 7 P.M. February 15 to March 15, 8 A.M. to 8 P.M. March 15 to April 30, 8 A.M. to 9 P.M.

PARC MONTSOURIS Boulevard Jourdan (14th) Métro stop: Cité Universitaire Buses: 21 and 62

This park, only 38 acres, is a copy of the Bey of Tunis' Palace. It has an observatory, a lake with waterfall, Punch and Judy shows, and a café-restaurant. Open daily in May, 7:30 A.M. to 10 P.M. June, July, and August, 7:30 A.M. to 11 P.M. September 1 to 15, 7:30 A.M. to 10 P.M. From September 15 to October 1, 7:30 A.M. to 9 P.M. October, 7:30 to nightfall. November 1 to March 1, 8 to nightfall. March and April, 7:30 to nightfall. No fee.

Botanical Gardens

For flower and plant lovers, there are several beautiful gardens where you can enjoy almost every variety of plant and blossom.

JARDINS ALBERT-KAHN 6, quai du 4-Septembre (2nd) Métro stops: Portes St.-Cloud and d'Auteuil Buses: 92 and 72
Seventy-one-and-a-half acres of French and Japanese gardens and a Vosgian forest. Open daily, March 15 to November 15, 2 to 6 P.M. Fee 8F ($2).

JARDINS FLEURISTES DE LA VILLE DE PARIS 3, avenue de la Porte d'Auteuil (16th) Buses: 52 and 62
Thirty-two acres on which 1,200,000 plants are grown each year. There is a rare arboretum, 94 hothouses with rare tropical plants, Camellias of 130 varieties, Orchids, a Caleceolaria and Croton collection, and a Palmarium. Open daily, March 1 to October 1, 10 to 6; October 1 to March 1, 10 to 5. Fee 5F ($1.25).

JARDIN MUSÉE RODIN 19, avenue Auguste-Rodin (7th) Métro stop: Varenne Bus: 69
Here you can see 2,000 rosebushes of 100 different varieties. Open at the same time as the museum.

JARDIN DES PLANTES Quai St.-Bernard (5th) Métro stop: Gare d'Orléans, Jussieu Buses: 67, 91, 62, 20, 61, 65, 89
Sixty acres of botanical gardens with menagerie, vivarium, labyrinth, and reptile house. Fee 5F ($1.25). Open daily, April 1 to October 1, 7 A.M. to sunset. October 1 to April 1, 8 A.M. to sunset.

ALPINE GARDEN In Jardin des Plantes
This is a winter garden and features rare flora from the Alps, Pyrenees, Himalayas, North Pole, etc. It's very interesting to see such unusual flowers from all over the world, and this may be your only opportunity to see them. Open daily April 15 to October 15, 9 to 12 and 2 to 5. Fee 1F ($.25).

JARDIN-ROSARIE BAGATELLE Bois de Boulogne Métro stop: Porte de Neuilly
The International Show from June 1–30 features 20,000 rosebushes of 2,650 varieties. Open daily in summer, 8:30 A.M. to 8 P.M.; in winter, 9 A.M. to 6 P.M. Fee 1F ($.25).

11
Excursions Out of Paris

Paris is Paris. There is no equal or comparison to this fabulous city. But it in no way represents France. When asked if they are French, Parisians often reply, "No, I am a Parisian." This pretty well indicates the aloof attitude and complacent personality of people living in Paris. And is probably one of the reasons that foreigners often say that the French are a rather stiff and unfriendly lot. However, this does not apply to regions outside of Paris, and if you want to get a feeling of the countryside you really should venture out into the surrounding areas. Time permitting, of course, you will want to go to other places mentioned in the book later on. But if time is limited, do at least take one or two excursions out of the city.

VERSAILLES

Versailles is one of my favorite places near Paris. I always manage to get out there on every one of my trips. There are tours that will take you there for a half or a full day, and I consider them very worthwhile. Here are a couple I would suggest:

TOUR Malmaison and Versailles
This tour takes you on a drive through northern suburbs to Malmaison, the beautifully furnished home of Napoleon and Josephine. Then via Marly to Versailles, where you will drive through the park, walk past the Trianons and the charming village of Marie-Antoinette. After a break for lunch (not included in tour price), visit the magnificent Palace of The Kings, with its beautifully decorated apartments, the chapel, the famous Hall of Mirrors, where the peace treaty was signed in 1919, and the unique gardens. This tour is really a bargain. I always make a point of coming to Versailles whenever I come to Paris because I consider it one of the most beautiful sights in the world—the palace, and especially the little hamlet of Marie-Antoinette. I

always lose myself here, and I think every woman would enjoy it as much as I do. The tour leaves at 10 A.M. and returns at 5:30 P.M. Price 40F ($10). November 11 to December 31; Sundays and Wednesdays only.

TOUR M   Versailles and Fontainebleau

In the morning, on this tour you drive by the Palais d'Art Moderne, Radio-TV Building, Statue of Liberty, Bois de Boulogne, and Saint-Cloud on the way to Versailles, the Royal City. In the afternoon, you drive through farming land (scenes of many famous pastoral paintings: *The Angelus, The Gleaners*) to Barbizon, picturesque village and important art center during the 19th century (studios of Millet, Rousseau, Corot). Then through the romantic forest of Fontainebleau to the Palace, built mainly during the French Renaissance (16th century) on the site of a medieval castle. It represents 700 years of French history. Its decoration, its unique collection of furniture, tapestries, and china, are wonderful examples of the evolution of art in France from François I through the Napoleons. Price of lunch is not included in cost of trip. Departure time 9:45 A.M., returning at 7 P.M. Price 50F ($12.50). Every day except Wednesday; in winter, only on Tuesday, Friday, and Sunday.

Or, if you prefer, you can also take a train from the Gare des Invalides. Its a half-hour ride at the cost of 3F ($.75) for first class or 2F ($.50) for second class. Once you arrive in Versailles you can take a taxi, or, if you feel like walking, it's a good brisk walk and not really too far. Anyone can tell you how to find the palace.

Once the hunting lodge of Louis XIII, the palace was built mainly by Louis XIV (the Sun King) after he developed a hate for Paris and Parisians since he and his mother were incarcerated there. He began the palace at the age of 23 and within three years there were 1,000 nobles in residence. This was also the official residence of Louis XV, the well beloved, and Louis XVI, who, with Marie-Antoinette, was arrested there during the revolution of 1789. At that time all the magnificent furniture of the palace was stolen or destroyed. Most of the furnishings there today are replicas of the period.

The back of the palace opens onto a breathtaking landscape of French gardens, fountains, and lakes, studded with lovely marble statues and a beautiful array of lovingly manicured flower and shrub hedges.

Only part of the palace is open for viewing purposes and this is divided into two sections. The first includes the apartments of Madame de Pompadour, the salons, and the Queen's private suites. The second portion includes the Hall of Mirrors, where the famous Treaty of Versailles was signed, the Grand Apartments, and the museum. To fully appreciate everything in this beautiful palace, take a guided tour in English and if possible spend the whole day there so that you can see every one of the public rooms as well as the park, the Petit Trianon, the Grand Trianon, and Marie-Antoinette's private little hamlet. You can also take a personally conducted tour for 45F ($11.25) which is well worth the money. These groups are limited to ten people or less; you can share the price of a guide among you. If you prefer, you can see the Hall of Mirrors, the Grand Apartment, and the Royal Chapel between 10 A.M. and 5 P.M. for 3F ($.75) without a guide; on Sundays 1.50F ($.38). After seeing the Grand Palace itself, go out the back entrance through the gardens, turn right, and visit the Grand Trianon. Built by King Louis XV and his mistress, the famed Madame de Pompadour. They used it as a retreat when they wished to escape the rigors of grand palace living. It is a good deal smaller of course, but no less elegant than the huge palace itself. The furnishings, though only replicas, are beautiful to see. Open daily except Tuesday from 2 to 5 P.M. Fee 3F ($.75); 1.50F ($0.38) on Sundays. From the Grand Trianon it is but a short walk to the Petit Trianon, built in 1768. Much smaller than the Grand Trianon and a bit shabbier, I'm afraid. However, this was a favorite of Marie-Antoinette, who also enjoyed getting away from the grand palace life. Here, too, Louis XV and Madame du Barry escaped from pressing matters in a more intimate setting. Open daily from 2 to 5 P.M. except Sundays. Fee 2F ($.50).

Between these two small palaces lies the Museum of Coaches housing a collection of 18th- and 19th-century coaches, including the one used by Napoleon I when he married Marie-Louise. Same hours as the Petit and Grand Trianon. Fee 2F ($.50); 1F ($.25) on Sundays.

Turning left when you leave the Petit Trianon, continue up the walk to the little hamlet once used by Marie-Antoinette when she felt like playing the little country girl. It's truly a fairy-tale setting with wee little houses, a millpond, a watchtower, etc., all set around a lovely little pond. For some reason or other many visitors coming to see Versailles are not even aware of this charming little hamlet and therefore miss a very unique and pleasant experience.

Dining in Versailles

If you're going to make a day of it, you will naturally want to have a meal sometime or other. There are several restaurants all over town of all descriptions and price ranges, but here are two suggestions. For a good budget lunch try the *Du Dragon,* 30 bis, rue des Réservoirs. There is an excellent *à la carte* menu as well as a fixed-price menu for 12F.($3). I was particularly fond of the frogs' legs, which were large and meaty, and the Provençale sauce as garlicky as I like it.

For a medium-price luncheon try the *Île-de-France,* 45, rue Carnot. The 35F ($8.75) fixed-price luncheon was a four-course affair and would please the keenest of gourmets. Closed in August.

No matter where you eat in Versailles, most restaurants are pretty well full at lunchtime, so it's wise to get there just prior to the rush at around 11:45 or after 1:00. Should you prefer a light snack there are lots of brasseries around for *croques monsieur* and other sandwiches.

FONTAINEBLEAU AND BARBIZON

Not as grand or as huge as Versailles, Fontainebleau Palace is still magnificent by any standards and perhaps a bit more personal than Versailles. Fontainebleau is the work of many but began primarily with Louis VII, though the hand of François I is far more prominent. Later Henri II and Diane de Poitiers, his mistress at the time, further embellished the palace. Louis XIV and finally Napoleon added the finishing touches, and the total result is what you see today. The furnishings you see were Napoleon's selection and it was here at Fontainebleau that he took his last farewell from his old guard before departing for Elba.

Surrounding Fontainebleau is a 40,000-acre forest the likes of which is seldom seen today. I have friends in Paris who come out here almost every Sunday just to hike the paths that are clearly laid out for this purpose.

I have particularly fond memories of this area inasmuch as a dear friend of mine, Alexander Mnouchkine, the well-known French film producer, was shooting *Stavisky,* with Jean-Paul Belmondo and Charles Boyer, while I was in Paris gathering material for this book. Therefore I was fortunate enough to spend a day in this beautiful forest where several scenes were filmed.

Bordering on the forest is the romantic and quaint little village of Barbizon. This was a very important art center in the 19th century and it was here that Millet, Rousseau, Corot, and Daumier lived and painted some of their best-known masterpieces. The village itself is very picturesque and if you have the time, it's well worth taking an hour or so just wandering in and out of the little streets and shops.

Fontainebleau and Barbizon are just over 40 miles from Paris. You can either take a fixed tour offered by Cityrama (Tour: Fontainebleau and Barbizon) for 35F ($8.75), or take a train from the Gare de Lyon. The train will stop in the suburb of Agon, which is approximately 2 miles from the château itself. Taxis are readily available; or you can take the bus, which runs every 10 or 15 minutes on weekdays and every 30 minutes on Sundays.

The Fontainebleau is open daily except Wednesday from 10 to noon and from 1 to 5 P.M. Entry fee 3F ($.75); 1.50F ($.38) on Sunday. There are guided tours and an audio guide also available for rental at 3F ($.75).

Dining in Fontainebleau

For the sake of convenience as well as an excellent meal, there are two good restaurants just opposite the château itself. One is the *Hôtel de L'Aigle Noir,* 27, place Napoléon Bonaparte. The building was once the home of the Cardinal de Retz, but became a hotel in 1720 and has been serving excellent food ever since. There are several fixed-price meals starting at 20F ($5). All offer a good choice of dishes and good value. The other is the *Napoléon* at 9, rue Grande. This too is a hotel, but in the dining room you have an excellent choice of several fixed-price meals from 22.50F ($5.63) to 60F ($15).

Dining in Barbizon

Auberge la Dague is located about one block before the forest on the main street—you can't miss it. This hotel is just beautiful and offers the perfect ambience as well as gourmet meals. I personally have not eaten here or checked the menu, but reports from those who have give it a high starred rating. The terrace out front is a perfect place to sit for your afternoon tea or coffee while recuperating from a hike in the forest or before starting back to Paris.

CHARTRES

A medieval city, known primarily for one of the world's most beautiful Gothic cathedrals, a masterpiece of medieval religious art. Twelfth- and 13th-century stained-glass windows flood the stony interior with a beautiful and majestic light. The numerous Renaissance statues have been wonderfully preserved and help considerably to soften the Gothic architecture.

After visiting the cathedral, take the time to wander through the picturesque narrow streets and to poke into the quaint little inns and shops scattered throughout the town. The old houses and the ancient town walls have both helped to preserve the medieval atmosphere of Chartres.

Chartres can be reached by a 2-hour train ride from the Gare Montparnasse. But I strongly recommend one of the guided bus tours instead, as you will get much more information and it will make the trip much more worth while.

Tours to Chartres

The following companies offer tours:

RAPID PULLMAN   Place des Pyramides (1st)   Tel: 266.10.11 or 260.31.01
TOUR C H: Departs at 1 P.M. every Tuesday, Thursday, and Saturday and returns about 7 P.M. all year round. Cost 45F ($11.25). The return journey is made by the pretty château of Maintenon and Rambouillet, summer residence of the French president.

CITYRAMA   2, rue du 29 juillet (1st)   Tel: 742.25.09
TOUR Q: Departs at 1 P.M. every Tuesday, Thursday, and Saturday during the summer period (in winter, Thursday only), and returning at 7 P.M. Cost 35F ($8.75).

PARIS VISION
Departure points from Rue de Rivoli alongside the Tuileries Gardens and near the Opéra. The coach departs at 1 P.M. Tuesdays, Thursdays, and Saturdays, from April 1 to March 31. Cost 45F ($11.25).

For any one of the above tours your concierge will be happy

to book you a ticket. Sandwich-board stands along the streets sell the tours and tell you where the departure point is.

COMPIÈGNE

A very quaint and picturesque town about 40 miles north of Paris, this little village has several claims to fame, one of which is the fact that Joan of Arc was imprisoned here before she was burned at the stake. Another is the palace built by Louis XV, which contains an excellent collection of First Empire furniture, and is well worth seeing.

This royal palace, built during the 18th century, has been the summer residence of several sovereigns, particularly of Napoleon III. The palace itself is supposed to be one of the three great palaces built by the French kings, ranking only below Versailles and Fontainebleau. At the palace too is the history of Don Quixote as well as a vehicle museum of carriages, bicycles, autos, etc. Not to be overlooked is the 16th century Hôtel de Ville, home of Louis XII. There is only one coach tour that can take you to Compiègne:

RAPID PULLMAN
Tour departure 8:15 A.M. Wednesday, Saturday, and Sunday from April to October 28. Price 60F ($15). This tour also goes to Pierrefonds, where you will see the restored medieval fortress, one of the castles of the Sleeping Beauty.

CHANTILLY

On the way to Compiègne one passes through Chantilly, a beautiful little town about 30 miles north of Paris, known for one of the finest racecourses in France as well as its forest, its fine Renaissance château, and its Chantilly cream. And what woman has not heard of Chantilly lace? Straddling two islands in the middle of a small lake are two beautiful buildings: a 19th-century grand château and a 16th-century petit château. The former is a beautiful sight with its sparkling blue slate roofs, trimmed with ginger-bready spires and turrets, and surrounded by shimmering waters of the lake and the plush greenery of the lawns and forest bordering it. The château houses the Musée Condé, and its collection of paintings and tapestries as well as the illuminated manuscript, *Les Très Riches Heures du Duc de Berry,* and a priceless collection of miniatures, books, and furniture. The 16th-century château was built on the site of a medieval castle, enlarged and remodeled to its present Renaissance style during the last century; it is one of the best examples of a royal residence.

Take the time to visit the racing stables before you leave. They are so richly decorated you'd swear they were the residence of a princely personage, rather than mere horses. During the racing season, June and September, the place is jammed with racing enthusiasts and the horsey set—a good time and place to meet someone interesting.

To reach Chantilly you can take an hour's train ride from the Gare du Nord or a bus from a tour.

Tours to Chantilly

RAPID PULLMAN   TOUR C Y
Departs 2 P.M. every Monday, Wednesday, and Saturday, from April 1 to October 31, and returns about 6:30 P.M. Price 45F ($11.75.) The tour also takes you through St.-Denis, with its important basilica that is the burial place of the kings of France, and Senlis, a quaint little town preserving its medieval aspect, with a Cathedral that represents an important step in the evolution of Gothic architecture. Here, too, are the ruins of a royal palace that housed the French kings from Charlemagne to Henry IX.

CITYRAMA TOUR C H
Departs at 1 P.M. every Wednesday and Saturday, March 25 to November 2, returns at 7 P.M. Price 35F ($8.75).

PARIS VISION
Departs 8:15 A.M., Wednesday, Saturday, and Sunday from April 4 to October 31. 60F ($15). This tour takes you to the Château of Compiègne, stopping for lunch at Pierrefonds, and then to Chantilly.

ROUEN

It was here in the marketplace in 1431 that Joan of Arc was burned at the stake. The marketplace is still almost as it was then, and one can just about visualize the horrible episode taking place. Rouen is almost a history book in itself, as here you will find buildings from the 4th century right up to the modern office buildings one sees scattered all over. Frankly, I am not at all impressed with the new ones. I feel they spoil the historical look of this beautiful old town. But many of the original buildings were unfortunately lost forever during the invasion of Normandy during the Second World War. Rouen can be reached by a train ride of just over an hour from the Gare St.-Lazare.

Tour to Rouen

PARIS VISION

Departs at 8:15 A.M. on Thursdays from March 29 to November 1. The tour takes a full day and costs 65F ($16.25), lunch not included. Departure is from the Rue de Rivoli. The tour goes through "Les Andelys" and stops at the ruins of the Château Gaillard, erected by Richard the Lion-Hearted on a rocky prominence overlooking one of the many branches of the Seine. In Rouen it also includes a visit on foot to the old town, a visit to the Gros Horloge (Great Clock), the Palace of Justice, the Gothic Rouen cathedral, and the churches of St.-Maclou and St.-Ouen.

12
Beauty Comes First

Sometime during our visit to this elegant city of "chic," take the time to treat yourself to "the works" à la Parisienne. The French beautician has a certain unique touch and style that must be experienced to be appreciated.

BEAUTY SALONS

In Paris you do not have to worry about who can safely color or bleach your hair, as just about any shop can be trusted to take care of your needs. In fact, the French are the originators of almost every technique used in the beauty business today.

Having decided to indulge yourself, why not go whole hog and allow yourself, at least once, the luxury of one of the posh "name" salons? Most of them provide a full range of beauty care: hair, manicure, pedicure, facials, etc. Prices vary, depending on your needs, but tend to be lower than in the United States, or at least close enough to be comparable. The prices listed here are as of this writing, and since the dollar is still bouncing around I can't vouch for what they will be when you get there. Hopefully, not too far off. Following is a list of the best beauty salons in Paris, where you will no doubt rub elbows with some famous faces.

Prices

Prices vary a bit from shop to shop. For the salons listed below, here are some prices and price ranges:

Shampoo and set *(shampooing et mise en plis)*	30F to 50F	$ 7.50 to $12.50
Cut *(coupe)*	20F to 40F	$ 5 to $10
Color *(teinture)*	50F to 100F	$12.50 to $25
Bleach *(décolorante)*	100F to 200F	$25 to $50
Touch-up *(teinture retouche)*	100F	$25
Manicure	20F	$ 5
Pedicure	30F to 40F	$ 7.50 to $10

PATRICK ALES 37, avenue F.-D.-Roosevelt (8th) (1st floor) Tel: 359.33.96 Métro stop: F.-D.-Roosevelt
A favorite of Brigitte Bardot and the Parisian *grandes dames.* Quiet, high-style atmosphere. Specializes in repairing damaged, discolored hair with special herb treatments. Hours: 9 A.M. to 6 P.M.

ALEXANDRE 120, rue du faubourg St.-Honoré (8th) Tel: 359. 40.09 Métro stop: Louvre
World renowned for super-special hairdos. Hours: 9:30 A.M. to 6:30 P.M. Closed Monday.

ANTOINE 5, rue Cambon (1st) Tel: 073.55.37 Métro stop: Concorde
Known as one of the best for years. A complete line of hair treatment. Hours: 9 A.M. to 6:30 P.M.

ELIZABETH ARDEN 7, place Vendôme (1st) Tel: OPE.42.42 Métro stop: Opéra
The Paris branch of this salon is well known the world over, and the Place Vendôme setting is unique. Hours: 9 A.M. to 6:30 P.M. Closed Saturday.

CARITA 11, rue du faubourg St.-Honoré (8th) Tel: 265.79.00 Métro stop: Concorde
Hilton Hotel, 18, avenue de Suffren (15th) Tel: 273.92.00 Métro stop: Louvre
Famous for wigs as well as hairstyling, men's hair care, and facial salon. Children's hair, too. Hours: 9:30 A.M. to 7 P.M.

THÉRÈSE CHARDIN 6, rue Lincoln (8th) Tel: 225.89.90 Métro stop: George-V
Excellent haircutting. Quiet, relaxed atmosphere. Hours: 9:30 A.M. to 6:30 P.M. Closed Monday.

CHARLES OF THE RITZ 51, avenue Montaigne (8th) Tel: 359. 55.39 Métro stop: F.-D.-Roosevelt
Friendly, quiet atmosphere. Interesting gift boutique. Hours: 9:30 A.M. to 6:30 P.M.

JEAN-LOUIS DAVID 47, rue Pierre-Charron (16th) Tel: 359. 75.16 Métro stop: Alma Marceau
As marvelously organized as a drugstore, includes a beauty-boutique, gadgets, travel and ticket agency, comb-out service, and wig rentals. Hours: 10 A.M. to 7 P.M.

JACQUES DESSANGE 37, avenue F.-D.-Roosevelt (8th) Tel: ELY.31.31 Métro stop: F.-D.-Roosevelt
Rental of wigs for special occasions is their specialty. Hours: 9 A.M. to 6 P.M.

DESFOSSE 19, avenue Matignon (8th) Tel: 359.95.13 Métro stop: F.-D.-Roosevelt
Well known for its services to both men and women, will book theater, air, train tickets, etc., while you're under the dryer. Hours: 9 A.M. to 7 P.M.

DIANE BOUTIQUES 37, rue de Bassano (8th) Tel: ELY.40.81 Métro stop: George-V
1, rue de l'Odéon (6th) Tel: DAN.09.64 Métro stop: Odéon
4, rue de Bourgogne (7th) Tel: INV.30.39 Métro stop: Varenne
17, rue de Châteaudun (9th) Tel: TRU.17.61 Métro stop: N.-D.-Lorette
A favorite of the younger set. They clean and set wigs very inexpensively. Hours: 9:30 A.M. to 7 P.M.

GALERIES LAFAYETTE SALON 40, boulevard Haussmann (9th) Tel: 073.01.54 Métro stop: Chaussée d'Antin
One of France's largest and most modern salons, in the famous department store. Hours: 9:15 A.M. to 6:15 P.M. Closed Monday.

GEORGEL 50 bis, rue Pierre-Charron (8th) Tel. 359.54.54 Métro stop: Alma-Marceau
Men's department in the basement.

GIN 47, rue Bonaparte (6th) Tel: 633.59.57 Métro stop: St.-Sulpice
Curly wigs and 1920s styles are a specialty in this small boutique-like shop. A favorite with artists, cover girls, and starlets. Hours: 9:30 A.M. to 6:30 P.M., Tuesday through Saturday; 2:30 P.M. to 6:30 P.M. Monday.

RENÉ GOUJEAN 6, rue Royale (8th) Tel: 073.60.58 Métro stop: Concorde
Favorite of cover girls. Great manicurist. Hours: 9:30 A.M. to 6:30 P.M.

GUILLAUME 5, avenue Matignon (8th) Tel: ELY.28.66 Métro stop: F.-D.-Roosevelt
Prices according to services rendered. Very social clientele. Hours: 9 A.M. to 6 P.M. Closed Monday.

JACY DE PARIS 6, avenue F.-D.-Roosevelt (8th) Tel: 359.32.97 Métro stop: F.-D.-Roosevelt
Micheline Jacy is usually there and speaks English as do two of her excellent hairdressers. Roland is marvelous. One of the few who start new trends in hair styling. Hours: 9 A.M. to 7 P.M.

JOFFO 8, boulevard de la Madeleine (9th) Tel: OPE.30.84 Métro stop: Madeleine
Also does men's hair. Hours: 9:30 A.M. to 6:30 P.M.; to 10 P.M. Monday and Friday.

MICHEL KAZAN 3, place du Théâtre Français (1st) Tel: 742.02.46 Métro stop: Palais-Royal

A good address near the Louvre, Avenue de l'Opéra, across from the Comédie-Française. Hours: 9 A.M. to 6 P.M.

LORCA   3, avenue Matignon (8th)   Tel: 225.57.90   Métro stop: F.-D.-Roosevelt

No dryers here. Everything done by hand, curl by curl with comb and brush only. Hours: 9 A.M. to 6 P.M.

MARC ET JEAN-MICHEL   42, avenue de Neuilly, Neuilly   Tel. 624.09.92   Métro stop: Pte. Maillot

Jean-Michel is Alexandre's ex-assistant. Very fancy styles and clientele. Hours: 9 A.M. to 6 P.M.

ROGER PASQUIER   40, avenue Pierre-1er-de-Serbie (8th)   Tel: 359.38.11   Métro stop: Iéna

Will do a quick comb-out, manicure, etc., without shampoo for 16F ($4). Hours: 9 A.M. to 6 P.M.; open Monday, closed Saturday.

JEAN-LOUIS ST.-ROCH   56, avenue Paul-Doumer (16th)   Tel: 870.97.60   Métro stop: Muette

Junior prices for juniors by junior staff. Hours: 9:30 A.M. to 6:30 P.M.

For Hair Problems

RAYMOND FURTERER   38, Chaussée d'Antin (9th) (just behind the Galeries Lafayette Department Store)   Tel: 874.33.23   Métro stop: Chaussée d'Antin

If your hair is breaking or falling out, or if you have a dry scalp or severe dandruff, this is the place for you. It's a very interesting clinic style salon, and every hair problem can be handled here. First, they take a couple of hairs from the front, temple, and center areas for analysis under a microscope. From this they can tell you exactly what's wrong—whether you've been eating irregularly, if your diet is wrong, if you've been under nervous tension, or whatever. After this, they clean the scalp with a special solution and then apply whatever treatments are necessary for your particular problem. After all the treatments are finished your hair is shampooed and set, and you're ready to leave. The treatment itself takes about an hour and a half, with additional time for the shampoo and set. Each treatment costs 48F ($12). All products used are of natural herbs and plants, and are available for sale at the salon so you can continue treatment on your own.

Most of the salons listed above can provide all your beauty needs, but the following ones specialize in facial and body aesthetics, such as massage, masks, hydrobaths and other forms of beautification.

STENDHAL INSTITUTE OF BEAUTY   36, rue Châteaubriand   Tel: 225.41.08   Métro stop: George-V

An extremely modern and well-equipped salon on several floors that offers you every type of facial treatment. First the skin is thoroughly cleansed and examined under a magnifying mirror, after which the pores are again cleaned with masks. There are electrical treatments for firming the muscles and eliminating wrinkles, moisturizing masks, etc. The cost of a 1½-hour treatment is 50F ($12.50). They also have paraffin treatment for losing excess liquid in the body; a half-hour session costs 40F ($10). And they have pressurized water massage for activating circulation, gym workouts, and other treatments; the all-inclusive cost is 70F ($17.50). After the facial treatment a complete new make-up is applied, so you walk out feeling like a queen. The tender, loving care, massage, etc., made me want to spend a week there, rather than an hour and a half, but it certainly did lift my morale and give me new energy. Ask for Mme. Baehr for an appointment.

DR. N. G. PAYOT BEAUTY INSTITUTE   10, rue de Castiglione (1st)   Tel: RIC. 18.65   Métro stop: Tuileries
The institute is located in what was once the ancient hotel of the Comtesse de Castiglione. Dr. Payot is well-known in the field of beauty and has developed many wonderful products. He specializes in treatment for the face and body. A complete routine for the face includes skin analysis, cleansing, depilitation, steam and ozone baths to eliminate toxic elements, deincrustation, mask and compresses for the eyes, an atomizing tone-up, and personalized make-up. This treatment takes about one hour and costs 45F ($11.25). Dr. Payot also has many treatments for the body. One complete treatment with a massage, and including your choice of jet spray or paraffin, or jet spray or Ionozone bath is 50F ($12.50). There is also wax depilitation for excess hair. The costs run from eyebrows alone at 6F ($1.50) to the lower leg at 28F ($7). Special beauty treatment of the feet given by a medical chiropodist costs 28F ($7).

ELIZABETH ARDEN   7, place Vendôme (1st)   OPE.42.42   Métro stop: Opéra

FERNAND AUBREY   5, rue du Cirque (8th)   BAL.48.34   Métro stop: Champs-Elysées–Clemenceau

JEANNE GATINEAU   116, boulevard Haussmann (9th)   LAB. 77.10   Métro stop: St.-Lazare

GUERLAIN   68, avenue des Champs-Elysées (8th)   ELY.31.10   Métro stop: George-V

JEANNE PIAUBERT   129, rue du faubourg St.-Honoré (8th)   ELY.16.02   Métro stop: Champs-Elysées–Clemenceau

SPECIAL PROBLEMS

The French have been the leaders in the beauty business since time immemorial. They have treatments that are still unavailable to Americans; so if you want to try them, what better time than when in Paris?

Obesity and Cellulite

One problem in particular that plagues American women is cellulite, that ugly, orange-skin appearance that usually is most evident on the thighs, hips, back, upper arms, and tummy. It is tiny lumps of fat and is terribly unattractive, especially on a person wearing a bikini or sleeveless dress. Americans rarely know what it is or how to eliminate it, which is why it is so prevalent in the United States. In Europe, especially in France, women recognize and get to work on it immediately.

It's not easy to get rid of but if you are determined to do so there is a place you can go. They also specialize in weight problems, nutritional illnesses, and an overall rebalancing of the entire system.

DR. DE LAVAL   7, rue le Sueur (16th)   Tel: KLE.30.90
Dr. de Laval is one of the top specialists in Europe for these problems and his results are marvelous. The fact that he has many celebrities from both Europe and America among his clients is a good barometer of his success. For the best results in eliminating the problem of cellulite, Dr. de Laval recommends 25 sessions, though after 10 sessions you definitely see the difference. If you are staying in Paris for any length of time you will have treatment three times a week for ten sessions without interruption. Each session is about two hours long and includes every possible kind of treatment from baths to electronic devices and air-pressure boots. I spent a great deal of time at this clinic and was very impressed. I consider it one of the most complete clinics for such problems I have ever seen. What impressed me most, and this of course will be of interest to those of you who cannot stay the length of time required for clinic treatment, is that Dr. de Laval will analyze your condition and give you a program to work out on your own after you leave Paris, thereby eliminating the problem of having to cease treatment. I got such a program from him including a special exerciser, a prescription for an iodine-based bath oil to bathe in three times a week, and a jelly to be massaged into the problem areas after the bath. Both these products are his special formula but are available from a druggist in Paris to whom Dr. de Laval can send you. For treatment in the clinic, each session costs 90F ($22.50) for the two-hour period. In order to see Dr. de Laval it is necessary to make an appointment 3 weeks in advance.

CLINIQUE MÉDICALE DE PHYTODIÉTÉTIQUE   43, avenue Foch, Vaucresson   Tel: 970.17.79
The clinic is only 15 minutes by cab on the expressway from the Arc de Triomphe and 5 minutes from Versailles. The rooms

are unpretentious but bright, pleasant, and comfortable. To some it may seem even a bit austere.

Treatment is by means of an exclusive detoxification cure, under strict supervision of a physician, who claims indisputable results. The cure requires a stay of five to seven days depending on the individual case, and the first three or four days are spent in your room without visitors. After that, visitors are allowed for three hours a day.

The daily rate is $50 and the price for the total treatment is approximately $215. There is an English-speaking staff.

Plastic Surgery

As long as we're on the subject of beauty, how can we ignore the subject of plastic surgery, the ultimate step in reshaping and rejuvenating the face and body. Why should I include it in a guide book? Because in Paris it is far less expensive than in the United States and you can take advantage of excellent surgeons as well as total privacy. When you return home no one is any the wiser and you can always tell your friends when they comment on how well you look, "I guess I really needed a vacation." Don't laugh, it's done all the time! At "Especially for Women," where we specialize in all forms of rejuvenation, many women are able to keep their secret even from their husbands. Of course a nose-bob or chin implant is far more obvious, so I'm afraid the truth will have to prevail in those cases.

In any case, should you wish to consider plastic surgery, check into the doctors listed below. I mention these because, after intensive research on doctors all over Europe, after observing their operations and considering all the available facts about them, these are the doctors in whom I have the greatest faith. All of them speak English and in every case their prices include surgeon's fee, anesthesia, all medications, consultations, and hospital stay.

These doctors do require certain blood tests to be taken before the operation, so it is best to have them done at home before leaving for Paris, if possible. Otherwise, allow a couple of days extra to get them done there. Since certain precautions must be taken before surgery, contact the doctor of your choice well in advance for an appointment and he will give you directions.

This should give you a general idea of what types of plastic surgery are available, how to go about it, and what to expect.

The prices alone are an inspiration when you realize that face-lifts in the U.S. cost from $1,500 to $5,000, with the accent on the $3,000 to $5,000 bracket. Then you must add approximately $116 a day for the hospital and anesthesia plus all medications. The difference in prices makes it worth considering on your trip to Paris, don't you agree?

DR. PIERRE POUTEAUX 21, rue Clément-Marot (8th) Tel: 359. 74.72 Métro stop: F.-D.-Roosevelt

Dr. Pouteaux is a member of the French Society of Plastic Surgeons and the European Society of Rhinology. He has also been lionized in *Elle,* the French version of *Vogue.* They even did several color layouts on his work—an indication of his fame as a plastic surgeon. Dr. Pouteaux is charming and friendly, with a great sense of humor as well as concern for his patients, especially if they are foreigners. We always recommend him to our clients and have had nothing but raves about him when they return, which speaks for itself. The details of his operations are as follows:

FACELIFT $990 all-inclusive. After a hospital stay of 4 days the patient feels fine and is fit enough to run around Paris without concern. The scar in front of the ear can be covered with a wisp of hair, a scarf or wig. Every other day the patient is required to drop by the doctor's office for a check-up and on the 10th day the stitches are removed and the patient can leave Paris without worry.

EYELIDS $440 all-inclusive. Only one night's stay at the hospital is required and the stitches are removed on the 4th day. All scars disappear after about 2 weeks. If the eyelids are done in conjunction with a facelift the price is only $350. This operation is done the day after the facelift.

NOSE-BOB $660 all-inclusive. The hospital stay is only 2 days and stitches are removed on the 10th day. There will be some swelling and bruising but not for long. After a couple of days the patient is presentable enough to go out.

FOREHEAD WRINKLES $550 all-inclusive, with a hospital stay of 1 or 2 days and stitches removed on the 10th day. There will be some swelling for awhile but it will soon go down. This operation is primarily for patients who have such deeply etched wrinkles or frown lines that a facelift can't remove them, or if a total facelift is not otherwise required.

DEEP WRINKLES For deep laugh lines or heavy furrows between the eyes silicone injections are advisable. They are not painful and there are no side effects. Depending upon the depth and the length of the wrinkles, one or two sessions at the doctor's office are sufficient and the cost is between $100 and $200 depending on the amount of work to be done.

DERMABRASION Dr. Pouteaux uses this method to remove wrinkles and scars, especially those of acne or small pox. It is accomplished by means of a high-speed metal brush, which gently brushes off the top layers of skin to the base of the scar. The face is first frozen of course and the procedure takes place right in the doctor's clinic so no hospital stay is necessary. After the operation there will be a crust on the face for about 10 days. For the whole face—forehead, cheeks, etc.—the price is $240, less for smaller areas.

ELECTROLYSIS   If the area to be done is small, such as the chin, it can be done in 1 or 2 sessions spaced 5 to 7 days apart, at the doctor's office. After treatment there is a small scab that disappears after 8 or 10 days, but can be covered with make-up in the meantime. Price $35 per half-hour session.

Chemosurgery

DR. JEAN-LOUIS CHERIF-CHEICK   21, rue Clément-Marot (8th) Tel: 359.74.72   Métro stop: Alma-Marceau

The price for the whole face is $150, and the entire face *must* be done when using this method to avoid discolorations or lines of demarcation. It is basically a chemical face-peeling used for light wrinkles or scars that do not require the deeper penetration of the steel brush method of dermabrasion. The skin generally consists of 12 layers and chemosurgical peeling removes 4 or 5 of these. Dr. Cherif-Cheick uses resorcin instead of the phenol used by U.S. doctors because phenol is considered too dangerous to the kidneys and has actually caused death in some instances. Its use is prohibited in France. He claims that resorcin has no side effects whatsoever. A cream is applied to the skin for 20 to 25 minutes. The skin turns brown, as with a suntan, and starts peeling 2 or 3 days later. A second application is applied to the skin 1 or 2 days after the first session and causes a sunburn type of peeling which disappears after 8 or 10 days. No make-up can be worn until the skin stops peeling. Acne scars are entirely removed, but small pox scars require dermabrasion.

Body Surgery

DR. JACQUES FAIVRE   23/25, rue Vital (16th)   Tel: 870.03.50 Métro stop: Passy

Dr. Faivre is President of the French Aesthetic Surgery Society and Tribunal Expert. His clinic is very modern and not at all like a hospital—each room done in a different style of décor. Even the operating theater, as sterile as it is, has stars painted on the ceiling to induce a feeling of relaxation.

BUST ENLARGEMENT $1,350 all-inclusive. A 2-day hospital stay is all that's necessary and the stitches are removed 10 or 12 days later. Dr. Faivre uses the under-arm incision so there are no body scars at all.

BUST REDUCTION $1,450 all-inclusive. This requires a 3 day hospital stay and stitches are removed in 10 or 12 days.

ABDOMINAL REDUCTION $1,550 all-inclusive. Five days in the hospital are necessary with stitches removed in 10 or 12 days. The scars border the pubic hairline and are quite undetectable even in a bikini. Many men have this operation today to eliminate the pot belly often associated with old age.

THIGH LIFT $1,760 all-inclusive. A hospital stay of approximately 6 days is required, though the patient can walk the day after the operation. Stitches are removed 8 days after the hospital release. The patient will be a bit stiff and unable to climb stairs easily for about a week, but gradually becomes more comfortable and in 6 weeks feels perfectly normal.

13
Shopping

What woman hasn't dreamed of shopping in Paris! Proudly sporting an *haute couture* label is half the joy of visiting this famed mecca of fashion. But unfortunately high fashion is synonymous with high prices. Few can afford originals of the *haute couture* today. For this reason most of the big names now also have ready-to-wear (*prêt à porter*) lines and boutiques. Fortunately these *are* affordable. Even the original collections are available at bargain prices after the collections and just prior to a new one. That is, if you can slither into these model-sized garments. But more about that later. First, some important tips:

Custom allowances are listed in the section on government requirements. But aside from these, the importation of almost all French perfumes is limited to one bottle per traveler when going through American customs, so check on the brand you buy first, or it may be confiscated.

When buying perfumes stick to the name brands. No matter how expensive they are, the price is still only one-third of the U.S. price.

American cigarettes are expensive in Europe, so bring as many as you can carry on the plane. Failing this, you will have to experiment with French brands—which are strong enough to knock you for a loop. Gitanes and Gauloises are the most popular, but of the two, I find the latter more agreeable. Gitanes are so strong that I can't even sit next to anyone smoking them.

STORE HOURS   Generally 9:30 A.M. to 6:30 P.M., Tuesday to Saturday. Many shops close for lunch from 12 noon to 2 P.M.

Shopping Tips

Shopping discounts up to 20% are still given in many shops in the form of a refund mailed to your home address. Some establishments require a minimum $25 purchase before discount is granted. When payment is made in any foreign currency (including personal check), a form is filled out, a copy of which (in a stamped envelope with the store's address) must be given to French customs when leaving the country. (There is a special desk on the main floor of Orly Airport for this purpose.) When buying in a couture house there is frequently an additional, on-the-spot reduction of 10%.

Sales (*soldes*) usually take place the first week in January, the last week in June and July. Couturier sales are in March and July. Then you can buy a "name" dress at almost half off, so it's almost worth planning your trip for sale time, especially if you wish to buy quite a few things.

Prisunic and Monoprix are stores similar to Woolworth's and can be found all over the city. There is a Prisunic on the Champs-Elysées and Monoprix just past the Galeries Lafayette on Boulevard Haussmann as well as one on the Avenue de l'Opéra, plus many other locations. They have a large cosmetic and toiletry department for all the odds and ends one always needs. They also have some nice lingerie—even Pierre Cardin lingerie—and sportswear, to name just a few departments. But important, too, is their *alimentation* (grocery) department for buying snacks for your room. I always load up on Boursin cheese and crackers and cookies the minute I arrive in Paris, for those times I'm too busy or too lazy to go out for a meal. It comes in handy, not to mention the savings to your budget.

French cosmetics are also a good buy—no duty to be paid. Orlane, Dior, Chanel, Guerlain, Stendhal, etc.

HOSTESSES INTERNATIONALES 119, rue de la Pompe (16th) Tel: 553.55.72

Run by two charming Parisians who will arrange for a guide to take you shopping, secure invitations to exclusive fashion showings, auction sales, and wholesale dealers. Prices range from $25 for four or five hours with guide and a car for one or two people to $37 for eight or nine hours in a larger, four-or-five-passenger car. Any Air France ticket office can make arrangements for you.

MAIN SHOPPING STREETS AND AREAS

Main Department Stores

Between the Madeleine and St.-Lazare

Couturiers

Rue Cambon (1st)
Rue François-ler (8th)
Avenue George-V (8th)

Avenue Montaigne (8th)
Rue Royale (8th)
Rue du Faubourg St.-Honoré
  (8th)

Boutiques

Champs-Elysées (8th)
Chaussée d'Antin (9th)
Rue du Four (6th)
Rue de Longchamp (16th)
Rue de Passy (16th)
Rue de la Pompe (16th)
Rue de Rennes (6th)

Boulevard St.-Germain (6th)
Rue du Faubourg St.-Honoré
  (8th)
Rue de Sèvres (6th)
Rue Tronchet (8th/9th)
Avenue Victor-Hugo (16th)

Shoe Boutiques

Champs-Elysées (8th)
Boulevard de la Madeleine (8th)

Rue du Faubourg St.-Honoré
  (8th)
Boulevard St.-Michel (5th/6th)

Jewelers

Place Vendôme (1st)

Rue de la Paix (2nd)

Art Galleries and Art

Rue du Bac (7th)
Rue des Beaux Arts (6th)
Rue La Boëtie (8th)
Rue Bonaparte (6th)
Place de Furstenberg (6th)
Rue Guénégaud (6th)

Rue Jacob (6th)
The Louvre
Avenue Matignon (8th)
Rue de Miromesnil (8th)
Montmartre
Montparnasse

Quartier St.-Germain-des-Prés

Antique Dealers

Rue du Bac (7th)
Rue Bonaparte (6th)
Rue Jacob (6th)
Marché aux Puces (18th)
Quartier St.-Germain-des-Prés

Rue du Faubourg St.-Honoré
  (8th)
Rue des Sts.-Pères (6th/7th)
Village Suisse (15th)
Quai Voltaire (7th)

Copies of Antiques and Furniture

Faubourg St.-Antoine (11th) and couturier boutiques (see listings)

Crystal and China

Rue du Paradis (10th)

DEPARTMENT STORES

BON MARCHÉ   22, rue de Sèvres (7th)
Excellent ready-to-wear department and leather goods.

FRANCK & FILS   80, rue de Passy (16th)
Higher prices than other big stores but excellent for shoes, lingerie. Has probably one of the best and largest selections of handbags in Paris.

GALERIES LAFAYETTE   30, boulevard Haussmann (9th)
First in quality and good taste. For ready-to-wear, hosiery, shoes, and knitwear, "Club 20 Ans" features a colorful grouping of 25 boutiques including Daniel Hechter, Mic-Mac, Pierre d'Alby, Sonia Rykiel, and Ted Lapidus.

INNO   53, rue de Passy (16th)
   15, rue des Bourdonnais (1st)
   18, boulevard de Charonne (20th)
   36, rue du Départ (14th)
Open daily 9 to 7; Fridays, 10 A.M. to 8:45 P.M. Supermarket style, category between Le Printemps and Prisunic.

MONOPRIX   20 chain stores in Paris, 30 outside
Very low prices, but good quality merchandise, even furs. Splendid supermarkets, especially the branch at 21, avenue de l'Opéra (1st).

AU PRINTEMPS   64, boulevard Haussman (9th)
Huge choice of dresses and coats; superb for handbags, wigs, and hairpieces at a fraction of the price charged elsewhere. Boutiques include "Primavera"—everything for the house; "New Boutique"—12 famous designers grouped together; "Bernard Quatrepingle"—boutique for men's clothing.

PRISUNIC   60, avenue des Champs-Elysées (8th)
   18, rue de Passy (16th)
Actually 95 chain stores throughout the city, modeled after our 5¢ and 10¢ stores but *the place* for inexpensive sportswear. Anything here is a bargain.

LA SAMARITAINE   75, rue de Rivoli (1st)
Very inexpensive Junior Department. Extraordinary pet shop.

LA SAMARITAINE DE LUXE   27, boulevard des Capucines (9th)
Especially good for household and kitchen items and low-priced furs.

AUX TROIS QUARTIERS   17, boulevard de la Madeleine (1st)
Classical ready-to-wear, good furniture, and household department. Rather than an "in" spot, it is the temple of tradition.

BOUTIQUES

The most fashionable shopping area for youthful fashions is Boulevard St.-Germain and Rue de Sèvres. From Sèvres-Babylone to the Boulevard St.-Germain and the area surrounding the Church of St.-Germain-des-Prés, there are dozens and dozens of shops, all of which you should poke into, since taste in clothes is a very personal thing.

N G STORES 38, rue Bonaparte (6th)
40, rue Jacob (6th)
Very avant-garde fashions.

AMIE 7, rue Pierre-Charron (8th)
Year-round headquarters for Tiktiner, the famous Nice sportswear house. All the well-cut, marvelous dresses, pants, and bathing suits, in exclusive, ravishing fabrics.

L'ARMOIRE DE GRAND'MÈRE 118, rue Mouffetard (5th)
Picturesque area and shop. The choice is varied and tasteful, the prices average.

L'ATELIER 1, Cité du Retiro (8th)
Ready-to-wear or choose your style and they will make up out of another material, or you can even bring in your own sample design. Prices vary according to detail of design but generally are very reasonable.

ATELIER 32 32, rue Médéric (17th)
Made-to-measure *haute couture*-style dresses, coats, shirts, and suits.

AURORE 195, rue du faubourg St.-Honoré (8th)
Large selection.

LA BAZARINE 18, place des Vosges (3rd/4th)
Boutique designed to dress the attractive, mature woman in modern and young way. Choose your own fabric from a big trunk of materials collected from the four corners of the world.

BELI 120, avenue Victor-Hugo (16th)
One of the first yé-yé boutiques in the 16th arrondissement. A smaller Dorothée Bis, very inexpensive.

NADINE BERGER 52, rue de Sèvres (7th)
Very popular, up-to-the-minute clothes at low prices.

LA BERGERIE Passage du Lido, Champs-Elysées (8th)
Young, rather expensive, but up-to-the-minute dresses, sportswear, bathing suits.

BIBA 18, rue de Sèvres (7th)
Branch of the popular, inexpensive London boutique.

DOROTHÉE BIS 35/39, rue de Sèvres (6th)
38, rue Marbeuf (16th)
One of the oldest, most successful Paris boutiques. Has launched many worldwide trends. Most fashionable Parisians stop here regularly for the latest styles. Very low-priced, fun, ready-to-wear.

BISTRO BOUTIQUE 13, rue des Amandiers (20th)

One of the first of the boutiques out near Père Lachaise Cemetery. Amusing things from $40 to $160. Many inspired by 1920s and '30s.

JEAN BOUQUIN   Rue St.-Benoît (6th)
A favorite of the Beautiful People of Paris for his elegant hippie garb.

LA BOUTIQUE FANTASQUE   18, rue Franklin (16th)
For young women who don't care to dress like teenagers. Large choice, reasonable prices for *haute couture* styles.

BUNNY   106, rue de Longchamp (16th)
Yé-yé clothes at reasonable prices.

BUS STOP   147, boulevard St.-Germain (7th)
Crammed with plenty of chic, avant-garde things, in the hub of the student quarter. Open until 11:30 P.M.

CARNABY   99, rue de Longchamp (16th)
British-made fashions for *monsieur,* too. An excellent tailor will also beautifully do women's made-to-measure sportswear.

CARNABY STREET   2, place du Marché Ste.-Catherine (4th)
In the Marais district, 6 little shops. Flirt, Shoes, Boys, Smoking, Girls, and Merchandise. Salespeople and atmosphere are reminiscent of London's Carnaby Street.

CATHERINE   52, rue Vavin (6th)
High-style sportswear 100% handmade. Novel ideas like Russian peasant-style and satin shirts, velvet jeans, 1900 vintage lingerie.

CERRUTI 1881   3, place de la Madeleine (8th)
Started as men's boutique but so many sales were going to women who wanted the clothes in small sizes for themselves that a women's section was added in the cellar. Fantastic jersey pants suits, most things here are "unisex"—adaptable to men and women.

CHEZ JULES   120, boulevard Montparnasse (14th)
A counter in this top men's tailoring shop stocks exclusive male coats, suits, and accessories in feminine forms and sizes.

CHIPIE   31, rue St.-André-des-Arts (6th)
Small boutique with very reasonable prices.

CLAUDE ET GILBERT   64, rue de Rennes (6th)
Glass, steel, and metal décor, with leather, suede, and fur the specialties.

LA DAME DE TRÈFLE   16, rue Jean-Mermoz (8th)
Giant two-story ferris wheel window display. Interesting sportswear, shoes.

DEBS   4, rue de Sèvres (6th)
83, rue de Passy (16th)
Rue du Havre (8th/9th)
Teenagers' temple of fashion.

DIBS   23, avenue des Gobelins (5th)
Mini-department store, 4 floors, young styles (some Ungaro copies for $60), jersey dresses, good sportswear, skirts, excellent raincoats and furs.

DON JUAN   157, boulevard St.-Germain (6th)

Classic-style boutique, everything *dans le vent*. Excellent quality, extremely well-cut pants.

ELLE BON MAGIQUE   127, avenue des Champs-Elysées (8th)
All the goodies from *Elle* magazine. Excellent selection and size range. Closed Monday mornings, otherwise open Tuesday to Saturday 10:30 A.M. to 6:30 P.M.

ELLE-ELLE   9, boulevard Malesherbes (8th)
Medium-priced adaptations of young styles for all ages.

ERES   2, rue Tronchet (8th/9th)
108, boulevard Haussmann (8th)
Specializes in rather avant-garde sportswear, bathing suits in every imaginable fabric and color.

ETAM   9, boulevard St.-Michel (5th)
39, avenue de l'Opéra (1st)
47, rue de Sèvres (6th)
Very inexpensive young lingerie a specialty in every one of their 80 branches.

EVA   121, boulevard St.-Germain (6th)
Courrèges-style dresses and coats at reasonable prices.

FAHRENHEIT   107, boulevard St.-Germain (6th)
Wild red décor with clothes dangling on a seemingly endless conveyor belt running up and around all the multi-levels. Good styles, moderate prices.

FELICE   2, rue de Sèvres (6th)
Very young and fashionable.

FIGUE   14, cour de Vincennes (12th)
Fashions go East too, East of Paris.

LIANE FRANCK   60, rue de Rennes (6th)
Sportswear for men too.

LA GAMINERIE   137, boulevard St.-Germain (6th)
Fanciful, cavelike Pueblo-village-style interior. Jazzy window displays. Sportswear, especially good pants. Each month a special 8-day exhibition of a new, different designer. Very reasonable prices, excellent quality.

GÉGÉ LA MARGUERITE   135, boulevard St.-Germain (6th)
Good Courrèges and Ungaro copies for $60 to $80.

GIRL   78, rue du Bac (7th)
Typical little boutique with the important distinction that *only* extremely well-finished, well-lined models are sold. Reasonably priced for impeccable quality.

GLADY   18, rue de Sèvres (6th)
41, boulevard Raspail (7th)
For teenagers and young women.

GUDULE   72, rue St.-André-des-Arts (6th)
Up-to-the-minute, young jersey dresses, pants suits, fantastic pullovers, and interesting jewelry.

HIT PARADE   35, Chaussée d'Antin (9th)
Yé-yé elegance, split-level profusion of inexpensive "with-it" clothes displayed on every inch of space.

HOBBY   53, Chaussée d'Antin (9th)
Good pants and sportswear.

JNS 3–47, Chaussée d'Antin (9th)

Drainpipe and conduit display shelves. Crazy décor but great clothes and selection. Here you'll find designer copies at very reasonable prices and some couturiers' ready-to-wear (Ted Lapidus, for example).

JONES 45, avenue Victor-Hugo (16th)

More a small department store than boutique. Very chic. Good selection of perfumes, dresses, and excellent leather goods.

LE KNACK 104, avenue Victor-Hugo (16th)
85, rue de Rennes (6th)

All the latest styles in dresses, pants suits, sweaters, elegant sportswear plus a large stock of complementary accessories. Prices range from $100 up to $240.

LAURA 104, avenue Général-Leclerc (14th)

Filled with fresh, young, inexpensive, trend-setting ready-to-wear, with a strong personality. The Sonia Rykiel style, tube sweaters and jersey things.

LOOK 91, rue de Longchamp (16th)

Frequented by young ladies of good family. Tea is offered all afternoon and the collection shown when the girls feel ready. Designs are created by ex-Chanel and ex-Carven cutters. Everything made to measure, with good choice of fabric. Reasonable prices for this class of workmanship.

LA MACHINERIE 54, rue de Passy (16th)

Same owner as Hit Parade. Up-to-the-minute apparel from excellent young designers and amusing gadgets displayed in an atmosphere of high-powered pop music.

MADD 20, rue Tronchet (8th)

Very popular, very low prices (dresses from $14 up). Browse to your heart's content.

MARIE MARTINE 8, rue de Sèvres (6th)

Really one of the first and most successful of the boutiques. Beautiful, chic though rather expensive ready-to-wear. Around the corner two new sections: "Weekend," 78, rue des Sts.-Pères; "Furs," 85, rue des Sts.-Pères.

MAYFAIR 128, rue de la Pompe (16th)

In an old butcher shop so the clothes are hung from meat racks. One of the first in the area and still one of the best, always filled with reasonable new ideas.

LA MERCERIE DE JUSTINE 88, rue du faubourg St.-Honoré (8th)

Where to find ready-to-wear copies of Louis Feraud's couture designs. Dresses ($70), suits ($90).

MIA & VICKY 21, rue Bonaparte (6th)

Modern pizzaz on the ground floor of a 17th-century mansion. Backed by Liz Taylor and Richard Burton.

MIC MAC 13, rue de Tournon (6th)
Galeries Lafayette

Whitewashed branch of the popular St.-Tropez shop. Chic sportswear, small custom order collection.

MINNY 37, avenue Victor-Hugo (16th)

Dresses, coats, marvelous sweater collection. Original styles are well cut, well made, and well finished, always in extremely good taste.

MOD IN   87, rue de Seine (6th)
Best known for pants and skirts (will also make to order).

ORPHÉE   5, rue du Four (6th)
Dress boutique, jerseys and sweaters.

PENTHOUSE   32, rue Poissonnière (2nd)
Wild décor with 9 outdoor TV screens, young clothes displayed on rail-riding racks.

PÉPIN   136, boulevard St.-Germain (6th)
High-fashion sportswear, famous for their trousers (made to measure and ready-to-wear with one fitting allowed free of charge).

LES PESTES   96, rue de Longchamp (16th)
Tiny shop with English and Scotch imports and very pretty French designs. One of the co-owners was a long-time mannequin at Balenciaga so the specialty here is a made-to-measure coat in the master's style, priced from $90 depending on your choice of fabric.

PHILOMÈNE   15, rue Vavin (6th)
New/old clothes, 1920s vintage in original old fabrics, marvelous beaded panels, buttons, curios, $50 and up for dresses.

PIA   5, rue du Four (6th)
Young, inexpensive models.

PLINE   9, rue Bélidor (17th)
A vast, bare workroom studio, just one model dress, a silk jersey in 75 fabulous colors for $45, not unlike those of a certain Florentine marchese. Can be made to measure in just one week.

POPARD   48, rue du Bac (7th)
Adorable dresses, suits, coats, 1920s styles, amusing accessories. Men's branch next door.

POPELINE   91, rue St.-Dominique (7th)
Very young styles in a gay and friendly setting. Good materials, quality, and finishing.

PULCINELLA   10, rue Vignon (9th)
Treasure chest of romantic Victorian accessories, knickknacks, old jewelry, copies and original things, clothes, handmade materials.

PUSSYCAT   41, rue Vital (16th)
Easy-to-wear little nothings. Every customer gets a tiny plush cat.

QUESAR   24, rue Boissy d'Anglas (8th)
Two designers. He sells his plastic airblown furniture on the ground floor. She is Emmanuèle Khanh and her clothes are upstairs.

PACO RABANNE   33, rue Bergère (9th)
The man who made plastic and metal important in fashion. Ultra-modern styles $200 and up.

RANCH   176, boulevard St.-Germain (6th)
Leathery, furry, sporty things plus a great shift in all sorts of materials.

RÉAL   65, rue du faubourg St.-Honoré (8th)
Small, rather expensive shop where you might run into Brigitte Bardot or Sylvie Vartan. Shows spring and fall collections with the *grands couturiers*.

RÉJA   10, rue de l'Ancienne-Comédie (6th)
Over 3,000 pairs of pants in stock. All materials. Even ski pants for men and women. Can also be made to measure for a 10% increase in price.

RÉMY   Lido Arcades, 76-78, avenue des Champs-Elysées (8th)
Principal outlet for "Choses," the famous St.-Tropez boutique. In winter and summer—jeans, tee shirts, and *dernier cri* bathing suits.

RETY   54, rue du faubourg St.-Honoré (8th)
Charming, friendly shop specializing in Chanel copies at one-fourth the price ($200).

SONIA RYKIEL   6, rue de Grenelle (6th)
In a cozy, ancient antique shop. Paradise for jerseys and great knits, jump suits, pants, sweaters, even "Future Maman Corner" for jersey maternity clothes adapted from regular models.

SASSAFRAS   6, rue Princesse (6th)
Owned by the daughter of Mme. Grès, the well-known couturier. Jaunty sporty things. For *monsieur* too.

SCOTTIE SHOP   134, avenue Victor-Hugo (16th)
Very up-to-the-minute styles, excellent sportswear.

SNOB   8, avenue Victor-Hugo (16th)
126, rue La Boëtie (8th)
For those inexpensive little nothings.

TASSY   32, rue du Four (6th)
Small, tasteful boutique collection around $70.

TIFFANY   12, rue de Sèvres (6th)
Excellent choice of models, with some exclusives created by the owner's brother. Average prices.

TINNY   137, boulevard St.-Germain (6th)
2, avenue Général-Leclerc (17th)
Very young clothes for very young people.

TIPHÈNE   33, rue du Four (6th)
Small, tasteful boutique collection around $70.

TORRENTE   79, rue du faubourg St.-Honoré (8th)
Small custom design house run by the sister of Ted Lapidus. Some ready-to-wear sportswear but the forte here is yummy fabrics plus couture-quality suits and coats. Expect to pay a minimum of $250–$300 but the materials and workmanship are superb.

LE TOURNIS   2, rue de Sèvres (6th)
Fanciful décor, good selection, reasonable prices.

TUB   48, Chaussée d'Antin (9th)
Long narrow shop with winding passageways displaying fashions for the whole family.

TWIGGY   35, boulevard des Capucines (1st)
Just the name's the same; not Twiggy's fashions though English oriented.

ANNE VALERIE   11, rue du faubourg St.-Honoré (8th)
  88, avenue Mozart (16th)
  Fantastic pants collection in silk, cotton, toile, shantung, and
  much more.
VENEZIANO   26, avenue Pierre-1er-de-Serbie (16th)
  Branches in Megève and St.-Tropez. A really chic Italian trend
  setter for tasteful, elegant sportswear, shoes, and accessories.
VICTOIRE   3 and 12, place des Victoires (2nd)
  Extraordinary boutique in an old house on a charming square.
  Reasonably priced, international selection of styles and design-
  ers represented. Hostess gowns, bags, belts, and accessories, plus
  fun home furnishings.
VOG   34, rue Tronchet (8th/9th)
  Chic, beautifully stocked, large selection of ready-to-wear. Very
  popular, always dependable, early with fads.
VROOM   62, rue de Rennes (6th)
  No counters or drawers. Young, kicky clothes displayed against
  a backdrop of crushed cars and machinery parts.
LE WEEK END   80, avenue de Suffren (7th)
  Off-beat address facilitates low prices for smart, color-coordi-
  nated sportswear in beautiful, specially dyed shades and mate-
  rials.

HAUTE COUTURE

All couturiers design two custom collections a year. Spring-
summer showings open the end of January and run through
May. Fall-winter showings begin end of July and go through
mid-December. Most have showings Monday to Friday at 3
P.M. Some have boutique showings at 11 A.M. Invitation cards
are needed for custom collections but these are relatively easy
to get (through the concierge at better hotels or request directly through the salon) except during the two opening weeks
of the collection when the press and buyers are in town. Then,
unless you are a client or a celebrity, they are virtually impossible to get.

If you are truly determined to attend a showing during its
opening weeks, I would suggest you try any of the following
measures. Write directly to the couturier of your choice, using
your best stationery, and suggest that you might become a
client and would appreciate an invitation, without specifying
a particular day. Or, if you're in Paris without having written
in advance, and are staying at one of the deluxe hotels, ask
their PR people to help you. If that doesn't work, go around
to the fashion house and trot out your most convincing argu-
ments in person. Who knows, it might even work. If all efforts

fail, content yourself with browsing in the various designer boutiques where the prices are much lower than those of the collections. Even if you don't buy, you will at least get the feel of the new trends. But a word of caution: if you do buy a designer gown, be prepared to pay duty on it even if you have snipped out the label. The customs men are very wily and knowledgeable; they can spot the fine detailing of a designer garment, and are quite *au courant* with the new designs.

Those salons marked with BOUTIQUE in the following list have their own boutiques which offer designer's label and equal styling at relatively modest prices (usually under $200), and accessories, gifts, and ready-to-wear. A customer should watch her timing in boutique buying. The best time is soon after a new collection is launched in the salon.

PIERRE BALMAIN   44, rue François-1er (8th)   Tel: 225.68.04
   BOUTIQUE   Small collection of *couture*, ready-to-wear, and accessories.
   BOUTIQUE   For men, just across the street.
PIERRE CARDIN   118, rue du faubourg St.-Honoré (8th)   Tel: 225.06.23
   BOUTIQUE   In the *couture* house. Colored stockings, coats, dresses with prices just under his made-to-order collection.
   BOUTIQUE   185, boulevard St.-Germain (6th). Elegant and professional, most price tags under $200.
CARVEN   6, Rond-Point des Champs-Elysées (8th)   Tel: 359.17.52
   BOUTIQUE   In the *couture* house.
CASTILLO   95, rue du faubourg St.-Honoré (8th)   Tel: 225.61.90
   BOUTIQUE   76, rue du faubourg St.-Honoré (8th).
CHANEL   31, rue Cambon (1st)   Tel: 073.60.21
   BOUTIQUE   Ground floor. Has accessories, bags, and jewelry only.
ANDRÉ COURRÈGES   40, rue François-1er (8th)   Tel: 359.72.17
No fashion show except twice a year for the press.
   BOUTIQUE   **Couture Future,** 67, rue du faubourg St.-Honoré (8th). Dresses run about $160, coats $200 (almost 50% below New York prices); all his accessories too.
JEAN DESSÈS   12, Rond-Point des Champs-Elysées (8th)   Tel: 225.45.63
   BOUTIQUE   In the *couture* house.
CHRISTIAN DIOR   30, avenue Montaigne (8th)   Tel: 359.93.64
   BOUTIQUE   **Miss Dior,** 11 bis, rue François-1er (8th). Dresses (about $60), coats ($110–$270), suits ($200), gloves, sweaters, blouses, skirts, jewelry, handbags. No fittings, but hems and sleeves are adjusted without charge.
   BOUTIQUE   **Baby Dior,** 28, avenue Montaigne (8th) (see section "For Children").

EKTOR 4, rue Cambon (1st) Tel: 073.93.97
Bright young Brazilian who took over Balenciaga's workroom boss, 22 cutters, fitters, and seamstresses. Showed his first collection in Paris this year.

JACQUES ESTEREL 85 bis, rue du faubourg St.-Honoré (8th) Tel: ELY.25.30

LOUIS FERAUD 88, rue du faubourg St.-Honoré (8th) Tel: ANJ. 27.29

GIVENCHY 3, avenue George-V (8th) Tel: 225.92.60
BOUTIQUE Ground floor of salon, for ready-to-wear, shoes, scarves, with prices only a fraction below the upstairs made-to-order salon.
BOUTIQUE 66, avenue Victor-Hugo (16th) Much less expensive.

GRÉS 1, rue de la Paix (2nd) Tel: 073.90.15
BOUTIQUE In the *couture* house.

JACQUES GRIFFE 5, rue Royale (8th) Tel: ANJ.02.21
BOUTIQUE In the *couture* house.

LANVIN 22, rue du faubourg St.-Honoré (8th) Tel: 265.27.21
Completely remodeled in 1969 into spacious, colorful, boutiques. First floor—accessories and ready-to-wear from $100. Second floor—same garments but alterations possible. Third floor—custom-made clothes with two fittings at higher prices.

TED LAPIDUS 37, avenue Pierre-1er-de-Serbie (16th) Tel: 225. 52.47
BOUTIQUE 6, place Victor-Hugo (16th)
BOUTIQUE Place St.-Germain (6th) and in large stores. A compromise between *haute couture* and very good ready-to-wear.

GUY LAROCHE 29, avenue Montaigne (8th) Tel: 225.87.45

MOLYNEUX 5, rue Royale (8th) Tel: 265.68.40

JEAN PATOU 7, rue St.-Florentin (2nd) Tel: 073.08.71
BOUTIQUE Very interesting rings created by artisans who also work for the more famous jewelers, watches, cuff links, tie pins at young prices. In the *couture* house.
BOUTIQUE 52, avenue Victor-Hugo (16th)

EMILIO PUCCI 37, rue Jean-Goujon (8th)
4, rue de Castiglione (1st)
Boutiques with all the goodies from the famed Italian designer.

MADELEINE DE RAUCH 37, rue Jean-Goujon (8th) Tel: ELY. 26.26

NINA RICCI 20, rue des Capucines (1st) Tel: 073.67.31
BOUTIQUE In the *couture* house.

MAGGY ROUFF 5, avenue Marceau (16th) Tel: POI.42.00

YVES ST.-LAURENT 30 bis, rue Spontini (16th) Tel: 727.43.79
BOUTIQUE Rive Gauche, 21, rue de Tournon (6th)/38, rue du faubourg St.-Honoré (8th)/and 46, avenue Victor-Hugo (16th). St.-Laurent's Rive Gauche boutiques are probably the most famous of the *haute couture* offshoots. Branches now sprouting in major European and American cities.

JEAN-LOUIS SCHERRER 17, rue du Vieux Colombier (6th) Tel: ELY.34.83

BOUTIQUE   182, rue du faubourg St.-Honoré (8th) Prices from $50 to $100.

UNGARO   2 bis, avenue Montaigne (8th)   Tel: 256.70.70
BOUTIQUE   In wide entry foyer of salon.

VALENTINO   42, avenue Montaigne (8th)
A boutique for the popular Italian couturier's ready-to-wear, shoes, bags, scarves.

PHILIPPE VENET   62, rue François-1er (8th)   Tel: 225.33.63
BOUTIQUE   32, avenue George-V (8th).

SALE SHOPS

The following shops offer you *haute couture* fashions at fantastic discounts. They buy up all the designers' collections after the big showings and you reap the benefits. Usually the price is just enough over the designer's cost for them to make a profit, but still very inexpensive for you, considering the savings. There are new things as well here at lower prices than in the regular boutiques. June and January are especially good months to pick up a bargain; November and May, the next best.

BAB'S   7, avenue Marceau (8th)
A good selection of Nina Ricci, Courrèges, and Cardin.

VIOLETTE BENISTAN   4, rue Chambiges (8th), 1st floor
Specializes in couturier sale clothes from $80 and up. Closed Saturday.

CABESSA   122, rue La Boëtie (8th) 4th floor
Haute couture models from the latest collections, with labels. Faultless alterations can be made here. Open Monday to Friday, 10:30 to 1 and 2:30 to 6.

DREYFUS MARCHÉ   Place St.-Pierre (18th)
This is the spot for *haute couture* fashions at bargain prices.

FABIENNE K   76, rue de Seine (6th)
Their specialty is nightgowns that are sold as evening gowns, no less. Very elegant. From 100F ($25).

FERNANDE   3, rue d'Anjou (8th)
Haute couture dresses from $20, suits from $40 with original labels.

ANNA LOWE   35, avenue Matignon (8th)
You can buy resale dresses (with *couture* labels) in like-new condition, sometimes worn only once. Closed Saturday.

NOIR ET BLANC   42, rue du Dragon (6th)
Very sophisticated atmosphere, with black walls serving as a background for stark white chantilly trees. They have superb silver fox scarves, silk mousse shirts, crêpe georgette dresses, plissé blouses—all in excellent taste from 150F to 400F ($37.50 to $100).

ROBE DES VEDETTES 28, rue Pierre-Demours (17th)
Couture designs mostly used in films. Run by Jules Verne's great-grandniece.

LA SOLDERIE 85, rue La Boëtie (8th)
Serve-yourself style for bargain-priced couturier clothes. Mannequins' sizes (38–42). Dresses from $14, suits from $20, coats from $30. Large selections and very popular.

KNITWEAR

LE BISTRO DU TRICOT 55–57, rue Bonaparte (6th)
Super knits, dresses, slacks at bargain prices in an 1880s bistro.

LA BOÎTE À PULL Passage du Lido, Champs-Elysées (8th)
All sorts of inexpensive knitwear displayed in huge baskets.

LA BOUCHERIE 139, rue Cardinet (17th)
In an old butcher shop. Handicrafts too, but knitwear is the specialty. Choose your own wool and colors and patterns to be knitted on-the-spot. Many crocheted designs, suits, long shirts, and handmade jewelry.

CASHMERE CLUB 72, avenue Kléber (16th)
A favorite for those who collect cashmere sweaters.

CASHMERE HOUSE 2, rue d'Aguesseau (8th)
Incredible prices for cashmere and lambswool sweaters, skirts, and dresses and the only place to find cashmere knitting yarn.

DELYA 9, boulevard Bonne-Nouvelle (2nd)
Sweaters and knits.

KORRIGAN 14, avenue Victor-Hugo (16th)
25, rue du Four (6th)
31, rue Marbeuf (8th)
11, rue du faubourg St.-Honoré (8th)
15, rue Daunou (2nd)
Many other large stores
Twice a year a wonderful collection of well-designed and well-cut sweaters, dresses, suits, and coats.

REMY 422, rue du faubourg St.-Honoré (8th)
Very smart knitwear. Furs on the third floor.

RODIER 17, rue Duphot (1st/8th)
7, avenue des Gobelins (5th)
85, rue de Rennes (6th)
18, avenue Victor-Hugo (16th)
30, rue Marbeuf (8th)
27, rue Tronchet (9th)
Reasonable knitwear for head to toe, in every color.

SÈVRES 33, rue de Sèvres (6th)
Sale knits, cashmere, lambswool, shetlands, all colors, all qualities. Rummage through to your heart's content.

SÈVRES BAZAAR Carrefour de la Croix-Rouge (6th)
Huge selection, including Lanvin and Corot sweaters, many sale items.

SPORT LOOK 52, rue Dauphine (6th)

SWEATERS BAZAAR 83, rue du faubourg St.-Honoré (8th)
Wide assortment. Jersey, shetland, silk, angora, cashmere, knitted dresses, sweaters, pants, coats.

TRICOT CLUB 82, rue de Passy (16th)
All kinds of knitwear. A Rodier boutique.

LA TRICOTIÈRE 15, rue Beautreillis (4th)
Everything is knit, and each item is different. Open 10:30 A.M. to 8:00 P.M., located on a very pretty little street.

FOR LARGE SIZES

CAROLINE 202, rue de la Convention (15th)
A good selection of dresses, suits, and sportswear for the well-endowed figure.

LEATHER GOODS

ADIGE 53, avenue Victor-Hugo (16th)
26, rue Cambon (1st)
6, rue Royale (8th)
Exact copies of famous *couture* shoes at about one-third the price. Also great boots in all colors.

AMARYLLIS 36, rue du faubourg St.-Honoré (8th)
Leather, leather, leather! Dresses, coats, hats, shirts, pants—everything cut from exceptional skins and available in exceptional colors.

ASTRE 10, 35, and 43, rue de Sèvres (6th)
Unique in that both extremely small and very large sizes are available. Will also make to order if you cannot be properly fitted, which is rare. Jourdan, Dior, Seducta, and Charlet models available.

À L'AVENUE MATIGNON 27, avenue Matignon (8th)
Luxurious handbags.

LA BAGAGERIE 13, rue Tronchet (8th)
41, rue du Four (6th)
74, rue de Passy (16th)
From a fashion standpoint, one of the best bag and belt boutiques in the world. Their designs inspire international fashions. Prices begin at $10.

BALLY 11, boulevard de la Madeleine (1st)
35, boulevard des Capucines (2nd)
146, avenue des Champs-Elysées (8th)
22, avenue de l'Opéra (1st)
91, rue de Passy (16th)
45, rue de Sèvres (6th)
Sports shoes, many Swiss imports, for men too.

CHARLES BLAIR-SCHERICK 374, rue du faubourg St.-Honoré (8th)
Stunning, original handbag line.

JEAN BRENIER 37, rue de Longchamp (16th)
Very inexpensive, latest style shoes.

CAREL 29, boulevard St.-Michel (6th)
9, avenue Mozart (16th)
122, avenue des Champs-Elysées (8th)
4, rue Tronchet (8th)
41, boulevard des Capucines (2nd)
Very much in vogue, rather avant-garde shoes.

CARVIL 22, rue Royale (8th)
135, boulevard St.-Germain (6th)
87, avenue Paul-Doumer (16th)
67, rue Pierre-Charron (6th)
Most up-to-the-minute styles, for men and children too.

CEDRIC 11, rue du faubourg St.-Honoré (8th)
Inexpensive, chic shoes.

CÉLINE 237, rue du faubourg St.-Honoré (8th)
3, avenue Victor-Hugo (16th)
47, avenue F.-D.-Roosevelt (8th)
58, rue de Rennes (6th)
Very elegant women's and children's shoes.

COLLON 2, rue Tronchet (8th)
Fabulous handbags and everything for the traveler.

CUIRAM 11, rue Meslay (3rd)
Lovely ultra-supple leather items, glove-fine lambskin.

DELICATA 126, boulevard St.-Germain (6th)
Avant-garde shoes and shoes for feet with a problem.

DEROCHE 67, avenue des Champs-Elysées (8th)
Very, very inexpensive, modern shoes.

CHRISTIAN DIOR 32, avenue Montaigne (8th)
15, rue François-1er (8th)
Deluxe shoe fashions. Exquisite jeweled and embroidered slippers. Can be made to measure too.

EILERS 5, boulevard des Capucines (2nd)
Good selection of Christian Dior and Jourdan shoes.

ELISABETH 81, rue St.-Dominique (7th)
23, rue d'Auteuil (16th)
Shoes in good taste, all styles, for all occasions.

ROGER FARE 22, rue d'Aguesseau (8th)
31, rue Tronchet (8th)
Glove maker to kings and queens.

FLASH 115, boulevard St.-Germain (6th)
Comfortable, exclusive models for men and women. Designed by the two owners, made in Italy.

DENISE FRANCELLE 244, rue de Rivoli (1st)
Tiny shop for belts, gloves, and scarves.

GALERIE DU CUIR 17, avenue Victor-Hugo (16th)
Handbags.

GANT PERRIN 22, rue Royale (8th)
Glove specialists, the very best quality.

GUCCI 350, rue St.-Honoré (8th)
Famous Italian leather goods.

GUIBERT 37, avenue de l'Opéra (2nd)
Gloves.

HERMÈS 24, rue du faubourg St.-Honoré (8th)
Only "the best," stunning accessories, gloves, belts, bags, scarves.
The quality justifies the price.

INNOVATION 104, avenue des Champs-Elysées (8th)
Bags and suitcases.

JOCELYN 134, boulevard St.-Germain (6th)
Boot maker, fancy leather goods.

CHARLES JOURDAN 5, boulevard de la Madeleine (8th)
12 and 54, rue du faubourg St.-Honoré (8th)
86, avenue des Champs-Elysées (8th)
High-fashion shoes always very much *en vogue*.

KORANIAN 19, rue Vignon (8th)
Made-to-measure shoes from $12 to $45.

LANCEL 8, place de l'Opéra (2nd)
Handbags and suitcases.

LEDERER 49, rue Cambon (1st)
Excellent copies of those Hermès bags, plus lovely designs of
their own.

MÉNESTRIER 33, rue de Navarin (9th)
For those big leather pouches all the models carry.

MILLNER 235, rue St.-Honoré (1st)
Shoes, handbags.

MORABITO 1, place Vendôme (1st)
Very deluxe handbags at luxury prices.

NEW DURER 36, boulevard St.-Michel (6th)
Excellent young boutique for ladies' and men's shoes.

CHRISTIAN PAUVERT 13, rue de Tournon (6th)
Espadrilles and embroidered shoes, summery styles from the
Midi.

JEAN PAX 8, rue Duphot (1st/8th)
Exclusive designs, hand-sewn bags, accessories.

PEAU DE PORC 67, rue du faubourg St.-Honoré (8th)
2 bis, rue Caumartin (9th)
240 bis, boulevard St.-Germain (7th)
Excellent pigskin items.

PHÈDRE 55, rue de Passy (16th)
Low-priced handbags.

POL 11 bis, avenue Victor-Hugo (16th)
Dior and Jourdan shoes.

ROGER VIVIER 24, rue François-1er (8th)
11, rue du faubourg St.-Honoré (8th)
Each season France's Dior of shoes sets world styles. Prices $25
and up. Will also make to measure for both men and women.

VUITTON 78 bis, avenue Marceau (8th)
Home of the sumptuous, famous, status-symbol luggage identified by yellow V's printed on brown. Also a good selection of
gifts, modest-to-expensive gadgets, toys, and games.

FOR HIM

ARNY   14, rue de Sèvres (6th)
Very British shoes, raincoats, and sweaters, also French and Italian styles.

CARDIFF   119, boulevard St.-Germain (6th)
Young styles, excellent shirts.

PIERRE CARDIN   118, rue du faubourg St.-Honoré (8th)
The name in men's clothing today. Cardin has revolutionized nearly every category of the male wardrobe. Now as famous for men as for women. Rather extreme, but elegant styles and very original ties.

CARNABY   99, rue de Longchamp (16th)
London-type fashions, mostly British-made. Good sportswear, shirts, and ties plus small, excellent tailoring shop with natty cuts, superb materials, and beautiful workmanship at low prices.

CERRUTI 1881   3, place de la Madeleine (8th)
Three floors of the most up-to-the-minute men's accessories, suits (ready-to-wear, $150–$225; made-to-order, $360) elegantly cut and exquisitely made.

CHEZ JULES   120, boulevard Montparnasse (14th)
Top men's tailor.

LES CRAVATES   8, rue Boudreau (9th)
Select your own material and in 48 hours you'll have a lovely made-to-order tie for $3 (a $10 value in New York City).

CHRISTIAN DIOR   30, avenue Montaigne (8th)
Men's boutique carries excellent sweaters, ties, hats, exquisite shirts, dressing gowns, leather goods.

EDDY   Lido Arcades, 76–78, avenue des Champs-Elysées (8th)
All good quality, Italian, English, French wools, shirts, and ties.

ELYSÉES SOIERIES   65, avenue des Champs-Elysées (8th)
One of the best for shirts and ties, ready to wear.

PIERRE FAIVRET   165, rue St.-Honoré (1st)
Most young and some not-so-young actors and celebrities dress here. Personalized service, wide range of articles, extraordinary fabrics, colors, and superb quality.

GIVENCHY GENTLEMAN   3, avenue George-V (8th)
Tiny modern boutique on the ground floor, almost everything is ready to wear.

DORIAN GUY   36, avenue George-V (8th)
One of the best ready-to-wear men's shops, very elegant.

HARVARD   120, rue de la Pompe (16th)
American styles, cut in Milan, finished in Paris. Excellent sportswear and shirts.

LANVIN 2   Corner of Rue Cambon and Rue de Rivoli (1st)
Warm and modern boutique with a bar and fireplace, plus everything for the fashionable male.

TED LAPIDUS   6, place Victor-Hugo (16th)
29, rue Marbeuf (8th)
37, avenue Pierre-1er-de-Serbie (16th)
Place St.-Germain (6th)

Elegant, inventive, and amusing men's fashions. Excellent cut and quality. Sportswear and shirts.

GUY LAROCHE 29, avenue Montaigne (8th)

In addition to usual accessories and clothes in men's boutique, also carries good-looking fur coats now so much in style.

NICOLL 29, rue Tronchet (8th/9th)

The most British, traditional-style men's shop in Paris.

POPARD 48, rue du Bac (7th)

Next-door to women's boutique. Very smart.

RACING STAND 9, rue Gustave-Courbet (16th)

Accessories, gadgets, car-minded fashions. Owned by ex-racing driver Claude Ballotte and his wife. Sleek leather goods, special luggage to fit every type of car.

RENOMA / WHITE HOUSE 129 bis, rue de la Pompe (16th)

Mecca for the chic young man who dares color and audacious articles. Mod, anticipates world fashion trends, snappy men's suits to order.

ROIENA 46, avenue Victor-Hugo (16th)
37, rue Marbeuf (8th)

Luxurious collection of shoes and boots.

SAINT GERMAIN DES PRÉS 37, rue du Four (6th)

Young styles, sometimes avant-garde, Jr. Cardin.

VICTOIRE 3, place des Victoires (2nd)

Men's branch of the nearby women's shop. Sophisticated sportswear to please the modern male.

WESTON 114, avenue des Champs-Elysées (8th)

Town and sport shoes. Young Parisians seem to adore shoes by Weston.

WIWAS 15, rue Gustave-Courbet (16th)

Offbeat place for avant-garde shoes and boots.

FOR CHILDREN

Children's wear departments of large department stores are a good place to find reasonably-priced clothes of the kind Parisian children wear.

AU NAIN BLEU 406–410, rue du faubourg St.-Honoré (8th)

Paris's oldest toy store. Celebrity customers from all over the world and a stock to fit.

BABY DIOR 28, avenue Montaigne (8th)

The name says everything. Ready-to-wear for children up to 4; baby gifts.

BABY TRAIN 9, rue du Petit-Pont (5th)

Fantastic miniature train store, bulk of whose customers, needless to say, are adults.

BELLINA 7, rue du faubourg St.-Honoré (8th)

Top luxury togs for kiddies.

CÉLINE   3, avenue Victor-Hugo (16th)
Shoes for boys and girls.
LE CHAPERON BLEU   14 bis, avenue Hoche (8th)
Superb continental toys.
LA CHATELAINE   170, avenue Victor-Hugo (16th)
The kind of togs visiting royalty buys to take home.
FARANDOLE   48, avenue Victor-Hugo (16th)
Toys, for young and old alike.
JONES   39, avenue Victor-Hugo (16th)
Extraordinary collection of clothes for boys and girls from infant to 18.
CLAUDE LABARRE   22, rue Dauphine (6th)
Everything but dolls. Toys, books, games, a child's dreamland.

JEWELRY

ALTAMIRA   29, rue des Sts.-Pères (6th)
Modern jewelry, hand-painted scarves. One of the tiniest shops in Paris.
JANE BEAUCAIRE   29, rue Marbeuf (8th)
Jewelry the couturiers used in their last collections at half-price.
BERNARD   34, avenue des Gobelins (13th)
Can copy any jewelry. Call for an appointment.
BIJOUX ANCIENS   16, boulevard Raspail (7th)
Extremely large choice, only good quality, reasonably priced antique jewelry.
CASTY   3, rue de Castiglione (1st)
Specializes in pearls, turquoise, coral, semi-precious stones, costume jewelry in the style of Chanel; fantastic choice.
LE COUSOIR   31, avenue Matignon (8th)
$30 for a copy of a Van Cleef bracelet. "Junk jewelry" that looks real.
DAUPHINE DIX   10, rue Dauphine (6th)
One-of-a-kind jewelry, belts, specially made ornaments to go with a special dress or gown. Dresses with built-in jewelry.
REINE FLEURMAY   204, rue de Rivoli (1st)
180, boulevard St.-Germain (6th)
Costume jewelry created by couture designers plus just-for-fun little bangles.
JACQUES GAUTIER   30, rue Jacob (6th)
Costume jewelry, creative wonders with glass, semi-precious stones, and enamel. Medium prices, from $18.
RAYMOND GILLET   19, rue d'Arcole (near Notre Dame) (4th)
Jewels at rock-bottom prices, antique wedding bands.
NIORT   420, rue St.-Honoré (1st)
Cabochon glass in a thousand colors. Clips, bracelets, rings are popular summer jewelry.
OBREY-NOVA   13, rue Tronchet (8th/9th)
Where the big watches began. Gold mine of solid fashion

watches, newest and best designs. Average price $60. Nova specializes in mini-rings, necklaces, and bracelets to match your watch.

AU VIEUX CADRAN 59, rue Bonaparte (6th)

Old jewelry, marvelous collection of watches dating from the Renaissance with working original movements.

PERFUMES AND GIFTS

JACQUES ANQUETIL 258, boulevard St.-Germain (7th)

Enamels, fabrics, jewelry, dolls.

FAUCHON 24–28, place de la Madeleine (8th)

Gourmet foods, candy, excellent perfume selection.

FREDDY 10, rue Auber (9th)

Well known by Americans for perfumes, gloves, bags, ties, scarves, umbrellas, dolls at very good prices.

LAFAYETTE GIFT SHOP 11, rue Scribe (9th)

In the basement of American Express. Low prices and big discounts on perfumes, scarves, jewelry, gloves, ties, leather goods, most everything your home drugstore has and then some.

LIZ 14, rue St.-Roch (1st)

194, rue de Rivoli (1st)

One of the best for perfumes, gloves, bags, ties, scarves, dolls, beauty products, unusual gifts. Simply call RIC.27.86 and a chauffeur-driven car will come to fetch you and take you back home if you so desire. For groups, 2 cars with 24 places are also available.

LUBIN 11, rue Royale (8th)

Elegant gifts, handmade jewelry, scarves, lingerie, lovely scented carriers, antique bottles, and boxes.

MADISON SHOP 57, avenue F.-D.-Roosevelt (8th) Tel: 359. 72.63

A wide variety of perfumes, cosmetics, scarves, bags, gifts, belts, and ties. If you spend 400F there you receive from 20% to 35% off. They give excellent counseling on perfumes and cosmetics. In fact, they have a special skin analyst who will give you the black light treatment, showing up every impurity and imperfection, and she will then counsel you properly on treatment. Call for an appointment.

MAXANDRE 42, rue du faubourg St.-Honoré (8th)

Large choice of Christian Dior gloves. Balenciaga scarves and stockings in fashion.

RIGAUD 41, rue François-1er (8th)

Original gifts by the well-known perfumer.

SWELLY 17, place Vendôme (1st)

Perfumes, gloves, evening bags.

ANTIQUES

AU 14, RUE DE L'UNIVERSITÉ   14, rue de l'Université (7th)
Most items have been chosen by a young American decorator, Dick Dumas; 18th-century furniture and a million amusing decorative *objets d'art* you'd love to have *chez vous.*

LA BROCANTERIE   26, boulevard St.-Germain (5th)
Very pleasant shop crammed with the unusual. Need a 17th-century dog collar? M. Moineau has a whole collection.

CAILLAT   24, rue du faubourg St.-Antoine (12th)
Five floors of furniture. Honestly run and fair prices.

LA DÉMARQUE   Rue St.-Placide (6th)
Sportswear and a wide variety of shetland sweaters for 45F.

GÉRONDEAU   33, rue Bonaparte (6th)
Unbelievable assortment of things, some very valuable, some just for fun. The owner, "Tonton," is most amusing and it's worth a visit just to chat with him.

LE GRAND DÉPÔT   21, rue Drouot (9th)
Exotic things from India, Kashmir, Mexico, and other ports of call from 3F to 30,000F.

HÔTEL DROUOT   6, rue Rossini (9th)
Huge auction house with good buys. Daily inspection 10–11 A.M. and all day Saturday. Sales take place Monday through Friday from 2 to 6 P.M. Closed August.

MANSART ART ET CURIOSITÉS   5, rue Mansart (9th)
Fabulous collections of pill-, cigarette-, stamp-, and other boxes from all periods; animals, antique jewelry, and other items. Great for gifts, huge choice. Presentation is fascinatingly done by collections. Something for every taste.

MARCHÉ AUX PUCES (FLEA MARKET)   Porte de Clignancourt (18th)
Here are 3,000 antique and secondhand dealers located in 5 markets, each with its own specialty. You'll find antiques at Biron, Vernaison, and Paul Bert, old clothes at Malik, and junk at Jules Valles. Open Saturday, Sunday, and Monday, 9 A.M. to 6 P.M. Bargaining is a must. Go early with the dealers and experts or late near closing time on Monday.

LA MAROTTE   16, rue Birague (4th)
A quaint little shop near the Place des Vosges said to be haunted by the Three Musketeers.

LES MUSES DE L'EUROPE   64, rue de Seine (6th)
Right out of the 18th century with its collection of bric-a-brac, matched accessories and ensembles, velour flowers, antique hat pins, rose satin lingerie, tunics.

LE PASSÉ COMPOSÉ   1, rue du Bourbon-le-Château (6th)
Old toys and assorted goodies like an antique French slot machine.

VILLAGE SUISSE   Corner Avenue de Suffren and Avenue de la Motte-Picquet (15th) near the Eiffel Tower
Smaller flea market with modern malls in a modern apartment

complex. Rather high prices but some good bargains and usually high quality. Very modern shops. Open Thursday through Monday, 10:30 A.M. to 7 P.M.

CRYSTAL / PORCELAIN / CERAMICS

BACCARAT   30 bis, rue du Paradis (10th)
Crystal famous the world over.
CHRISTOFLE   12, rue Royale (8th)
   31, boulevard des Italiens (2nd)
   95, rue de Passy (16th)
Silver, the most famous although not necessarily the most expensive.
LE GRAND DÉPÔT   21, rue Drouot (9th)
All the best in porcelain and china for over a century.
LALIQUE   11, rue Royale (8th)
Beautiful crystal.
LE PETIT DÉPÔT   21, rue de Provence (9th)
Low, low prices. Porcelain, china, fine crystal, casseroles. All seconds but it would take an expert to tell.
TALMA   10, rue des Sts.-Pères (7th)
Specializes in white porcelain of all kinds, including limoges. Good choice of reasonable gifts.
VERRERIE DES HALLES   15, rue du Louvre (1st/2nd)
Excellent for things like soup tureens and the temple for bistro-style glasses.

KNICKKNACKS / GADGETS / GIFTS

BISTRO BAZAAR   2, rue Récamier (7th)
Knickknacks and a place for snacks.
BOUTIQUE LE DRUGSTORE   133, avenue des Champs-Elysées (8th)
   149, boulevard St.-Germain (6th)
   6, boulevard des Capucines (9th)
Drugs, cigarettes, newspapers, perfumes, gadgets, clothes, jewelry, food. Not exactly what you'd expect a drugstore to be.
BOUTIQUE DU PALAIS-ROYAL   9, rue de Beaujolais (1st)
Marvelously situated in the Palais-Royal gardens. A million amusing items. French, Italian, and Scandinavian handicrafts, provincial artisans.
CHARADE   Rue de Longchamp (16th)
Gadgets from glass bubbles; mobiles; paper flowers.
ÉTAGÈRE   37, rue de Seine (6th)
Tiny shop with circa 1880s inexpensive curiosities.
EXPRESSIONS   31, rue de l'Université (7th)
A gold mine of little gifts from around the world, especially folkloric dolls. Run by a charming American.
LA FACTORERIE   5, boulevard Malesherbes (8th)
Jungle décor, with furnishings, animals, and furs from every-

where, though mainly Africa, Canada, the Orient. Le Zoo sells monkeys and small leopards.

NICOLE FROMENTIN   17, rue St.-Florentin (8th)
Handmade silk flowers, like a dream.

LA GADGETIÈRE   1, rue Georges-Bizet (16th)
Filled with all kinds of practical and absurd gadgets.

GALERIE PITTORESQUE   133, boulevard Raspail (6th)
Antique jewelry, lovely toys, and many curiosities at very reasonable prices.

MAURICE GENIS   1, rue St.-Benoît (6th)
Amusing, well-chosen little things, perfect for an original gift. Reasonable prices.

KITCHEN BAZAAR   11, rue d'Alençon (15th)
A must in the country of good cooking. Modern, gay, practical kitchen equipment from the world over.

JANIE PRADIER   78, rue de Seine (6th)
31, rue des Poissonniers, Neuilly-sur-Seine
Filled with new ideas and lovely purely fun, decorative objects. One of the most popular and best known in Paris. You'll be sure to find just that amusing little thing you've been looking for.

RAM DAM   130, rue de la Pompe (16th)
Best-known gadget center in Paris.

STRITCH   5, rue d'Arcole (4th)
Small gift shop for jewelry matchboxes, practical things, sophisticated gadgets, odds 'n' ends. One of the best for selection and quality.

TROUSSELIER   73, boulevard Haussmann (8th)
Handmade, fabric, artificial flowers.

MISCELLANEOUS MARKETS

FOIRE À LA FERRAILLE   Boulevard Richard-Lenoir (11th)
Twice-a-year large flea market with wrought-iron specialties. Spring: the week before Holy Week; fall: first and second weeks in October.

MARCHÉ AUX FLEURS (FLOWER MARKET)   Place Louis-Lépine and Quai de Corse (4th)
Open Monday through Saturday 8 A.M. to 7 P.M.; closed Sunday, holidays.

MARCHÉ DE LA FRIPERIE   Carreau du Temple (4th)
Open all week except Monday, 8 A.M. to 7:30 P.M.; Sunday 8 A.M. to 1 P.M.

MARCHÉ AUX TIMBRES (STAMP MARKET)   Corner avenues Marigny and Gabriel, Jardins des Champs-Elysées (8th)
Open Thursdays, Saturdays, and Sundays from 8 A.M. to 7 P.M., and holiday afternoons.

LES PUCES DES CHAMPS-ÉLYSÉES   48, rue de Ponthieu (8th)
Antiques, bibelots, secondhand items, 11 A.M. to 8 P.M. every day but Monday.

CLEANERS

ARC-EN-CIEL   146, rue de Rivoli (1st)   Tel: 488.18.52   Métro stop: Louvre
ANN-MARIE COMMARIN   11, rue de Longchamp (16th)   Tel: 727.11.62   Métro stop: Iéna
ÉLYSÉES PRESSING   6, rue de Ponthieu (8th)   Tel: 359.18.17   Métro stop: George-V
PRESSING DE LA MADELEINE   12, rue de l'Arcade   Tel: 265. 30.11   Métro stop: Madeleine–St.-Lazare
TEINTURERIE MARBEUF, ANAURY   14, rue Marbeuf (8th)   Tel: 359.70.39   Métro stop: Alma-Marceau

REPAIR SERVICES

Shoe repair is to be found in little shops along the Champs-Elysées and in most department stores. There is generally a "while you wait" service.

JIMMY   7, rue Godot-de-Mauroy (9th)   Tel: 073.01.08   Métro stop: Madeleine

For all other leather goods, handbags, luggage, etc., try:

MME. FLEURY   37, rue Laugier (17th)   Métro stop: Ternes
This is an inexpensive shop and very good.
JACOMO   2, rue Treilhard (8th)   Tel: 522.74.50   Métro stop: Villiers–Ch. Vincennes
ROMAN   213, rue St.-Honoré   Tel: 073.36.73   Métro stop: Tuileries
A very expensive shop for your better things.
F. BRUNET   99, rue Aristide Briand   Tel: 270.07.39   Métro stop: Chambre des Députés
They specialize in Samsonite luggage.

If none of these shops is convenient to you, feel free to call and ask if they can suggest one closer to your location; or ask the concierge at your hotel.

Part III
The Château Country

14
Welcome to the Château Country

The kings of France were known for their love of beauty and elegance. Nowhere is this more evident than in the region of the Val de Loire, south of Paris.

Here the Loire River seductively snakes its way through the French countryside, dispensing the even mildness of an oceanic climate deep into the heart of the country and bringing with it all of the elements that have created what is known as the "Garden of France."

With such beauty to behold in every direction, and with such a perfect climate, it is no wonder that the French monarchs chose this area for their royal residences. In the Middle Ages these residences were built as fortresses, but eventually, as security and peace were established, they evolved into the beautiful châteaux we see standing so regally today.

A visit to France is incomplete without a visit to this beautiful region. Unfortunately, most tourists spend only a couple of days here, which is truly a pity. A week to ten days is so much more worthwhile.

A unique experience is not only to visit, but actually to spend a night or a few days in one of the châteaux whose owners have opened their homes to overnight guests. Taxes and upkeep being as astronomical as they are, many aristocratic families have turned to this means of maintaining these beautiful and historic monuments. A list of châteaux with overnight accommodations will be given later in this chapter.

The château country covers a large area; however, the most important châteaux are between Angers and Orléans. Orléans is famous for the siege that was waged by Joan of Arc, though few monuments to her remain as most of the city was destroyed during the last war.

Though a lot of people use Tours as their base while visiting the château country, I happen to prefer Angers and will use that here. You will find listings here to regular hotels in Angers only, in addition to listings for the various châteaux you can stay in, as I've mentioned.

HOW TO GET THERE

There is a train from Paris, leaving from the Gare Montparnasse, that takes about 2½ hours.

There are also various tours you can take if time is a problem:

PARIS VISION ONE-DAY TOUR

May 15—November 16	Tuesday
May 3—October 4	Thursday
May 15—October 9	Friday
April 15—November 11	Sunday

This is a full-day tour, lunch and dinner included.

ITINERARY Departure at 7:30 A.M. from the Rue de Rivoli, to Chartres by the Western Motorway. Visit the Chartres Cathedral. Then Châteaudun, Vendôme, Tours (visit and lunch), Chenonceaux (visit), Amboise (visit), Chaumont (visit), Blois (visit), Chambord (dinner and sound-and-light show). Return to Paris late at night.

This is, of course, a very tiring tour, though you do see some of the highlights. I find when you're that tired you can't enjoy them as much. But if it is the only chance you'll have to see at least part of this beautiful valley, take it.

PARIS VISION TWO-DAY TOUR

Takes in all the major châteaux, including all meals and overnight accommodations, for 325F ($81.25), which is very worthwhile.

CITYRAMA TOUR

Cityrama offers a two-day tour from April through the middle of November. Price: 295F ($73.75), all meals and hotel accommodations included. The tour visits Chartres, Tours, Langeais, Azay-le-Rideau, Vouvray, and the sound-and-light spectacle at Chambord. For singles there is an additional charge of 55F ($13.75).

CALENDAR OF EVENTS

Spring/Summer

SOLESMES Easter Festival in the Abbey Easter
ROYAN Festival of contemporary art April

ORLÉANS   Festival of Jeanne d'Arc   May
MONT ST.-MICHEL   Festival of St. Michel   May
ANGERS   Festival of Dramatic Art   June
NANTES   Artistic Games   June
CHARTRES   Musical Saturdays   June
LE MANS   The 24-hour Le Mans Motor Car Race   June
MOHANT   Romantic Festival   June
TOURS   Musical Festival   End of June or beginning of July
LA BOUILLE   Festival of Dramatic Art   July
MONT ST.-MICHEL   Great Pilgrimage   July
SAINTS' FESTIVAL OF DRAMATIC ART   August
CONFOLENS   International Folkloric Festival   August
CHARTRES   Pilgrimage, Louis XVIII vows   August

Fall/Winter

TOURS   West European Agricultural Fair   September
RENNES   Variety Festival   November
NANTES   Wine Festival   November
SOLESMES, ST.-BENOÎT-SUR-LOIRE   Midnight masses   December

There are many sound-and-light shows in the Val de Loire which, while not officially festivals, certainly qualify as such. "Le Carrousel du Cadre Noir," at Saumur, given by the famous French Cavalry School, should also be seen.

HOTELS IN ANGERS

Four Star

HÔTEL CONCORDE 18, boulevard du Maréchal-Foch A-B-C
Tel: 88.63.19
Modern hotel right in the central area and very convenient to
all shops. All rooms have baths. Single: 71F ($17.75); double:
90F ($22.50); breakfast: 10F ($2.50).

Three Star

HÔTEL D'ANJOU 1, boulevard du Maréchal-Foch A-B-C Tel:
88.24.82
Facing the main square. Newly renovated. Single: 29F to 69F
($7.25 to $17.25); double: 33F to 79F ($8.25 to $19.75).

Two Star

LA BOULE D'OR 27, boulevard Carnot A-B-C Tel: 88.68.26
Near the city center. Single: 21F to 42F ($5.25 to $10.50);
double: 42F to 63F ($10.50 to $15.75). This remarkable small
hotel has been completely renovated in a rather elegant manner.
HÔTEL DE CHAMPAGNE 17, place Sémard A-B-C Tel: 88.
78.06
Single: 40F to 47F ($10 to $11.75); double: 32F to 50F ($8 to
$12.50). About two blocks from the railroad station.
HÔTEL DE LA CROIX DE GUERRE 23, rue de Châteaugontier
A-B-C Tel: 88.66.59
Single: 30F to 35F ($7.50 to $8.75); double: 38F to 55F ($9.50
to $13.75). This is a rather new hotel on the same square as the
Hôtel de France, near the railroad station.
HÔTEL DE FRANCE 8, place de la Gare A-B-C Tel: 88.49.42
Single: 30F to 60F ($7.50 to $15); double: 44F to 75F ($11 to
$18.75). This recently renovated hotel is just opposite the rail-
road station and the tourist office. It is one of my favorites,
primarily because the manager, M. Buyer, just has to be one of
the kindest, most helpful men in all of France. Coming from an
old, established family of the area, he knows everything and
everyone and can be extremely helpful. He is also president of
the Hotel Associates.

Where to Stay   181

HÔTEL JEANNE DE LAVAL   34, boulevard du Roi-René   A-B-C
Tel: 88.51.95
Single: 27F to 50F ($6.75 to $12.50); double: 32F to 56F ($8
to $14).
HÔTEL D'ORLÉANS   20, rue Denis-Papin   A-B-C   Tel: 88.70.04
Single: 32F to 48F ($8 to $12); double: 37F to 78F ($9.25 to
$19.50). Near the railroad station and the tourist office.
HÔTEL DU PROGRÈS   26, rue Denis-Papin   A-B-C   Tel: 88.
10.14
Single 27F to 57F ($6.75 to $14.25); double; 32F to 68F ($8 to
$17). Very nice, modern hotel. Comfortable, warm, kind service.

CHÂTEAUX IN THE VAL DE LOIRE

There can be no greater thrill for the tourist than to actually spend a night, or several if possible, in any of the beautiful
châteaux in this area. It will give you an experience never to
be forgotten.

These listed are just a few of the châteaux in the Loire
Valley that take paying guests. However, there are châteaux
scattered all over France; in fact, all over Europe. Should you
be traveling elsewhere, and enjoy the idea of staying at a
château, you can get listings with photos from the following
two addresses:

RELAIS DE CAMPAGNE   1, passage de la Visitation, Paris,
75007   Tel: 222.71.10
SECRÉTARIAT-GÉNÉRAL   160, rue de Belleville, Paris, 75020
Tel: 636.11.11
CHÂTEAU D'ARTIGNY   Montbazon, 37250, Indre-et-Loire   Tel:
(47) 56.21.77
An absolutely sumptuous castle offering outstanding cuisine and
royal accommodations. The manager, M. Alain Radier, certainly
does make you feel at home. During the off-season they have
musical weekends, and all year long you can take advantage of
the large park and beautiful French gardens surrounding the
château. There is a heated pool and tennis, with riding and
golfing nearby. Open from January 20 to November 20. Rooms
from 81F to 219F ($20.25 to $54.75), including service. There
is an outstanding restaurant in the château. The *menus* run from
45F to 83F ($11.25 to $20.75) plus an *à la carte* menu.
DOMAINE DES HAUTS DE LOIRE   Chaumont-sur-Loire, 41150,
Onzain, Loir-et-Cher   Tel: (39) 79.88.04
Owned by M. and Mme. Bonnigal, this is a large and very lovely
château close to Tours. It is closed from December 1 to February
20. The rates are the same whether single or double, and all
prices include service and taxes but not breakfast. Double room

with bath: 120F to 180F ($30 to $45). Breakfast is 10F ($2.50). Price of room including breakfast and dinner is 220F to 300F ($55 to $75). They have a private swimming pool on the grounds and tennis courts less than a mile away.

CHÂTEAU DE MARÇAY   Marçay, Chinon, 37500, Indre-et-Loire
Tel: (47) 93.03.47
Open all year round and managed by M. and Mme. Gagnat. This is a historical castle situated very close to Chinon and has its own private little park and terrace. Rooms from 70F to 130F ($17.50 to $32.50). The restaurant offers good food from 30F to 40F ($7.50 to $10).

LE PRIEURÉ   Chênehutte-les-Tuffeaux, Gennes, 49350, Maine-et-Loire   Tel: (41) 51.01.01
Five miles west of Saumur on the right bank of the Loire River, this is a little Renaissance manor with an incomparable view of the Loire. There is a heated pool and mini-golf, with standard golf and trap-shooting nearby. Open from March 1 to January 5. Some of the rooms are in the pavillion with a private garden and terrace, and the rates run from 46F to 150F ($11.50 to $37.50). They have a good restaurant with *menus* from 35F to 69F ($8.75 to $17.25), plus *à la carte*.

CHÂTEAU DE TEILDRAS   Cheffes-sur-Sarthe, Châteauneuf-sur-Sarthe, 49330, Maine-et-Loire   Tel: 8 Cheffres
This is one of my favorites, not only because of the charming hosts, M. and Mme. de Bernard and their lovely 20-year-old daughter, Yolaine, but because the château itself is absolutely exquisite. All the rooms have just been decorated this year by the de Bernards themselves, one room more beautiful than the next. The bathrooms are huge, all tiled, and each has a double marble basin. You will surely feel like a queen staying in any of these lovely chambers. The whole atmosphere of the château is one of elegant French living. There is no lobby or hotel desk. You have your own key and simply make use of the château as if it were your very own. The dining room is small and intimate, and the food fit for any gourmet. There is a huge stretch of woodland surrounding the château which allows you to take relaxing walks and enjoy the countryside. If you wire your arrival time at either Anjou or Tours, the de Bernards will pick you up at the station.

DOMAINE DE LA TORTINIÈRE   Montbazon en Touraine, 37250, Indre-et-Loire   Tel: (47) 56.20.19
In the heart of the château country, this twin-towered beauty, surrounded by a beautiful park, was once the lodging of Napoleon III. South of Tours and ten miles from the Tours Airport, it is central to the most famous châteaux mentioned later on and an ideal choice from which to start your sightseeing. Room with bath: 100F to 140F ($25 to $35) plus 12F for breakfast ($3). For the room, breakfast, and dinner, the rate is 228F to 318F ($57 to $79.50). All rates include taxes and service. There is a private swimming pool, and it's just under a mile to the nearest tennis courts.

16
Wining and Dining

The Loire Valley is famous for its excellent wines and there are many places where they invite you to taste their products free of charge. As for food, naturally the Loire River spawns many excellent fish which are served as a main course in most restaurants. You can find excellent pike, shad, trout, and salmon here.

In the Loire Valley you will find mostly white wines. A good selection of dry white wine could be Quincy, Sancerre or Pouilly-sur-Loire, or Reuilly. If you prefer sweet wines, try the Saumur Coteaux de Layon or Vouvray. But if red wine is your preference, try Bourgueil or Chinon. One of America's favorites, Anjou Rosé, comes from this area.

RESTAURANTS

Expensive

LA CROIX DE GUERRE 23, rue de Châteaugontier Tel: 88. 66.59
Classic décor and very pleasant. Smiling personnel and good food. *À la carte* menu around 40F ($10). Three fixed-price menus: 18F, 26F, and 38F ($4.50, $6.50, and $9.50). Good selection of wines.

L'ENTR'ACTE 10, place de Ralliement Tel: 87.33.76
Rustic style with a very warm welcome. Excellent service, honest prices, and especially good food make this a popular place. Daily special at 40F ($10), and there is a tourist *menu* at 20F ($5). Closed Saturday.

LE LOGIS 17, rue St.-Laud Tel: 87.44.15
Very pleasant, with attractive décor and good, quiet service. Three fixed-price menus: 16F, 25F, and 45F ($4, $6.25, and $11.25).

PLANTAGENETS 8, place de la Gare Tel: 88.49.42
One of the most agreeable in Angers, located in the Hôtel de France. Very pleasant and comfortable, with good service and good food. Wines personally chosen by the manager, M. Buyer. *À la carte* about 40F ($10). There is a fixed-price menu at 20F ($5).

LE VERT D'EAU 9, boulevard Gaston-Dumesnil Tel: 88.42.74
A well-known restaurant with a very large selection of over 20
hors d'oeuvres, 14 fish dishes, 18 main courses, and 16 desserts,
plus several more from time to time. Fixed-price menu at 24F
($6) and 30F ($7.50). Closed Monday.

Moderate and Inexpensive

LE BARBÈQUE 9, boulevard Arago Tel: 88.56.11
Good, simple, rustic décor. This restaurant is owned by a very
gay, sympathetic couple, who do everything possible to make
you comfortable. Main dish about 10F to 20F ($2.50 to $5).
Closed Sunday.

CLUB 925 Rue d'Anjou Tel: 87.62.36
A lovely little dining room, serving simple but good food and
featuring good service. Fixed-price menu 13F, 18F, and 22F
($3.25, $4.50, and $5.50). Open until 2 A.M.

L'ENTRECOTE Avenue Joxé Tel: 88.76.99
An immense restaurant, well decorated, with good service and
remarkably good cuisine. Tourist menu from 12F ($3). Lunch
only. Closed on Sunday.

LA RÉGENCE 7, rue Cordelle Tel: 88.59.92
Regency-style dining room that makes you feel extremely comfortable and elegant. The food is not superb but it certainly is
good. *Menus* at 12F, 18F, and 23F ($3, $4.50, and $5.75).
Closed Monday.

17
Nighttime Entertainment

NIGHT CLUBS

KANDY PALMER'S   15, rue de la Roë   Tel: 88.59.69   A-B-C
This place might very well be in Paris. Beautifully done, very posh, smart, and sophisticated. A large bar, low tables, soft lights, and telephones on the tables for ordering. The food here is excellent. From about 50F ($12.50).

KING CLUB   38, rue St.-Laud   Tel: 87.48.98   A-B
Good place for young people. They have good records, but the music is a little too loud for my taste. Drinks from 12F ($3). Closed Monday.

ST.-GEORGES   Just out of Angers on the way to Nantes   A-B
Pleasant place, very soft lights, rustic wood décor. Younger set. Entrance fee 15F ($3.75).

18
Sightseeing

Angers itself has a few things to put on your agenda. Primarily the **Castle of Angers**, built by King Louis IX (Saint Louis). This is a huge feudal castle, boasting seventeen round towers and moats over three hundred feet deep. From the ramparts there is a fantastic view of the city and, if the weather is good, almost all the way to Tours. Here at the castle is kept the largest and oldest collection of tapestries in the world, including the famous *Tapestry of the Apocalypse* of the 14th century, 170 meters long.

The **Hôtel de Pincé** (a museum) is the work of a 16th-century Angevin architect, and contains an excellent collection of painted Greek vases and an important collection of Oriental art (ceramics, statuettes, and engravings). **The Hôpital St.-Jean**, another museum, was built by Henry II and is the oldest in France. Further examples of fine Angevin architecture can be seen in its refectory, chapel, cloisters, and storehouses. It also contains the famous contemporary tapestries *Hymn of the World* by Jean Lurçat.

The House of Adam is also worth a visit. A magnificent 15th-century half-timbered house with rich carvings, typical of this area many centuries ago.

Le Logis Barrault, the fine arts museum, is a remarkable piece of 15th-century architecture. Here, in its municipal library, are works of David d'Angers, primitive painters of the 14th and 15th centuries, plus a fine 18th-century collection.

It is also worthwhile just to wander around the quiet little streets of the city, especially in the district called "La Doutre," which contains houses dating from the 15th to 18th centuries, including several fine half-timbered houses, notably the **Apothecary** (1582).

THE CHÂTEAUX

Now let's begin our visits to the famous châteaux of the area. Most of the châteaux listed below are open from 9 to 12 and 2 to 6, closing for lunch in the summertime and a bit earlier in winter. However, to get the exact times at which a château can be visited, check with the tourist office in Angers.

Starting at the far end of the line with the most famous châteaux just west of Orléans, we will work our way back toward Angers. All the châteaux listed will be convenient for you to see without going much out of your way.

ILLUMINATIONS   Seeing these châteaux by daylight is a great experience in itself, but seeing them at night when they are illuminated is absolutely spectacular and really should be included in your itinerary if you have time. Blois, Chambord, Chenonceau, Amboise, and Azay-le-Rideau all offer a *son et lumière* (sound-and-light) spectacle in the evening. Check with the tourist office to see what time the shows begin. The average fee is 5F ($1.25).

BLOIS

A famous castle built at three different periods and with three separate wings: 1) the Louis XII wing, built of brick at the beginning of the 16th century, 2) the François I wing of the same century, influenced by the Italian Renaissance (note the beautiful spiral staircase), and 3) the Gaston d'Orléans wing of the 17th century, more classic in style. It was at Blois, in 1588, that one of the most gory murders in French history took place —when Henry III had the Duke de Guise dismembered and then burned in the huge fireplace you can still see in the castle today. It was here too that Louis XIII imprisoned his mother, Marie de Medici. In spite of her gross weight, she managed to swim the moat and escape. Rich in ancient history, there is also a bit of modern history attached to the château. When the Germans invaded the nearby city of Orléans in 1940, they ignited an enormous fire that threatened to engulf the château itself. In an effort to save this symbol of their heritage, the townspeople dynamited all the buildings surrounding the Château in order to prevent the flames from reaching it.

CHAMBORD

Chambord is just a few miles east of Blois and is the largest château in the entire Loire Valley. It is surrounded by almost 15,000 acres of forest, the same forest through which François I and his royal entourage once galloped on their hunts. Looking very much like a fortress, Chambord was nevertheless built in the Renaissance period. Today, uninhabited and almost completely without furnishings, it stands as a lonely sentry guarding the memory of days gone by.

CHEVERNY

A much smaller 17th-century château with a somewhat cold exterior but a truly magnificent classic décor inside. Unlike the others, this was not a royal residence, but was built instead by a wealthy family. It is still inhabited by their descendants, and the interior reflects the love and pride with which they have maintained their beautiful ancestral possessions.

VALENÇAY

This lovely château was purchased by Napoleon for his minister of foreign affairs, Talleyrand, in order to entertain other monarchs and heads of state in a very regal manner. Talleyrand was buried here in 1838, and the museum which you see today contains many mementos and personal possessions of this famous historical figure. It was here too that Ferdinand VII of Spain was imprisoned for six years. Still to be seen is the magnificent Empire furniture of that era.

CHAUMONT

A big fortress with magnificent, low, round towers, it is a bit foreboding. However, the inside is quite elegant; notice the staircase, faïence tiling, and antique furniture. This was the rather temporary abode of Diane de Poitiers, a mistress of Henry II, who was exiled to Chaumont by Henry's wife, Catherine de Medici, after his death. The château, now owned by the state, houses a beautiful collection of medallions, the works of Nini of Italy. There is even one with the likeness of our great Benjamin Franklin, who was a guest there.

AMBOISE

Amboise is the little town where Leonardo da Vinci lived and eventually died. The Château d'Amboise dominates the area. It was here that Charles VIII died of a brain concussion. It was also here, in 1560, that almost 2,000 Protestants were executed for their part in a plan to kidnap François II, then living at the château. The executions—hangings and decapitations—were carried out on the balcony of the château and were supposedly watched by François II and his queen. Only about one-third of this original 15th-and-16th-century fortress remains: the king's residence with its series of dormer windows; St. Hubert Chapel, which contains the remains of Leonardo da Vinci; and the two towers, one with its spiral ramp for horsemen. You simply must try to see the *son et lumière* (sound-and-light) spectacle at Amboise. It is said to be the very finest in the area and is most impressive. The spectacles take place only in the summer and there are two shows per evening, one at 9:45 P.M. and one at 10:30 P.M. Entrance 5F ($1.25).

CHENONCEAUX

An exquisite 16th-century castle furnished by Catherine de Medici, comprising a long two-floor gallery over the water. This huge, luxurious Renaissance building borders an extremely beautiful park, which is in flower all year long. The interior contains priceless furniture, tapestries, and paintings. Chenonceaux is perhaps best known for the famous women associated with its history. Starting with Catherine Briçonnet, who had the major hand in the construction of the château itself, there was Diane de Poitiers, who lived there until Catherine de Medici, the jealous wife of her lover King Henry II, unceremoniously dethroned her. Subsequently, the "White Queen," widow of Henry III, took up residence. In the 18th century, George Sand's grandmother, Madame Dupin, acquired the château, and that pretty much marked the end of its feminine dominance.

AZAY-LE-RIDEAU

Built on a small island on the Indre River, this beautiful Renaissance château is just the place to sit and relax after all your château-hopping. The gardens are filled with multicolored sculptured masterpieces, lovingly maintained. The interior contains beautiful furniture and tapestries. Built originally by Gilles Berthelot, the finance minister of François I, it was eventually wrested from him by François in later years.

CHINON

Chinon does not have a château such as those we have been visiting. All that remains there are the ruins and walls of a castle begun in the 9th century, fortified by the Plantagenets. This is the same castle where Joan of Arc experienced her first miracle, when she recognized King Charles VII in disguise as one of his entourage. The chief interest at Chinon is the ancient town itself, where Rabelais lived as a child. Wander through the little winding streets of half-timbered, slate-roofed houses, with their traditional protruding second stories. It's quite an adventure into history.

LANGEAIS

A medieval fortress, built in the 15th century and left totally intact. Considered one of the most impressive fortresses in the Loire, the interior is furnished entirely with Gothic furniture, tapestries, and mantelpieces. The wedding chamber where Charles VIII married Anne of Brittany in 1491 can still be visited today.

LOCHES

Forty kilometers south of Tours, Loches dominates one of the most beautiful spots in this area. It is an outstanding royal residence, built in the reign of Charles VII, and contains the tomb of Agnès Sorel, who was Charles's first official mistress and celebrated for her rare beauty. It also contains the oratory of Anne de Bretagne.

SAUMUR

The poet king, René II of Anjou, called Saumur "the Castle of Love" in one of his court romances. It is indeed a beautiful castle, built at the end of the 15th century as a country seat by King René's pleasure-loving ancestor, Louis I of Anjou, brother of Charles V, king of France. It was embellished with bell turrets, gilded weathercocks, and finely sculpted gable windows. The castle was built on the foundations of a fortress erected to enable the crown to reconquer Anjou, while St. Louis was still a minor. Only the layout and the round base of the towers of the old fortress were preserved by the builders of the castle. The Reformation brought about many changes. In 1590 Governor Duplessis-Mornay, the erudite friend of Henry IX and the founder of the Protestant Academy, had an Italian architect build the surrounding line of redoubts and bastions in order to fortify the site. These fortifications remind one strangely of those that the great Vauban was to build in France eighty years later. The castle was turned into a state penitentiary under the Empire, and later became a barracks and a military arsenal. Finally, in 1908, it was bought by the town of Saumur. The authorities, with government help, set about restoring and renovating the castle and installed in it the town's museums. Thanks to the way the remarkable collections of furniture, ceramics, and works of art belonging to Count Charles Lair have been installed there, it seems almost inhabited once again. Recently too, medieval tapestries, depicting secular subjects, which were originally in the Church of Notre-Dame-de-Nantilly, have been moved to the castle and make a visit to it more interesting. The town of Saumur itself is the seat of a world-famous cavalry school founded in 1768, and the home of the well-known riding group, Le Cadre Noir. Not surprisingly, the authorities have also installed in the old castle of the Dukes of Anjou a cavalry museum, retracing the history of the horse and riding through the ages.

MONTGEOFFROY

This is one château in Anjou where nothing has changed since the Maréchal de Contades, Governor of Strasbourg, had it built, decorated, and furnished in 1772. A Parisian architect, Nicholas Barre, built it in three years around the chapel and two fine towers of a former château. The result was one of the master-pieces of French 18th-century architecture—a white façade softened by a slate roof with pink brick chimneys. If the choice of the architect was a happy one, so was the choice of decora-tors and cabinetmakers. When, at the end of the 19th century, one of the Maréchal's descendants decided that the long-aban-doned building should once again be lived in, he found every-thing exactly as it was in 1775 when the Maréchal de Contades took possession of it. Nothing had been changed, nothing mod-ernized. Since then, members of the Contades family have al-ways lived at Montgeoffroy in this perfectly decorated house of the *ancien régime,* miraculously intact throughout the centuries.

BRISSAC

The name of the Cossé family recurs in the history of France throughout the centuries, and their château at Brissac bears witness to their durability. Each generation seems to have added to its opulence—tapestries, paintings, fine furniture, magnificent ceilings with decorated beams—and to its variety of architec-tural styles from the 15th to the 17th centuries. The Aubance River flows at its foot through a large park. Today this park is often the scene of various hunts, organized by the young, handsome Marquis de Brissac and his beautiful wife (who still rides sidesaddle), who invite all the nearby aristocrats to par-ticipate.

The château can be visited and all the rooms you will see are still used by the marquis for his guests. There is a huge dining room with a balcony at one end for musicians, installed by the marquis's grandmother, a beautiful *grand salon* and also a hall of armor. The descendants of the original Cossé still live at Brissac, which has been in the family since 1502.

PLESSIS BOURRÉ

Built of white *tuffeau* rock, the château is mirrored in the immense moat which surrounds it and has come down to us practically intact from the end of the 15th century. It was built by Jean Bourré, who is also responsible for the building of Langeais. Constructed according to logical and functional plans, it is fortified but comfortable, with windows opening out on the surrounding countryside. The living quarters and chapel contain a large selection of furniture and works of art. The ceiling of the guardroom is decorated with humorous and ribald scenes, illustrating the jovial, common-sense proverbs and fables.

LE PLESSIS-MACE

Set among lush meadows and old trees, this is perhaps the most accessible of all the châteaux of Anjou. More than a château, it is an elegant manor house, built of white *tuffeau* and slate, dating from the reign of Louis XI. Joachim du Bellay here composed his poems celebrating *la douceur angevine*. The chapel contains fine Renaissance paneling and the art collection of the last owner may be seen in the château itself. Buried under a thicket of undergrowth are the vestiges of the original château.

SERRANT

West of Anjou, this large, severely symmetrical building, set in a large park and surrounded by a moat, is the last of the châteaux in Anjou. The plans were drawn up by Philibert Delorme, architect of the châteaux of the Tuileries and Fontainebleau. A chapel, to house the mausoleum of Voubrun, was later added by Hardouin-Mansart, who also designed the chapel and the Palace of Versailles. The château, which once belonged to the Irish family, Walsh, is now the property of the La Trémoille family and houses a large library and collection of furniture and works of art in the sumptuous public rooms. The château itself is a rather harmonious building, although its construction covered a period from the 16th to the 18th centuries. The richly decorated apartments, furniture, and tapestry, and very beautiful sculptures, make this a very worthwhile visit.

WINE-TASTING

It is possible to taste wine at many places along your way through the Loire Valley. However, if you want not only to taste one of the world's finest wines, but also meet a most interesting and charming woman and inspect the vineyards as well, then by all means go to Roche aux Moines, where the famous Coulée de Serrant wine is grown. Ask at your hotel or the tourist office in Angers for directions on how to get there.

The history of the vineyards is interesting. They were planted in the 12th century by the monks of St.-Nicholas-d'Angers, which is how the name Roche aux Moines (Rock of the Monks) originated. The proprietress of the vineyard, Mme. Joly, is extremely friendly and charming, speaks fluent English, and is always happy to explain the history of the vineyard as well as the ruins of the fortress that stands behind the magnificent château. She will take you through a tree-shaded lane and point out the various vineyards, the monastery below, and the other interesting characteristics of this particular part of the country. Then you will have the opportunity to taste her rare wine.

Part IV
Deauville

19
Welcome to Deauville

This attractive seaside town with wide avenues was founded by the Duc de Morny in the 19th century, and has been a fashionable resort ever since. Because of its beautiful gardens, which flourish in the mild channel climate, it is called "the beach among flowers." As I sit in Deauville writing this, the sun is pouring through my balcony windows, diamond bright, blinding to the naked eye. The air is mild and the gardens below, plushly verdant. All is fresh, balmy, and invigorating.

In spite of the mid-summer weather, it is November, the so-called "off-season" in Deauville. There are few people around and most of the hotels are closed. How much more enjoyable it is to be in this beautiful city now than during summer season. Then it becomes so jammed with people that it is hard to see, much less admire, Deauville itself. Now, without tourists, without the *haute couture* window dressing, without the Jaguars and Mercedes cluttering its streets, Deauville comes into its own. Now, when the city is stripped of its summertime distractions, one can really take the time to study and appreciate the beautiful architecture of its fine old half-timbered Norman buildings, with their tiled and thatched roofs, rounded storybook towers, balconies, and dormer windows. Even some of the new mansions being built today are often painstakingly constructed of ancient stones and of timbers, old beams, and antique roofing tiles.

When most of these slumbering masterpieces along the waterfront are closed for the winter you can stroll or drive at night through the back streets, where other homes are alive with light, peering into the windows as you go by for a quick glimpse of French domestic life.

Be sure to have a look at the Grand Casino, the last stronghold of a truly elegant way of life. In summer, it draws the wealthiest, most famous people in the world, its cloakrooms become a sea of furs, and rare dogs sport diamond collars to glitter in unison with their mistresses. At the Grand Casino one can see such glamorous figures as the Rothschilds, Frank Sinatra, Anthony Quinn, and Kirk Douglas at the gambling tables.

The summer season lasts from March to September. June, July, and August—especially August—are usually totally sold out. So if you wish to visit this beautiful city by the sea, try to come either in early spring or in the fall. I found October and November to be absolutely beautiful and don't hesitate to recommend your coming at that time. Of course, it's much quieter then but if you wish to enjoy the city itself, this is the time to do it. In November, during the yearling sales, the hotels get very crowded again with the horsey types. Just across a narrow little bridge from Deauville is the city of Trouville. Not as posh, but yet with its own Casino and other highlights. We are including information on Trouville in this section, too.

HOW TO GET THERE

Deauville is only 110 miles from Paris and therefore quite a short and easy trip from the capital. It's a 15-minute flight on Air-Inter, which has daily flights. Or you can take the train: two hours on the Autorail Rapide, or one hour and 40 minutes on the Turbotrain. The train station in Deauville is right in the center of town.

If you are coming from England, Air France has flights from London that take only 45 minutes. An alternate route from England is to take the car ferry to Le Havre or Cherbourg; it runs twice a day. Le Havre is only ten miles from Deauville.

USEFUL ADDRESSES

Physicians

JACQUOT 18, rue R.-Fossorier Tel: 88.23.57
RIPOLL Résidence Olliffe, Rue Olliffe Tel: 88.32.99

Dentists

DRUT 170, avenue de la République Tel: 88.23.86
HULIN 196, avenue de la République Tel: 88.33.91

Hospital

POLYCLINIQUE   Avenue Florian de Kergorlay   Tel: 88.14.00
A very modern clinic with specialists in every form of medicine available, including an ophthalmologist and a gynecologist.

Drugstores*

PHARMACIE ANGLAISE   2, place de Morny   Tel: 88.20.28
PHARMACIE DE L'HORLOGE   14, place de Morny   Tel: 88.20.47
LEGRIS   68, rue Mirabeau   Tel: 88.37.14
TOUZE   29, rue Désiré-Le-Hoc   Tel: 88.22.39

CALENDAR OF EVENTS

March to September

The "season." Numerous events and gala dinners at the Grand Casino, center of night life: gambling rooms, theater, musicals, concerts, night clubs. Check with your concierge to find out what is going on while you are there.

September to March

The Winter Casino is open every day. The Cabaret Restaurant is open for dinners and dancing, as are the night clubs and cinemas.

July and August

The racing season at the two racecourses. In August, the two most famous polo teams meet: French champions against the world champions. In July, international racing events. August is also the time of the important sales of race horses.

November

The yearling sales.

* Strictly for prescriptions and drugs.

20 Where to Stay

HOTELS IN DEAUVILLE

Deluxe

Note: Generally only double rooms are quoted, as a single is the price of a double room during the season. Since the age group of the people who come to Deauville is generally from 25 and up, we will not categorize the hotels or the restaurants according to A, B, and C age groups.

GOLF   Sur le Mont Canisy   Tel: 88.19.01
Single: 137F to 208F ($34.25 to $52); double: 168F to 242F ($42 to $60.50); includes breakfast. Full pension (three meals) 89F ($22.25); half-pension (breakfast and lunch or dinner) 48F ($12). All rooms are large, well-appointed, and furnished in traditional style. First-floor rooms all have terraces. The hotel is located in the middle of a golf club, high up on a hill with a view overlooking all of Deauville and Le Havre. Absolutely breathtaking! The bar is like a pub with caricatures of celebrities who made the Golf famous: the Aga Khan, M. Dubonnet, Mr. Hennessey, Baron Rothschild, and many others. The dining room is exquisite with three windowed walls overlooking the sea. During the day it looks like a garden with a bright outdoorsy feeling, but at night it's quite different—very romantic with all the lights twinkling below and the candlelight. There is a beauty salon, bar, and boutiques, a magnificent golf course, and three tennis courts to lure the sports-minded.

NORMANDY   Rue J.-Mermoz   Tel: 88.09.21
Rates: Single with bath and toilet: 126F to 194F ($31.50 to $48.50); double: 158F to 225F ($39.50 to $56.25); includes breakfast. If you wish to have your meals at the hotel, add 88F ($22) per day for full pension (lunch and dinner); or 42F ($10.50) for half-pension (lunch or dinner). If you wish to book for August, you must make your reservations several months in advance and then keep your fingers crossed. Out of season—from September 16 to March 15—they offer a special weekend including one night at the hotel with breakfast, lunch at Ciro's, and dinner at the Casino: single 185F ($46.25); double 285F ($71.25). The front of the hotel faces onto the city

square and the Winter Casino, while the back opens onto the sea. Just next door is the Summer Casino. All rooms are extremely large and are done in French Traditional style. The baths are well-equipped with a large tub, large wall mirror over the basin, and separate toilet. This hotel is too beautiful even to begin to describe. It's like something out of a fairy tale with its many gables; and the landscaping that surrounds it stretches out across the entire block. The large restaurant faces onto an outdoor courtyard. The food and wines are excellent, as is the service. There is a little paneled bar off the lobby with caricatures of all the famous people who have stayed here. To sit there sipping a drink and listening to people chat about which one of their horses won the race that day can be most entertaining. Needless to say, it's also an excellent place to meet exciting people. On the other side of the hotel you will find the Galeries Lafayette department store under a lovely, picturesque arcade, and many famous boutiques. The hotel is open all year round.

ROYAL   Sur la plage   Tel: 88.16.41

This hotel is just across the street from the Normandy, with the same facilities I outlined above. The rates are also the same, since they are owned by the same management. The difference is in the building. Where the Normandy is done in a picturesque, Norman style, the Royal is a huge, stucco-type building with a wide verandah in front facing the beach. The rooms are Directoire in style. This hotel too gets the horsey types but not from the racing set. Here, you'll find polo enthusiasts: owners, trainers, players, etc. Open only from May through September. The hotel is just across the street from the tennis courts and miniature golf, and just down the way from the Thermes-Marins Spa and its adjacent indoor pool. It is also just a block from the beach itself, with its boardwalk, cafés, and shops.

Four Star

LA BAJOCASSE   83, rue Général-Leclerc   Tel: 88.30.38

Quiet hotel with pretty rooms. Double without bath: 76F to 94F ($19 to $23.50); double with bath and shower: 113F ($28.25); breakfast included. No restaurant on the premises. This is owned by an elderly couple and they are very particular about their clientele. No noisy parties! Open all year round.

LA FRESNAYE   81, avenue de la République   Tel: 88.09.71

Centrally located with large, pretty rooms and a fine restaurant. Double without bath: 43F ($10.75); double with bath and shower: 100F ($25); breakfast included. Open all year.

Three Star

CENTRAL   158, boulevard F.-Moureaux   Tel: 88.13.68

On the main boulevard opposite the channel. Double with shower, bath, and breakfast: 50F to 63F ($12.50 to $15.75).

CHATHAM   Sur la plage   Tel: 88.06.71
Near the beach promenade. Double without bath: 53F ($13.25);
double with bath and shower: 75F ($18.75); breakfast included.
The Chatham is open during the season.

THE FLAUBERT   Sur la plage   Tel: 88.37.23
Conveniently located right on the beach promenade; good service. Double without bath: 50F ($12.50); double with shower
and bath: 80F to 107F ($20 to $26.75); breakfast included.

PLAGE   2, place Maréchal-Foch   Tel: 88.08.45
Conveniently located opposite the Maréchal-Foch square and
across from the casino. Double without bath: 58F ($14.50);
double with bath: 106F ($26.50); breakfast included. Restau-
rant serves excellent food.

LES SABLETTES   15, rue Paul-Besson   Tel: 88.10.66
Double without bath: 42F to 53F ($10.50 to $13.25); double
with shower and bath: 74F to 85F ($18.50 to $21.25); breakfast
included. Small but very clean and comfortable.

ST. JAMES   16, rue de la Plage   Tel: 88.05.23
Very good hotel. Double with shower, bath, and breakfast: 85F
to 95F ($21.25 to $23.75). Intimate atmosphere, lovely rooms.
They have a bar and the cooking in the restaurant is done by
the proprietor; very good. Open all year long.

Two Star

BRISE MARINE   15, rue Olliffe   Tel: 88.27.66
A quiet place very near the beach and the marina. It gets a
lot of yachting people. Double without bath: 42F to 45F ($10.50
to $11.25); double with shower and bath: 74F to 85F ($18.50
to $21.25); breakfast included. No restaurant. Open only dur-
ing the season.

HÔTEL CONTINENTAL   1, rue Désiré-Le-Hoc   Tel: 88.21.06
Just opposite the boat basin and near the sports stadium, at the
end of Avenue de la République, the main street. Double without bath: 40F to 44F ($10 to $11); double with bath and
shower: 89F ($22.25); breakfast included. No restaurant.

MARIE-ANNE   142, avenue de la République   Tel: 88.38.32
Centrally located; simple, but comfortable and convenient. Double without bath: 27F to 47F ($6.75 to $11.75); double with
shower and bath: 69F ($17.25); breakfast included. No res-
taurant.

LE NID D'ÉTÉ   121, avenue de la République   Tel: 88.36.67
Double room with shower, bath, and breakfast: 64F ($16).
Restaurant on premises with good food. Open only during the
season.

OCÉAN   1, quai de la Marine   Tel: 88.09.92
Excellent hotel, well-known among boating people; comfortable;
and very good food at their restaurant. Double without bath:
50F to 60F ($12.50 to $15); double with shower and bath:
85F to 86F ($21.25 to $21.50); breakfast included.

LE PATIO   180, avenue de la République   Tel: 88.25.07

All newly remodeled, with very good service. Double with shower, bath, and breakfast: 70F to 80F ($17.50 to $20). There is a bar as well as a restaurant, where the food is excellent. They also have a discothèque and an American-type bar.

PAVILLON DE LA POSTE   25, rue R.-Fossorier   Tel: 88.38.29
Centrally located. Double without bath: 50F ($12.50); double with shower and bath: 80F ($20); breakfast included. All newly remodeled; quite nice for the money. No restaurant. Open all year.

LA RÉSIDENCE   55, avenue de la République   Tel: 88.07.50
Double without bath: 53F ($13.25); double with shower: 69F to 74F ($17.25 to $18.50); breakfast included.

HOTELS IN TROUVILLE

Deluxe

BELLEVUE   1, place Maréchal-Foch   Tel: 88.14.85
The main hotel of Trouville, right on the main boulevard along the channel, opposite the Maréchal-Foch square. Double without bath: 75F to 92F ($18.75 to $23); double with shower and bath: 115F to 178F ($28.75 to $44.50); breakfast included. Good service and food; restaurant and bar. Open open during the season.

LA RÉSIDENCE   Rue St.-Michel   Tel: 88.04.66
Double without bath: 64F to 74F ($16 to $18.50); double with shower and bath: 85F to 132F ($21.25 to $33). No restaurant. Open only during the season.

21
Wining and Dining

The cuisine of Normandy is something very special; it includes a variety of dishes, including fish and seafood, and is especially known for the butter and cream that go into its famous sauces. Be sure to try the Camembert, Livarot, and especially the Pont l'Evêque (like Camembert but with a stronger taste), which are the special cheeses of this region. *Tarte aux pommes à la Normandie* is a delicious dessert to top off any meal. It consists of a hot apple tart flamed with Calvados and served with a rich cream. How's that for calories?

The Normandy region is famous for its apple orchards and the two favorite drinks of this region are "cidre," which is much better than any at home, and, of course, the famous Calvados, an apple brandy. Cidre is usually drunk with crepes instead of wine. In fact, many people drink it throughout the meal in place of wine. Cidre Bouche is called the champagne of cidre as it has bubbles. It is particularly good with fish and cheese.

RESTAURANTS IN DEAUVILLE

Restaurants are open for lunch from noon to 3 P.M. and for dinner from 7 to 10 P.M.

Expensive

CHEZ AUGUSTO   27, rue Désiré-Le-Hoc   Tel: 88.34.49
French and Italian specialties and a very *intime* atmosphere.

LES EMBASSADEURS   In the Summer Casino   Tel: 88.29.55
In the same casino as the Grill Room but with a different atmosphere, with its green carpets and the gamblers around for local color. This is more of a pub-type place, primarily for the convenience of those at the tables. *Menu* from 35F to 48F ($8.75 to $12).

GRILL ROOM DU CASINO   In the Summer Casino   Tel: 88.29.55
Open only for dinner. Another one of the best in town, and not just for the millionaires and gamblers who frequent the casino.

It's intimate, warm, and lovely. Excellent food, wine, and service. Music in the evening. Good *à la carte* menu from 60F to 70F ($15 to $17.50).

RESTAURANT DE L'HÔTEL DU GOLF   Sur le Mont Canisy   Tel: 88.19.01

Wonderful dining room with marvelous view, surrounded by flowers and trees that give you the illusion of sitting in a garden. Excellent food and wines. *Menu* from 38F ($9.50).

RESTAURANT DE L'HÔTEL NORMANDY   Sur la plage   Tel: 88.09.21

It is always a pleasure in good weather to have a meal here in the garden under the umbrellas or in the dining room itself facing the sea. Watching the other diners come and go is a show in itself. Many of them are millionaires, or celebrities, and the impromptu fashion show is unbelievable. *Menu* from 70F to 80F ($17.50 to $20), though there are some dishes from 35F ($8.75).

RESTAURANT DE L'HÔTEL ROYAL   Boulevard Cornuché   Tel: 88.16.41

Done in Louis XVI décor. Not quite as charming as the Normandy, but the food and wines are good, as is the service. *Menu* from 38F ($9.50).

LE KRAAL   Place du Marché   Tel: 88.30.58

Charming restaurant done in typical Normand décor. Comfortable and relaxing. Good food and very kind service in this intimate atmosphere. About 40F to 50F ($10 to $12.50).

MAMAN   38, avenue Hocquart-de-Turtot   Tel: 88.33.37

"Maman" is taking very good care of this homey-type bistro. Honest and abundant cuisine about 30F ($7.50).

AU PETIT GAMBETTA   70, rue Général-Leclerc   Tel: 88.34.11

Here you can find a good meal. The service isn't so fast, but the prices are not as expensive as most places either. From 18F to 26F ($4.50 to $6.50). *À la carte* menu from 40F to 50F ($10 to $12.50).

PROMENADE DES PLANCHES   Tel: 88.22.62

One of the best in town, right on the beach; open only for lunch. This is a VIP's rendezvous and you must make a reservation or you'll be out of luck. The food is exquisite, especially the fish and seafood. You can pick your lobster or crab right out of the tank. The restaurant is on two levels, with a glass front so that you can see out on the beach. Lovely during the summer. Excellent service. Specialties of the day and also good *à la carte* menu from 50F to 70F ($12.50 to $17.50).

Moderate

CHEZ CRI CRI MULLER   20, rue Désiré-Le-Hoc   Tel: 88.26.90

"Cri Cri," once on the stage, gives new life to the old restaurant "de France." Stone walls and mirrors give the place a warmth and liveliness that makes it a good spot for lunch or dinner. *Menu* from 16F ($4), which is not easy to find anymore.

LA JOYEUSE 172, avenue de la République Tel: 88.24.51
A lovely little villa converted into a small hotel. Gay décor, warm welcome. Lovely in the garden under the umbrellas. *Menus* from 20F to 25F ($5 to $6.25).

LE LUTRIN 48, rue Gambetta Tel: 88.32.38
A Norman-style bistro with a rustic atmosphere. Good food at low prices from 16F to 24F ($4 to $6).

CAFÉ DE PARIS Place de Morny Tel: 88.31.60
Small brasserie-type place, 16F ($4) and up.

LE PETIT GAMBETTA 70, rue Gambetta Tel: 88.87.83
A little place, good atmosphere, and good food for about 20F ($5).

PETIT VATEL 129, avenue de la République Tel: 88.21.56
Good meals at good prices, 16F to 20F ($4 to $5).

Inexpensive

Open only in season.

CHEZ MIOCQUE 81, rue E.-Colas Tel: 88.09.52
LA ROSERAIE 77, rue E.-Colas
LA SÉLECT 83, rue E.-Colas Tel: 88.05.32

RESTAURANTS IN TROUVILLE

All restaurants open all year round.

BAR DES PLANCHES Bord de la mer Tel: 88.15.04
Good food, clean and comfortable. Varied *menu* from 20F ($5).

LE BIVOUAC Sur la plage Tel: 88.00.64
Deluxe brasserie. *Menu* from 55F ($13.75).

LE GRILLADIN 38, avenue Hocquart-de-Turtot Tel: 88.33.37
Good enough, but particularly so whenever there are horse events in town. Around 20F ($5).

CHEZ MARINETTE 156, boulevard F.-Moureaux Tel: 88.03.21
Excellent restaurant, very good food for 28F ($7). Nice atmosphere.

LA RÉGENCE 132, boulevard F.-Moureaux Tel: 88.10.71
Very elegant with chandeliers and silver service plates, reminiscent of the old Trianon. They get an extremely aristocratic and wealthy clientele. *Menu* from 60F ($15).

LES VAPEURS 160, boulevard F.-Moureaux Tel: 88.15.24
Brasserie with good food, around 30F ($7.50).

22
Nighttime Entertainment

BARS AND NIGHT CLUBS

CASINO D'ÉTÉ (Summer Casino) Boulevard Cornuché A-B-C
Open all day, every day from March to September.

CASINO D'HIVER (Winter Casino) Rue E.-Colas B-C
Opposite the Place François André d'Hôtel and the Normandy Hotel. There is also a theater, a concert hall, and a cinema. The program is listed in the casino and at your hotel. Open from September to March.

KRAAL Place du Marché A-B-C
In the underground cave of the Kraal restaurant, a small bar where you may dance and listen to some good records or old jazz.

MÉDUSE CLUB 16, rue Désiré-Le-Hoc A-B
A pleasant club for young people, with music and a disc jockey. I find it a little bit too loud.

NEW BRUMMEL At the Summer Casino A-B-C
The most popular discothèque in town. A sexy, red-and-gold interior, red velvet oriental-style ottomans and chairs, dim lights, and never-ending music. "The" spot for all the Beautiful People in town. The funny part of it is, you don't have to be with a date to dance. A woman just gets up and dances alone. It's a great way to meet people. About $5 a drink, which is a bit expensive, but then the waiters don't hover around you to coax you to drink, so you can very easily enjoy the atmosphere and the show that the dancers put on, on just one drink. During the season the fashion show alone is worthwhile; slinky leather pants with see-through tops, sparkling gowns or embroidered jeans, and furs of every description. It's a must at least once while you're in Deauville.

TCHAKACHA Boulevard de la Mer A-B
An elegant discothèque for young people who haven't yet discovered the casino or gotten into gambling.

23
Excursions Out of Deauville

CAEN

A short drive from Deauville, Caen is situated in the center of a very prosperous agricultural region. Although three-quarters of it was destroyed during the battle of Normandy in 1944, the town has been rebuilt and is now a fine example of modern town planning. Most of its ancient monuments survived intact. The towers of the 11th-century **Abbaye-aux-Dames** and **Abbaye-aux-Hommes** still stand at opposite ends of the town. The monastery buildings of the latter are now the town hall. The churches of **St.-Pierre** and **St.-Jean** have been restored in all their ancient splendor. The massive ramparts of **William the Conqueror's castle** are now well in evidence and the foundations of its keep, built by Henry I, have been brought to light. The rebuilt university, with about 15,000 students, has theaters, museums, and an art gallery. Caen is still the cultural and artistic center it was in the Middle Ages. It is also an important shopping center and a still-expanding business and industrial area. Many coach tours start from Caen, which is a very good center for exploring the Calvados area by public or private transport.

TOUQUES

Very close to Deauville and an interesting village to visit. The remains of the **château of William the Conqueror** can be visited here. A fortress dating from the 12th and 13th centuries consisting of the outer wall with its 6 towers and a moat, it was built on the site of an 11th-century building that William the Conqueror often visited. It was here that he conferred the regency of the duchy of Normandy on his wife, Queen Matilda, before leaving for England. Many buildings in Touques illustrate the former wealth of the town. The visitor's eye is caught by the silhouettes of several fine, stone-built houses. The churches of St.-Pierre and St.-Thomas are of considerable artistic interest. The **Church of St.-Pierre** dates from the 11th century but is no longer in use. Worthy of mention, too, are the magnificent manor houses, **Fleurigny, Mesnil St.-Germain, Epinay,** and **Meautry.**

CHÂTEAUX AND MANOR HOUSES

Ever since the 12th century, an age of grim fortresses, of which Falaise is the best preserved, right up to the end of the 18th, the lush countryside of Calvados has seen the building of private residences. Some are stately homes, such as **Fontaine-Henry** (16th century), **Balleroy** (17th), and **Benouville** and **Versainville** (18th).

Most, however, are humbler manor houses, the homes of farmers, but distinctive and varied in architectural style. There are many in the **Pays d'Auge,** where they are seen at their best in the spring sunshine that brings out the harmony of the colored tiles and the half-timbering, the brick and stonework. Places such as **Coupesarte, St.-Germain-de-Livet, Victot,** and **Grandchamp** are a joy indeed. The Bessin coastal area and the plain of Caen have many fine examples of stone manor houses, built from the 15th through the 18th century, with elaborate porches, turrets, and spiral stairs. Some villages, such as Crepon near Arromanches, are quite unspoiled.

Even in the **Bocage,** for many centuries a poor region, there are some elegant 18th-century residences, of which **Pontecoulant** is a fine example.

The capital of the Bessin, **Bayeux,** has some marvelous, old châteaux and manor houses to see. Take the time for a drive through this beautiful area and you will never want to leave.

ECCLESIASTICAL ARCHITECTURE

The region of Calvados is rich in gems of ecclesiastical architecture. In Caen, the two abbeys and the Church of St.-Nicholas are outstanding examples of the Romanesque style, introduced into England by the Normans at the time of the Conquest. They are stark in character, built to impress rather than to charm. Priories such as St.-Gabriel, and simple country churches like the one at Thaon, are more homely examples of Norman architecture. The towers and steeples in the region, dating from the 11th to the 14th century, are many and varied. There are also some superb examples of the Gothic style: the cathedrals at Bayeux and Lisieux, the abbey-church of St.-Pierre-Dives, and the Church of St.-Pierre at Caen (the apse of which shows the beginnings of Renaissance architecture in the region). The Abbey of Juayé-Mondaye will appeal to those who appreciate neoclassical architecture, and there are many interesting modern churches which have replaced old ones destroyed in 1944. Despite the ravages of war, a number of country churches still have impressive features, notably the 13th-century frescoes at Ste.-Marie-aux-Anglais and the 14th-century stained glass at St.-Hymer.

WORLD WAR II SITES

If you are at all history-minded you may wish to see the site of the famous Normandy landing on June 6, 1944, known as D–Day. You will remember the names of some of the famous beachheads—Omaha, Utah, etc.—that stretch from an area south of Deauville almost to Barfleur. Numerous landing monuments, cemeteries, photographs, and relief maps tell the entire story of this momentous day. The site is open every day from 9 A.M. to noon and 2 P.M. to 7 P.M. You can check with the Office Tourisme (also called Syndicat d'Initiative) for the best way to get to the various villages or cities you wish to visit. Tel: 88.21.43.

24
Sports

Golf

HÔTEL DU GOLF   Sur le Mont Canisy
18- and 9-hole courses.

Mini-Golf

Boulevard de la Mer, adjacent to the tennis courts
Open all year.

Horseback Riding

PONY-CLUB
Boulevard de la Mer, just in front of the Hôtel Royal   Tel:
88.37.21
Open all year round.

Swimming

Beach
Heated Indoor Swimming Pool   Boulevard de la Mer, next to
the Thermes-Marins
The large, very modern, covered pool is open every day 9 A.M.
to 7 P.M. all year round. Admission Monday through Friday 8F
($2), Saturday and Sunday 10F ($2.50). Snack bar for sandwiches, salads, and soft drinks.

Tennis

Boulevard de la Mer in front of the Normandy Hotel   Tel: 88.
02.26

Yachting

THE DEAUVILLE YACHT CLUB   Quai de la Marine   Tel: 88.38.19
This is a good place to wander around if you're interested in
seeing all the Beautiful People arrive on their gorgeous yachts.
Whether you're interested in yachting or not, it's worth a stroll,
since you never know whom you might meet.

25
Beauty Comes First

BEAUTY SALONS

Prices are similar to those in Paris.

ANDRÉ 104, rue Victor-Hugo Tel: 88.27.93
It is said he is the best in Deauville.

BEAUSSIER 43, rue Désiré-Le-Hoc Tel: 88.34.95

BODARD 206, avenue de la République Tel: 88.03.87

JEAN CLÉMENT 97, rue E.-Colas Tel: 88.33.47

FONTAIN 34, rue Gambetta Tel: 88.27.64

JACY Boulevard de la Mer Tel: 88.34.00
The same excellent hairdressers that Micheline Jacy employs in her Paris and Riviera branches.

LORVENN At the Normandy corner
Ask the hotel concierge to make an appointment for you. Excellent service. This salon and André's handle all the beautiful belles when they come to Deauville.

LE VASLOT 44, rue de Verdun Tel: 88.30.19

MASSAGE

ANDRIEU 17, rue Hoche Tel: 88.08.44

DEÇOIX 59, rue R.-Fossorier Tel: 88.21.85

SOTIRA 57, rue Gambetta Tel: 88.36.09

THERMES MARINS Rue Edmond-Blanc Tel: 88.09.47
This is a spa, but you can make an appointment for just a massage.

PEDICURES

ANDRÉ 104, rue Victor-Hugo Tel: 88.27.93

ODETTE GUÉRIN 81 bis, rue Général-Leclerc Tel: 88.21.44

TIPHAGNE 12, rue R.-Fossorier Tel: 88.24.48

SPA

THERMES-MARINS   Rue Edmond-Blanc, at the corner of Boulevard de la Mer, just across from the Royal and Normandy hotels   Tel: 88.09.47
This is an extremely modern, fully equipped Spa specializing in thalasso therapy, treatment with sea water. Here you can reduce, relax, get rid of all the aches and pains in your body and arthritis, rheumatism, cellulite, skin problems, etc. There are mud baths, algae baths (which use a mud-like substance made of seaweed), jet-stream water massage, hand massage, sauna, and just about anything else you can think of. A few hours spent here is like heaven. The staff is more than kind and helpful. The entire operation is carefully watched over by Dr. Pierre Chapelle, a handsome young doctor, who speaks English, and has a smile that will dazzle you. The usual cure for any of the problems mentioned above is 21 days. However, if you're only staying a few days, you can be accommodated for whatever treatment you like. If you wish to tip the girls, just put it in an envelope and give it to the receptionist; she will take care of it. I feel 8F ($2) per day is a good tip.

26
Shopping

During the off-season, everything is half-price.

DEPARTMENT STORES

AU PRINTEMPS 104, rue E.-Colas Tel: 88.21.81
In the little square between the Normandy Hotel and the Winter Casino. A branch of the Paris store, but more picturesque here in Deauville with its quaint arcade flanking the square. Closed on Monday in winter.
PRISUNIC 49, avenue de la République Tel: 88.30.52
One of the chain of inexpensive department stores described in the Paris shopping section.

BOUTIQUES AND SMALL SHOPS

BOUTIQUE AUX PANTALONS 76, rue E.-Colas Tel: 88.34.37
CARDIN Rue Gontaut-Biron Tel: 88.09.23
The famous Paris designer. Everything for men, women, and even children.
CASHMERE HOUSE 33, rue E.-Colas Tel: 88.04.90
Good cashmeres but expensive.
DUBOSQ 50, rue Gambetta Tel: 88.29.69
À L'ÉLANTINE (Marguerin) 45, rue Désiré-Le-Hoc Tel: 88. 30.78
GALIA 60, rue Désiré-Le-Hoc Tel: 88.23.08
GESYLCA 9, place du Casino Tel: 88.32.62
HELEN SPORT 98, rue E.-Colas Tel: 88.33.56
TED LAPIDUS Place du Casino Tel: 88.30.56
A branch of the famous designer, carrying a good selection of boutique items—sportswear, scarves, jewelry, belts, and other accessories.
MARCELLIN 50, rue Désiré-Le-Hoc Tel: 88.08.75
MARIE-MARTINE At the entrance of the Casino Tel: 88.39.13
Good selection, but expensive.
MORELLI Sur le Marché Tel: 88.30.89
PATOU Rue Gontaut-Biron Tel: 88.33.65
Jean Patou is a famous designer and stocks very elegant things.
À LA PLACE DE MORNY 9, place de Morny Tel: 88.06.96
POINT D'INTERROGATION 29, rue Olliffe at Place de Morny Tel: 88.07.01
REINOLD 5, avenue du Général-de Gaulle Tel: 88.33.72
Especially for junior sizes.
VALENTINE BOURGADE Rue Gontaut-Biron Tel: 88.30.64

LEATHER GOODS

DOMINIQUE CASSEGRAIN   At the entrance of the Casino   Tel:
88.05.97
ÉLYSE ET HONORÉ   7, avenue du Général-de Gaulle   Tel:
88.36.16
FORMENTIN   Boulevard Mauger
HERMÈS   Rue du Casino   Tel: 88.04.42
A good selection of Hermès' famous scarves.
LA PEAU DE PORC   Rue Gontaut-Biron
All pigskin products.

SHOES

CYPRIS   Rue Gontaut-Biron   Tel: 88.09.23
ÉLYSE ET HONORÉ   7, avenue du Général-de Gaulle   Tel: 88.
36.16
JACQUOT   55, rue Désiré-Le-Hoc   Tel: 88.34.41
POINT D'INTERROGATION   29, rue Olliffe at Place de Morny
Tel: 88.07.01
ROYALDAME   92, rue E.-Colas   Tel: 88.32.08

JEWELRY

ARAX   86, rue E.-Colas   Tel: 88.26.45
BINET   32, rue Gambetta   Tel: 88.32.91
HERMÈS   Rue du Casino   Tel: 88.04.42
SERVIAN   99, rue E.-Colas   Tel: 88.30.11
VAN CLEEF ET ARPELS   1, rue Gontaut-Biron   Tel: 88.36.87
WATOS   3, rue du Casino   Tel: 88.22.27

GIFTS / GAMES / SOUVENIRS

BADOU   32, rue Désiré-Le-Hoc   Tel: 88.07.07
DAVID   35, rue Olliffe   Tel: 88.22.85
AU DIABLOTIN   64, rue Désiré-Le-Hoc   Tel: 88.20.62
GALERIES DE DEAUVILLE   Sur la plage
SUZANNE GODARD   2, avenue du Général-de Gaulle   Tel: 88.
37.66
PEGOTTY   5, place François-André   Tel: 88.34.98
ROYALE SOUVENIRS   3, rue Désiré-Le-Hoc

SPORTS EQUIPMENT

CALLAC   33, rue Olliffe   Tel: 88:36.32
DAVID   35, rue Olliffe   Tel: 88.22.85
NADAL   Sur la plage   Tel: 88.20.62
VOILE NORMANDE   Quai de la Gare   Tel: 88.31.33

LAUNDRY AND DRY CLEANING

BODARD   206, avenue de la République   Tel: 88.03.87
CHÂTELIER   35, rue R.-Fossorier   Tel: 88.23.87
DEAUVILLE PRESSING   9, rue Désiré-Le-Hoc   Tel: 88.23.87
MIRABEAU   27, rue Mirabeau   Tel: 88.25.06
SELF SERVICE LAVOMATIQUE   1, rue Victor-Hugo
   A good spot for a hurry-up job of laundry.
SYMDENS   4, rue de l'Avenir   Tel: 88.31.36

Part
V
The
Riviera

27
Welcome to the French Riviera

The timeless Riviera, between Toulon and Menton, has an allure of surprising endurance. The Côte d'Azur, as it is called in French, has been a magnet for more than 2,000 years. Ancient Greeks and Romans set up villas, crowned heads of Europe held winter court here. From Cézanne to Delacroix, and Tolstoi to F. Scott Fitzgerald, writers and painters have taken to the Riviera as to an elixir. The luminous sunshine and flowers in winter first caught the eye of Lord Brougham and the British aristocracy in the 19th century. Since then, such varied personalities as Winston Churchill, Brigitte Bardot, D. H. Lawrence, Billy Rose, Katherine Mansfield, the Aga Khan, Sir Laurence Olivier, Queen Victoria, W. Somerset Maugham, Juliette Greco, Frank Harris, Pablo Picasso, Isadora Duncan, Aldous Huxley, and Jean Cocteau have only served to further the mystique of this lovely year-round Mediterranean paradise.

The Riviera proper used to be some 40 miles long, stretching from Menton to Cannes. Now it has doubled in length to include St.-Raphaël and St.-Tropez. It consists of a bright stretch of resort towns, lively beaches, bays, and isolated inlets along the coast. Inland are fascinating hill towns, where Riviera sophisticates spend more and more of their time, as do discerning visitors who prefer the quiet and the inexpensive rates.

The Côte d'Azur is a patchwork of styles and amazing variety. Eze-Village is a cul-de-sac of doll-like houses and rocky, tunneled streets. Cap-Ferrat has grand villas discreetly secluded behind huge gates and hedges. Juan-les-Pins is young and lively, and since 1925 greatly expanded through the interest of American millionaire Frank J. Gould. The steep, layered streets of Villefranche slant to the quays, making it a 17th-century house of cards. Antibes is a fortified town, a mecca for the rich, and a market that sells lilies and carnations as others do stringbeans and carrots.

The appeal of the Côte d'Azur as a vacation spot is its variety of attractions. Visitors are often surprised by the ski facilities of the Riviera mountains. But swimming and skiing are not the only sports along the coast; the 20 miles between Cannes and Nice boast 18 tennis clubs, a half-dozen 18-hole golf courses, a race track, a polo field, and numerous riding stables.

Cannes itself has 22 tennis courts and two golf courses. Mandelieu Golf Club, about three miles from Cannes, is considered one of the Riviera's finest challenges. The Cannes Country Club, excellent too, is near the fashionable village of Mougins. Two new yacht basins have sprouted in Cannes, while the Palm Beach Casino is perhaps the coast's most elegant indoor-outdoor spot.

With the Alps forming a natural protective shelter, and the Mediterranean currents warming this lovely stretch of land, the temperature along the Côte d'Azur is always much higher than in the rest of the country. It is not at all unusual to walk around in shirtsleeves in November or December. Though the actual season is from June through September, the Riviera has become very popular as early as April, and sometimes up to the middle of November.

With this beautiful climate, it is no wonder that so many famous artists have come here to live and paint. Matisse lived out his days in Nice. His work can be seen in the beautiful little chapel at Vence in the hills above Nice. Picasso was so fond of the Riviera that there is hardly a town or village that doesn't boast a sketch or painting of his. Jean Cocteau painted a chapel in Villefranche as a token of his great admiration and love for this part of France. The great master Renoir chose to end his days on the Côte d'Azur. The country house where he lived from 1903 till his death in 1919 still stands in Cagnes with his studio and some paintings, sketches, and sculpture done while he lived there.

Less than 20 kilometers from Cannes stands the town of Grasse, atop a hill. The traveler's nose will tell her exactly when she has arrived. Hillsides of jasmine and wild flowers, plus crowded hothouses, serve the town's 35 perfume factories.

The scent industry first came to Grasse in the 16th century, via the Medici's perfumer, M. Tombarelli. By the 19th century, essence of flowers was distilled here by Molinard and Fragonard, manufacturers whose factories still receive numerous visitors daily. Well over 160 million pounds of fresh flowers are treated annually by a 75-million-dollar industry.

Will your womanly curiosity make you want to know more about the extraordinary landmarks, ancient ruins, fortified villages to be discovered here? They are all around you. The Riviera's extravagant past, featuring the Phoenicians, ancient Greeks, and ancient Romans, is literally at your feet.

You can trace the origins of the Grimaldi family from the medieval castle at Cagnes through to the palace at Monaco, criss-cross the destiny of Napoleon in Antibes, St.-Raphaël, Cannes, and Grasse, or discover the beginnings of the modern Riviera in Nice on the Promenade des Anglais (eight yards wide), first built by an English clergyman in the early 19th century.

Most of the activity of the Riviera naturally centers on the lovely beaches, and this is where you will find the luxury hotels. Most of the beaches are silky and inviting, with the exception, perhaps, of Nice, where the beach itself consists of stones —not at all comfortable. However, air mattresses and the like are available for rent, as are sun umbrellas and chairs.

Naturally you will want to bring your most glamorous and colorful wardrobe to the Riviera, and believe me, you will use it. You will see all manner of dress in the street from bikinis with an Indian cloth wrapped around for a skirt to gorgeous pants suits. Anything goes, so long as it's bright and comfortable. You may wish to bring a little shawl or stole to wear over your shoulders at night as most of the hotels and restaurants are air-conditioned.

The ambience all along the Côte d'Azur is one of such friendliness that it is very easy to meet people. If not at the beach itself, then surely at any of the sidewalk cafés or bars along the promenade. At any of these you may be sitting next to a duke, a Greek millionaire, an Italian count, or a wealthy American industrialist. All it takes is a smile, a few pleasant words, and who knows, you too may be off to the races. Don't think "it can't happen to me," because it can and does!

CLIMATE

Sea breezes temper the summer heat and the nights are renowned for their ideal temperature; they have been called "the velvet nights of the Côte d'Azur." There are 2,500 to 2,800 hours of sunshine per year, with fewer than 75 rainy days. A few heavy downpours in the autumn and the sky soon becomes clear again. There are only about three days of frost in Nice each year.

Average Maximum Winter Temperatures at Nice

October	75.2–78.8° F
November	64.4–69.8
December	60.8–64.4
January	60.8–62.6
February	60.8–62.6
March	64.4–68
April	64.4–71.6

HOW TO GET THERE

By Air

The Nice/Côte d'Azur Airport is the second most important in France and serves the entire Riviera. Nineteen airlines land there.

From	Flying Time
Paris	1 hour, 20 minutes
London	1 hour, 55 minutes
Geneva	50 minutes
Rome	1 hour
New York	8 hours

See Chapter 3 for further flight information.

By Rail

From	Train Time
Paris	10 hours, 35 minutes
Geneva	9 hours, 20 minutes
London	20 hours

Seven express trains run between Paris and Cannes, including the celebrated "Blue Train" and the "Mistral," and one train daily from Geneva.

HOW TO GET AROUND

Trains

They link major towns on the Riviera coast. Fast and comfortable. For instance, the train from Nice to Cagnes costs 6F ($1.50) and takes only a half-hour.

Buses

There is a regular and very comfortable coach service between the Riviera cities. Timetables can be picked up at Gare des Autobus on the Promenade du Paillon or the tourist office at Place Masséna in Nice, and at the Gare Routière on the Place de l'Hôtel de Ville in Cannes. Average costs: Nice to Monte-Carlo, 4F ($1); Nice to Menton, 6F ($1.50); Nice to Cagnes, 6F ($1.50); Nice to Grasse, 6F ($1.50).

Departures from Nice every 15 minutes in the morning, every 30 minutes in the afternoon.

There is also extensive service out of Cannes to the other lovely towns. Here are some of the schedules:

CANNES TO NICE, MONACO, MENTON, INTERMEDIATE STOPS Rapides Côte d'Azur, Gare Routière, Place de l'Hôtel de Ville   Tel: 39.11.39

CANNES TO GRASSE AND INTERMEDIATE STOPS Rapides Côte d'Azur, at the railroad station   Tel: 39.21.37

The bus departs from Cannes every 15 minutes from 7 A.M. to 8:30 P.M. After 9 P.M., service every hour until 12:30 A.M.

CANNES TO ST. RAPHAËL, ST.-TROPEZ, AND INTERMEDIATE STOPS Buses of the Corniche d'Or and the Société Méridionale d'Autocars   Tel: 39.08.87

Buses depart from the Gare Routière, on the Place de l'Hôtel de Ville, 10 times daily.

CANNES TO VALLAURIS, GOLFE-JUAN Buses Bolleri Tel: 63.88.82

Departure from the Gare Routière, Place de l'Hôtel de Ville, 8 times daily; from the railroad station, 17 departures per day.

Taxis

Plentiful at the airport and in all larger towns. Fares are indicated on meters as with U.S. taxis. Initial flag drop 4F ($1) plus 70 centimes for every kilometer. Charge of .50F ($.12) for each bag, though hand bags are carried free. At night between 10 P.M. and 5 A.M., there is a 25% additional fee. From the airport to Nice you will pay approximately 15F ($3.75).

Boat Trips

Day or night excursions may be arranged in Cannes, Nice, and Monte-Carlo.

GAMBLING

Rates of admission are standard in all casinos. You must be over 21, dress correctly, and be able to show identification. Admittance fees are usually under $2 or $3.

TOURIST OFFICES
(SYNDICATS D'INITIATIVE)

Nice

13, place Masséna Tel: 85.47.89

Cannes

Corner of Rue J.-Jaurès and Rue de Laugier Tel: 99.19.77

TOUR AGENTS

Nice

AMERICAN EXPRESS 11, promenade des Anglais Tel: 87.29.82
HAVOS/EXPRINTER 14, place Masséna Tel: 88.30.92
WAGON-LITS COOK 2, avenue de Verdun Tel: 87.19.84
RIVIERA TOURISME 10, rue du Paradis Tel: 88.68.92

Cannes

AMERICAN EXPRESS La Croisette Tel: 38.15.88
HAVOS VOYAGERS 3, rue Maréchal-Foch Tel: 39.26.32
WAGON-LITS COOK 1, la Croisette Tel: 39.17.61

CALENDAR OF EVENTS

The Riviera season is in full swing from January through April, with festivals, "battles of flowers," international regattas, etc.

Winter

MONTE-CARLO Christmas Water Ski Contest December
ENTIRE RIVIERA Carnations, tuberoses, violets, and anemones, orange and lemon blossoms bloom in profusion December and January
MONTE-CARLO Monte-Carlo Auto Rally Second and third weeks of January
MONTE-CARLO Fête of St. Dévote January 27
CANNES Water Skiing Cup January
ENTIRE RIVIERA Almond blossoms in bloom January
NICE Carnival
In February, two weeks before Ash Wednesday, the Carnival celebrates the ancient rites of spring during 12 confetti-filled, fanciful days of colorful floats, cavalcades, masked balls, battles of flowers, fireworks, and the burning in effigy of "King Carnival."
CANNES Mimosa Festival February
Mimosa has flourished here since its importation from Santo Domingo in 1835. There are 1,500 to 1,600 acres of it, thousands of tons cut for export.
MENTON Lemon Festival February
Exhibitions of citrus fruits and exotic plants. The lemon tree blooms year round here, and Menton lemons are highly prized. In the same month you will also find apricot and peach blossoms all over the Riviera. At the end of February and in March rock roses, thyme, asphodel, and rosemary fill the air with fragrance.

Spring

MENTON Spring Festival April 2
CANNES International Tennis Tournament, International Trap Shooting Competition, International Regatta April
VENCE Folklore Festival Easter Sunday and Monday
NICE International Trade Fair Easter week
GRASSE Jasmine and roses are at their height April and May
MONTE-CARLO Monte-Carlo automobile Grand Prix May

CANNES International Film Festival May
A glittering highlight of the Côte d'Azur, this is the most important film festival in the world. For two weeks Cannes teems with film stars, directors, producers, and other titans of the international movie industry. The town goes wild with festivities, parties, personalities, and press. You have to book way in advance for this event.

ST.-TROPEZ The "Bravado" May 16 and May 18
The whole town celebrates the 17th-century victory of its fishermen against 20 Spanish galleons. Drums, fifes, musket fire, fireworks, and a glorious sham battle.

Summer

ALL OVER THE RIVIERA Bougainvillea and Loral Rose are at their height in June

ANTIBES Feast of St. Peter Ceremony of the Blessing of the Sea June 29

ALL OVER THE RIVIERA Tour de France bicycle race passes along the entire cheering Riviera July

ALL OVER THE RIVIERA Bastille Day July 14
Fireworks, music, outdoor dancing, and fun, as all France celebrates its revolution.

NICE Flower festivals and galas. August

MONTE-CARLO Losange d'Or August
International sailing and motorboat race.

MENTON International Festival of Chamber Music August
Nightly concerts at the Place de l'Eglise.

CANNES *Son et Lumière* (sound-and-light) spectacles of Ste.-Marguerite Castle, Lérins Islands June to October

Fall

CANNES-MENTON Painting and Music Biennial September
Famous since 1951.

NICE Auto Race begins September

MONTE-CARLO Monégasque National Holiday November 19

28
Wining and Dining

The Riviera menu offers most of the great classic dishes of France. In addition, it features specialties unique to this area, and which are famous throughout the epicurean world. Like all regional dishes, these make the most of local foods. We can approximate these specialties with the products we're able to obtain back home, but it won't be the real thing. The local dishes served only on the Riviera are the very quintessence of the region. Following is a list of some of these:

Soup

Soupe au pistou vegetable soup seasoned with basil, garlic, grated cheese, and olive oil

Fish and Seafood

daurade gilt-head
langoustine prawn
loup local bass

oursins sea urchins, served raw
rouget red mullet
stockfisch dried cod

Other Specialties

aïoli the famous Provençal specialty, served as a mayonnaise with steamed fish, or boiled beef or hard-boiled eggs. Made of garlic, egg yolk, salt, pepper, olive oil, and lemon juice. (A dear friend of mine also uses this sauce on hot or cold London Broil, and it's delicious.)

artichauts artichokes, small and delectable; often served cold

bouillabaisse dish made with Mediterranean fish (*rascasse, rouget, vive, roucau*), onion, tomato, olive oil, and seasoning (saffron, garlic, thyme, sage, fennel, bayleaf, orange peel, salt and pepper). Gourmets disagree as to whether other Mediterranean shellfish such as lobster, mussels, or crabs should be added.

bourride a variation of bouillabaisse that some prefer to the original, made with bass, whiting, and other local fish, plus aïoli

brandade a kind of mousse or paste of dried cod, served only in winter. May be hot or cold.

pan bagnat a sort of *salade niçoise* sandwich, the bread buttered with olive oil

pissaladière delectable pie of onions, leeks, olive oil, garlic, anchovies, black olives, seasoning *ratatouille* tomatoes, eggplant, summer squash, pimentoes, olive oil, garlic, and eggs

rouille very hot blend of pepper and garlic used to flavor various kinds of fish soup

salade niçoise made with tomatoes, string beans, potatoes, and anchovies with such additions as onion, red and green peppers, black olives, quartered hard-boiled eggs, tuna fish. The dressing is of wine, vinegar, olive oil, hot mustard, salt and pepper.

Fruit

figues figs

grenades pomegranates

oranges de Tanger tangerines

LOCAL WINES   Rosé de Provence, especially produced in Vence area. Also white wines: Bellet, Escare, Villars.

See the chapters on Nice and Cannes for lists of restaurants in those cities.

29
Sightseeing

From Nice you can visit any one of the other cities along the Riviera by an organized tour. I recommend this to anyone traveling alone, because you do see so much more and get a better grasp of what you do see. See the chapters on Nice, Cannes, Monaco, and the other towns for sights to see in each of them.

There are too many tours to mention them all; we have listed just a sampling to give you an idea of prices and what is included.

Special note: Excursion rates may differ, as new fares were coming out just as we were going to press.

MENTON Depart from Nice 9:15 A.M. Return 6.30 P.M. Every day Price 20F ($5)
Drive along the "Grande Corniche" road, built by Napoleon I in 1806, with its magnificent view of Nice below. Stop at the Village of Eze, founded by the Phoenicians several centuries before Christ, and again at La Turbie to admire the Tower of Augustus. Drive past the medieval castle of Roquebrune to the border of Menton below. There you can spend some time, after lunch. Stop to see the famous Casino of Monte-Carlo, then on for a close view of Princess Grace's palace, after which you will stop to see the Oceanographic Museum with its remarkable aquarium and exotic gardens. On the return along the lower Corniche Road you pass through tropical Beaulieu and Ville-franche.

MONTE-CARLO Depart from Nice 1:45 P.M. Return 6.30 P.M. Every day Price 20F ($5)
The same itinerary as for Menton except you do not stop in Menton.

GRASSE AND CAGNES Depart from Nice 9:15 A.M. Return 6:30 P.M. Price 20F ($5)
Cross the Var River bridge, which was the border between France and Italy before 1860. Bypassing the Grimaldi Castle of Cagnes, on to St.-Paul-de-Vence and into the Roman town of Vence, famed for its mineral springs and mosaic pottery, as well as the Matisse Chapel. Pass through the one-time Saracen stronghold, Tourettes-sur-Loup, a quaint village welded onto the rock, to the Point du Loup where a stop is made for lunch. After a drive through the famous Gorges du Loupe, you go up

the cliff to Gourdon, perched on its hill at 2,200 feet, then down to Grasse to visit an important perfume factory. Home along the coast of Cagnes, passing along the "Croisette" to Nice.

ST.-TROPEZ AND THE GOLDEN CORNICHE Depart from Nice 8:45 A.M. Return 6:30 P.M. Price 30F ($7.50)

Travel through the heart of Antibes and Cagnes along the beautiful motorway cut through the pine forest of the Esterel Mountains. Stop near the arena of the once-important Roman town Fréjus (founded by Julius Caesar in 49 B.C.). Then back to the continuous "Garden of the Seaside" to St.-Tropez—a fishing village artists and now the Beautiful People have turned into a famed resort. Lunch on the famous harbor with its luxurious yachts and poke around the boutiques. Return through St.-Raphaël, a Gallo-Roman holiday center, and the Golden Corniche of breathtaking beauty. Pass by the landing beaches of Le Drammont (Allied Forces, 1944) and on through the artists' haunts of Agay, Anthéon, Le Trayes and back to Cagnes with its wide, sandy beaches. Return home along the national road through Golfe-Juan and Juan-les-Pins.

THE LÉRINS ISLANDS (FROM CANNES) Esterel Chanteclair Company, Gare Maritime of the Islands Tel: 39.11.02 June to September: departs from Cannes at 7, 10, 11:20 A.M., 2, 2:30, 3, 3:30 P.M.; from the islands at 12 noon, 3, 4, 5, 6 P.M. October to June: departs from Cannes at 7:30, 10, 11:20 A.M., 2, 2:45 P.M.; from the islands at 12 noon, 4, 5 P.M. Daily round-trip fare 8F ($2) to both islands, 6F ($1.50) to Ste.-Marguerite only.

A 20-minute boatride from Cannes will bring you to the island of Ste.-Marguerite, the highest and largest of the two islands. Here you will visit the famous and legendary castle, the Prison of the Iron Mask, the cells where the Protestant pastors were incarcerated after the French Revolution. From the château's terrace there is a beautiful view of the Bay of Cannes, with the Alps serving as a backdrop. Open every day on arrival of the ferry.

Near the island of Ste.-Marguerite, separated only by a narrow channel called Plateau du Milieu, is the island of St.-Honorat. Its Cistercian Abbey, with an old fortified monastery dating back to the 15th century, also belongs to the legends of Cannes. The new monastery has a museum containing stone fragments of the Roman and Christian era that were discovered on the island. From the monastery you have access to the church. St.-Honorat is traceable to the fourth century, when he founded the monastery, which became one of the most illustrious in Christendom. In the 5th-century chapel of the Trinity, located at the extreme end of the island looking eastward, you may attend religious services held by one of the monks of the Abbey of Lérins, at 11 A.M. on Sundays and holidays from Easter to All Saints' Day. You will also find souvenir shops on the island, and the famous "Lurina" liquor.

Tickets are purchased at the station upon departure.

THE LÉRINS ISLANDS (FROM NICE)   Price: 25F ($6.25)

You can also visit the islands from Nice. A bus leaves from Nice at 8:45 A.M., crosses the Var River, passes through Cagnes (see the medieval Grimaldi Castle), the old town of Antibes, and the famous residential Cap d'Antibes. From there, a boatride to Ste.-Marguerite; after lunch, a second boatride to St.-Honorat. Back in Cannes, you have time to stroll the streets a bit before returning via bus to Nice, arriving back at 6:30 P.M.

30
Beauty Comes First

The average prices at beauty salons on the Riviera are as follows:

Shampoo and set	15F to 30F	$3.75 to $7.50
Cut	7F to 20F	$1.75 to $5
Bleaching (just the roots)	14.50F to 25F	$3.62 to $6.25
Manicure	8F to 20F	$2 to $5
Facial	25F to 30F	$6.25 to $7.50
Make-up	15F to 20F	$3.75 to $5

See the chapters on Nice and Cannes for lists of beauty salons and saunas there.

31
Shopping

While basking in the sun, sea, and the unique civilization of this delightful area of the Mediterranean, you will undoubtedly be looking out of the corner of your eye at the glamorous shops of Nice and Cannes, the antique stores of Monte-Carlo, the potteries of Vallauris, and the swinging boutiques of St.-Tropez.

Here the emphasis is on the fun items that make holidays and their memories happier: real Riviera bikinis, wild sunglasses, resort RTW (ready-to-wear), local arts and crafts, as well as practical items for vacationers.

Shopping Hours

Stores are generally open Monday through Saturday, 9:30 to 12:30 and 2:30 to 6:30. Most shops remain open later during the peak months of July and August. Lunchtime closing is a custom on the Riviera as in other Mediterranean regions, but increasing numbers of shops are giving it up. "Closed for vacation" signs usually go up in November, traditionally the Côte d'Azur's quietest month.

Shopping Tips

Export discounts of up to 20% are given on purchases to be taken out of France. When payment is made in any foreign currency, a form is filled out and a copy of it must be given to French customs at the point of embarcation. In many cases, the refund is granted on the spot, while in other cases, it is sent to the purchaser's home address.

Perfume dealers usually make deliveries to ships and planes on duty-free sales.

Remember, there is no U.S. customs duty on original artwork or antiques over 100 years old. Just don't forget your certificate of origin.

SHOPPING NOTE   The Tourist Office in Cannes offers you a very interesting booklet of coupons, called a *carnet de séjour*, which you can use all over Cannes for discounts at various shops for free gifts. You pay nothing for it and it does come in handy. Just drop into the Tourist Office on the Croisette and ask for it.

Nice / Côte d'Azur Airport

Have a few minutes before departure time? The airport has the following shops: *Rodier*, knits and silks; *Parfumerie*, perfumes and beauty products; *Bureau de Tabac*, smoker's needs, periodicals, postcards, souvenirs, games, and film.

32
Welcome to Nice

Nice is the capital and reigning queen of the Riviera. It is the sixth-largest and the most rapidly expanding city in France. You will notice its beauty first, then its vitality and variety.

Nice is famous for its magnificent Promenade des Anglais, a boardwalk bordering the beach; for its casinos; its festivals and carnivals; its onion-domed churches, elegant shops, radiant flower market; picturesque port; luxury hotels; and for the winding, narrow, surprising Old Town as well as fabulous, time-honored restaurants serving every kind of food.

With all this to offer, it is natural to use Nice as a central point for all our Riviera sightseeing, though Cannes would also do quite well. Nice is the larger of the two, and Cannes is undeniably the greater mecca of high society. The range of prices is very much the same in both cities so your choice will depend on which location you want.

33
Where to Stay in Nice

The Promenade des Anglais is the preferred location in Nice since it is right on the beach. Most of the better hotels on the Promenade have their own private beaches, which is, of course, very convenient. However, there are also good hotels on the Avenue de Verdun and the Rue de France, both only one short block behind the Promenade and an easy distance to the beach. Then there are other excellent hotels scattered around the city. We will only list the more central ones here so that you will be within walking distance of wherever you wish to go. We will use the A, B, C system after each hotel name to indicate the age group that frequents this particular hotel.

All rates are for the season. There is a reduction during the off-season of approximately 20%.

HOTELS

Deluxe

HÔTEL NÉGRESCO   37, promenade des Anglais   B-C   Tel: 88. 39.51

All rooms here are double, but the rate for one person is 110F to 205F ($27.50 to $51.25); for a double: 132F to 235F ($33 to $58.75); including taxes and service. This is by far the most elegant hotel in town, with every room decorated in a different way. It would be impossible to describe the magnificent décor in the various rooms, but take my word for it, it is out of this world. Some resemble Arab tents; some are furnished entirely with antiques, their walls covered in silk; some have leopard carpeting; and all are beautiful. Over 70% of the back rooms have been remodeled in a very modern style, whereas the front and side rooms are traditional. Most of the décor is inspired by the manor houses and châteaux of France. They feature a wide collection of tapestries, paintings, and antique furniture. And the staff is dressed in 18th-century costume! The bar, with its gleaming parquet floors, balcony, and red-and-blue plush seats, is a popular meeting place for guests. The elegant restaurant, though very expensive, is well worth the prices. Beauty salon.

HÔTEL PLAZA   12, avenue de Verdun   B-C   Tel: 87.80.41

Single: 130F to 150F ($32.50 to $37.50); double: 195F to 230F ($48.75 to $57.50); includes taxes and service, but no breakfast. The hotel faces the main plaza of the city, with its beautiful trees and shrubbery, where there are concerts in the summer. From the higher floors and the roof you can look right out over the city. The front rooms facing the sea have balconies. All have modern baths with showers. Most are air-conditioned and most have mini-bars. There is a delightful roof garden for sunbathing, drinks, or snacks; especially beautiful at night. During the season, dinner dancing on Saturday night. There are two restaurants and three bars for your pleasure. Beauty salon.

Four Star NN

HÔTEL ADRIATIC   81, rue de France   B-C   Tel: 88.79.68

Single: from 56F to 77F ($14.00 to $19.25); double: from 88F to 110F ($22 to $27.50); including breakfast, taxes, and service. Very comfortable and convenient hotel, all rooms quite large, well furnished, with good-sized modern baths.

HÔTEL ATLANTIC   12, boulevard Victor-Hugo   B-C   Tel: 88.40.15

Single: from 88F to 110F ($22 to $27.50); double: 120F to 154F ($30 to $38.50); including breakfast, taxes, and service. The rooms are large and well furnished and the baths very spacious. Right in the center of the city, this hotel is elegant as well as convenient.

HÔTEL MERIDIEN   1, promenade des Anglais   B-C   Tel: 82.25.25

Single: from 135F to 210F ($33.75 to $52.50); double: 165F to 245F ($41.25 to $61.25); *no* breakfast, taxes, or service included. A brand-new hotel owned by Air France, offering all the latest comforts and conveniences. Though right on the beach it still has its own 240-square-foot swimming pool on the roof. There is also a solarium where you can bronze up before you go out onto the beach, plus a sauna and massage room and a beauty salon. And if that is not enough, how about a cinema, a theater, a concert hall, and a casino, all right in the hotel! All rooms are air-conditioned and have terraces or balconies.

MÔTEL NAPOLÉON   6, rue Grimaldi   B-C   Tel: 87.70.07

Centrally located on a side street running just a few blocks between Rue Victor-Hugo and Rue Masséna. Single: from 50F to 70F ($12.50 to $17.50); *not* including breakfast, service, or taxes. Medium-size, comfortable, traditionally decorated rooms with large baths.

PARK HÔTEL   6, avenue Gustave-V   B-C   Tel: 87.80.25

Single: 77F to 152F ($19.25 to $38); double: 105F to 176F

($26.25 to $44); including breakfast, service, and taxes. Large, simply furnished rooms. The front rooms all have balconies looking onto the park and the sea. The hotel is situated just a few doors down from the Hôtel Plaza and overlooks the central plaza of the city. It is just a short block to the beach. The hotel is also close to Masséna Square. Very conveniently situated for all the shops and restaurants on the street directly behind the hotel. There is a restaurant in the hotel but I found it very dreary.

HÔTEL ROYAL   21, promenade des Anglais   B-C   Tel: 88.40.91
Single: from 60F to 110F ($15 to $27.50); double: from 88F to 143F ($22 to $35.75); taxes and service included, but no breakfast. Right on the beach, all front rooms face the sea and have balconies. The rooms are rather small but very nice. The hotel itself is very comfortable and has a good clientele.

HÔTEL SPLENDID SOFITEL   50, boulevard Victor-Hugo   B-C
Tel: 88.59.64
Single: from 100F to 110F ($25 to $27.50); double: from 148F to 175F ($37 to $43.75); including breakfast, taxes, and service. The hotel has been here since 1890, was entirely reconstructed in 1964, and has now been redecorated throughout. All rooms are very modern and some have balconies. It is completely air-conditioned and has an open-air swimming pool on the roof with beautiful views of the city and the mountains.

HÔTEL WESTMINSTER   27, promenade des Anglais   B-C   Tel: 88.29.44
Single: from 72F to 105F ($18 to $26.25); double: from 105F to 128F ($26.25 to $32); including breakfast, taxes, and service. An older-style hotel with traditional rooms and décor. Quiet, comfortable, and very convenient.

Three Star NN

HÔTEL ALBERT-Ier   4, avenue des Phocéens   A-B-C   Tel: 85.74.01
Single: from 44F to 132F ($11 to $33); double: from 66F to 158F ($16.50 to $39.50); breakfast, taxes, and service included. Facing the main plaza of the city, just a block down from the Place Masséna, and a short block to the beach, this is a very convenient hotel, though not very modern. The rooms are a bit small, but though simply furnished they are comfortable and many have balconies.

HÔTEL AMBASSADOR   8, avenue de Suède   A-B-C   Tel: 87.75.79
Single: from 72F to 83F ($18 to $20.75); double: from 110F to 132F ($27.50 to $33); breakfast, taxes, and service included. Very nice, clean, comfortable hotel just one block from the beach and opposite the main park. Modern rooms and especially modern bathrooms, except the toilets.

HÔTEL BRICE ET BEDFORD   44–45, rue du Maréchal-Joffre   A-B-C   Tel: 88.14.44

Single: from 36F to 65F ($9 to $16.25); double: from 64F to 103F ($16 to $25.75); including breakfast, taxes, and service. Centrally located. The rooms are rather small and simple but comfortable.

HÔTEL BUSBY 38, rue du Maréchal-Joffre A-B-C Tel: 88. 19.41

Single: 66F ($16.50); double: 88F ($22); including breakfast, taxes, and service. An older hotel, centrally located. The rooms are quite adequate, simply furnished but very comfortable and clean.

HÔTEL CHATHAM 9, rue Alphonse-Karr A-B-C Tel: 87.80.61

Single: 64F ($16); double: 84F ($21); including breakfast, taxes, and service. Newly renovated in 1973, the hotel is conveniently located in the center of town, and is quiet and very comfortable. All rooms are large and modern and have modern baths. There is a TV lounge just off the main lobby. The young and handsome proprietor and manager, M. Venaud, will do his best to make you comfortable here.

HÔTEL CONTINENTAL-MASSÉNA 58, rue Gioffredo A-B-C Tel: 85.49.25

Single: from 80F to 90F ($20 to $22.50); double: from 110F to 120F ($27.50 to $30); including breakfast, taxes, and service. Just a couple of blocks off the Promenade and from the Place Masséna, the hotel is well located and still very quiet. Amazingly enough for a three-star hotel, this one has a number of modern comforts. For example, a Telecommand at every bed which allows you to make immediate contact with the desk or the outside world by phone, TV, or radio. All rooms are soundproof, modern, and large.

GRAND HÔTEL DE FLORENCE 3, rue Paul-Déroulède A-B-C Tel: 88.46.87

Single: 60F to 82F ($15.00 to $20.50); double: 88F to 120F ($22 to $30); including breakfast, taxes, and service. Centrally located just off Boulevard Victor-Hugo, the hotel is entirely new. The rooms are fairly large and very nicely done in the French traditional manner, but very colorful and all have TV and air-conditioning. There is a bar in the hotel.

HÔTEL LA MALMAISON 48, boulevard Victor-Hugo A-B-C Tel: 88.34.28

Single: 66F ($16.50); double: 110F to 120F ($27.50 to $30); including breakfast, taxes, and service. Centrally located, quiet, and very comfortable. The rooms are medium size and traditionally furnished.

HÔTEL MARINA 11, rue St.-Philippe A-B-C Tel: 88.69.76

One of the best budget hotels in Nice, very good for young people. Single: from 35F to 57F ($8.75 to $14.25); double: 63F to 86F ($15.75 to $21.50); including breakfast, taxes, and service. The hotel is rather small but adorable; it is extremely clean and comfortable and has very fine service. Only a half-block from the beach and next-door to a good shopping area.

There is a snack bar just behind the hotel for lunches and dinners, though no restaurant in the hotel itself.

HÔTEL VENDÔME   26, rue Pastorelli   A-B-C   Tel: 85.77.90
Single: 38F to 53F ($9.50 to $13.25); double: 50F to 77F ($12.50 to $19.25); including breakfast, taxes, and service. Just a couple of blocks from the Place Masséna, the railway station, bus station, stores, and restaurants. A small hotel, rather old, but certainly clean and comfortable, and a good buy for the money.

HÔTEL WEST-END   31, promenade des Anglais   B-C   Tel: 88.79.91
Right on the beach and yet not as expensive as the four-star and deluxe hotels, this too is an excellent choice. Single: from 35F to 70F ($8.75 to $17.50); double: 88F to 110F ($22 to $27.50); including breakfast, taxes, and service. An old, traditional-style hotel. The rooms are quite lovely and very comfortable. There is a restaurant in the hotel itself.

Two Star NN

HÔTEL AVENIDA   41, avenue Jean-Médecin   A-B-C   Tel: 88.55.03
Single: 28F ($7.00); double: 55F ($13.75); including breakfast, taxes, and service. Very centrally located on one of the main avenues so you need only walk out the door and find whatever you wish. The hotel is very comfortable; the rooms are medium size, simply furnished, and clean. For the price the location is very good.

HÔTEL DE BRUSSELS   17, rue de Belgique   A-B   Tel: 88.47.61
Single: from 31F to 50F ($7.75 to $12.50); double: 42F to 70F ($10.50 to $17.50); including breakfast, taxes, and service. Not at all near the beach; in fact, just across the street from the railroad station and a couple of blocks off of the main avenue of Jean-Médecin. The hotel is old but has balconies on the rooms facing front. Very quaint and European in style, which I rather like. The rooms are medium size, clean, and comfortable.

HÔTEL LES CAMÉLIAS   3, rue Spitalieri   B-C   Tel: 85.20.14
Single: from 25F to 39F ($6.25 to $9.75); double: 43F to 60F ($10.75 to $15); including breakfast, taxes, and service. Quietly situated in its own garden on the north end of town, just to the right of Avenue Jean-Médecin and good shopping. The rooms are medium size, and simply furnished but clean and comfortable. Even though the rates are low I wouldn't recommend this for a younger group because it is rather quiet and gets an older, steady clientele.

HÔTEL CARLTON   26, boulevard Victor-Hugo   A-B-C   Tel: 88.87.83
Single: from 25F to 28F ($6.25 to $7); double: from 36F to 50F ($9 to $12.50); including breakfast, taxes, and service. A very good location for such a low-priced hotel. The rooms are quite adequate, simply furnished but comfortable.

HÔTEL COLBERT   34, rue Lamartine   A-B-C   Tel: 85.14.38
Single: 45F ($11.25); double: 65F ($16.25); including breakfast, taxes, and service. On the north side of town near Avenue Jean-Médecin for good shopping, etc. The hotel is rather nicely situated considering its budget price. This is an older hotel, but only in the sense that it offers you all the nice old traditional touches. The rooms are large, done in modern style; one can be extremely comfortable here. The elegant restaurant with its chandeliers and touches of gilt offers an excellent cuisine and even has its own garden. An excellent buy for the money.

HÔTEL COLUMBIA   17, boulevard Victor-Hugo   A-B-C   Tel: 87.78.32
Single: 24F to 48F ($6 to $12); double: 40F to 66F ($10 to $16.50); including breakfast, taxes, and service. Well located in the center of town. Adequate rooms with simple furnishings; a good budget hotel.

HÔTEL CÔTE D'AZUR   57, boulevard Gambetta   A-B-C   Tel: 88.98.04
Single: 25F ($6.25); double: 38F to 55F ($9.50 to $13.75); including breakfast, taxes, and service. On one of the main boulevards of the south end of town. Well located for shopping and restaurants. The rooms are medium size, simply furnished, and quite adequate.

HÔTEL FRANCK-ZÜRICH   31, rue Paganini   A-B-C   Tel: 88.36.77
Single: from 27F to 64F ($6.75 to $16); including breakfast, taxes, and service. An old hotel, completely renovated, located near the railroad station. The rooms are simply but very nicely furnished in modern style. The baths are large, tiled, and also very modern. They've really done a nice job of sprucing up this hotel. If you don't want to be near the beach, this is a good location. There is a lounge and TV room.

HÔTEL LOCARNO   4, avenue des Baumettes   A-B-C   Tel: 88.54.94
Single: from 40F to 55F ($10 to $13.75); double: from 50F to 77F ($12.50 to $19.25); including breakfast, taxes, and service. A new building about 50 yards from the sea. Done in a rather sterile modern style but very comfortable. The hotel is located at the far south end of town, which means a bit of a walk to the center of the city.

HÔTEL MASSENET   11, rue Massenet   B-C   Tel: 87.11.31
Doubles only, from 55F to 75F ($13.75 to $18.75); including breakfast, taxes, and service. Very well located just off the boulevard and near the park—yet at prices far less than the Promenade hotels charge. Rooms are simple but attractive and the hotel offers good service.

HÔTEL PLM   60, avenue Jean-Médecin   A-B-C   Tel: 85.10.29
Single: from 22F ($5.50); double: from 30F to 40F ($7.50 to $10); no breakfast included. Very centrally located on one of the main avenues; excellent shopping at hand. This hotel belongs

to the PLM chain owned by the Rothschilds—who do a good job of management. The service is very good, and the rooms are always well decorated and very comfortable.

HÔTEL RÉGENCE 22, rue Masséna B-C Tel: 87.75.08

Single: 40F ($10); double: 48F to 55F ($12 to $13.75); no breakfast included. Just a short distance from the Promenade, the Place Masséna, and the park, it is very convenient to everything. Newly renovated, all rooms are done in a rather modern style and are very colorful. They are simply furnished but adequate. The baths are all tiled, with modern fittings.

HÔTEL ST.-GEORGES 7, avenue Georges-Clemenceau A-B-C Tel: 88.17.33

Single: from 32F to 42F ($8 to $10.50); double: from 48F to 72F ($12 to $18); including breakfast, taxes, and service. An older hotel with all the typical elegant touches. Centrally located, very convenient to everything. There is a lovely garden out back and a TV lounge. The rooms are rather small and simply furnished, but they are comfortable. The baths are all up-to-date modern with colored tile and very good fixtures.

HÔTEL ST.-PIERRE 2, avenue des Fleurs A-B-C Tel: 88.55.20

Single: 30F to 50F ($7.50 to $12.50); double: from 40F to 72F ($10 to $18); including breakfast, taxes, and service. Not too far from the center of town and not too long a walk to the Promenade. The rooms are medium size, simply furnished but very comfortable.

34
Wining and Dining in Nice

This will give you a general idea of the good restaurants all over the city. However, wherever you go you're bound to find choices of your own. Don't hesitate to step in anywhere; I'm sure the food will be of high quality.

RESTAURANTS

Expensive

BONG LAI 14, rue Alsace-Lorraine Tel: 88.75.36
Vietnamese and Chinese food. Located near the railroad station.

DRAGON 5, boulevard Gambetta Tel: 87.64.78
Chinese and French food. Right in the center of town.

GARAC 2, boulevard Carnot Tel: 89.57.36
Specializes in fish, *bouillabaisse,* and lobster.

LE GRILL Pizzeria (Chez Pierrot) 54, avenue Bellevue Tel: 82.41.43
Pizza, grilled meat and fish, brochettes. In the center of town. Closed Thursday.

MARSOUIN 2, rue St.-François-de-Paule Tel: 85.78.21
Fish fins, shellfish, seafood, *bourride,* and *bouillabaisse.* In the old city.

CHEZ LES PÊCHEURS 18, quai des Docks Tel: 85.59.61
Specializes in *bouillabaisse* and *bourride.* Closed Wednesday.

PÉRIGORD 7, avenue Georges-Clemenceau Tel: 88.79.23
Périgourdin and classic French cuisine. They also have an attractive summer garden. Located in the center of town.

PETIT BROUANT (Chez Puget) 4 bis, rue G.-Deloye Tel: 85.25.84
Specialty: *bouillabaisse.*

LE PORTOFINO 67, quai des Etats-Unis Tel: 85.67.21
Fish, grilled meats, and good Italian specialties. Seafront.

IL POZZO Hotel Westminster 1, rue Meyerbeer Tel: 87.02.87
Good Italian cuisine. Seafront.

PRINCE'S 57, quai des Etats-Unis Tel: 85.71.56
Specialties: lamb, *bouillabaisse,* and local fish. There is a terrace right on the sea. Closed Thursday.

RASCASSE   18, cours Saleya   Tel: 85.70.93
Local fish, *bouillabaisse, bourride,* paella, grilled bass with fennel. In the old city.

RAYNAUD   59, quai des Etats-Unis   Tel: 85.66.54
Specialty: fish.

LA ROUSTICA   11, rue Biscarra   Tel: 85.20.31
Niçois and Oriental foods and pizza. In the center of town.

TCHIM-TCHIM   3, quai des Deux-Emmanuel   Tel: 89.46.54
Seafood; Indonesian dishes on request.

VIETNAM   40, rue de la Buffa   Tel: 88.30.18
Chinese, Japanese, and Vietnamese food. Thursday opens at 7 P.M. Located in the center of town.

ZORBA   8, rue d'Italie   Tel: 87.32.58
Greek and Lebanese food. The moussaka and the lamb kebabs are delicious. Greek music. Open from 9 P.M. to midnight, closed Tuesday. Near the railroad station.

Moderate

LA BONBONNIÈRE   18, rue Biscarra   Tel: 85.29.70
Fish soup and *niçois* dishes. Closed Saturday.

LA BRÉSILIENNE   75, quai des Etats-Unis   Tel: 80.06.40
Seafood and traditional French cooking, with a large menu. Open every day.

LE CAPITOLE   52, promenade des Anglais   Tel: 87.31.82
Specialties: paella, scampi. Center of town.

LA CASITA   12, passage Masséna   Tel: 87.78.43
Specialties: *couscous* and paella. Near the center of town.

COMMERCE   11, place Garibaldi   Tel: 85.90.80
Couscous served every day. Center of town.

LE CUL DE POULE   32, rue de Assalit   Tel: 85.21.52
Normand seafood. Closed on Sunday. Center of town.

DALPOZZO   33, rue de la Buffa   Tel: 88.97.06
Oriental dishes. Center of town.

LE DAMIER   45, rue de France   Tel: 88.13.09
Algerian and Tunisian dishes. Located in the center of town. Open 7 A.M. to 11 P.M.

DEPALLE   11, rue Meyerbeer   Tel: 88.25.95
Regional cuisine. In the center of town.

EMBASSY ET DU COMMERCE   18 bis, rue Biscarra
Niçois and Provençal dishes, especially *bouillabaisse.* In the center of town.

FLORIAN   22, rue Alphonse-Karr   Tel: 88.47.83
Specialty: Alsatian dishes. Closed in November. Located near the center of town.

GRAND CAFÉ DE LYON   33, avenue Jean-Médecin   Tel: 88.13.17
Specialties: rabbit and duck. Center of town.

MICHEL   12, rue Meyerbeer   Tel: 88.77.42
Specialties: oysters and seafood. Closed Monday. Center of town.

LA PAGODE   4, rue Paul-Déroulède   Tel: 88.56.14
Vietnamese and Chinese food.

CHEZ PIERRE   8, avenue St.-Jean-Baptiste   Tel: 85.41.51
Seafood, fish, *bouillabaise.*
POZNANSKI   1, rue Longchamps   Tel: 87.96.40
Specialty: perch. Located in the center of town.
LA REINE PÉDAUQUE   9, rue Paul-Déroulède   Tel: 88.86.01
Grills and seafood.
CHEZ SUZANNE ET NOÉ   26, boulevard Victor-Hugo   Tel: 88.
49.75
Wild boar a specialty, as well as seafood and fish soup. Center of
town.

Inexpensive

At these prices, naturally most of these are brasseries or little
cafés. You certainly won't find the intimate atmosphere you
would in restaurants that cost a bit more. However, the food
is good and service fast.

BRASSERIE CASSINI   30, rue Cassini   Tel: 85.54.14
Snacks and all varieties of pizza. Open day and night, closed on
Thursday. Seafront.
LA CANISSE   2, rue Barillerie
Hungarian dishes. In the old city.
FÉLIX-FAURE   14, avenue Félix-Faure   Tel: 85.49.58
Snacks and all varieties of pizza. Center of town.
AUX GOURMETS   12, rue Dante   Tel: 88.53.61
Specialties: *coq au vin,* braised chicken in cream, veal kidneys,
and filet of sole with champagne. Located in the center of town.
L'INTERLAKEN   26, avenue Durante   Tel: 88.81.36
Specialties: Pepper steak and *soufflé Grand Marnier.* In the cen-
ter of town.
LE KRONENBOURG   55, rue Gioffredo   Tel: 85.46.84
Specialty: cold meats. In the center of town.
DE LILOU   9, rue Penchianatti   Tel: 85.61.95
Regional dishes. Near the center of town.
LA PETITE CAVE   43, rue Pastorelli   Tel: 85.24.33
Specialties: *bouillabaisse, couscous,* paella. Located in the center
of town.
LE PRONY   3, rue Alsace-Lorraine   Tel: 87.20.39
Niçois dishes. Located in the center of town.
LE PROVENÇAL   19, rue Pertinax   Tel: 80.58.78
Aïoli, frogs' legs, grills. In the center of town.
LA ROMANTICA   19, avenue Durante   Tel: 88.18.05
Specialties: *bourride, caneton à l'orange,* duck with olives. In the
center of town.
AU SOLEIL   7 bis, rue d'Italie   Tel: 88.77.74
Specialty: provincial dishes. In the center of town.
TAVERNE DU CHÂTEAU   42, rue Droite   Tel: 85.88.30
Niçois dishes. In the Old City.

35
Nighttime Entertainment in Nice

The theater season runs from November to April and includes a magnificent calendar of performances. For programs of the opera, and the various theaters, check with your concierge or the daily paper.

OPERA

OPÉRA   Rue St. François-de-Paule, just off the Promenade near Albert Park   Tel: 85.67.31

THEATERS

THÉÂTRE DES ARÈNES   (Cimiez)
Ballet and opera performances in the open air during the summer.
CAFÉ THÉÂTRE   Mille-Pattes 1, rue du Congrès   Tel: 88.39.75
THÉÂTRE DU CASINO   In the Casino Municipal
For drama, ballet, and recitals.
CERCLE MOLIÈRE   Théâtre Municipal du Vieux-Nice   Rue St.-Joseph   Tel: 80.00.73
COUSIN BIBI   2, rue Alberti   Tel: 85.37.17
THE HALL DU CASINO   In the Casino Municipal
Features excellent musical productions.
THÉÂTRE DE NICE   Esplanade des Victoires   Tel: 80.69.17
Box office open every day except Monday from 9 A.M. to noon and 3 to 7 P.M.
THÉÂTRE DE VERDURE
Variety shows in the open air; only in the summertime. Some of the world's top singing stars perform here and you can hear them in the entire surrounding area, whether you buy a ticket or not.

CINEMAS

All over the place. Check your daily newspapers to see what's playing.

CABARETS

The Place de la Méditerranée is really the best bet for a woman alone, for here you can have dinner and see the show without feeling conspicuous. However, if you have a companion, either male or female, do try the Showboat, Candy, Folies Club, and Mayfair (a real Parisian-style cabaret).

NIGHT CLUBS

Only if you are with two or three other people or have a date. They are: Le Gorille, Whiskey-à-Go-Go, Cha-Cha-Club.

GAMBLING

Throughout the year at the Casino Municipal, Place de la Méditerranée, and Nouveau Casino.

36
Sightseeing in Nice

NEW TOWN Place Masséna

This is the focal point of every visit to Nice. Many of the activities center around this famous square, which consists of a fine group of Genoese style buildings with arcades dating back to the 17th century. The Jardins Albert I, planted with exotic trees and palm trees, extend from the Place Masséna to the Promenade des Anglais. It contains an open-air theater where some of the world's greatest artists perform. In fact, if you're staying at the Park or Plaza hotels, you need not even buy a ticket. You can hear the entire performance, and I dare you to sleep!

OLD NICE

A maze of lively, picturesque streets, containing churches, residences, and shops dating from the 17th century. Here you will find Ste.-Réparate Cathedral with its onion dome, and the churches of Gesú, St.-Augustin, and Ste.-Rita. Most of the sanctuaries of Old Nice contain rich furniture and interesting works of art. In the Chapelle de la Miséricorde, you can see the painting of the Virgin by Miralhet dating from the beginning of the 15th century.

Old palaces of the 17th century are generally of Genoese style, as are the prefecture of the Old Senate, Lascaris Palace, and the former Town Hall.

THE CHÂTEAU

This is actually a hill where the Greek town, founded in the fifth century B.C., originally stood. In 1705, the citadel of the town was razed to the ground, and today only public gardens stand in their place. They can be reached by a lift; the view from the top of the hill of the town below and the sea is beautiful.

EXHIBITION GALLERIES Les Pouchettes 77, quai des Etats-Unis Tel: 85.65.23

Open daily from 10 to 12 and 2 to 6 P.M., except Monday. Here are displayed the works of Matisse, Chagall, Picasso, Dufy.

THE FLOWER MARKET

One of the most glorious of all flower markets. Open mornings (mid-October to mid-May) on Rue St.-François-de-Paule. In the summertime it is held on Boulevard Jean-Jaurès.

BEAUX-ARTS MUSEUM 33, avenue des Baumettes

Here you may see 17th-century Gobelins tapestries, frescoes by Raphael, paintings by Jules Chéret, Carpeaux, Matisse, Dufy;

sculpture from China and Japan; and the history of the Nice Carnival. Open every day except Monday and holidays from 10 to 12 and 2 to 5 P.M.

MASSÉNA MUSEUM   65, rue de France;   35, promenade des Anglais (two entrances)

This Italian-style villa was built originally for Victor Masséna, Prince of Essling, in 1900. Its treasures include the richly decorated reception suite, *niçois* primitives, paintings of the Impressionist school. Arms, faïence, jewels. Regional folklore. Valuable library bequeathed by the Chevalier de Cessole. Open every day, holidays excepted, from 10 to 12 and 2 to 5 P.M.

MUSEUM OF NATURAL HISTORY   60 bis, boulevard Risso   Tel: 85.07.83

Open daily from 10 to 12 and 2 to 4 P.M., from October through February; and from 10 to 12 and 2 to 5 P.M., from March through August; closed Monday and public holidays. They have some extraordinary collections here, and it's worth a couple of hours. Admission 1F ($.25).

PALAIS LASCARIS   15, rue Droite   Tel: 80.38.16

Belonging to an old Nice family of the aristocracy, the palace was constructed in the 18th century and partly transformed in the 19th. Baroque style was influenced by local form. Many ceilings are believed to have been painted by J. B. Carole in the 17th century. Collection of Italian-style furniture. Open in the summertime from July to September, 9 to 12 and 2 to 6 P.M. every day. In the winter: Wednesday, Thursday, Saturday, and Sunday, 9 to 12 and 2:30 to 3:30 P.M. Entrance 4F ($1) for tour with commentary; 2F without tour.

PRIEURÉ DU VIEUX-LOGIS   59, avenue St.-Barthélemy

In an ancient provincial farm house, a complete reconstruction of an ancient priory, with furniture, *objets d'art,* paintings, and sculpture of the 15th and 16th centuries. Open Thursday and Saturday and the first Sunday of the month, from 3 to 5 P.M.

IN CIMIEZ

ROMAN RUINS   Villa des Arènes, 164, avenue des Arènes   Tel: 85.97.25

Open daily in winter, every afternoon except Monday, from 2 to 5 P.M.; summer: daily from 10 to 12 and 2 to 7 P.M.

MATISSE MUSEUM   Hill of Cimiez

In the very lovely setting of an 18th-century mansion with admirable interior proportions, and facing archaeological excavations of ancient Nice (a temple and a Christian basilica), a remarkable collection of works by Matisse has just been opened. It contains more than 40 canvases and drawings by the artist, who spent the last years of his life in Nice. Open in summer daily from 10 to 12 and 2 to 7 P.M., and in winter every afternoon except Monday from 2 to 5 P.M.

37
Sports in Nice

Beaches

Most big hotels have private beaches with salt-water swimming pools, solariums, pool-side service, and bar.

The price of admission to main public beaches is nominal, about 2F to 8F ($.50 to $2), plus charges for anything else you want: cabana, umbrella, or whatever.

Skin Diving

EXPLORATION SOUS-MARINE ET ÉCOLE DE PLONGÉE

Tennis

NICE LAWN TENNIS CLUB

Water Skiing

BAINS DE LA PLAGE
OPÉRA PLAGE
RUE PLAGE
SPORTING PLAGE

38 Beauty Comes First in Nice

Here is a list of beauty salons and hairdressers in Nice. For price ranges, see the Riviera chapter, page 230.

COIFFEUR L'AIGLON   20, rue Verdi   Tel: 87.06.20
ANDRÉ-LUC   2, rue Offenbach   Tel: 88.11.15
ANTONIO ET ALBAN   6, avenue Gustave-V   Tel: 87.93.79
JEAN CANESTRIER   20, rue Pertinax   Tel: 85.61.88
JOSEPH CARLIN   1, boulevard Carnot   Tel: 85.30.61
DAURELLE   6, avenue de la Californie   Tel: 86.55.38
LES ENTRERURS   8, rue Spitalieri   Tel: 85.49.55
SALON DES GALERIES LAFAYETTE   (in the store)   6, avenue Jean-Médecin   Tel: 85.39.65
GEORGE SALON DAMES   168, avenue St.-Lambert   Tel: 84.20.58
ILDY   254, avenue de la Californie   Tel. 86.34.45
JACQUES ET ROBERT   5, rue de Rivoli   Tel: 88.23.45
JACY DE PARIS   25, promenade des Anglais   Tel: 88.15.24
DANY JADE   29/31, avenue Georges-Clemenceau   Tel: 87.61.42
COIFFEUR JEANNE   7, rue Verdi   Tel: 88.30.37
COIFFEUR JOEL   4, rue Molière   Tel: 88.30.37
MAJUY SABATIER   5, rue Meyerbeer   Tel: 88.70.73
MARIO AND CHRISTIAN   11 bis, rue Massenet   Tel: 87.13.47
NEGRESCO   1, rue de Rivoli   Tel: 88.60.44
COIFFEUR PARIS-RIVIERA   5, rue Lamartine   Tel: 80.02.97
SALON POMPADOUR   24, rue de France   Tel: 88.17.50
TONYA   8, avenue de Verdun   Tel: 87.70.57

39
Shopping in Nice

DEPARTMENT STORES

CAP 3000 St.-Laurent-du-Var
The biggest, brightest, and newest shopping center in the South of France, Cap 3000 is located next to the Nice/Côte d'Azur Airport, 4 miles west of Nice. The huge complex houses a large Nouvelles Galeries department store, supermarket, garden center, auto service center, cinema, and four restaurants. Among the ladies' boutiques at Cap 3000 are names like Banane, Carnaby, Paola, Rodier, Thierry et Sigrand, and Terrible. Beauty establishments are the Elysées 3000 and Coiffure N.G. Shoe stores are André, Byron, Montclair, and Rémy. Other shops include those offering home furnishings and appliances, photographic equipment and supplies, watches and jewelry, gifts, sporting goods, stationery, pharmaceuticals, and books. Open 10 A.M. to 1 A.M. Monday through Saturday.

GALERIES LAFAYETTE 6, avenue Jean-Médecin
One of a major French chain. The emphasis is on good taste and quality. The Nice stores have a "20 Ans" boutique selling youthful ready-to-wear by top Paris designers. Also a delightful gadget and souvenir department.

PRISUNIC 42, avenue Jean-Médecin
One of the nationwide chain described in the section on shopping in Paris. A good place to stock up on suntan lotion, cosmetics, and notions. Budget to moderate prices.

À LA RIVIERA 46, avenue Jean-Médecin
The Côte d'Azur's own department store, fully stocked and very popular with the local residents.

UNIPRIX 54, avenue Jean-Médecin
Similar in operation to Prisunic, with a slightly wider selection of casual clothing.

BOUTIQUES AND SMALL SHOPS

AMIE 14, avenue de Verdun
Smart Côte d'Azur styles in sportswear and swimsuits. Moderate prices.

BANANE   33, avenue Jean-Médecin
Youthful, modish ready-to-wear.

BRIGITTE BEL   10, rue Croix de Marbre
Très chic ready-to-wear. Same owner as Pink, listed below.

BIG BEN   45, rue Hôtel des Postes
Rendezvous of the young set.

CATHERINE BOUTIQUE   2, rue Masséna
Up-to-date sporty things for young ladies.

DALVIN   2, rue de la Liberté
A deluxe boutique offering classic styles in the grand manner.

FERNAND DESGRANGES   16, avenue de Verdun
Dresses, bags, belts, costume jewelry.

GIGI   10, rue de la Liberté
Good selection of daytime wear and a grand choice of evening dresses.

LA GOULUE   19, rue de la Liberté
For the "in" and the exotic. Different and diverting.

HARRY'S SPORT   26, avenue Jean-Médecin
Clothes for every sport, popular with the *Niçoises.*

HENRIETTE   5, rue de la Liberté
Well-known Riviera house of high fashion. Quality with matching prices.

BERNARD LAURENT   9, avenue Jean-Médecin
Specialists in leather, with the emphasis on Cardin.

MARIE-THÉRÈSE   Avenue de Suède et Avenue Gustave-V
Très très haute couture. Patronized by the Begum Aga Khan.

NON-STOP SOLDES   21, rue de la Buffa
Designer clothes with the labels deleted. Full range of minis, maxis, midis, dresses, suits, and coats, all at cost or below cost.

PAOLA   5, rue Masséna
Wide-ranging assortment of young-ish, Côte d'Azur–styled sportswear.

PINK   7, rue de France
Cardin and Riviera styles. Very chic ready-to-wear.

SONIA ROLLAN   25, promenade des Anglais
Open Sundays from 11 A.M. to 5 P.M., Sonia sells junior Riviera-styled dresses, pants, and blouses.

SAINT-LAURENT/RIVE GAUCHE   7-9, rue du Paradis
Like its Parisian namesake, it offers the latest ready-to-wear from the noted couturier.

SIR OLIVER   10, rue du Paradis
The youthful "now" look clearly in evidence.

SOLDINE   2, rue Dalpozzo
Favored by the young set, this outlet shop offers top name ladies' wear at bargain prices. Selection includes skirts and dresses (in all lengths), suits, and coats.

WINDY   26, rue Masséna
Yé-yé, for the young, wild, and willing.

LEATHER GOODS

LA BAGAGERIE 9, rue de la Liberté
Branch of the well-known Paris shop specializing in trend-setting town-and-country handbags, belts, and original luggage.

BALLY 30, avenue Jean-Médecin
The local outlet of the highly reputed Swiss chain. Fashionable footwear for ladies.

AU CAIMAN 2, place Magenta
High-style leather and crocodile handbags.

AU DÉPART 37, rue Masséna
Handbags, luggage, and classic umbrella styles. Also a nice selection of gadgets for the gift-minded.

HEYRAUD 3, place Masséna
Traditionally styled shoes for ladies and gents.

MARCELLE LADOUSSE 11, rue Masséna
Dressy day gloves and dressier evening gloves by Dior and others. Large selection of handkerchiefs and scarves.

LANCEL 9, avenue Jean-Médecin
Classic styles in handbags and luggage.

JULIE LANDS Rue Croix de Marbre
Au courant lace-up ladies' boots and short boots.

MARLY 24, rue Masséna
Brand-name shoes at reasonable prices.

OFAL 10, rue du Paradis
Pretty leather odds and ends, gift items, and gadgets.

OFRE 4, rue Dalpozzo
Shoes for the younger set at lower prices.

YOLANDE PERUGIA 6, avenue de Suède et avenue Gustave-V
Dress-up handbags for the evening, including pearl bags and the like. Will custom-make bags and shoes.

JEAN PIERRE Place Magenta
All the latest of the big continental names in shoes.

VUITTON 2, avenue de Suède et avenue Gustave-V
Home of the status-symbol luggage identified by yellow LV initials on brown leather. Matched sets are a specialty.

FOR HIM

BARCLAY 12, avenue de Verdun
Gentlemen's outfitters with a tendency toward the mod. Also fun fashions for the ladies.

COUCKE 4, avenue de Suède et avenue Gustave-V
Specialists in shirts for all occasions, but particularly casual wear.

DARON 8, avenue de Verdun
Wide array of sports- and beachwear for him.

FASSONABLE 9, rue du Paradis
Fine quality gentlemen's apparel for all seasons.

JANA FOR MEN   Place Magenta
  Haberdashers, featuring shirts, ties, odd trousers, and jackets.
J. JELLY   48–50, avenue Jean-Médecin
  For the younger and livelier set. If it's "in," it's here.

JEWELRY

AUGIER   10, avenue de Verdun
  Silver, deluxe costume jewelry and—a girl's best friend, diamonds.
BARICHELLA   14, avenue de Verdun
  Diamonds, pearls, quality costume jewelry, Swiss and French watches and larger timepieces.
BETTETINI   27, rue Alphonse-Kerr
  Rubies, diamonds, pearls, and silver. Also Swiss watches by the score.
BONET   24, rue de France
  Classic designs, costume pieces, and a treasure trove of silver doodads.
BOYER   1, rue du Paradis
  Precious stones and a good variety of watches.
CARTIER   Hôtel Négresco   Promenade des Anglais
  A Cartier representative with a desk at the hotel is pleased to show visitors selections from Cartier's very elegant stock on request.
MARTIN   2, avenue de Verdun
  Good array of rubies, other gemstones, and costume jewelry. Silver services for "tea for two" and more.
MORABITO   13, avenue Jean-Médecin
  Christofle silver, china, crystal, and watches.
PEYROT-RUDIN   11, avenue Jean-Médecin
  Costume jewelry to diamonds. Also watches and silver tea and coffee sets.

PERFUMES / GIFTS

ARINBO   8, rue Masséna
  Single porcelain and crystal gift items as well as sets of high quality.
ANNE ET FRÉDÉRIC   41, rue de France
  For gifts and a good stock of fascinating French gadgetry, try this shop.
ART ET CRISTAUX   6, avenue de Suède et avenue Gustave-V
  Fine Saint-Louis and Saxe porcelains.
CANTILÈNE   1, rue du Paradis
  Original selection of gifts for the home. Also Porcelaine de Paris and silver table service.

GALERIE DES GLACES   3, place Masséna
Baccarat, Bohémie, Daum, and Murano crystal, plus Saxe porcelains.

JACY DE PARIS   25 bis, promenade des Anglais
A parfumerie operated by the celebrated Paris coiffeur. All the brand-name scents. Also a good place to pick up a beret.

ROYAL PARFUMS   9, avenue Jean-Médecin
Good selection available in this popular shop on Nice's main shopping street.

ANTIQUES

ART ET JOIE   7, rue Maccarini
Antique jewelry from most any era.

BIANCHARELLI   26, rue Ségurane
Stashes of old silver adornments.

FIRMIN   20, rue Ségurane
Port-of-call for rare maritime curiosities.

LORD BYRON   2, avenue de Verdun
Furnishings and small doodads.

LA PETITE MARQUISE   50, promenade des Anglais
Far Eastern things, precious stones, and ivory.

40
Welcome to Cannes

The origins of Cannes are uncertain, although we do know that it goes back at least as far as the 10th century. The arrival of Lord Brougham from England in 1834 changed the face of what was still a tiny hamlet and began the evolution toward what it is today, the glamour capital of the Riviera.

Cannes is situated on an inlet of the Golfe de la Napoule. Its promenade along the beach, the Boulevard de la Croisette, has seen some of the most famous and celebrated people in the world. But in spite of all its glamour and fame it has a history as well. The old town, called Le Suguet, overlooking the harbor, is a very picturesque point; it contains an 11th-century tower, museums of Mediterranean civilization, pre-Columbian archaeology, Polynesian ethnography. From Cannes you can take a short excursion over to the Lérins Islands; Ste.-Marguerite, with its 17th-century castle; and St.-Honorat, with its fortified monastery and watch tower. So whether your preference is for glamour and games or for history, Cannes will not disappoint you.

HOTELS

Deluxe

All have telephone, radio, TV, wall-to-wall carpeting, and air-conditioning.

CARLTON HÔTEL 58, boulevard de la Croisette A-B-C Tel: 38.21.90

One of Cannes's palaces. Single: 68F to 200F ($17 to $50); double: 105F to 278F ($26.25 to $69.50); including breakfast, taxes, and service. This one was totally renovated in 1971 and is beautifully done. All the rooms are large and have double washbasins in the large, modern baths. The hotel has no swimming pool but is right on the beach. The gastronomic reputation of its restaurant with its gold frescoes is universal. There is also a beauty salon, a bar, and a magnificent terrace that draws a lot of celebrities for after-theater *tête-à-têtes*. The tennis courts are currently being redone and should have reopened by the time you read this.

GRAND HÔTEL 45, boulevard de la Croisette B-C Tel: 38.15.45

Single: 105F to 157F ($26.25 to $39.25); double: 136F to 220F ($34 to $55); including breakfast, taxes, and service. This too, is a palace. Unlike the other traditional types we have mentioned, this one is totally modern—in fact, very Scandinavian in its appearance, with bright colors and straight-line design. The rooms are large and have every convenience, including terraces. There is a beauty salon.

HÔTEL MAJESTIC Boulevard de la Croisette A-B-C Tel: 39.17.92

Right on the seafront, this is an absolutely beautiful hotel and certainly my very favorite. Single: from 100F to 255F ($25 to $63.75), including breakfast, taxes, and service. The entire hotel is constantly under renovation, and if you look at rooms that were done five years ago, you wouldn't believe that they weren't done the day before yesterday. They are truly elegant, done in silks and with French traditional furniture. The modern baths are all done in marble and each contains a double wash-basin. They are so lovely you wouldn't mind living in the bath-room alone, much less the room. Most front rooms have bal-conies but even those facing the back are attractive indeed. Elegance prevails everywhere, from the crystal-chandeliered main hall, to the high-ceilinged corridors. There is an excellent restaurant, a bar, beauty salon, and outdoor swimming pool, surrounded by a lovely patio and lawn.

HÔTEL MARTINEZ Boulevard de la Croisette B-C Tel: 39. 25.21

Single: from 68F to 210F ($17 to $52.50); including break-fast, taxes, and service. Although the rooms have been newly dec-orated, I find them rather plain—though they are large and very comfortable. The bathrooms in particular are huge, with double sinks. I wasn't too fond of the plain parquet floors in the restau-rant or of the garishness of the lobby, but the service is good and that's important. There is a beauty salon.

HÔTEL RÉSERVE MIRAMAR 66, boulevard de la Croisette B-C Tel: 38.24.70

Double: 136F to 210F ($34 to $52.50); no breakfast included. No singles available. The rooms are large but rather plain; all have terraces, which is worth something. The generally unim-pressive bathrooms have double washbasins. There is a beauty salon.

Four Star

All have wall-to-wall carpeting, radio, and TV. Most have air-conditioning.

CANBERRA HÔTEL 120-122, rue d'Antibes A-B-C Tel: 38. 28.70

Single: from 73F to 158F ($18.25 to $39.50); including break-fast, taxes, and service. A new modern hotel in the center of the city, not too far from the beach. The rooms are medium size, rather plain, but modern and very comfortable.

CANNES PALACE HÔTEL 14, avenue de Madrid A-B-C Tel: 38.28.36

Single: 84F to 157F ($21 to $39.25); including breakfast, taxes, and service. Situated at the end of the Croisette and not too far from the beach. It is done in a modern décor that I find a bit cold. The rooms are smallish but brightly colored. There is a restaurant, grill room, bar, color-TV room, sauna, beauty salon.

HÔTEL GONNET ET DE LA REINE 42, boulevard de la Croisette A-B-C Tel: 39.02.84

Single: 73F to 105F ($18.25 to $26.25), including breakfast, taxes, and service. Very conservative, small hotel, recently re-modeled. The rooms are a nice size, though some bathrooms are still old-fashioned.

HÔTEL SAVOY Rue F.-Einesy B-C Tel: 38.17.74

Single: 80F to 95F ($20 to $23.75); double: 84F to 100F ($21 to $25); including breakfast, taxes, and service. The rooms are large enough, traditionally furnished, and very comfortable. This is really a nice hotel.

HÔTEL SOFITEL MÉDITERRANÉE 1, boulevard Jean-Hibert B-C Tel: 99.22.75

Single: 80F to 126F ($20 to $31.50); double: 102F to 162F ($25.50 to $40.50); including breakfast, taxes, and service. Over-looking the yacht basin, the hotel is quiet and very comfortable. The rooms are medium size, done in a simple, modern style that is very adequate. The rooms also have a terrace overlooking the yacht basin. There is a swimming pool and solarium on the roof.

Three Star

HÔTEL ATHÉNÉE 6, rue Lecerf A-B-C Tel: 38.69.54

Doubles only, at 61F to 95F ($15.25 to $23.75). Conveniently located in the center of town, rather than on the beach, this is a very nice little hotel with adequate, clean, and comfortable rooms.

HÔTEL BEAU RIVAGE 61, boulevard de la Croisette A-B-C Tel: 38.24.25

Single: from 58F to 68F ($14.50 to $17); double: 79F to 89F ($19.75 to $22.25); including breakfast, taxes, and service. On the beach front. A pleasant enough hotel with simple but ade-quate rooms. There is a bar, a garden, and a TV lounge.

HÔTEL BEAU SEJOUR 100, rue Georges-Clemenceau A-B-C Tel: 99.06.99

Single: 106F ($26.50); double: 116F ($29); including break-fast, taxes, and service. A brand new hotel just opened in 1974, 150 meters from the beach. Rather nice from what I've been able to see of it, which was not too much. All rooms have bal-conies, mini-bars, and TV. There are a restaurant, bar, and pool at the hotel, plus a very lovely garden. Since it's so recently built it should offer the latest in comfort and service.

HÔTEL CLARICE 44, boulevard Alexandre-III A-B-C Tel: 38. 07.55

Single: 47F to 52F ($11.75 to $13); double: 53F to 89F ($13.25 to $22.25); including breakfast, taxes, and service. This charming new hotel is in an ideal situation, with a shady garden, a meadow, flower-filled terraces, and modern comfort. It is near the Croisette and the Palm Beach Casino. From the terraces you have a good view of the sea and mountains. The rooms are fur-nished in traditional French manner but the baths are large and modern. The public rooms too are done in traditional fur-nishings with tapestries. There is a snack bar and a restaurant with excellent cuisine.

HÔTEL EMBASSY 8, rue de Bône A-B-C Tel: 38.79.02

Single: 73F to 105F ($18.25 to $26.25); double: 84F to 126F ($21 to $31.50); including breakfast, taxes, and service. A very modern hotel, well located in the center of the city, quiet, and extremely nice. The rooms are large and furnished in good, modern style. All have air-conditioning, telephones, and very luxurious marble bathrooms. There is a solarium on the roof for sunbathing and a lovely private garden in front of the lounge. A good restaurant and grill room complete the picture. Extremely good value for the money.

HÔTEL ÎLES BRITANNIQUES 9, boulevard d'Alsace A-B-C
Tel: 39.05.85
Single: from 40F to 52F ($10 to $13); double: from 55F to 78F ($13.75 to $19.50); including breakfast, taxes, and service. Centrally located in the city, rather than on the beach, this hotel offers kitchenettes, which does help save on eating out. The rooms are small but comfortable.

HÔTEL LA MADONE 2–5, avenue Justinia A-B-C Tel: 38.57.87
Single: 53F to 105F ($13.25 to $26.25); double: 68F to 126F ($17 to $31.50); including breakfast, taxes, and service. About 150 meters from the Croisette and the beaches, this charming hotel is in a peaceful residential district. It has been renovated and is really very nice. The baths especially are very modern and colorful. The rooms are furnished in traditional French style and have a warm family air about them, as do the public rooms. The hotel has a garden terrace and a solarium.

HÔTEL LES ORANGERS 90, rue Georges-Clemenceau A-B-C
Tel: 39.99.93
Single: 53F to 63F ($13.25 to $15.75); double: 56F to 68F ($14 to $17); including breakfast. taxes, and service. Five minutes from the center of Cannes and 200 meters from the beach, this is a newly modernized hotel in a very quiet area. The rooms are rather small and simply furnished, but do provide a make-up table. There is also a heated outdoor swimming pool and a patio for sunning around it. The lobby is very modern and attractive with marble floors and modern furniture. The restaurant is done in typical provincial style with excellent food. There is also a bar.

HÔTEL DE PARIS 34, boulevard d'Alsace A-B-C Tel: 38.30.89
Single: from 53F to 95F ($13.25 to $23.75); double: 68F to 115F ($17 to $28.75); including breakfast, taxes, and service. About 200 meters from the Croisette in the center of town, this is a newly remodeled hotel. The rooms are rather large and all are furnished in provincial style with beautiful wallpaper, spreads, and draperies. The bathrooms are modern, with colored tiles. The front rooms have a balcony overlooking the garden in front. There is a colorful provincial bar as well.

HÔTEL DE PROVENCE 9, rue Molière A-B-C Tel: 38.44.35
Centrally located, quite close to the Palais du Congrès, this is a very nice little hotel with only 30 rooms. All are air-conditioned and have refrigerator, radio, and telephone; many have a balcony. Only 100 yards from the beach and close to all shopping and the Palais des Festivals, this is an excellent choice. The rooms are medium size, furnished rather nicely in traditional style with beautiful spreads and draperies. There is also a cute little bar. I don't have the rates on this, as it is rather new and

I couldn't get them when I was in Cannes, but I should think they would be about the same as the Clarice. It is worth checking out.

HÔTEL SPLENDID 4, rue Félix-Faure A-B-C Tel: 39.02.47

Single: 79F to 105F ($19.75 to $26.25), breakfast not included. Two blocks from the seafront, this is a newly remodeled hotel with small to medium-size rooms, some of which have balconies. The singles are small but have double beds. The back rooms too are smaller and cheaper, but they do have large bathrooms.

HÔTEL WESTMINSTER 55, boulevard d'Alsace B-C Tel: 38.56.47

Single: from 63F to 74F ($15.75 to $18.50); double: 79F to 95F ($19.75 to $23.75); including breakfast, taxes, and services. Not on the beach, but a very pleasant atmosphere, located in the middle of a quiet flower garden. Entirely renovated in a simple manner, the large rooms are very comfortable and homey. South-facing rooms have balconies. There is a restaurant, a bar, and a TV room.

Two Star

HÔTEL ALBERT 68, avenue de Grasse B-C Tel: 39.24.04

Double: 53F to 69F ($13.25 to $17.25); including breakfast, taxes, and service. Conveniently located, very comfortable hotel with medium-size, adequate rooms.

HÔTEL DES ALPES 15, rue St.-Givier A-B-C

Single: from 40F to 48F ($10 to $12); double: 48F to 68F ($12 to $17); including breakfast, taxes, and service. Quiet, comfortable hotel with its own garden. The rooms are medium size, comfortable, simply furnished but adequate. It also has a TV lounge.

HÔTEL CORONA 55, rue d'Antibes Tel: 39.69.85

Single: 35F to 53F ($8.75 to $13.25); double 30F to 65F ($10 to $16.25); no breakfast. On a main avenue, convenient to all the shops and restaurants, a good comfortable hotel with good-size rooms and baths. They have air-conditioning and a TV lounge.

DEVIHOTEL 7, rue Molière A-B-C Tel: 38.60.24

Single: 53F to 58F ($13.25 to $14.50); double: 58F to 95F ($14.50 to $23.75). Another new hotel about 100 yards from the Croisette and centrally located. The rooms are medium size but very well furnished in good, modern furniture including a make-up table. The baths are small but again modern and very convenient. The front rooms have balconies overlooking a lovely garden. It's worthwhile.

HÔTEL DE FRANCE 85, rue d'Antibes A-B-C Tel: 39.23.34

Single: 42F to 58F ($10.50 to $14.50); double: 62F to 73F ($15.50 to $18.25); including breakfast, taxes, and service. On the main avenue, traditional and comfortable hotel with medium-size rooms, simply furnished and very comfortable.

MOTELIA HÔTEL 283, avenue de Grasse A-B-C Tel: 99.16.21

Single: 32F to 53F ($8 to $13.25); double: 52F to 95F ($13 to $23.75); including breakfast, taxes, and service. Centrally located, a very modern hotel with large rooms done in simple modern furniture with louvered doors on the closets and colorful modern baths. Some rooms have balconies and there is a garden as well as a TV lounge. Some of the rooms have kitchenettes, which is worth looking into if you feel like saving money on eating out.

HOSTELLERIE DE L'OLIVIER 90, rue Georges-Clemenceau A-B-C Tel: 39.53.29

Single: from 32F to 42F ($8 to $10.50); double: from 58F to 78F ($14.50 to $19.50); including breakfast, taxes, and service. Very quaint and homey. Modern, but with the right touch of warmth and friendliness that overcomes the sterility of some modern hotels. Greenery everywhere you look, from the moment you approach the steps until you step out onto the deck, lends an additional warmth to the place. The little lanterns out front and the yellow sun umbrellas, too, offer a very cheerful welcome. The rooms are medium size with modern furniture, dressing tables, and balconies. The gardens form a lovely frame of green around this charming place. There is a TV lounge.

HÔTEL PLM 3, rue Hoche A-B-C Tel: 38.31.19

Doubles only: 42F to 74F ($10.50 to $18.50); including breakfast, taxes, and service. The usual PLM style; modern, clean, comfortable. The rooms are medium size, nicely done, and very adequate.

HÔTEL UNIVERSE 29, rue d'Antibes A-B-C Tel: 39.00.43

Single: 42F to 50F ($10.50 to $12.50); double: 50F to 60F ($12.50 to $15); including breakfast, taxes, and service. Located near the station and in the heart of the city, it is close to everything and only one block from the beach. I didn't see the rooms in this one but it has been recommended to me by other travelers. The lobby is very modern, clean, and comfortable and I found the desk clerk warm and friendly.

HÔTEL VENDOME 37, boulevard d'Alsace B-C Tel: 38.34.33

Single: 33F to 64F ($8.25 to $16); double: 62F to 76F ($15.50 to $19); including breakfast, taxes, and service. A completely renovated hotel, much more like a private residence than a hotel, situated in very pleasant surroundings, only 200 meters from the beach, and near the train station. The rooms are large and colorful, and have luxurious bathrooms. There is a very pleasant garden as well.

HÔTEL WAGRAM 140, rue d'Antibes B-C Tel: 38.55.53

Another quaint hotel that I heartily recommend as homey, friendly, and much more like a private residence than a hotel. Rates on single rooms only on demand. Double: 68F to 80F ($17 to $20); no breakfast included. Excellent value for the money. All rooms are rather large, traditionally furnished, and very comfortable. The lovely dining room overlooks a quiet, peaceful garden. The garden gate is only 75 yards from the Croisette. There is also a TV lounge.

42
Wining and Dining in Cannes

The following list, which gives only a few samples, is far from complete, but is quite enough to keep a visitor of even two or three weeks happy and well fed while in Cannes. Of course, in addition to places listed here, there are excellent restaurants located in the good hotels, where the food and service are always good.

Regional and Provençal Specialties

LE BISTINGO In front of the Suguet on the Jetée Albert-Edouard Tel: 39.34.66
Menu at 35F ($8.75).

THE BLUE BAR Palais des Festivals Boulevard de la Croisette Tel: 39.03.04
Regional and Provençal specialties.

LA CIGOGNE 8, boulevard de Strasbourg Tel: 38.65.35
Service at all hours.

LE FESTIVAL 55, boulevard de la Croisette Tel: 38.04.81
Large *à la carte* menu.

GEDEON BEDEON 23, rue Forville Tel: 99.01.27
À la carte menu.

LOU SOULEOU 16, boulevard Jean-Hibert Tel: 39.85.55
Menus from 16F to 20F ($4 to $5); also *à la carte*. Closed Tuesday.

LE MADRID RESTAURANT Cannes Palace Hotel 14, avenue de Madrid Tel: 38.28.36
Menus at 32F ($8); and *à la carte*. Regional specialties.

LA MÈRE BESSON 13, rue des Frères-Pradignac Tel: 39.59.24
The day's special is 20F ($5); also *à la carte*. Closed Sunday.

LA MÈRE FRANÇOISE 8, rue Meynadier (1st floor)
Menus at 16F, 18F, 20F ($4, $4.50, $5); also *à la carte*.

REINE PÉDAUQUE 4, rue Maréchal-Joffre Tel: 39.40.91
Menus from 40F to 50F ($10 to $12.50); also *à la carte*.

Seafood Specialties

ASTOUX ET BRUN   24, rue Félix-Faure   Tel: 31.21.87
Seafood specialties at all hours.
ASTOUX ET FILS   43, rue Félix-Faure   Tel: 39.06.22
Menus from 28F to 52F ($7 to $13) and extensive *à la carte*.
Closed Tuesday except in season.

Italian, International, and Regional Specialties

LA BUCCA DA BOUTTAU   10, rue St.-Antoine   Tel: 39.29.00
À la carte menu.
FÉLIX   63, boulevard de la Croisette   Tel: 38.00.61
LA PÊCHERIE   Restaurant of the Clubhouse of the New Harbor
Tel: 38.48.90
Seafood specialties, large *à la carte* menu.
LA TAVERNE SICILIENNE   16, quai St.-Pierre   Tel: 29.46.79
Italian specialties and *à la carte* menu.
VENEZIA   Rond-Point du Bois d'Angers   Tel: 38.37.60
Italian specialties. *Menu* at 25F ($6.25) and *à la carte*.

Bordelaise and Périgourdine Specialties

L'AUBERGE FLEURIE   102, avenue Michelle-Jourdan   Tel: 47.
19.88
Menus at 25F ($6.25); also *à la carte*.
LE FLAMBUSQUET   51, avenue de Vallauris   Tel: 99.53.22
Scandinavian and Périgourdine specialties. *Menus* starting at
25F ($6.25); also *à la carte*.

Lyonnaise and Provençal Specialties

LYONNAISE À LA PROVENÇAL   8 bis, rue des Frères-Pradignac
Tel: 39.26.65
Menus at 15F and 20F ($3.75 and $4); special of the day at
12F ($3). Tourist *menus* at 16F ($4).

Pizzerias

CHEZ MARIO   5, rue Jean-Dollfus   Tel: 39.58.61
LA PIZZA   3, quai St.-Pierre   Tel: 39.22.56
LA SOCCA   1, rue Rigué   Tel: 39.91.39

Oriental Specialties

CHEZ ROGER   16, rue des Frères-Pradignac   Tel: 39.14.68
Menus starting at 32F ($8).

Chinese Specialties

LE MANDARIN   Rond-Point du Bois d'Angers   Tel: 38.37.60
Menu at 26F ($6.50) and *à la carte*.

Vietnamese Specialties

L'ASIE   17, rue du Commandant-André   Tel: 39.39.55
Choice *menu* at 25F ($6.25); also *à la carte*.

FLEUR DE JASMIN   4, place de l'Hôtel de Ville   Tel: 39.44.86
Vietnamese, especially Hanoi, specialties. *Menu* at 25F ($6.25);
also *à la carte*.

HONG KONG   38, rue Georges-Clemenceau   Tel: 39.27.28
Menu at 20F ($5) and *à la carte*.

Fondues

ROMANENS   5, rue Notre-Dame   Tel: 39.35.16
Swiss fondue, fondue Bourguignonne, and specialties of hors
d'oeuvres in a cheese pastry.

LA TABLE IMPÉRIALE   8, galeries Fleuries   Tel: 39.12.29
Fondue saigonnaise.

LE TONNEAU   10, rue de Grasse   Tel: 39.48.33

43
Nighttime Entertainment in Cannes

CONCERTS AND SHOWS

SYMPHONIC CONCERTS On the Esplanade des Allées, in the gardens of the Croisette

During the summer months, particularly July and August, these concerts take place on Monday, Wednesday, and Friday at 9 P.M., and last about 1½ hours. Rates for seats: armchairs 5F ($1.25), chairs 2F ($.50); there is room for about 1,000 standees.

MUNICIPAL CASINO Esplanade des Allées, in the gardens of the Croisette Tel: 39.34.66

Open from November through May 31. A variety of plays, galas, shows, and concerts take place here all through the season. Check for performances scheduled.

PALM BEACH CASINO Tel: 38.25.00

Open from June 1 to October 15. Here, in the music hall of the Casino, are various orchestral performances, ballets, galas, and international attractions.

CASINO DES FLEURS Tel: 39.19.40

For plays, operettas, and musicals. Open all year.

PALAIS DES FESTIVALS On the Croisette

In May, the International Film Festival takes place here—screenings, receptions, galas, all attracting the film celebrities of the world. Other festivals during the year include jazz, TV, and advertising films. There is always bound to be something of interest on.

CINEMA

There are 12 movie houses in Cannes showing French and international films. Five of them are on the Rue d'Antibes. The average price for seats is 12F ($3). At the Lido, 32, boulevard de la République, and the Alexander III, on Boulevard Alexander-III, the seats are only about 6F ($1.50). Consult the local newspaper for the programs.

CABARETS AND NIGHT CLUBS

It is best to have a male escort, but, if not, another woman or two will do. You won't be refused admittance.

THE NEW BRUMMEL At the Gardens of the Casino Municipal Tel: 39.34.66 A-B
From November through May, starting at 10 P.M. There is a bar and a popular discothèque. Good crowd.

CASINO DES FLEURS 5–7, rue des Belges Tel: 39.19.40 A-B
Hi-fi and pop orchestra every evening from 10 P.M. till dawn. Matinee on Sunday and on holidays.

CAFÉ DES ALLÉES 2, rue Félix-Faure and Allées de la Liberté Tel: 39.00.95 A-B
Bar and dancing.

CHARLESTON 5, rue La Fontaine Tel: 28.57.84 A-B
Behind the Festival Palace. Every night from 10 P.M. Done in the style of 1925. This is a very popular discothèque, cabaret, and snack bar.

LA CHUNGA 1, rue Latour-Maubourg Tel: 38.11.29 A-B-C
Open all night. Bar, underground night club.

CYRANO 26, rue Meynadier Tel: 39.84.41 A-B-C
10 P.M. till dawn. Show—discothèque—dancing.

ROXY-CLUB 10, rue Teisseire Tel: 39.24.67 A-B-C
Open every night till dawn. A very atmospheric place, where you may have dinner and watch a show of international performers.

SHOW CLUB 28, rue Commandant-André Tel: 39.09.05 A-B-C
Every night from 9 P.M. till dawn. Bar, discothèque, good music and ambience, refined décor.

SPEAKEASY 72, rue Macé Tel: 39.31.31 A-B
Open every night, Sunday matinee. Bar-discothèque.

WHISKY À GO-GO 115, avenue de Lérins, facing the Palm Beach Casino Tel: 38.20.63 A-B
Open every night from 10 P.M. till dawn.

GAMBLING

CASINO MUNICIPAL
All game rooms closed from November through April.

PALM BEACH CASINO
All game rooms open from June 1 to October 15.

44
Sightseeing in Cannes

MONT CHEVALIER

Taking a pleasant walk, you may leave the Boulevard du Midi through Rue Jean Dollfus to the old town of Le Suguet on Mont Chevalier. By Rue Louis-Perrisol, you will find your way to the Place de la Castre, which is still surrounded by an old fortified wall. You will finally arrive in front of the **Church of Notre Dame d'Espérance** (17th-century church, Renaissance gate, and Gothic interior). Walking under the bell tower, you will reach Place St.-Anne, a long shady terrace with a view which extends over Cannes, the harbor, and the island of Ste.-Marguerite. While there, visit Le Suguet's 11th-century square tower, 72 feet high. Then walk through the ancient town with its quaint steps, winding roads, and shops.

MUSÉE DE LA CASTRE In the old castle near the Tour de Mont Chevalier, Le Suguet.

Here, there is a remarkable Grecian, Egyptian, Roman, and Cyprian collection left by the Dutch Baron Lycklama to the town of Cannes in 1871. Open daily except Monday from 10 to 12 and 2 to 4 P.M. in winter; in summer open till 6 P.M.

45
Sports in Cannes

CLUB MONTFLEURY Parc François-André, Avenue Beauséjour Tel: 38.75.78

I was tremendously impressed with this beautiful club because it offers you absolutely everything you could want in the way of sports and entertainment during the day and even during the evening. It is brand new and wasn't quite opened when we were there, but I could see exactly what it would be like when it was finished. There is an ice-skating rink (imagine, in this climate!), tennis courts, an open-air pool with a telescopic roof for the winter, bowling, and mini-golf. The beauty of it is that you can buy a lifetime membership for only 10F ($2.50) and this entitles you to make use of all the facilities at half-price any time you wish. The Club is laid out like a park, which you approach through a palm-lined lane. The clubhouse, at the end of the lane, has wall-to-wall glass that enables you to look out at the park, the swimming pool, courts, or whatever from the lounge and the public rooms. There is also a pizzeria, a brasserie, a cafeteria, a tea salon, and a bar. The center of the lounge is built around a huge tree that grows right through the building. It's the most interesting club of its kind that I have seen. The club is about a five-minute walk from the Hôtel Martinez on the beach or a short taxi ride, and you could easily spend the entire day and evening here if you like. All sporting equipment is available for rent so you need not bring anything with you.

The skating rink is open from October through April, from 8 A.M. to 11:30 P.M. The tennis courts, swimming pool, and bowling are open from 8 A.M. to 10 P.M. all year round, as are all the restaurants and bars. With your membership card, tennis will cost you 10F per hour ($2.50); the pool is 6F ($1.50), and you can stay in all day if you like; skating, 7F per entrance ($1.75), which means you pay only when you arrive and here, too, you can stay all day if you wish.

The beauty of it is that you meet not only other tourists such as yourself but important people who live in Cannes or those who visit for the entire season. And that, of course, is exactly what one is looking for on a trip. Who knows? You could quite easily be invited to someone's home or out to dinner, etc. One way or another, you're bound to meet someone interesting at the Club.

Public Beaches

BEACHES ON THE CROISETTE   Near the Municipal Casino
  In front of the Rue Macé
  In front of the Zamenhoff
  2 public beaches south of Port Canto
  Along Boulevard Eugène-Gazagnaire
BEACHES ON BOULEVARD JEAN-HIBERT
  There are seven public beaches scattered along this boulevard.
BEACHES ON THE BOULEVARD DU MIDI
  At the beginning of the Boulevard du Midi, going toward La
  Napoule, there are two beaches: the Méditerranée and Du Riou.
  From the Cannes city limits going toward La Napoule, there are
  three miles of public beaches.

Private Beaches

There are seven private beaches on Boulevard Jean-Hibert
and 27 private beaches on the Croisette. At all of them, various accommodations are available. The average prices (which
may be cheaper off-season) are as follows:

Cabin for two	6F	($1.50)
Dressing room	2F	($.50)
Dressing room with hot showers	2.50F	($.62)
Mattress	3.50F	($.87)
Umbrella	2.50F	($.62)
Deck chair	2F	($.50)

Golf

GOLF CLUB DE CANNES   In Mandelieu, 3 miles from town
  Tel: 38.95.39
  With an 18-hole golf course. Entrance fee for the entire day
  is 30F ($7.50), except on Saturday, Sunday, and holidays, when
  it is 40F ($10). Lessons are 25F ($6.25) per half-hour. All
  equipment may be rented at the club, and there is a restaurant
  and bar. Open daily except Tuesday.
GOLF BASTIDE DU ROY   In Biat, 7 miles west of Cannes   Tel:
  34.50.27
  Open every day. Entrance fee for the entire day is 30F ($7.50);
  lessons: 20F ($5) per half-hour. Equipment may be rented at
  club. Restaurant, bar.
GOLF DE VALBONNE   Tel: 67.00.08
  Open every day. Entrance fee for the day is 30F ($7.50), dur-
  ing the week. Lessons 30F ($7.50) per half-hour. Equipment
  rental at club. Restaurant, bar.

GOLF DE MOUGINS   Tel: 90.00.04
Open November through May. Entrance fee for the day is 30F ($7.50) during the week; 40F ($10) on Saturday, Sunday, and on holidays. Lessons 25F ($6.25) per half-hour. Equipment may be rented at the club. Restaurant, bar.

Horseback Riding

CERCLE DE L'ÉTRIER   Domaine de la Bacquerie, Mandelieu
Tel: 38.93.01
Lessons, riding in groups, training for competitions: 20F per hour ($5), insurance included. The great international horse show takes place here with the participation of the best French and foreign horsemen and -women. In October there are interesting riding and dressage competitions. Closed on Monday.

CLUB HIPPIQUE   Domaine du Maure Vieil, Mandelieu   Tel: 38. 82.56
Lessons, accompanied rides, cross-country rides: 12F to 16F ($3 to $4) per hour. Clubhouse and bar. Closed on Thursday.

SANT'ESTELLO SPORTING CLUB   Domaine de Barbossi, R.M. 7, Mandelieu   Tel: 38.91.78
Lessons, group riding, cross-country rides. Lessons from 14F to 20F ($3.50 to $5) per hour. Clubhouse, snack bar, salon. Open every day.

Horseracing

Interesting from the point of view of racing—and the kind of people you may meet there.

RACETRACK AT CAGNES-SUR-MER   Tel: 31.21.15
Built in 1956, the track has three runs allowing three separate categories of racing: Steeplechase, Trot, and Gallop. The Steeplechasing is to be seen in January; the Grand Prix Steeple Competition is at the end of the month. Trots are in February. The night trot races take place at 8:30 P.M. on Sundays, Tuesdays, and Thursdays, from the beginning of July to mid-September. Gallop racing: from December 16 to March 27. There is a panoramic restaurant. Frequent bus and rail connections from Cannes to the track.

Ice Skating

CLUB MONTFLEURY   Parc François-André, Avenue Beauséjour
Tel: 38.75.78

Polo

Another very interesting sport as well as a good place to meet people. The Cannes polo season opens in April and is the occasion for the International Polo Weeks, which attract some of the most prestigious French and foreign players.

POLO GROUNDS   At the Vacquerie, Mandelieu, only about 3 miles from Cannes   Tel: 38.92.48

Your concierge or the tourist office can tell you how to get there.

Skin Diving

CLUB ALPIN SOUS-MARIN

Swimming Pools

PALM BEACH CASINO POOL   Tel: 38.25.00

Open June through September. 15F ($3.75) per person.

PORT CANTO CLUBHOUSE POOL   Tel: 38.49.92

Heated seawater pool. December 1 to May 15: open every day except Tuesday; May 15 to October 31: open every day including Tuesday. 10F to 15F ($2.50 to $3.75) per person.

GALLIA TENNIS CLUB   Boulevard de Strasbourg   Tel: 38.63.30

Open every day from July through September. 5F ($1.25) per person.

Tennis

CANNES LAWN TENNIS CLUB   Résidence Fleurie, Rue Lacour
Tel: 38.58.85

Open every day from 8 A.M. to 7 P.M. (from April through September, from 7:30 A.M. to 8 P.M.). Six courts; reception hall, bar, and dressing room.

CLUB MONTFLEURY   Parc François-André Avenue Beauséjour
Tel. 37.75.78

GALLIA TENNIS CLUB   Boulevard de Strasbourg   Tel: 38.63.30

HÔTEL MONTMORENCY   Boulevard du Midi   Tel: 39.21.61

Three courts, open all year.

SANT'ESTELLO SPORTING CLUB   Domaine de Barbossi, R.M. 7, Mandelieu   Tel: 38.91.78

Open every day from 8:30 A.M. to 6:30 P.M. (from April through September, from 7:30 A.M. to 8 P.M.). Eleven courts; swimming pool; restaurant.

Water Skiing

CENTRE NAUTIQUE, SKI CLUB DE CANNES

46
Beauty Comes First in Cannes

HAIRDRESSERS

For prices, see the section on beauty salons in the chapter on the Riviera (page 230); the same apply in Cannes.

ANTOINE Rue Jean-Baptiste-Daumas Tel: 38.53.64
ANTONY 62, rue d'Antibes Tel: 39.47.10
He also does facials, make-ups, and other beauty treatments.
L'ARGENTINE 98, boulevard Carnot Tel: 99.21.97
L. CHOLLET 22, avenue des Tignes Tel: 99.19.10
Other beauty treatments available.
P. DENNY 37, boulevard de la Croisette Tel: 39.16.43
LE DURANGO 116, boulevard Carnot Tel: 39.54.38
COIFFURE MARCEL-RAYMOND 15, rue du 24 Août Tel: 38.39.07
Specializing in magnificent cuts and special treatment for damaged hair.
RIMAY 52, rue d'Antibes Tel: 39.20.86
STARLETTE PARFUMS 18, rue d'Antibes Tel: 39.23.77
LE VICTORIA 124, rue d'Antibes Tel: 99.16.11
VIRGILE J. P. 1, square Mérimée Tel: 39.17.64

SAUNAS

E. COHEN & RACELINE 51, boulevard Victor-Hugo Tel: 88.31.74
ESTHETICA (Beauty Institute) 60, avenue de-Lattre-de-Tassigny Tel: 39.66.66
Open from 8 to 12 and 2 to 3 P.M. by appointment; closed Saturday afternoon, Sunday, and Monday. Each session 25F ($6.25). Massage is also available.
J. GARSI 84, rue d'Antibes Tel: 39.98.30
Open Monday through Friday, from 2:30 to 8 P.M. 20F per person ($5.00); 15F for two persons ($3.75).

ALAIN GUARY   53, boulevard Carnot   Tel: 99.14.68
Open from 9 to 12 and 2 to 4 P.M., by appointment. Closed Saturday afternoon and Sunday. Tariff per session 15F ($3.75), reduced according to number of persons or sessions.

STARLY BEAUTY INSTITUTE   84, rue d'Antibes   Tel: 39.40.85
Open 9 to 12 and 2 to 7 P.M. Closed on Sunday and Monday mornings. Tariff 18F ($4.50). Massage also available.

JEAN WOHL   1, rue Félix-Faure   Tel: 39.82.65
Open from 8:30 A.M. to 7:30 P.M.; closed Saturday afternoon and Sunday. Tariff 18F to 20F per session ($4.50 and $5). Reduced tariff depending on number of persons or sessions.

THALASSO THÉRAPIE

MARINE THERMAL SPRINGS (Bellamar)   Tel: 99.30.99
Clubhouse of Port Canto.

47
Shopping in Cannes

Home of the world-famous film festival, playground of princes, and an important port of call for cruise ships, Cannes is a deluxe resort in every possible sense. For this reason, many of the best shops in Paris and New York have opened branches here over the years.

Special note: If bargain shopping is your cup of tea, be sure to wander through Rue Meynadier, the picturesque commercial center of old Cannes. This is where you can get the best bargains for the least cost.

DEPARTMENT STORES

GALERIES DE LA CROISETTE Boulevard de la Croisette
Something for everyone. Vacationers will appreciate the large selection of beach towels and bags from $2. Fold-up beach mats from $7.50, bikinis and sun hats. Also good assortment of ready-to-wear and accessories. There is a separate store for *monsieur* across the street.

LA GRANDE MAISON DE BLANC 49, rue d'Antibes
Long established and well stocked with resort necessities. Popular with the people of Cannes.

V.R.A.C. 73, rue Félix-Faure
Côte d'Azur equivalent of the American bargain store. Everything you need for the beach at low prices.

BOUTIQUES AND SMALL SHOPS

ADRIENNE 87, rue d'Antibes
Designs of first quality. Dresses, trousers, ensembles.

ARIANE 77, rue d'Antibes
Latest by Céline, Courrèges, Féraud, Pucci, Ungaro.

ELIZABETH D'ASTRÉE 69, rue d'Antibes
High fashion, furs and jewels.

HENRI BARRAU 63, rue d'Antibes
Pace-setting designs by Pierre Cardin, Jacques Heim, Ted Lapidus, and the like.

DOROTHÉE BIS   3, rue d'Antibes
Branch of the style-setting Paris boutique. Bikinis and sportswear in season; midis, trousers, and chic ensembles.

BOUTIQUE 94   94, rue d'Antibes
Wide array of resort wear, especially bright Tahitian prints and generally fun clothes.

CARINA JEUNE   Rue d'Antibes
Mod clothes for the fashion-conscious junior miss.

CASHMERE SHOP   83, rue d'Antibes
Cashmere, of course, but also relatively inexpensive cotton and wool knits, tops, and beach dresses.

DARON   Boulevard de la Croisette
Wide selection of quality sports- and beachwear.

FERNAND DESGRANGES   Boulevard de la Croisette
Dresses, belts, bags, costume jewelry.

ROSELYNE FARD   Boulevard de la Croisette
Top assortment of Patou ready-to-wear and accessories.

LAFAYETTE SHOP   Boulevard de la Croisette
High fashion to low-slung bikinis and virtually everything in between.

LANVIN   Boulevard de la Croisette
Best for ladies and their beaux. "Super sale" during August.

MARCY BOUTIQUE   79, rue d'Antibes
Appealing array of resort wear, especially tunics and slacks. Belts, bathing suits, and even fun watches.

MIGUEZ-CARTON BOUTIQUE   90, rue d'Antibes
Deluxe ready-to-wear and a full line of fashion accessories.

NAT'S   Rue Macé and Rue d'Antibes
Combines chic and elegance for dresses, trousers, and suede specialties.

NOEL   Boulevard de la Croisette
Sportswear for the sun set.

STEHLY   Boulevard de la Croisette
Slacks and skirts for him and her.

ROSELYNE VARCH   Boulevard de la Croisette
Designs by Carven, Castillo, Madeleine de Rauch, and Patou.

ZORA COUTURE MODES   2, galeries Fleuries
2, rue des Serbes
Home of the custom-made bikini (from about $27; ready-mades begin at about $22). Smart beachwear, including robes, skirts, and hats. Louis Féraud scarves.

LEATHER GOODS

YVES DRY   Rue d'Antibes
Emphasis is definitely on dressy footwear. Some casuals and purses.

CHAUSSURES HEYRAUD   64, rue d'Antibes
One of a chain all over France. The latest in reasonably priced shoes for men and women.

HERMÈS Boulevard de la Croisette
Ultimate in leather, scarves, and sportswear.
MAROQUINERIE 60 70, rue d'Antibes
Purses, wallets, and dog collars for dogs and people.
REGICIA 22, rue d'Antibes
Inexpensive shoes for men, women, and children. Good array
of reasonably priced sandals.

FOR HIM

ARMAND THIÈRY & SIGRAND Rue d'Antibes
Avant-garde styling for men for the year round. Also includes
the Atsel women's boutique.
CARLIN 42, rue d'Antibes
Large assortment of moderately priced sweaters, shirts, pants.
Fittings for odd-size trousers is a specialty.
IMPERIAL HOUSE 64, rue d'Antibes
Conservatively styled trousers, shirts, and sweaters.
TRABAUD 48, rue d'Antibes
Suits, jackets, pants, shoes, and boots—all in the latest cuts and
colors. Features designer items by Balmain and Cardin.
WORLDLY TAILOR & OUTFITTER Boulevard de la Croisette
Dressy, well-cut men's clothes made to measure. Large selection
of jersey knits for ladies as well as men.

JEWELRY

CARTIER Boulevard de la Croisette
Branch in Monte-Carlo
High quality with prices to match.
JULIAN ET FILS 71, rue d'Antibes
Tissot and Vacheron Constantin watches, wide selection of gold
jewelry.
NOEL 74, rue d'Antibes
Costume bracelets, gold jewelry, and pearls.
VAN CLEEF & ARPELS Boulevard de la Croisette
Branch in Monte-Carlo
Diamonds and doodads delivered to your door. Good and ex-
pensive.

PERFUMES / GIFTS

ELLE ET LUI 68, rue d'Antibes
6, rue Félix-Faure
Good selection of scents. Also small gift items.
FRANCE PERFUMES 78, rue d'Antibes
Perfumes, plus beach bags and mats.

PARFUMERIE BOUTEILLE 59, rue d'Antibes
  Finest perfumes in France are featured, as well as a broad range of beauty products. English-speaking staff.
STARLETT PERFUMES 18, rue d'Antibes
  Especially scintillating, reasonably priced scents.

ANTIQUES

L'ÉCRIN Rue d'Antibes
  Good range of glassware, lamps, porcelain, and gifts.
FLORENCE & VENISE 75, rue d'Antibes
  Italian craftsmanship at its finest—antique desks, tables, armoires, chandeliers, Florentine *objets d'art*.
HENNOCQUE/QUIRIN Boulevard de la Croisette
  Smart gift items, *objets d'art*, opalines, porcelains.

48 Welcome to Monte-Carlo

Though Monte-Carlo is not actually a part of France, but in the principality of Monaco, I am including it anyway, since it is right next door and most tourists are anxious to see it. For more than six centuries Monaco has been a sovereign state, separated from France only by an invisible frontier. Here Prince Rainier and Princess Grace (our own Grace Kelly) reign supreme.

The life of Monte-Carlo centers pretty much on the famous casino and its yachting basin where some of the largest and most beautiful yachts in the world can be seen on any day during the season, and its fabulous galas. Princess Grace lends an aura of modern beauty unsurpassed by any other reigning queen in the world today. (I guess I'm a bit chauvinistic.)

This small principality dazzles the eye, with its green foot-hills, the vibrant blue of the Mediterranean below, and the Alps as a backdrop. The mountains screen Monaco from the north winds and account for a very pleasant temperature year round. No visit to the Riviera is complete without at least a day's trip to this fairy-tale principality, easily reached from Nice or Cannes by coach tour or bus. Take the time to wander around its winding streets and look in its many fashionable boutiques.

CALENDAR OF EVENTS

Following is a list of the most important events in Monte-Carlo which are attended by many famous international celebrities.

MONTE-CARLO AUTOMOBILE RALLY   January
INTERNATIONAL TELEVISION FESTIVAL OF MONTE-CARLO
  February
"MONTE-CARLO OPEN," International Tennis Tournament   April

MONACO AUTOMOBILE GRAND PRIX   May
MONTE-CARLO INTERNATIONAL FESTIVAL OF ARTS   July
MONÉGASQUE RED CROSS GALA   August
   Presided over by Princess Grace.
OPERA, THEATER, AND BALLET SEASON   Casino in the Salle
   Garnier   October through April
   Seats for the premiere, 40F to 75F ($10 to $18.75); for other
   performances, 25F to 40F ($6.25 to $10).

During July and August classical concerts are given in the
courtyard of the royal palace with world-renowned soloists.
Who knows, you may even see Princess Grace.

49
Where to Stay in Monte-Carlo

Generally tourists use Nice or Cannes as a base and come to Monte-Carlo on a sightseeing jaunt. However, in case you wish to stay over a night or two, we will list a few hotels in each category for your selection. All are centrally located. All are B-C category.

HOTELS

Deluxe

HÔTEL ALEXANDRA 35, boulevard Princesse-Charlotte Tel: 30.63.13
Single: 48F to 66F ($12 to $16.50); double: 60F to 88F ($15 to $22).

HÔTEL BALMORAL 12, avenue de la Costa Tel: 30.62.37
Single: 53F to 80F ($13.25 to $20); double: 102F to 110F ($25.50 to $27.50).

HÔTEL BRISTOL 25, boulevard Albert-1er Tel: 30.16.61
Single: 60F to 95F ($15 to $23.75); double: 83F to 120F ($20.75 to $30).

HÔTEL D'EUROPE 6, avenue Citronniers Tel: 30.83.65
Single: 44F to 66F ($11 to $16.50); double: 45F to 88F ($11.25 to $22).

HÔTEL HELDER 2, avenue de la Madone Tel: 30.63.07
Single: 48F to 66F ($12 to $16.50); double: 60F to 88F ($15 to $22).

HERMITAGE Square Beaumarchais Tel: 30.67.31
Single: 80F to 190F ($20 to $47.50); double: 126F to 276F ($31.50 to $69).

HOLIDAY INN Avenue Princesse-Grace Tel: 30.98.80
Single: 95F to 155F ($23.75 to $38.75); double: 115F to 180F ($28.75 to $45).

HÔTEL DU LOUVRE 16, boulevard des Moulins Tel: 30.65.25
Single: 53F to 66F ($13.25 to $16.50); double: 66F to 92F ($16.50 to $23).

MÉTROPOLE   Avenue de la Grande-Bretagne   Tel: 30.57.41
   Single: 70F ($17.50) to 127F ($31.75); double: 120F to 220F
   ($30 to $55).

HÔTEL DE PARIS   Place du Casino   Tel: 30.80.80
   The most elegant hotel in Monte-Carlo, just across from the
   Casino. Two restaurants and a pool. Single: from 115F to 224F
   ($28.75 to $56); double: 150F to 368F ($37.50 to $92).

Three Star

HÔTEL DE BERNE   21, rue du Portier   Tel: 30.77.42
   Single: 44F ($11); double: 50F to 60F ($12.50 to $15).

CAROLL'S HOTEL   29, boulevard Princesse-Charlotte   Tel: 30.
64.69
   Single: 44F to 52F ($11 to $13); double: 55F to 60F ($13.75
   to $15).

HÔTEL MIRAMAR   1 bis, avenue President-J.-F.-Kennedy   Tel:
30.86.48
   Single: 59F to 70F ($14.75 to $17.50); double: 70F to 88F
   ($17.50 to $22).

HÔTEL DE ROME   11, boulevard de Suisse   Tel: 38.69.17
   Double: 60F to 88F ($15 to $22).

HÔTEL DE RUSSIE   25, avenue de la Costa   Tel: 30.62.66
   Single: 48F to 66F ($12 to $16.50); double: 60F to 88F ($15
   to $22).

HÔTEL SPLENDIDE   4, avenue Roqueville   Tel: 30.65.93
   Single: 48F to 66F ($12 to $16.50); double: 66F to 88F
   ($16.50 to $22).

50 Sports in Monte-Carlo

Beaches

Both public beaches, with nominal admission fees and equipment rentals, and private beaches at the hotels.

Tennis

MONTE-CARLO COUNTRY CLUB

Water Skiing

CLUB DE MONACO

51
Sightseeing in Monte-Carlo

THE CASINO DE MONTE-CARLO

Surrounded by beautiful gardens, this is the second most important building in Monte-Carlo, second only to the Palace, of course. The gaming rooms are open every day from 10 A.M. Here, too, is the famous Salle Garnier, where all the important shows of Monte-Carlo take place.

THE OCEANOGRAPHIC MUSEUM (and Aquarium)

"The Temple of the Sea" was erected by Prince Albert I at the extreme point of the Rock of Monaco. Its rooms are devoted to oceanography and to the memory of its illustrious founder. The Aquarium presents the "Silent World" with thousands of wonderfully colored fish and marine animals of the Mediterranean as well as the tropical seas of the world. Underwater movies are continuously shown in the lecture room. Open all year from 9 to 7.

WAX MUSEUM 27, rue Basse

A magnificent wax museum with 24 scenes and 40 life-size figures from the François Grimaldi family, who have reigned over Monaco from 1297 to the present. Open every day from 9:30 to noon, and 2 to 6. Closed November 6 through December 15. Fee 5F ($1.25).

At the Palace

CHANGING OF THE GUARD

Every day at 11:55 A.M., July 1 to October 1. During this time Prince Rainier and Princess Grace open a part of their palace to visitors. Open daily 9 A.M. to 5:30 P.M. Entrance 5F ($1.25).

THE PALACE MUSEUM

Napoleonic souvenirs and collections of palace archives. Prince Albert left the museum all the works he collected during his reign: 23 paintings, 78 pieces of ceramic, 32 drawings. 11 oils, one tapestry, two sculptures, and 37 lithographs. The museum contains the largest collection of Picasso works assembled in one museum today. It also contains Ligurian, Greek, and Roman antiquities, relics of Napoleon's return from Elba, and Cap d'Antibes primitives. Open daily except Monday, 9 to 11 and 2 to 5:30 P.M. Entrance 5F ($1.25).

53
Other Riviera Towns

All the little Riviera towns are fascinating—each with its own style and attractions for you to discover. Here are some brief notes on the most popular and interesting ones.

They are arranged in order from West to East along the Côte d'Azur.

ST.-TROPEZ

Like most Riviera towns, St.-Tropez is ancient. In A.D. 68 in Pisa, Nero martyred one of his officers, named Trop. The body was placed in a small boat and floated from Pisa to what came to be called St.-Tropez. So much for history. Today, St.-Tropez is known primarily for Brigitte Bardot and her famous teeny-weeny bikini, which is what started the influx of the wild and wealthy set. Since then the beaches have become overrun with young gorgeous suntanned beauties hoping to meet a millionaire, and millionaires in their magnificent yachts looking for some young beauty to play games with.

Unless you're one of the above set, except for a quick look-see St.-Tropez probably won't be for you. And if you don't have it all together—gorgeous face, gorgeous body, gorgeous hair, gorgeous clothes—you'll get nothing out of your trip but a gorgeous inferiority complex!

Shopping

Shopping here is mainly for fun. Look for the latest and kookiest styles in "Trop's" ever-shifting bevy of boutiques. Also: sandals, sunglasses, sportswear, olive-wood objects, espadrilles (rope-soled shoes), and whatever is faddish in France at the moment. The majority of boutiques are found along the Quai, which borders the tiny and ancient harbor. Most are open year round from early morn till late evening.

LUIS AZZARO   The Quai
An elegant approach to tie-dyes. Also Indian fashions.

BRUYÈRE DES MAURES   The Quai
M. Roux, a local artist, specializes in olive-wood ware and, as the name implies, briar pipes.

CAPRICE   The Quai
Things in clingy crêpe are all the rage here. Reasonable prices on ladies' belts, bags, and slacks.

CHOC   10, rue des Commerçants
Fabulous collection of leather hats, belts, bags, and shoes. Minis and midis coexist here. The bikinis are not bad either.

CHOSES   The Quai
The house of 20,000 tee-shirts, tie-dyes being the most tempting. Also bathing suits, children's wear, men's shirts and shorts.

À LA CONFIANCE   Place de Lices
Run by Peggy Roche of *Elle,* one of Paris's fashion bibles, this fetching boutique is big on midis. Crêpes, silks, and slacks are also in abundant supply.

FRÉJUS

Fréjus was an important trading post on what was to become the famous Aurelian Way. Julius Caesar built it in 49 B.C. as a small village, the "Forum Julli." The ancient ramparts encircle a town five times larger than Fréjus today, and its Roman amphitheater held 10,000 strong. Octavius made Fréjus his naval base and in 31 B.C., before he became emperor, he sailed out to defeat Cleopatra's massive galleys in the Battle of Actium.

Near Fréjus is the famous **Roman Aqueduct,** a model of engineering so well preserved that it was used in 1832 and again in 1918 to supply the area with water. See the arena, or **Amphitheater,** ruins of the most ancient arena of Gaul. Bullfights are held here during July and August.

There is also a lovely **Renaissance cathedral** with magnificent sculptured wooden doors, early Gothic arches, 15th-century stalls, and a wooden altarpiece by Jacques Durand. The Baptistry, a 5th-century building, is one of the oldest in France. Its fine columns are actually Roman.

ST.-RAPHAËL

This is where Gounod composed *Romeo and Juliet,* and it is easy to see why this city inspired him. Originally a Roman city, today's casino stands on the site of an ancient Roman bath. Napoleon was a frequent visitor to St.-Raphaël and there is still a pyramid here commemorating his Egyptian campaign, his departure for Elba, and his return en route to Waterloo.

GRASSE

Famous for its perfume industry, your nose can tell when you're getting close to this lovely little city, for the air is heavily perfumed with the tons of flowers that are processed here. Aside from the perfume industry, Grasse is also well known for its jams and crystalized fruits.

Fragonard was born here in 1732 and the museum bearing his name today presents his works as part of its remarkable collection. The **Fragonard perfume factory** is open daily to the public; you can see exactly how perfume is made and sample some of the famous Fragonard perfumes.

VALLAURIS

Thanks to Picasso's fame, Vallauris is, nowadays, the world's center for ceramics. Local production is on display in the summer and during the Easter holidays. There is even one shop in the town that is authorized to sell ceramics the master himself designed. You must not fail to see two important works of Picasso's: the statue of *L'Homme au Mouton* (The Sheep Man) and the painting *La Guerre et al Paix* (War and Peace).

VENCE

Vence was once a great power, the capital of Roman Gaul, a favorite subject of the Provençal troubadours. In the 13th century, one daughter of the Count of Vence became Queen of England; a second, Empress of Austria; and a third, Queen of the two Sicilies. One of the most important things to see is the **Chapel of the Rosary,** a Dominican chapel built under the direct supervision of the great artist Matisse. The interior shows all the value of its varied simplicity. Two great mural compositions show the Virgin and St.-Dominic, while the stained glass in vivid colors suggests the forms of plants. Matisse considered the Chapel at Vence his masterpiece and the culminating point in his career. Open Tuesday and Thursday from 10 to 11:30 A.M. and from 2:30 to 5:30 P.M.

BIOT

Most famous for its **Fernand Leger Museum.** This is the place Léger had chosen to work and where he died. His widow and his friends have made this museum into something light and gay as he wished his own paintings to be. The galleries contain an incomparable collection of his canvases, drawings, sketches, and mosaics. This is the most complete collection of the work of a pioneer of 20th-century art. Open daily from 10 to 12 and 3 to 6; closed Monday.

JUAN-LES-PINS

One of the liveliest spots on the coast, with all kinds of amusements, jazz, and games. Juan-les-Pins is the favorite of the younger set. Not as expensive or as fashionable as any of the others along the Riviera, but it certainly does swing. The only clothes you need here is a selection of bikinis and blue jeans and you're off to the races. It's a great place to meet people.

ANTIBES

Home of the legendary Eden Roc, Antibes is said to resemble Greece, and in fact the ancient Greeks of Marseilles built "Antipolies" here. Napoleon lived here in 1794 and was imprisoned at **Fort Carré** after the fall of Robespierre. You can still inspect the fort and its ramparts today. The **Grimaldi Museum** was the château of the Grimaldi family, lords of Antibes from 1385 to 1608. Picasso worked at the château while he lived there in 1946.

CAGNES

Cagnes is really two towns, Haut-de-Cagnes, 300 feet above the sea, and Cros-de-Cagnes, directly on the coast. Haut-de-Cagnes is typically provincial with steep, winding streets and mellow old houses. Cros-de-Cagnes is a fishing village, with a beach and a beautiful, new, modern Hippodrome racetrack. Renoir lived here between 1890 and 1919. The charming home and studio containing his personal effects can still be visited. See, too, the **Museum of Modern Mediterranean Art,** which contains the work of painters such as Matisse and Chagall.

Index

Index

[*Where not indicated otherwise, or obvious, all entries refer to or are in Paris.*]

L'Abbaye (night club), 104
Abbaye-aux-Dames (Caen), 206
Abbaye-aux-Hommes (Caen), 206
L'Absinthe (restaurant), 71, 97
Académie Française, 110
Adige (leather), 164
Hôtel Adriatic (Nice), 235
Adrienne (boutique, Cannes), 274
Hôtel Albert (Cannes), 260
Hôtel Albert-ler (Nice), 236
Patrick Ales (beauty salon), 140
Hôtel Alexandra (Monte-Carlo), 280
Alexandre (beauty salon), 140
Alexandre (restaurant), 74
Allard (restaurant), 88
Hôtel des Alpes (Cannes), 260
Alpine Garden, 129
Altamira (jewelry), 169
Amaryllis (leather), 164
Hôtel Ambassador (Nice), 236
Amboise, Château of, 178, 188
Ambulance, 43
American Express, 5
Amie (boutique), 153
Amie (boutique, Nice), 250
L'Ancien Chartier (restaurant), 92, 97
À l'Ancien Trocadéro (restaurant), 93
André (beauty salon, Deauville), 210
André-Luc (beauty salon, Nice), 249
Andrieu (massage, Deauville), 210
Angers, 178, 179–187
Angers, Castle of, 186
Angkor (restaurant), 74, 97
Hôtel d'Anjou (Angers), 180

Anne et Frédéric (gifts, Nice), 253
Jacques Anquetil (gifts), 170
Anthony (hairdresser, Cannes), 272
Antibes, 218, 219, 224, 228, 229, 289
Antoine (beauty salon), 140
Antoine (hairdresser, Cannes), 272
Antonio et Alban (beauty salon, Nice), 249
Apothecary (Angers), 186
Arax (jewelry, Deauville), 213
Arc-en-ciel (cleaners), 174
Arc Élysée (hotel), 58
Arc de Triomphe, 39, 65, 95, 109–110, 112, 113, 128
restaurants near, 95
Hôtel de l'Arcade, 56
Aux Arcades (restaurant), 83–84, 96
L'Archestrate (restaurant), 71
Elizabeth Arden (beauty salon), 140, 143
L'Argentine (hairdresser, Cannes), 272
Ariane (boutique, Cannes), 274
Arinbo (gifts, Nice), 253
L'Armoire de Grand'mere (boutique), 153
Arny (for men), 167
Hôtel Arromanches, 58
Arrondissements, 38–40
Art et Cristaux (porcelain, Nice), 253
Art et Joie (antiques, Nice), 254
L'Asie (restaurant, Cannes), 264
L'Assiette au Beurre (restaurant), 74–75, 97
Astoux et Brun (restaurant, Cannes), 263

Astoux et Fils (restaurant, Cannes), 263
Astre (leather), 164
Elizabeth d'Astrée (boutique, Cannes), 274
L'Atelier (boutique), 153
Atelier 32 (boutique), 153
Hôtel Athénée (Cannes), 258
Hôtel Atlantic (Nice), 235
L'Auberge Basque (restaurant), 75
Auberge la Dague (restaurant, Barbizon), 134–135
L'Auberge Fleurie (restaurant, Cannes), 263
Auberge du Vert-Galant (restaurant), 75, 97
Fernand Aubrey (hair problems), 143
Augier (jewelry, Nice), 253
August, restaurants open in, 97–99
Aurore (boutique), 153
Hôtel Avenida (Nice), 238
Hôtel de l'Avenir, 62
À l'Avenue Matignon (leather), 164
Azay-le-Rideau, Château of, 178, 189
Luis Azzaro (boutique, St.-Tropez), 287

Bab's (couturier discounts), 162
Baby Dior (for children), 168
Baby Train (for children), 168
Baccarat (crystal), 172
Badou (gifts, Deauville), 213
La Bagagerie (leather), 164
  Nice, 252
La Bajocasse (hotel, Deauville), 199
Balleroy, 207
Bally (leather) 164
  Nice, 252
Pierre Balmain (couturier), 160
Hôtel Balmoral (Monte-Carlo), 280
Le Baltard (restaurant), 84, 97
Banane (boutique, Nice), 251
Bar du Combat Roggero (restaurant), 93, 98
Bar des Planches (restaurant, Trouville), 204
Le Barbèque (restaurant, Angers), 184
Barbizon, 131, 133–134
Barclay (for men, Nice), 252
Barichella (jewelry, Nice), 253
Henri Barrau (boutique, Cannes), 274
Bateau Mouche tour, 111
Bayeux, Cathedral of, 208
La Bazarine (boutique), 153
Hôtel Beau Rivage (Cannes), 258
Hôtel Beau Séjour (Cannes), 258
Jane Beaucaire (jewelry), 169
Beaussier (beauty salon, Deauville), 210
Beaux-Arts Museum (Nice), 246–247
Bedford (hotel), 50–51
Beli (boutique), 153
Bellevue (hotel, Trouville), 201
Bellina (for children), 168
Violette Beniston (couturier discounts), 162
Benouville, 207
Nadine Berger (boutique), 153
La Bergerie (boutique), 153
Berkeley, The (restaurant), 75
Bernard (jewelry), 169
Hôtel de Berne (Monte-Carlo), 281
Bettetini (jewelry, Nice), 253
Biancharelli (antiques, Nice), 254
Biba (boutique), 153
La Bière (restaurant), 93, 95
Big Ben (boutique, Nice), 251
Bijoux Anciens (jewelry), 169
Binet (jewelry, Deauville), 213
Biot, 289
Dorothée Bis (boutique), 153
  Cannes, 275
Le Bistingo (restaurant, Cannes), 262
Le Bistro (restaurant), 71, 97
Bistro Bazaar (gifts), 172
Bistro Boutique, 154
Bistro des Halles (restaurant), 84

Le Bistro du Tricot (knitwear), 163

Le Bistrot de Paris (restaurant), 75

Le Bivouac (restaurant, Trouville), 204

Charles Blair-Scherick (leather), 164–165

Blanc (restaurant), 90, 97

Blois, Château of, 178, 187

Blue Bar, The (restaurant, Cannes), 262

Blue Note, The (jazz), 107

Boat tours, 111, 228–229

Bobino, The, 102

Bodard (beauty salon, Deauville), 210

Bodard (cleaners, Deauville), 214

Body surgery, 147–148

Bois de Boulogne, 40, 42, 126, 127, 131

Bois de Vincennes, 127–128

La Boîte à Pull (knitwear), 163

Le Bon Bock (restaurant), 94, 96

Bon Marché, 152

La Bonbonnière (restaurant, Nice), 242

Bonet (jewelry, Nice), 253

Bong Lai (restaurant, Nice), 241

La Bonne Table (restaurant), 94–95, 96

Les Bosquets (restaurant), 95, 96

La Boucherie (knitwear), 163

La Boucherie (restaurant), 89, 97

Bougnat's Club (restaurant), 76, 98

La Bouille, 179

La Boule d'Or (hotel, Angers), 180

La Boule Rouge (restaurant), 92–93

Jean Bouquin (boutique), 154

Valentine Bourgade (boutique, Deauville), 212

Hôtel de Bourgogne et Montana, 60–61

Boutique le Drugstore (gifts), 172

La Boutique Fantasque, 154

Boutique des Jeunes (Monte-Carlo), 284

Boutique 94 (Cannes), 275

Boutique du Palais-Royal (gifts), 172

Boutique aux Pantalons (Deauville), 212

Boutique à Sandwich (restaurant, 91

Boyer (jewelry, Nice), 253

Brasserie Bofinger (restaurant), 76, 98

Brasserie Cassini (restaurant, Nice), 243

Brasserie de l'Île-St.-Louis (restaurant), 87, 96

Brasserie Lipp (restaurant), 76, 98, 120

Brasserie Munichoise (restaurant), 76, 98

Brasserie de l'Opéra (restaurant), 84, 96

Brasserie-Tabac des Invalides (restaurant), 90, 95

Brasserie de la Tour Eiffel (restaurant), 90, 97

Jean Brenier (leather), 165

La Brésilienne (restaurant, Nice), 242

Hôtel Brice et Bedford (Nice), 236–237

Hôtel Brighton, 56

Brigitte Bel (boutique, Nice), 251

Brise Marine (hotel, Deauville), 200

Brissac, Château of, 190–191

Le Bristol (hotel), 47

Hôtel Bristol (Monte-Carlo), 280

La Brocanterie (antiques), 171

Brouillet (restaurant), 86, 99

F. Brunet (repair), 174

Hôtel de Brussels (Nice), 238

Bruyère des Maures (pipes, St.-Tropez), 287

La Bucca da Bouttau (restaurant, Cannes), 263

La Bumbarde (night club), 104

Bunny (boutique), 154

Bus Stop (boutique), 154
Hôtel Busby (Nice), 237

Cabaret Restaurant (Deauville), 197
Cabessa (couturier discounts), 162
Cables, 27
Le Cadre Noir, 179, 190
Caen, 206
Café des Allées (cabaret, Cannes), 266
Café de Flore, 78, 120
Café de la Huchette (jazz), 108
Café de la Paix (restaurant), 52, 76
Café de Paris (Deauville), 204
Café-Restaurant de la Mairie, 85, 96
Café Théâtre (Nice), 244
La Cage (jazz), 107
Cagnes, 218, 219, 227, 228, 290
Caillat (antiques), 171
Au Caiman (leather, Nice), 252
California, The (hotel), 51
La Calvados (night club), 104
Hôtel les Camélias (Nice), 238
Canberra Hôtel (Cannes), 257
Candy (cabaret, Nice), 245
Jean Canestrier (beauty salon, Nice), 249
La Canisse (restaurant, Nice), 243
Cannes, 217, 218, 219, 221, 222, 223, 224, 233, 255–277
Cannes Country Club, 218
Cannes International Film Festival, 224, 265
Cannes Lawn Tennis Club, 271
Cannes Palace Hôtel (Cannes), 257
Le Canon de Montmartre (restaurant), 95, 96
Cantilène (gifts, Nice), 253
Cap d'Antibes, 229
Cap-Ferrat, 217
Cap 3000 (Nice), 250
Le Capitole (restaurant, Nice), 242
Caprice (boutique, St.-Tropez), 287
Cardiff (for men), 167

Pierre Cardin (couturier), 160, 167
Carel (leather), 165
Carina Jeune (boutique, Cannes), 275
Carita (beauty salon), 140
Carlin (for men, Cannes), 276
Joseph Carlin (beauty salon, Nice), 249
Carlton Hotel (Cannes), 256
Hôtel Carlton (Nice), 238
Carnaby (boutique), 154, 167
Carnaby Street (boutique), 154
Au Carnet des Dames (boutique, Monte-Carlo), 284
Carnet de séjour, 231–232
Caroline (large sizes), 164
Caroll's Hotel (Monte-Carlo), 281
Carrousel (night club), 104
Carrousel, Place du, 96, 109, 123
  restaurants near, 96
"Le Carrousel du Cadre Noir," 179
La carte, 65
Cartier (jewelry):
  Cannes, 276
  Monte-Carlo, 285
  Nice, 253
Carven (couturier), 160
Carvil (leather), 165
Cashmere Club (knitwear), 163
Cashmere House (knitwear), 163
  Deauville, 212
Cashmere Shop (Cannes), 275
Casino d'Été (Deauville), 199, 202, 205
Casino des Fleurs (Cannes), 265, 266
Casino d'Hiver (Deauville), 199, 202, 205
Casino de Monte-Carlo, 227, 283
Casino Municipal (Nice), 245
Le Casino de Paris, 101
La Casita (restaurant, Nice), 242
Dominique Cassegrain (leather, Deauville), 213

Le Casserole (restaurant), 76, 98

Hôtel Castille, 51

Castillo (couturier), 160

Casty (jewelry), 169

Catherine (boutique), 154

Catherine Boutique (Nice), 251

Caveau de la Huchette (night club), 104–105

Caveau des Oubliettes (night club), 105

Cecilia, The (hotel), 51

Cedric (leather), 165

Céline (for children), 169

Céline (leather), 165

Cellulite, 144–145

Celtic Hotel, The, 51

Central (hotel, Deauville), 199–200

Cercle de l'Étrier (Cannes), 270

Cercle Molière (Nice), 244

Cerruti 1881 (boutique), 154, 167

Cha-Cha-Club (Nice), 245

Le Chambiges (restaurant), 91–92

Chambord, Château of, 178, 187

Chambre des Députés, 109

Champ de Mars, 121

Hôtel de Champagne (Angers), 180

Champollion (restaurant), 76–77

Champs-Élysées, 39, 103, 110, 112

Chanel (couturier), 160

Chantilly, 136–137

Chapel of the Rosary (Vence), 289

Chapelle de la Miséricorde (Nice), 246

Le Chaperon Bleu (for children), 169

Charade (gifts), 172

Thérèse Chardin (beauty salon), 140

Charles of the Ritz (beauty salon), 140

Charleston (cabaret, Cannes), 266

Chartres, 135–136, 178, 179

Le Chat qui Pêche (night club), 105

Château The (Nice), 246

Château d'Artigny, 181

Château Frontenac (hotel), 52

Château Gaillard, 138

Château of Maintenon and Rambouillet, 135

Château de Marçay, 182

Château de Teildras, 182

Château de Vincennes, 128

La Châtelaine (for children), 169

Châtelier (cleaners, Deauville), 214

Chatham (hotel, Deauville), 200

Hôtel Chatham (Nice), 237

Chaumont, Château of, 178, 188

Chaussures Heyraud (leather, Cannes), 275

Chemosurgery, 147

Chenonceaux, Château of, 178, 188–189

Dr. Jean-Louis Cherif-Cheick (chemosurgery), 147

Cherry Lane (jazz), 107

Cheval d'Or (jazz), 107

Cheverny, Château of, 187–188

Chez André (restaurant), 74

Chez les Anges (restaurant), 74, 97

Chez Augusto (restaurant, Deauville), 202

Chez Babette (restaurant), 94, 96

Chez Bosc (restaurant), 75–76

Chez Edgard (restaurant), 78, 98

Chez Isidore (restaurant), 79

Chez Jules (boutique), 154, 167

Chez Marinette (restaurant, Trouville), 204

Chez Mario (restaurant, Cannes), 263

Chez Miocque (restaurant, Deauville), 204

Chez Cri Cri Muller (restaurant, Deauville), 203

Chez Paulette (restaurant), 87, 99

Chez les Pêcheurs (restaurant, Nice), 241

Chez Pierre (restaurant, Nice), 243

Chez Roger (restaurant, Cannes), 263

Chez Suzanne et Noé (restaurant, Nice), 243

Chez Vania (restaurant), 83

Chinon, Château of, 189

Chipie (boutique), 154

Choc (boutique, St.-Tropez), 287

L. Chollet (hairdresser, Cannes), 272

Choses (boutique, St.-Tropez), 287

Christofle (silver), 172

Chrysanthemum Show, 44

La Chunga (cabaret, Cannes), 266

Cigale (jazz), 107

La Cigale (restaurant), 90, 98

À la Cigogne (restaurant), 77

La Cigogne (restaurant, Cannes), 262

Cityrama, 109, 111, 134, 135, 137, 178

Hôtel Clarice (Cannes), 258

Claridge Hotel, 51–52

Claude et Gilbert (boutique), 154

Hôtel Claude-Bernard, 63

Jean Clément (beauty salon, Deauville), 210

Clinique Médicale de Phytodiététique, 144–145

Closerie des Lilas (restaurant), 77, 98

Les Cloyères (restaurant), 92

Club Écossais (jazz), 107

Club de l'Etoile (night club), 105

Club Hippique (Cannes), 270

Club de Monaco, 282

Club Montfleury (Cannes), 268, 271

Club 925 (restaurant, Angers), 184

Coach tours, 109–111, 130–131, 135, 136, 137, 138, 178, 221–222, 227–228

Coconnas (restaurant), 77, 98

E. Cohen & Raceline (sauna, Cannes), 272

Coiffeur l'Aiglon (Nice), 249

Coiffeur Jeanne (Nice), 249

Coiffeur Joel (Nice), 249

Coiffeur Paris-Riviera (Nice), 249

Coiffure Marcel-Raymond (Cannes), 272

Hôtel Colbert (Nice), 239

Collon (leather), 165

Colonne Vendôme, 114

Hôtel Columbia (Nice), 239

Comédie-Française, 103, 115

Comité de Tourisme de Paris, 47

Ann-Marie Commarin (cleaners), 174

Commerce (restaurant, Nice), 242

Commissariat Central (Police), 43

Compiègne, 136

Conciergerie, 110, 117, 118

Hôtel Concorde (Angers), 180

À la Confiance (boutique, St.-Tropez), 287

Confolens, 179

Conservatoire, 103

Consulates, 43–44

Hôtel Continent, 58–59

Hôtel Continental (Deauville), 200

Hôtel Continental-Masséna (Nice), 237

Les Copains (restaurant), 90, 98

Copenhague (restaurant), 77

La Coquille St.-Jacques (restaurant), 87–96

Corniche d'Or, 221

Hôtel Corona (Cannes), 260

Corsaire Basque (restaurant), 77

Côte d'Azur (*see* Riviera)

Hotel Côte d'Azur (Nice), 239

Coucke (for men, Nice), 252

Le Coupe-Chou (restaurant), 77, 98

Coupesarte, 207

André Courrèges (couturier), 160

Cousin Bibi (Nice), 244
Le Cousoir (jewelry), 169
Les Cravates (for men), 167
Crazy Horse Saloon, 105–106
La Croix de Guerre (restaurant, Angers), 183
Hôtel de la Croix de Guerre (Angers), 180
Cuiram (leather), 165
La Cuisine est un jeu d'enfants (book), 75
Le Cul de Poule (restaurant, Nice), 242
Cypris (shoes, Deauville), 213
Cyrano (cabaret, Cannes), 266

Dalpozzo (restaurant, Nice), 242
Dalvin (boutique, Nice), 251
La Dame de Trèfle (boutique), 154
Le Damier (restaurant, Nice), 242
Hôtel Danube, 63
Dany Jade (beauty salon, Nice), 249
Daron (boutique, Cannes), 275
Daron (for men, Nice), 252
Dauphine Dix (jewelry), 169
Daurelle (beauty salon, Nice), 249
David (gifts, Deauville), 213
Jean-Louis David (beauty salon), 140
Deauville, 196–214
Deauville Pressing (cleaners), 214
Deauville Yacht Club, 209
Debs (boutique), 154
Deçoix (massage, Deauville), 210
Delacroix Museum, The, 125
Delicata (leather), 165
Delya (knitwear), 163
La Démarque (antiques), 171
P. Denny (hairdresser, Cannes), 272
Depalle (restaurant, Nice), 242
Au Départ (leather, Nice), 252
Deroche (leather), 165
Desfosse (beauty salon), 141
Fernand Desgranges (boutique):

Cannes, 275
Nice, 251
Jacques Dessange (beauty salon), 141
Jean Dessès (couturier), 160
Aux deux Dragons (restaurant), 78
Aux deux Magots (restaurant), 78, 120
Devihotel (Cannes), 260
Au Diablotin (gifts, Deauville), 213
Diane Boutiques (beauty salon), 141
Dibs (boutique), 154
Christian Dior (couturier), 160, 165, 167
Discounts:
   couturier, 162–163
   shopping, 150, 231
Domaine des Hauts de Loire, 181–182
Domaine de la Tortinière, 182
Le Dôme (restaurant), 90, 97
Don Juan (boutique), 154–155
Dragon (restaurant, Nice), 241
Du Dragon (restaurant, Versailles), 133
Dreyfus Marché (couturier discounts), 162
Drouant (restaurant), 71–72
Hôtel Drouot (antiques), 171
Le Drugstore de l'Avenue Matignon (restaurant), 78
Le Drugstore Berry (restaurant), 78
Le Drugstore Opéra (restaurant), 78
Le Drugstore Ouest (restaurant), 78
Le Drugstore St.-Germain (restaurant), 78, 120
Le Drugstore St.-Lazare (restaurant), 78
Dubosq (boutique, Deauville), 212
Le Durango (hairdresser, Cannes), 272

L'Écrin (antiques, Cannes), 277
L'Écuelle (restaurant), 84, 98
Eddy (for men), 167

Église St.-Gervais, 115
Eiffel Tower, 40, 42, 97, 109, 110, 120–121
    restaurants near, 97
Eilers (leather), 165
Ektor (couturier), 161
À l'Élantine (boutique, Deauville), 212
Elisabeth (leather), 165
Elle Bon Magique (boutique), 155
Elle-Elle (boutique), 155
Elle et Lui (night club), 106
Elle et Lui (perfumes, Cannes), 276
Elle & Lui (boutique, Monte-Carlo), 284
Élyse et Honoré (leather, Deauville), 213
Élysées-Bretagne (restaurant), 78, 98
Élysées Matignon (restaurant), 78–79
Élysées Pressing (cleaners), 174
Élysées Soieries (for men), 167
Les Embassadeurs (restaurant, Deauville), 202
Hôtel Embassy (Cannes), 258–259
Embassy et du Commerce (restaurant, Nice), 242
Emergency medical services, 30, 43
À l'Enclos de Ninon (restaurant), 87, 98
L'Entr'acte (restaurant, Angers), 183
L'Entrecôte (restaurant, Angers), 184
Entrées, 66
Les Entrerurs (beauty salon, Nice), 249
Epinay, 207
Eres (boutique), 155
L'Escale Bleu (restaurant), 90
L'Espadon (restaurant), 72, 98
Essca-pade, 45
Jacques Esterel (couturier), 161
Esthetica (sauna, Cannes), 272
Étagère (gifts), 172
Etam (boutique), 155
Etchegorry (restaurant), 84, 98

Étoile (see Place de l'Étoile)
Étoile Park (hotel), 52
Eurailpass, 22
Hôtel d'Europe (Monte-Carlo), 280
Eva (boutique), 155
Exhibition Galleries (Nice), 246
Expressions (gifts), 172
Eze-Village, 217, 227

Fabienne K (couturier discounts), 162
La Factorerie (gifts), 172–173
Fahrenheit (boutique), 155
Dr. Jacques Faivre (body surgery), 147–148
Pierre Faivret (for men), 167
Family Hotel, 59
Farandole (for children), 169
Roselyne Fard (boutique, Cannes), 275
Roger Fare (leather), 165
Fassonable (for men, Nice), 252
Faubourg St.-Germain, 115
Faubourg St.-Honoré, 113, 115
Fauchon (perfume), 170
À Feijoada (restaurant), 79
Felice (boutique), 155
Félix (restaurant, Cannes), 263
Félix-Faure (restaurant, Nice), 243
Louis Feraud (couturier), 161
Ferme St.-Hubert (restaurant), 84, 98
Fernande (couturier discounts), 162
Le Festival (restaurant, Cannes), 162
Festival du Marais, 45
Fête des Vendanges, 44
Figue (boutique), 155
Firmin (antiques, Nice), 254
Le Flambusquet (restaurant, Cannes), 263
Flash (leather), 165
Flaubert, The (hotel, Deauville), 200
Flea Market, 171
Fleur de Jasmin (restaurant, Cannes), 264
Fleurigny, 207

Reine Fleurmay (jewelry), 169
Mme. Fleury (repair), 174
Florence & Venise (antiques, Cannes), 277
Florian (restaurant, Nice), 242
Flower Market, 173
Flower Market (Nice), 246
Foire à la Ferraille, 173
Folies Club (Nice), 245
Folies-Bergère, 101
Fontain (beauty salon, Deauville), 210
La Fontaine de Mars (restaurant), 90, 97
Fontainebleau, 131, 133–134, 136
Fontaine-Henry, 207
Formentin (leather, Deauville), 213
Fort Carré (Antibes), 289
Fouquet's (restaurant), 72, 98
Au 14, rue d el'Université (antiques), 171
Fragonard perfume factory (Grasse), 288
Hôtel de France (Angers), 180
Hôtel de France (Cannes), 260
France Perfumes (Cannes), 276
Denise Francelle (leather), 165
Francis Coiffeur/Parfumeur (Monte-Carlo), 285
Franck & Fils, 152
Liane Franck (boutique), 155
Hotel Franck-Zürich (Nice), 239
Freddy (perfume), 170
Fréjus, 228, 287
Fréjus, Cathedral of, 287
French National Railroad, 21–22
French Tourist Office, 28
La Fresnaye (hotel, Deauville), 199
Nicole Fromentin (gifts), 173
Raymond Furterer (hair problems), 142

La Gadgetière (gifts), 173
Galerie du Cuir (leather), 165
Galerie des Glaces (gifts, Nice), 154
Galerie Pittoresque (gifts), 173
Galerie Saint-Charles (antiques, Monte-Carlo), 285
Galeries de la Croisette (Cannes), 274
Galeries de Deauville (gifts), 213
Galeries Lafayette, 150, 152
    Deauville, 199
    Nice, 250
Galeries Lafayette Salon (beauty salon), 141
Galia (boutique, Deauville), 212
Gallia Tennis Club (Cannes), 271
La Gaminerie (boutique), 155
Gant Perrin (leather), 165
Garac (restaurant, Nice), 241
J. Garsi (sauna, Cannes), 272
Jeanne Gatineau (hair problems), 143
Jacques Gautier (jewelry), 169
Gedeon Bedeon (restaurant, Cannes), 262
Gégé la Marguerite (boutique), 155
Maurice Genis (gifts), 173
George V (restaurant), 72, 98
Hôtel George V, 48
George Salon Dames (beauty salon, Nice), 249
Georgel (beauty salon), 141
Gérondeau (antiques), 171
Gesylca (boutique, Deauville), 212
Gigi (boutique, Nice), 251
Raymond Gillet (jewelry), 169
Gin (beauty salon), 141
Girl (boutique), 155
Givenchy (couturier), 161
Givenchy Gentleman (for men), 167
Glady (boutique), 155
Les Gobelins, 126
Suzanne Godard (gifts, Deauville), 213
Golf (hotel, Deauville), 198
Golf Bastide du Roy (Cannes), 269
Golf Club de Cannes, 269
Golf de Mougins (Cannes), 270

Golf de Valbonne (Cannes), 269

Golfe-Juan, 222, 228

Gonella (leather, Monte-Carlo), 285

Hôtel Gonnet et de la Reine (Cannes), 257

Gorges du Loupe, 227

Le Gorille (night club, Nice), 245

René Goujean (beauty salon), 141

La Goulue (boutique, Nice), 251

Aux Gourmets (restaurant, Nice), 243

Grand Café de Lyon (Nice), 242

Grand Casino (Deauville), 195–196, 197

Le Grand Dépôt (antiques), 171

Le Grand Hôtel, 52–53

Grand Hôtel (Cannes), 256

Grand Hôtel de Florence (Nice), 237

Grand Palais, 110, 112

Le Grand Vefour (restaurant), 70

Grandchamp, 207

Grande Corniche, 227

La Grande Maison de Blanc (Cannes), 274

Grasse, 218–219, 221, 223, 227, 228, 288

Mary Grayo (boutique, Monte-Carlo), 284

Grés (couturier), 161

Jacques Griffe (couturier), 161

Le Grill (Nice), 241

Grill Room du Casino (Deauville), 202–203

Le Grilladin (restaurant, Trouville), 204

La Grillerie (restaurant), 87, 96

Grimaldi Museum (Antibes), 289

Alain Guary (sauna, Cannes), 273

Gucci (leather), 166

Gudule (boutique), 155

Odette Guérin (pedicure, Deauville), 210

Guerlain (hair problems), 143

Guibert (leather), 166

Guignol Lyonnais Marionette Theater, 112

Guillaume (beauty salon), 141

Guy (restaurant), 72, 98

Dorian Guy (for men), 167

Jacques Hairoumiantz (boutique, Monte-Carlo), 284

Hall du Casino, The (Nice), 244

Hall of Mirrors, 132

Hansom cabs, 42

Harry's New York Bar (jazz), 107–108

Harry's Sport (boutique, Nice), 251

Harvard (for men), 167

Hôtel Helder (Monte-Carlo), 280

Hotel Sport (boutique), Deauville), 212

Hennocque/Quirin (antiques, Cannes), 277

Henriette (boutique, Nice), 251

Hermès (leather), 166
  Cannes, 276
  Deauville, 213
  Monte-Carlo, 285

Hermitage (hotel, Monte-Carlo), 280

Heyraud (leather, Nice), 252

Hit Parade (boutique), 155

Hobby (boutique), 155

Holiday Inn (Monte-Carlo), 280

Hong Kong (restaurant, Cannes), 264

Hôpital St.-Jean (museum), 186

L'Horizon (restaurant), 93, 96

Hostellerie de l'Olivier (Cannes), 261

Hostesses Internationales, 150

L'Hôtel (restaurant), 72, 98

Hôtel de l'Aigle Noir (restaurant, Fontainebleau), 134

Hôtel d'Aumont, 116

Hôtel de Beauvais, 116

Hôtel des Invalides (see Les Invalides)

Hôtel de Pincé (museum), 186

Hôtel de Sens, 115, 116

Hôtel de Sully, 116
Hotel taxes, 28–29
Hôtel de Ville, 109, 110
Hotels, classifications of, 46
House of Adam, The, 186

Ildy (beauty salon, Nice), 249
Île de la Cité, 39, 109, 111, 116–117
Île-de-France (restaurant, Versailles), 133
Île St.-Louis, 39, 96, 109, 111, 118
    restaurants near, 96
Hôtel Îles Britanniques (Cannes), 259
Imperial House (for men, Cannes), 276
Inno, 152
Innovation (leather), 166
Institut de France, 117
Hôtel Inter-continental, 48
L'Interlaken (restaurant, Nice), 243
International Boat Show, 44
International Television Festival of Monte-Carlo, 278
Les Invalides, 40, 95, 109, 110, 120, 127
    restaurants near, 95
Hôtel d'Isly, 63

Jacomo (repair), 174
Jacques et Robert (beauty salon, Nice), 249
Le Jacques-Coeur (restaurant), 79
Jacquot (shoes, Deauville), 213
Jacy de Paris (beauty salon), 141
    Deauville, 210
    Nice, 249, 254
Jana for Men (Nice), 253
Jardin Musée Rodin, 129
Jardin des Plantes, 129
Jardin du Ritz (restaurant), 72
Jardin-Rosarie Bagatelle, 129
Jardin des Tuileries (see Tuileries Gardens)
Jardins Albert-ler (Nice), 246
Jardins Albert-Kahn, 129
Jardins Fleuristes de la Ville

de Paris, 129
J. Jelly (for men, Nice), 253
Jeton, 27
Galerie du Jeu de Paume, 123, 128
Jimmy (repair), 174
JNS (boutique), 156
Jocelyn (leather), 166
Joffo (beauty salon), 141
Jones (boutique), 156
Jones (for children), 169
Jour et Nuit (restaurant,) 72, 98
Charles Jourdan (leather), 166
La Joyeuse (restaurant, Deauville), 204
Juan-les-Pins, 217, 228, 289
Julian et Fils (jewelry, Cannes), 276

Michel Kazan (beauty salon), 141–142
King Club (night club, Angers), 185
Kitchen Bazaar, 173
Le Knack (boutique), 156
Koranian (leather), 166
Korrigan (knitwear), 163
Kraal (night club, Deauville), 205
Le Kraal (restaurant, Deauville, 203
Le Kronenbourg (restaurant, Nice), 243

Claude Labarre (for children), 169
Marcel Ladousse (leather, Nice), 252
Lady and the Unicorn, 125
Lafayette Gift Ship (perfume), 170
Lafayette Shop (Cannes), 275
Lamazère (restaurant), 72, 98
Lancaster, The (hotel), 49
Lancel (leather), 166
    Nice, 252
Julie Lands (leather, Nice), 252
Langeais, Château of, 178, 189
Lanvin (couturier), 161
    Cannes, 275
    Monte-Carlo, 284

Lanvin 2 (for men), 167
Lapérouse (restaurant), 70
Ted Lapidus (couturier), 161, 167–168
Deauville, 212
Le Lapin Agile (night club), 106
Guy Laroche (couturier), 161, 168
Latin Quarter, 39, 60, 96, 109, 110, 118–119
restaurants near, 96
Laura (boutique), 156
Lauré Nouveautés (boutique, Monte-Carlo), 284
Laurent (restaurant), 72, 98
Bernard Laurent (boutique, Nice), 251
Dr. de Laval (obesity), 144
Hôtel Jeanne de Laval (Angers), 181
Lederer (leather), 166
Ledoyen (restaurant), 72–73
Left Bank, 39, 60–64, 109
Fernand Léger Museum (Biot), 289
Legris (pharmacy, Deauville), 197
Leonardo's tomb, 188
Lérins Islands, 228–229, 255
Lido, 103, 110
Hôtel Lido, 56
De Lilou (restaurant, Nice), 243
Lisieux, Cathedral of, 208
Littré (hotel), 63
Liz (perfume), 170
Hôtel Locarno (Nice), 239
Loches, Château of, 189
Le Logis (restaurant, Angers), 183
Le Logis Barrault, 186
Loire Valley, 177–192
calendar of events in, 179
Longchamps, 127
Look (boutique), 156
Lorca (beauty salon), 142
Lord Byron (antiques, Nice), 254
Lorvenn (beauty salon, Deauville), 210
Hôtel Lotti, 53

Le Louis XIV (restaurant), 84–85
Louvre, 37, 39, 96, 109, 110, 117, 122–123, 128
restaurants near, 96
Hôtel du Louvre (Monte-Carlo), 280
Hôtel Louvre Concorde, 53
Anna Lowe (couturier discounts), 162
Lubin (gifts), 170
Lucas-Carton (restaurant), 73, 98
Le Lutrin (restaurant, Deauville), 204
Luxembourg Palace, 109, 128
Aux Lyonnais (restaurant), 86
Lyonnaise à la Provençal (restaurant, Cannes), 263

La Machinerie (boutique), 156
Madd (boutique), 156
Madeleine, Church of the, 110, 113, 114
Madeleine-Plaza (hotel), 56–57
Madison, The (hotel), 63
Madison Shop (perfume), 170
Hôtel la Madone (Cannes), 259
Le Madrid Restaurant (Cannes), 262
La Maison du Caviar (restaurant), 92, 98
La Maison du Valais (restaurant), 79–80
Hôtel Majestic (Cannes), 256–257
Malmaison, 130
Hôtel la Malmaison (Nice), 237
Maman (restaurant, Deauville), 203
La Manade (restaurant), 73, 99
Le Mandarin (restaurant, Cannes), 263
Madelieu Golf Club, 218
Le Mans, 179
Mansart Art et Curiosités (antiques), 171
Marais, The, 115, 121
Marc et Jean-Michel (beauty salon), 142

Marcellin (boutique, Deauville), 212

Marché aux Fleurs, 173

Marché de la Friperie, 173

Marché aux Puces (Flea Market), 171

Marché aux Timbres, 173

Marcy Boutique (Cannes), 275

Marie Martine (boutique), 156

Marie-Anne (hotel, Deauville), 200

Marie-Martine (boutique, Deauville), 212

Marie-Thérèse (boutique, Nice), 251

Hôtel Marigny, 59

Hôtel Marina (Nice), 237–238

Marine Thermal Springs (Cannes), 273

Marius (restaurant), 91, 95

Marlo and Christian (beauty salon, Nice), 249

Marly (leather, Nice), 252

Marmottan Museum, 126–127

Maroquinerie 60 (leather, Cannes), 276

La Marotte (antiques), 171

Marsouin (restaurant, Nice), 241

Martin (jewelry, Nice), 253

Hôtel Martinez (Cannes), 257

Masséna Museum (Nice), 247

Hôtel Massenet (Nice), 239

Matisse Chapel (Vence), 227, 289

Matisse Museum (Nice), 247

Maxandre (gifts), 170

Maxim's (restaurant), 65, 70–71, 99

Mayfair (boutique), 156

Mayfair (cabaret, Nice), 245

Meautry, 207

Le Medicis (restaurant), 89, 96

La Méditerranée (restaurant), 80

Méduse Club (Deauville), 205

Le Menestrel (restaurant), 80

Ménestrier (leather), 166

Menton, 217, 221, 223, 224, 227

Menu, 65

Le Mercerie de Justine (boutique), 156

Le Mercure Galant (restaurant), 73, 99

La Mère Besson (restaurant, Cannes), 262

La Mère Françoise (restaurant, Cannes), 262

Hôtel Méridien, 53

Hôtel Méridien (Nice), 235

Mensil St.-Germain, 207

La Méthode (jazz), 108

Métro, le, 40–41

Métropole (hotel, Monte-Carlo), 281

Hôtel Meurice, 49

Mia & Vicky (boutique), 156

Mic Mac (boutique), 156

Michel (restaurant, Nice), 242

Miguez-Carton Boutique (Cannes), 275

Millner (leather), 166

Minny (boutique), 156

Mirabeau (cleaners, Deauville), 214

Hôtel Miramar (Monte-Carlo), 281

Le Mistral, 119

Mod In (boutique), 157

Mohant, 179

Molyneux (couturier), 161

Monaco, 219, 221, 278–285

Monaco Automobile Grand Prix, 279

Le Monde des Chimères (restaurant), 87

Monégasque Red Cross Gala, 279

Monoprix, 150, 152

Mont St.-Michel, 179

Montalembert (hotel), 61

Mont-Blanc (hotel), 63–64

Monte-Carlo, 223, 224, 227, 278–285

Monte-Carlo (restaurant), 93, 95

Monte-Carlo Automobile Rally, 278

Monte-Carlo Country Club, 282

"Monte-Carlo Open," 278

Monte-Carlo, Casino of, 227, 283

Montgeoffroy, Château of, 190

Montmartre, 40, 110, 121–122

Hôtel Montmorency (Cannes), 271

Montpensier (hotel), 59

Hôtel-Mont-Thabor, 57

Morabito (leather), 166

Morabito (jewelry, Nice), 253

Morelli (boutique, Deauville), 212

Motelia Hotel (Cannes), 260–261

Motor Show, 44

Mougins, 218

Moulin Rouge, 103, 110

Au Mouton de Panurge (restaurant), 80

Muncihe (restaurant), 80, 99

Municipal Casino (Cannes), 265, 266

La Musardière (restaurant), 94, 95

Musée de l'Armée, 120, 124

Musée d'Art Moderne, 124, 131

Musée des Arts Décoratifs, 124

Musée Carnavalet, 124, 125

Musée de la Castre, 267

Musée Cernushi, 124–125

Musée Cluny, 125

Musée Cognacq-Jay, 125

Musée Condé (Chantilly), 126–137

Musée de Costume, 125

Musée d'Ennery, 125–126

Musée Guimet, 126

Musée de l'Homme, 121

Musée Instrumental du Conservatoire National Supérieur de Musique, 126

Musée Jacquemard-André, 126

Musée de la Marine, 121

Musée des Monuments Français, 121

Musée Municipal d'Art Moderne, 124

Musée Nissim de Camondo, 127

Musée de l'Opéra, 127

Musée de l'Orangerie, 123–124, 128

Musée Rodin, 127

Musée Victor Hugo, 127

Les Muses de l'Europe (antiques), 171

La Musette (night club), 106

Museum of Coaches (Versailles), 132

Museum of Modern Mediterranean Art (Cagnes), 290

Museum of Natural History (Nice), 247

Au Nain Bleu (for children), 168

Nantes, 179

Napoléon (restaurant, Fontainebleau), 134

Môtel Napoléon (Nice), 235

Napoleon's Tomb, 40, 120, 124, 127

Nat's (boutique, Cannes), 275

Hôtel Negresco (Nice), 234

Negresco (beauty salon, Nice), 249

New Brummel, The (cabaret, Cannes), 266

New Brummel (night club, Deauville), 205

New Durer (leather), 166

New Jimmy's (night club), 107

N G Stores (boutique), 153

Nice, 218, 219, 221, 223, 224, 233–251

Nicoll (for men), 168

Le Nid d'Été (hotel, Deauville), 200

Niort (jewelry), 169

Noel (jewelry, Cannes), 276

Noel (boutique, Cannes), 275

Noir et Blanc (couturier discounts), 162

Non-Stop Soldes (boutique, Nice), 251

Normandy (hotel), 53–54

Normandy (hotel, Deauville), 198–199

Notre Dame, Cathedral of, 39, 96, 109, 110, 116–117
restaurants near, 96

Notre Dame d'Espérance, Church of, 267

Nouveau Casino (Nice), 245

Nouvelle Eve, 110

Obelisk from Luxor, 113

Obrey-Nova (jewelry), 169–170

Océan (hotel, Deauville), 200
Oceanographic Museum (Monte-Carlo), 227, 283
Ofal (leather, Nice), 252
Office de Tourisme de Paris, 41
Ofre (leather, Nice), 252
Olympia, The, 101–102
Hôtel, Opal, 57
Opéra, 39, 42, 96, 102, 110, 114
  restaurants near, 96
Opéra (Nice), 244
Opéra Comique, 101, 102
Hôtel les Orangers (Cannes), 259
Orléans, 179
Hôtel d'Orléans (Angers), 181
Orphée (boutique), 157
Orphéon (jazz), 108
O.R.T.F. Auditorium, 102

Le Pactole (restaurant), 80–81
La Pagode (restaurant, Nice), 242
Palace Museum (Monte-Carlo), 283
Palais-Bourbon, 113
Palais de Chaillot, 40, 101, 103, 109, 120, 121
Palais de l'Élysée, 110, 113, 121
Palais des Festivals (Cannes), 265
Palais de Justice, 117, 118
Palais Lascaris (Nice), 246, 247
Palais-Royal, 115
Palais des Sports, 101
Palm Beach Casino (Cannes), 218, 265, 266, 271
Kandy Palmer's (night club, Angers), 185
Le Panorama (restaurant), 85, 96
Panthéon, 96, 109, 119
  restaurants near, 96
Paola (boutique, Nice), 251
Parc Buttes-Chaumont, 128
Parc Monceau,, 128
Parc Montsouris, 128–129
Parfumerie Bouteille (Cannes), 277
Parfumerie de la Costa (Monte-Carlo), 285
La Parfumerie "Le Helder"
  (Monte-Carlo), 285
Paris, 37–129
Hôtel de Paris (Cannes), 259
Hôtel de Paris (Monte-Carlo), 281
Paris-Athens (restaurant), 86, 96
Paris Club, The (jazz), 107
Paris-Dinard (hotel), 61
Paris Hilton (hotel), 60
Paris International Dance Festival, 44
Paris International Trade Fair, 45
Paris 25 (restaurant), 73, 99
Paris Vision, 135, 137, 138, 178
Paris Weekly Information, 100, 103
Park Hôtel (Nice), 235–236
Hôtel du Pas-de-Calais, 61
Roger Pasquier (beauty salon), 142
Le Passé Composé (antiques), 171
Le Passy (restaurant), 94
Le Patio (hotel, Deauville), 200–201
Jean Patou (couturier), 161
  Deauville, 212
  Monte-Carlo, 284
François Patrice (night club), 106–107
Paul (restaurant), 85, 96
Paule (boutique, Monte-Carlo, 284
Christian Pauvert (leather), 166
Pavillon de la Poste (hotel, Deauville), 201
Jean Pax (leather), 166
Dr. N. G. Payot Beauty Institute, 143
Peau de Porc (leather), 166
  Deauville, 213
La Pêcherie (restaurant), 81, 99
La Pêcherie (restaurant, Cannes), 263
Pegotty (gifts, Deauville), 213
Hôtel Peiffer, 59
Penthouse (boutique), 157
Pépin (boutique), 157
La Pergola (restaurant), 92, 95, 99

Périgord (restaurant, Nice), 241
Yolande Perugia (leather, Nice), 252
Les Pestes (boutique), 157
Le Petit Bar (jazz), 108
Le Petit Bedon (restaurant), 73
Petit Bosso (restaurant), 81, 99
Petit Brouant (restaurant, Nice), 241
Le Petit Dépôt (porcelain), 172
Au Petit Gambetta (restaurant, Deauville), 203
Le Petit Gambetta (restaurant, Deauville), 204
Petit Palais, 112
Le Petit St.-Benoît, 89, 97, 99
Le Petit Tonneau (restaurant), 91, 95
Petit Vatel (restaurant, Deauville), 204
Petit Zinc (restaurant), 89
La Petite Cave (restaurant, Nice), 243
La Petite Duchesse (restaurant), 81, 99
La Petite Marquise (antiques, Nice), 254
Peyrot-Rudin (jewelry, Nice), 253
Pharmacie Anglaise (Deauville), 197
Pharmacie de l'Horloge (Deauville), 197
Phèdre (leather), 166
Philomène (boutique), 157
Pia (boutique), 157
Jeanne Piaubert (hair problems), 143
Jean Pierre (leather, Nice), 252
Pigalle, 40
Pink (boutique, Nice), 251
La Pizza (restaurant, Cannes), 263
Place de la Bastille, 109, 114, 116
Place de la Concorde, 39, 96, 109, 110, 112–113, 114, 123, 128
restaurants near, 96
Place Dauphine, 117
Place de l'Étoile, 39, 95, 112
restaurants near, 95

Place de la Madeleine, 39, 96, 114
restaurants near, 96
Place de la Méditerranée (cabaret, Nice), 245
À la Place de Morny (boutique, Deauville), 212
Place de l'Opéra, 110, 114
Place du Tertre, 40, 121
Place du Théâtre Français, 115
Place Vendôme, 39, 50, 110, 114
Place des Vosges, 109, 116
Plage (hotel, Deauville), 200
Plan de Paris par Arrondissement, 38
Plantagenets (restaurant, Angers), 183
Hôtel Plaza (Nice), 235
Plaza-Athénée (hotel), 49
Plessis Bourré, Château of, 191
Le Plessis-Mace, Château of, 191
Pline (boutique), 157
Hôtel PLM (Cannes), 261
Hôtel PLM (Nice), 239–240
PLM St.-Jacques (hotel), 54
Point d'Interrogation (boutique, Deauville), 212
Pol (leather), 166
Polyclinique (Deauville), 197
Pontecoulant, 207
Pont-Neuf, 109, 110
Pony-Club (Deauville), 209
Popard (boutique), 157, 168
Popeline (boutique), 157
Le Portofino (restaurant, Nice), 241
La Poule au Pot (restaurant), 91, 95
Dr. Pierre Pouteaux (plastic surgery), 146–147
Powers (hotel), 57
Poznanski (restaurant, Nice, 243
Il Pozzo (restaurant, Nice), 241
Janie Pradier (gifts), 173
Pressing de la Madeleine (cleaners), 174
Le Prieuré, 182
Prieuré du Vieux-Logis (Nice), 247
Prince's (restaurant, Nice), 241

Hôtel Prince des Galles, 49–50
Les Princes (restaurant), 92, 99
Au Printemps, 152 (Deauville), 212
Prison of the Iron Mask, 228
Prisunic, 150, 152
    Deauville, 212
    Nice, 250
Prix fixe, 70
Le Procope (restaurant), 81, 97
Hôtel du Progrès (Angers), 181
Promenade des Anglais (Nice), 219, 233, 234, 246
Promenade des Planches (restaurant, Deauville), 203
Le Prony (restaurant, Nice), 243
Le Provençal (restaurant), 85, 96
Le Provençal (restaurant, Nice), 243
Hôtel de Provence (Cannes), 259–260
Prunier Duphot (restaurant), 73
Prunier Traktir (restaurant), 73, 99
Pub Renault (restaurant), 81
Pub St.-Jacques (jazz), 108
Pub St.-Michel (restaurant), 88, 96
Emilio Pucci (couturier), 161
Les Puces des Champs-Élysées, 173
Pulcinella (boutique), 157
Pussycat (boutique), 157

Hôtel du Quai Voltaire, 61–62
Quesar (boutique), 157

Paco Rabanne (boutique), 157
Racing Stand (for men), 168
Ram Dam (gifts), 173
Ranch (boutique), 157
Rapid Pullman, 135, 136, 137
Rapides Côte d'Azur, 221
Rascasse (restaurant, Nice), 242
RATP, 41
Madeleine du Rauch (couturier), 161
Raynaud (restaurant, Nice), 242

Réal (boutique), 158
Le Récamier (restaurant), 91, 99
La Régence (restaurant, Angers), 184
La Régence (restaurant, Trouville), 204
Hôtel Régence (Nice), 240
Régence-Étoile (hotel), 54
Régence-Plaza (restaurant), 73, 99
Regent's Hôtel, 64
Regicia (shoes, Cannes), 276
Regina, The (hotel), 54
Reginskaia (night club), 107
Reine Pédauque (restaurant, Cannes), 262
La Reine Pédauque (restaurant, Nice), 243
Reinold (boutique, Deauville), 212
Réja (boutique), 158
Le Relais du Bois (restaurant), 94
Le Relais de la Butte (restaurant), 81
Relais de Campagne, 181
Relais Paris-Est (restaurant), 73–74, 99
Rémy (boutique), 158
Remy (knitwear), 163
Rennes, 179
Renoma/White House (for men), 168
Hôtel Réserve Miramar (Cannes), 257
La Résidence (hotel, Deauville), 201
La Résidence (hotel, Trouville), 201
La Resserre (restaurant), 82, 99
Restaurant des Arts, 88–89, 97
Restaurant des Chauffeurs, 93
Restaurant du Dragon, 89, 97
Restaurant de Madame Fauré, 85, 96
Restaurant de l'Hôtel de la Bourdonnais, 90–91, 97
Restaurant de l'Hôtel du Golf (Deauville), 203
Restaurant de l'Hôtel Normandy (Deauville), 203

Restaurant de l'Hôtel Royal (Deauville), 203
Restaurant St.-Antoine, 85, 96
Restaurants open in August, 97–99
Rety (boutique), 158
Nina Ricci (couturier), 161
Le Richepanse (restaurant), 85
Rigaud (perfume), 170
Right bank, 39, 40, 47–60, 117
Rimy (hairdresser, Cannes), 272
Ritz (hotel), 50, 114
La Rive d'Ott (restaurant), 91, 97
Riviera, 217–290
À la Riviera (Nice), 250
Robes des Vedettes (couturier discounts), 163
Robin-Maroquinier (leather, Monte-Carlo), 285
Hôtel Roblin, 54–55
Roche aux Moines, 191–192
Rodier (knitwear), 163
Roiena (for men), 168
Sonia Rollan (boutique, Nice), 251
Roman (repair), 174
Roman Amphitheater (Fréjus), 287
Roman Aqueduct (Fréjus), 287
Roman ruins (Cimiez), 247
Romanens (restaurant, Cannes), 264
La Romantica (restaurant, Nice), 243
Hôtel de Rome (Monte-Carlo), 281
Rond-Point des Champs-Élysées, 42, 112
Roquebrune, 227
La Roseraie (restaurant, Deauville), 204
Rôtisserie de la Reine Pédauque (restaurant), 82
Rouen, 137–138
Rouen, Cathedral of, 138
Maggy Rouff (couturier), 161
Le Roussin d'Arcade (The Jackass) (restaurant), 88, 96
La Roustica (restaurant, Nice), 242

Aux Routiers (restaurant), 86
Roxy-Club (cabaret, Cannes), 266
Hôtel Royal (Nice), 236
Royal Parfums (Nice), 254
Royaldame (shoes, Deauville), 213
Royale Souvenirs (Deauville), 213
Royan, 179
Le Rude (restaurant), 94, 95
Rue de la Paix, 114
Hôtel de Russie (Monte-Carlo), 281

Majuy Sabatier (beauty salon, Nice), 249
Les Sablettes (hotel, Deauville), 200
Sabot de Bernard (restaurant), 74, 99
Le Sabot Rouge (restaurant), 95, 96
Sacré-Coeur, Basilica of, 40, 96, 110, 121–122
  restaurants near, 96
St.-Antoine (restaurant), 82
St.-Denis, Basilica of, 137
St.-Georges (night club, Angers), 185
Hôtel St.-Georges (Nice), 240
Blvd. St.-Germain, 39
St.-Germain-de-Livet, 207
St.-Germain-des-Prés, 97, 109, 110, 119–120
  Abbey of, 119
  restaurants near, 97
Saint Germain des Prés (for men), 168
St.-Honorat, Island of, 228–229, 255
St.-Hymer, Church of, 208
St. James (hotel, Deauville), 200
St.-Julien-le-Pauvre, 109
Yves St.-Laurent (couturier), 161
Saint Laurent/Rive Gauche (boutique, Nice), 251
Hôtel St.-Louis, 59–60
Ste.-Marguerite, Island of, 228–229, 255, 267

Blvd. St.-Michel, 119
St.-Pierre, Church of (Caen), 206, 208
St.-Pierre, Church of (Touques), 207
Hôtel St.-Pierre (Nice), 240
St.-Raphaël, 217, 219, 221, 228, 288
Ste.-Réparate Cathedral, 246
Jean-Louis St.-Roch (beauty salon), 142
Hôtel St.-Simon, 64
St.-Tropez, 217, 221, 224, 228, 286–287
Sainte-Chapelle, 117–118
St.-Marie-aux-Anglais, Church of, 208
Saints' Festival of Dramatic Art, 179
Sales, 150
Salle Gaveau, The, 103
Salle Pleyel, 102
Salon des Artistes-Décorateurs, 44
Salon des Galeries Lafayette (beauty salon, Nice), 249
Salon Pompadour (beauty salon, Nice), 249
Salon de Thé-Patisserie Hammes, 85–86, 96
Charles Salzanik (boutique, Monte-Carlo), 284
La Samaritaine, 152
La Samaritaine de Luxe, 152
Samoura (restaurant), 88, 99
Sant'Estello Sporting Club (Cannes), 270, 271
S.A.P.J.O. (antiques, Monte-Carlo), 285
Sassafras (boutique), 158
Saumur, Château of, 179, 189–190
Hôtel Savoy (Cannes), 257–258
Jean-Louis Scherrer (boutique), 161–162
Scottie Shop (boutique), 158
Hôtel Scribe, 55
Secretariat-General, 181
La Sélect (restaurant, Deauville), 204
Select Latin (restaurant), 89, 96
Self Service Lavomatique (Deau-ville), 214
Senlis, Cathedral of, 137
Serrant, Château of, 191
Servian (jewelry, Deauville), 213
"Service compris," 29, 65
Sévigné (hotel), 64
Sèvres (knitwear), 163
Sèvres Bazaar (knitwear), 163
"Shades of Glory," 110
Show Club (cabaret, Cannes), 266
Showboat (cabaret, Nice), 245
Sir Oliver (boutique, Nice), 251
Size charts, 24–25
Smoking, 7
Snob (boutique), 158
La Socca (restaurant, Cannes), 263
Société Méridionale d'Autocars, 221
Hôtel Sofitel Méditerranée (Cannes), 258
La Solderie (couturier discounts), 163
Soldine (boutique, Nice), 251
Au Soleil (restaurant, Nice), 243
Solesmes, 179
Son et Lumiére:
  Château d'Amboise, 187
  Château d'Azay-le-Rideau, 187
  Château de Blois, 187
  Château de Chambord, 178, 187
  Château de Chenonceaux, 187
  Château de Saumur, 179
  Hôtel des Invalides, 45, 110
Sonia Rykiel (boutique), 158
Sorbonne, 39, 60, 109, 118
Sotira (massage, Deauville), 210
Le Soufflé (restaurant), 82
Lou Souleou (restaurant), Cannes), 262
Speakeasy (cabaret, Cannes), 266
Hôtel Splendid (Cannes), 260
Hôtel Splendid Sofitel (Nice), 236
Hôtel Splendide (Monte-Carlo), 281

Sport Look (knitwear), 163
Square Monge (hotel), 64
Square du Vert-Galant, 117
Stamp Market, 173
Starlett Perfumes (Cannes), 277
Starlette Parfums (hairdresser, Cannes), 272
Starly Beauty Institute (Cannes, 273
Statue of Liberty, 131
Stehly (boutique, Cannes), 275
Stendhal Institute of Beauty, 142–143
Stritch (gifts), 173
Le Suguet, 255, 267
Summer Casino (Deauville), 199, 202, 205
Sweaters Bazaar, 164
Swelly (perfume), 170
Symdens (cleaners, Deauville), 214
Syndicats d'Initiative (*see* Tourist offices)
Syndicat d'Initiative de Paris, 41

Table d'hôte, 70
La Table d'Hôte (restaurant), 88, 96, 99
La Table Impériale (restaurant, Cannes), 264
Taillevent (restaurant), 74
Talma (porcelain), 172
Tapestry of the Apocalypse, 186
Tassée du Chapitre (restaurant), 82, 99
Tassy (boutique), 158
Taverne du Château (Nice), 243
La Taverne Sicilienne (restaurant, Cannes), 263
Tchakacha (night club, Deauville), 205
Tchim-Tchim (restaurant, Nice), 242
Teinturerie Marbeuf, Anaury (cleaners), 174
Théâtre des Arènes (Cimiez), 244
Théâtre du Casino (Nice), 244
Théâtre des Champs-Élysées, 101, 102
Théâtre des Nations, 45

Théâtre de Nice, 244
Théâtre de Verdure (Nice), 244
Thermes-Marins (spa, Deauville), 199, 210, 211
Armand Thièry & Sigrand (for men, Cannes), 276
Tiffany (boutique), 158
Tinny (boutique), 158
Tiphagne (pedicure, Deauville), 210
Tiphène (boutique), 158
Tomb of the Unknown Soldier, 112
Le Tonneau (restaurant, Cannes), 264
Tonya (beauty salon, Nice), 249
Torrente (boutique), 158
Toulon, 217
Touques, 206–207
La Tour d'Argent (restaurant), 65, 71, 99
Tour Eiffel (*see* Eiffel Tower)
Tour Eiffel (restaurant), 74, 99
Tour de France, 224
Tour de Jade (restaurant), 87
Tourettes-sur-Loup, 227
Tourist offices:
    Cannes, 222, 231
    Nice, 222
    Paris, 41
Le Tournis (boutique), 158
Tours (Val de Loire), 178, 179
Tours:
    boat, 111, 228–229
    coach, 109–111, 130–131, 135, 136, 137, 138, 178, 221–222, 227–228
Tourtour (restaurant), 82, 99
"Tout compris," 29
Touze (pharmacy, Deauville), 197
Trabaud (for men, Cannes), 276
Hôtel la Trémoille, 55
Les Très Riches Heures du Duc de Berry, 136
Trianon-Palace (hotel), 62
Trianons, 130, 132
Tricot Club (knitwear), 164
La Tricotiere (knitwear), 164

Trocadéro, 121
Le Trocadéro (restaurant), 94
Les Trois Maillets, 119
Trois Nailletz (night club), 106
Aux Trois Quartiers, 152
Le Trou dans le Mur (restaurant), 82–83
Trousselier (gifts), 173
Trouville, 196
Le Tromilou (restaurant), 87, 99
Tub (boutique), 158
Tuileries Gardens, 42, 109, 113, 123, 128
Les Tuileries (hotel), 60
La Turbie, 227
Twiggy (boutique), 158

Ungaro (couturier), 162
Uniprix (Nice), 259
Hôtel Universe (Cannes), 261
Hôtel de l'Université, 62

Vagenende (restaurant), 89, 97
Valençay, Château of, 188
Valentin (restaurant), 92
Valentino (couturier), 162
Anne Valerie (boutique), 159
Vallauris, 222, 231, 288
Van Cleef & Arpens (jewelry, Cannes), 276
  Deauville, 213
  Monte-Carlo, 285
Les Vapeurs (restaurant, Trouville), 204
Roselyne Varch (boutique, Cannes), 275
Le Vaslot (beauty salon, Deauville), 210
Le Vauban (restaurant), 91, 95
Vedettes Paris Tour Eiffel, 111
Vence, 218, 223, 227, 288–289
Hôtel Vendôme (Cannes), 261
Hôtel Vendôme (Nice), 238
Philippe Venet (couturier), 162
Venezia (restaurant, Cannes), 263
Veneziano (boutique), 159
Verrerie des Halles (glass), 172
Versailles, Palace of, 130–133, 136

Versailles Music and Drama Festival, 45
Versainville, 207
Le Vert d'Eau (restaurant, Angers), 184
Victoire (boutique), 159, 168
Le Victoria (hairdresser, Cannes), 272
Victoria Palace (hotel), 55
Victot, 207
Le Vieil Écu (restaurant), 86, 99
Vietnam (restaurant, Nice), 242
Au Vieux Cadran (jewelry), 170
Hôtel Vignon, 57
Village Suisse (antiques), 171–172
Villefranche, 217, 218, 227
Virgile J. P. (hairdresser, Cannes), 272
Visa, 22
Roger Vivier (leather), 166
Vog (boutique), 159
Vouvray, Château of, 178
V.R.A.C. (Cannes), 274
Au Vrai Saumur (restaurant), 94
Vroom (boutique), 159
Vuitton (leather), 166
  Nice, 252

Hôtel Wagram (Cannes), 261
Watos (jewelry, Deauville), 213
Wax Museum (Monte-Carlo), 283
Le Week End (boutique), 159
Hôtel West-End (Nice), 238
Hôtel Westminster (Cannes), 260
Hôtel Westminster (Nice), 236
Weston (for men), 168
Le Westphalie (restaurant), 92, 99
Whiskey-à-Go-Go (night club, Nice), 245
Whisky à Go-Go (cabaret, Cannes), 266
William the Conqueror's Castle (Caen), 206

William the Conqueror's Château (Touques), 206
Windy (boutique, Nice), 251
Winter Casino (Deauville), 197, 199, 205
Wiwas (for men), 168
Jean Wohl (sauna, Cannes), 273
World War II sites, 208

Worldly Tailor & Outfitter (Cannes), 276

Yves Dry (leather, Cannes), 275

Zéro de Conduite (restaurant), 89, 96
Zora Couture Modes (Cannes), 275
Zorba (restaurant, Nice), 242

Gerie Tully is an expert on women's interests and problems, and deals daily with the particular needs of women travelers. She is president of a New York based travel agency specializing in trips and tours for women, the only one of its kind in the world. Gerie has traveled all over the world, written articles for leading women's magazines, produced film and TV programs, headed a woman's market research company, and worked with a major cosmetic company. Her extensive experience, her sympathy, knowledge and research combine in **France Especially for Women.**